The Individual in a Social World

ESSAYS AND EXPERIMENTS

McGraw-Hill Series in Social Psychology

CONSULTING EDITOR
Philip G. Zimbardo

The
Individual in
a Social World

ESSAYS AND EXPERIMENTS

SECOND EDITION

❖

Stanley Milgram

*Late Distinguished Professor
of Psychology
Graduate School and University Center
City University of New York*

Edited by
John Sabini
University of Pennsylvania

Maury Silver
St. Francis College

McGraw-Hill, Inc.

New York St. Louis San Francisco Auckland Bogotá Caracas
Lisbon London Madrid Mexico Milan Montreal New Delhi Paris
San Juan Singapore Sydney Tokyo Toronto

To Sasha, Michèle, and Marc

THE INDIVIDUAL IN A SOCIAL WORLD
Essays and Experiments

2 3 4 5 6 7 8 9 0 DOC DOC 9 0 9 8 7 6 5 4 3 2

ISBN 0-07-041936-1

This book was set in Palatino by General Graphic Services, Inc.
The editors were Christopher Rogers and Fred H. Burns;
the production supervisor was Louise Karam.
The cover was designed by Carla Bauer.
R. R. Donnelley & Sons Company was printer and binder.

Cover painting: Gustave Caillebotte, *Paris, A Rainy Day*, 1876/77.
Oil on Canvas, 212.2 × 276.2 cm., Charles H. and Mary F. S. Worcester Collection,
1964.336. Copyright ©1988 The Art Institute of Chicago. All rights reserved.

Library of Congress Cataloging-in-Publication Data

Milgram, Stanley.
    The individual in a social world: essays and experiments /
Stanley Milgram; edited by John Sabini, Maury Silver.—2nd ed.
        p.   cm.—(McGraw-Hill series in social psychology)
    Includes bibliographical references and index.
    ISBN 0-07-041936-1
    1. Social psychology.   2. Social psychology—Experiments.
I. Sabini, John, (date).   II. Silver, Maury, (date).
III. Title.   IV. Series.
HM251.M4639   1992
302—dc20
                                                          91-33256

About the Author

--- ❖ ---

Stanley Milgram was born in 1933 in New York City. He took a bachelor's degree from Queens College in political science and received his Ph.D. in the social relations program of Harvard University in 1960 under the direction of Gordon Allport.

Milgram spent from 1960 to 1963 at Yale University conducting the obedience experiments for which he quickly became internationally famous, and for which he received many honors including the American Association for the Advancement of Science prize in sociopsychology. The first reports of this work appeared in 1963, but the full series of experiments was first published in his 1974 book *Obedience to Authority*, which was nominated for a National Book Award.

Milgram returned to Harvard in 1963 and remained there until 1967, when he moved to the Graduate Center of the City University of New York as head of the social psychology graduate program. In 1980 Milgram was named a distinguished professor of psychology by the Graduate School and University Center of the City University of New York. Milgram passed away in December of 1984.

At the City University of New York, Milgram conducted a seminal series of experiments on the psychology of urban living, and he wrote and produced an award-winning movie, *The City and the Self*, as a further expression of his insights into urban life.

Milgram was a fellow of the American Psychological Association and the American Academy of Arts and Sciences. In 1972 he won a Guggenheim Fellowship to spend a year in Paris developing his work on mental maps of Paris and New York. He was, in addition to all of this, an amateur songwriter, photographer, and inventor of games and gadgets.

Contents

———— ❖ ————

Foreword

———— ❖ ————

During the many decades when American psychology was held captive by a limited scientific doctrine of behaviorism, the pathfinders who dared to venture beyond these intellectually limited boundaries and explore new horizons were largely social psychologists. They valued the personal perspectives of the human actor in life's dramas, honored the alternative interpretations of reality held by different observers, and defended the subtle interplay of dynamic forces between and within cultures, social situations, and individual psyches.

Long relegated to a subordinate position within psychology's status hierarchy for these points of view, social psychology has steadily moved to the center of contemporary psychology. It did so by establishing a cognitively flavored brand of psychology, which, in recent years, has become the banner flown by mainstream psychology. Social psychology was the home of generalists within psychology, a haven for scholars interested in understanding the depth and breadth of the nature of human nature. It was neither too shy to ask the big questions that have intrigued social philosophers for centuries, nor too orthodox to venture into alien territories with new methodologies that have provided empirically grounded answers to the more vital questions of our time. Finally, social psychologists have become the vanguard of the movement to extend the boundaries of traditional psychology into realms vital to contributing solutions for real-world problems, the areas of health, ecology, education, law, peace and conflict resolution, and much more. Indeed, it is not immodest to declare that nothing of human nature is too alien to social psychological inquiry and concern.

Our McGraw-Hill Series in Social Psychology celebrates the fundamental contributions being made by researchers, theorists, and practitioners of social psychology to a richer understanding of the human condition. The authors of each book in the series are distinguished researchers and dedicated teachers, committed to sharing a vision of the excitement inherent in their particular area of investigation with their colleagues, graduate students, and seriously curious undergraduates. Taken as a whole the series will cover a wide path of social psychological interests, allowing instructors to use any of them as supplements to their basic textbook or, for the more daring, to organize a challenging course around a collection of them.

Among contemporary social psychologists, few have attained the international recognition accorded to Stanley Milgram. The core of that acclaim surely is his powerful laboratory demonstration of the phenomenon known as "blind obedience to authority." This uniquely original research disturbed the sensibilities of many people by revealing the power of social situations to induce the majority of ordinary people to behave in ways that were thought to be the province only of those with pathologies of mind or spirit. It is never comforting to be exposed to the truth of the "banality of evil," the knowledge that any wrong which any human being has ever done to another person, we too could do—under the wrong circumstances. The universal appeal and controversy surrounding that research continues even to this day with students of a generation so different from those Milgram studied several decades ago.

But that is the genius which formed Milgram's approach to social psychology: asking fundamental questions about human nature, about the resourcefulness and vulnerabilities of the individual ever buffeted by a complex array of social forces from groups, institutions, culture, and environment. Milgram's dedication to social psychology came from an insatiable curiosity about why people behave as they do when confronted with an assortment of social pressures from everyday life situations— from group norms to conform, to compliance pressures from authority figures, to the adaptations necessitated by living in urban centers, and to the forces of electronic communications media.

Milgram was a keen observer of the human landscape, with an eye ever open for a new paradigm that might expose old truths or raise awareness of hidden operating principles. Not only did he ask the big questions that most other psychologists shun, he found ways to answer them using an always creative mix of methods, observation, introspection, interview, and, of course, the laboratory experiment. His answers never depended solely on paper-and-pencil antiseptic questionnaire or survey research so characteristic of today's investigators.

Paradoxically, Milgram's popular success came from his phenomenological approach to social psychology, starting always with vital phenomena to be understood, but his approach also limited the appeal Milgram's work held for his peers. Milgram's disdain for theory and reliance on his personal insights and observational abilities is not the stuff from which new Ph.D. dissertations are built. In that sense, Milgram is more like a Picasso than a Freud. To some extent, we can trace the influence here of his mentor, Solomon Asch, whose classic study of group conformity and independence is similarly nontheoretical.

The new student of social psychology will find in this book of essays by a master researcher and gifted writer a treasury of creative views on different slices of the human experience. One cut is on the many ways in which individuals adapt to the physical, social, and cognitive aspects of life in the city. Another considers the dynamic interplay of individuals and social groups. A third focuses on the aspects of the communicative web that is so much a part of our daily lives. In addition to Milgram's classic studies of the small-world problem and the lost-letter technique, you will find a rich, previously unpublished gem. Milgram presents pilot research on the cyrano effect, the impact of presenting the words of another person, as in *Cyrano de Bergerac*. This research is bursting with new directions for research. Finally, of course, is the section on the confrontation between individuals and authority. Many readers will be pleased to discover here a fuller context in which to better appreciate the basic study of obedience to authority, including Milgram's concerns for the ethics of this sensitive research.

Before sending the reader on this journey of seeing the social world through the vision of one of the most important social psychologists of our times, I must take you back in time. It is 1949 and seated next to me in senior class at James Monroe High School in the Bronx, New York, is my classmate, Stanley Milgram. We were both skinny kids full of ambition and desire to make something of ourselves so that we might escape life in the confines of our ghetto experience. Stanley was the smart one, who read the *New York Times* (which I never could fold properly to read on the subway so I stuck to the *Daily News*). We went to him for authoritative answers. I was the popular one, the smiling guy other kids would go to for advice, even though many of my friends ended up in prison.

When we met years later at Yale University as beginning faculty members (in what my mother would forever call an "Ivory League" school), it turned out that Stanley really wanted to be popular, and I wanted to be smart. So much for unfulfilled desires. Now I have the bittersweet task of sending you, our reader, to enjoy the wisdom of my old friend, smart Stanley, sadly deceased long before his time. It is with childhood pride then that I give you this lasting legacy to his creative scholarship, that will ensure his popularity among a new generation of students, just as his peers can rediscover the depth of his smarts.

Philip G. Zimbardo
Series Editor

Preface to the
Second Edition

———— ❖ ————

Bubble chambers are devices physicists use to make powerful, but normally invisible, forces visible. Photographs of the tracks are permanent records of these evanescent events. Such photos have been sold as art because there is an elegance about them, an elegance derived from their simplicity. Had Milgram been a physicist, he would have invented the bubble chamber; instead as a social psychologist his genius expressed itself in finding powerful, covert social forces and making them tangible in a direct, simple, elegant way. The passion for elegance and simplicity drove Milgram's prose as much as it did his design of experiments.

In a graduate seminar a student once asked Milgram about the style the student should use in writing his paper. Milgram replied that there was but one way to write—for the intelligent layman. Milgram believed that if one had something to say, one could say it simply—so that your grandparent could understand it. Jargon, he believed, announced that one had nothing to say. The essays here all have something to say.

Some psychologists are driven by the urge to create theories. Others are driven to understand phenomena which are compelling in their own right. Milgram's work was clearly of the latter sort. Indeed Milgram had little use for theories, at least theories in social psychology.

Milgram saw experimental social psychology as a way of finding out what was really true, and he saw theories as a kind of speculation, no better, and often worse, than commonsense theories. Theory-driven research seemed to him to swell, rather than resolve, speculation. Now, this way of putting the matter is naive—and Milgram knew it was naive, which is why he never put it this way. It is naive because we all know, or so modern philosophy tells us, that all knowledge is theoretical. But still, Stanley Milgram was distrustful of social psychological theories and indeed believed that commonsense "theories" were less speculative grounds for raising questions and doing experiments.

He had a particular antipathy to theories that explained everything and illuminated nothing—for instance, learning theory circa 1960 (when Milgram went to Yale). Milgram did not waste his time, at least as he saw it, elaborating "grand theory." Milgram's aim in conducting research was always to provide insight into concrete phenomena, rather than to articulate an abstract theory.

His eschewing theory had a certain cost. For one thing, the original report of the obedience experiments was *rejected* by the *Journal of Abnormal and Social Psychology;* perhaps the experiments were thought not theoretically important enough. Other articles in this collection met a similar fate. One we know of was rejected by the *Journal of Personality and Social Psychology* with a reviewer's comment that it should be resubmitted to *Parade Magazine.*

The same insightfulness that erupts from the articles collected here was easy to enjoy in conversations with Milgram. Conversations with Milgram were wide-ranging (even more wide-ranging than the scope of the articles collected here), intense, and exhilarating. But they were also a bit scary; we once reported to Milgram that we were no longer going to do an experiment he had encouraged us to do (for our theses) because we were afraid—from experience—of being beaten up and arrested on the subway. Milgram sat back in his chair, thought about the matter for a moment, and then remarked that anthropology graduate students might have to do field work in cultures where eating foreigners was common, so he didn't see why we should stop the experiment on the subway just out of fear of being beaten up. He was kidding, of course; well, maybe he was kidding. One often didn't know with Stanley just when he was serious about an idea and when he was playing with it. One didn't know because Stanley didn't know; playfulness was a part of thinking about things for Stanley, an intrinsic part.

Stanley Milgram died on December 20, 1984; he was 51 years old. His genius is now frozen as his published work. In 1977 he collected much of this work as *The Individual and the Social World.* This edition is a revision of that collection and includes most of the articles he had selected for the 1977 edition (with three exceptions). This edition also includes additional articles written since the publication of the first collection.[1] The final

---

[1]The three articles not reproduced from the original collection are Ethical Issues in the Study of Obedience, Conformity and Norwegian Life, and Crowds, which we regret that we could not include because of space constraints. The new articles are: (1) On Maintaining Social Norms: A Field Experiment in the Subway; (2) The Vertical City; (3) Subject Reaction: The Neglected Factor in the Ethics of Experimentation; (4) Candid Camera; (5) Reflections on News; (6) Cyranoids; (7) Response to Intrusion into Waiting Lines. We wish to express our appreciation to the original publishers of these works for their permission to reprint them here.

chapter is a transcript of an address Milgram gave to the American Psychological Association in August of 1984 on his work with what he called "Cyranoids." A report of this work was never published by Milgram, so this transcript is as close as we can come to his thinking about this unfinished project.

John Sabini
Maury Silver

Preface to the First Edition

———— ❖ ————

The late Gordon W. Allport taught that social psychology examined how the thought, action, and feelings of the individual were affected by the implied, actual, or imagined presence of others. At the center of his definition was the individual; the individual remains at the center of my own conception of the field. Thus, I have loosely structured this volume in terms of four domains of social facts confronted by the individual: the city, authority, groups, and media.

The volume describes research I have carried out over a period of twenty years, and it is impossible to thank here all those who helped me in carrying out particular studies. But I wish to indicate a general intellectual debt to a few people who have been especially important to my professional development: first, to the late Gordon W. Allport, who always encouraged me to think I could contribute something useful to social psychology, and to three inspiring teachers: Solomon E. Asch, Roger Brown, and Jerome S. Bruner.

Many of the experiments reported here were carried out in the context of my courses in social psychology at Harvard, Yale, and The City University of New York. The many students who participated in these projects were true partners in research, and I wish to express my appreciation to each of them.

Alice B. Kornblith and Alexandra Milgram provided helpful editorial and secretarial assistance in the preparation of this volume and Joan Gerver prepared the index.

Finally, I wish to acknowledge my appreciation to the several publishers who allowed me to reprint my articles, which first appeared in their journals and books.

Stanley Milgram

Introduction

———— ❖ ————

A s a social psychologist, I look at the world not to master it in any practical sense, but to understand it and to communicate that understanding to others. Social psychologists are part of the very social matrix they have chosen to analyze, and thus they can use their own experience as a source of insight. The difficulty is to do this in a way that does not drain life of its spontaneity and pleasure.

A wish to understand social behavior is not, of course, unique to psychologists; it is part of normal human curiosity. But for social psychologists, this need is more central, more compelling, and thus they go a step further and make it their life's work.

The studies in this collection, carried out over a period of twenty years, examine the way in which the social world impinges on individual action and experience. The implicit model for the experimental work is that of the person influenced by social forces while often believing in his or her own independence of them. It is thus a social psychology of the reactive individual, the recipient of forces and pressures emanating from outside onself. This represents, of course, only one side of the coin of social life, for we as individuals also initiate action out of internal needs and actively construct the social world we inhabit. But I have left to other investigators the task of examining the complementary side of our social natures.

The social world does not impinge on us as a set of discrete variables, but as a vibrant, continuous stream of events whose constituent parts can be dissected only through analysis, and whose effects can be most compellingly demonstrated through the logic of experiments. Indeed, the creative claim of social psychology lies in its capacity to reconstruct varied types of social experience in an experimental format, to clarify and make visible the operation of obscure social forces so that they may be explored in terms of the language of cause and effect.

The source for the experiments in this volume is neither textbooks nor abstract theory, but the texture of everyday life. They are imbued with a phenomenological outlook. Even so apparently technical a study as "The

Lost Letter Technique" begins with the imagined experience of encountering such a missive, the consciousness of choice which the letter stimulates, and the ultimate resolution of conflicting tendencies in a decisive and measurable act.

Every experiment is a situation in which the end is unknown; it is tentative, indeterminate, something that may fail. An experiment may produce only a restatement of the obvious or yield unexpected insights. The indeterminancy of its outcome is part of its excitement.

Although experiments may be objective, they are rarely entirely neutral. There is a certain viewpoint that is implicit in the experiments that were carried out. Thus, in my studies of conformity and obedience, the moral value always rests with the person who rejects the group or authority. Going it alone seems to be the preferred value. But of course the experimenter himself set up the situation in a way in which only such rejection could constitute a morally adequate choice. The pervasive effects of such implicit values do not in themselves undermine the validity of the experiments; they do, however, given them a specific coloration that is not scientifically derived.

I do not mean thereby to reduce experimental social psychology to an emotional catharsis in which the feelings and needs of the investigator are paramount. Far from it! Even if a study originates in a personal interest, problem, or bias, it cannot long remain at this level. Emotional factors are severely disciplined by the experimental method and the ideal of scientific objectivity.

The most interesting experiments in social psychology are produced by the interplay of naivete and skepticism. The experimenter must be sufficiently naive to question what everyone thinks is a certainty. Yet he must be skeptical at every point—in his interpretation of data, and in the too hasty assimilation of a discovery to a preexisting framework of thought.

Although most of the papers in this volume deal with the presentation of experimental ideas, several represent attempts to justify or defend those ideas in the face of criticisms. Or they apply the experimental conclusions to issues of larger scope. Thus, in the section on "The Individual and Authority," I include a defense of the ethics of the obedience experiment. Another paper defends its methodological suppositions. Papers such as these, however necessary a part of the social psychologist's work, have always seemed to me a deflection from the more pleasurable activity of experimental invention.

The following interview, conducted by Carol Tavris for *Psychology*

Today, expands on the remarks in this introduction and touches on a broad range of my substantive and methodological concerns.

CAROL TAVRIS: Much of your work is directed toward the experience of living in cities, isolating the intangibles that make Oslo different from Paris, Topeka different from Denver, and New York different from anything. How do you go about defining those intangibles?

STANLEY MILGRAM: First, you keep your eyes open; you generalize on the basis of numerous specific incidents; you try to determine whether particular incidents lead up to a definable pattern; you attempt to find an underlying coherence beneath the myriad surface phenomena in a particular city. You generalize from your own experience and formulate a hypothesis.

Then you become systematic about it. You ask people what specific incidents seem to them to characterize a particular urban setting, and you see whether any patterns or dimensions emerge. When you ask Americans to cite specific incidents they think typical of London, for example, they often center on the civility of the Londoner. Typical comments about New York focus on its pace of activity, and diversity. The psychologist differs from the novelist or travel writer in that he tries to measure whether these features—pace, friendliness, diversity—actually correspond to what is out there, and differ from one urban setting to the next. *Measurement* of ambience, then, is the special contribution that social psychology makes to centuries of travelogues.

TAVRIS: What features of urban life have interested you most recently?

MILGRAM: For years I've taken a commuter train to work. I noticed that there were people at my station whom I had seen for many years but never spoken to, people I came to think of as *familiar strangers*. I found a peculiar tension in this situation, when people treat each other as properties of the environment rather than as individuals to deal with. It happens frequently. Yet there remains a poignancy and discomfort, particularly when there are only two of you at the station: you and someone you have seen daily but never met. A barrier has developed that is not readily broken.

TAVRIS: How can you study the phenomenon of the familiar stranger?

MILGRAM: Students in my research seminar took pictures of the waiting passengers at one station. They made duplicates of the photographs, numbered each of the faces, then distributed the group photographs the following week to all the passengers at the station. We asked the commuters to indicate those people whom they knew and spoke to, those whom they did not recognize, and those whom they recognized but had never spoken to. The commuters filled out the questionnaires on the train and turned them in at Grand Central Station.

Well, we found that the commuters knew an average of 4.5 familiar strangers, and the commuters often had many fantasies about these people. Moreover, there are sociometric stars among familiar strangers. Eighty percent of the commuters recognized one person, although very few had ever spoken to her. She was the visual high point of the station crowd, perhaps because she wore a miniskirt constantly, even in the coldest months.

TAVRIS: How do our dealings with familiar strangers differ from those with total strangers?

MILGRAM: The familiar-stranger phenomenon is not the absence of a relationship but a special kind of frozen relationship. For example, if you wanted to make a trivial request or get the time of day, you are more likely to ask a total stranger, rather than a person you had seen for many years but had never spoken to. Each of you is aware that a history of noncommunication exists between you, and you both have accepted this as the normal state.

But the relationship between familiar strangers has a latent quality to it that becomes overt on specific occasions. I heard of a case in which a woman fainted in front of her apartment building. Her neighbor, who had seen her for 17 years and never spoken to her, immediately went into action. She felt a special responsibility; she called the ambulance, even went to the hospital with her. The likelihood of speaking to a familiar stranger also increases as you are removed from the scene of routine meeting. If I were out strolling in Paris and ran into one of my commuter strangers from Riverdale, we would undoubtedly greet each other for the first time.

And the fact that familiar strangers often talk to each other in times of crisis or emergency raises an interesting question: is there any way to promote solidarity without having to rely on emergencies and crises?

TAVRIS: To study the familiar stranger, your students directly confronted commuters for information. Is this typical of your experimental style?

MILGRAM: Methods of inquiry must always be adapted to the problem at hand, and not all of life's phenomena can be assembled in a laboratory. You must often go out to meet the problem, and it doesn't require a license to ask someone a question. My experimental style aims to make visible the social pressures that operate on us unnoticed.

And an experiment has a tangible quality to it; you see people really behaving in front of you, which stimulates insight. It is a matter of bringing issues down to a level where you can see them clearly, rendering processes visible. Social life is highly complex. We are all fragile creatures entwined in a cobweb of social constraints. Experiments often serve as a beam that helps clarify the murky aspects of experience. And I do believe that a Pandora's box lies just beneath the surface of everyday life, so it is often worthwhile to challenge what you most take for granted. You are often surprised at what you find.

TAVRIS: For example?

MILGRAM: We've recently looked at the subway experience which is so characteristic of New York life. If you consider that at rush hour total strangers are pressed against each other in a noisy hot car, surrounded by poking elbows, it is astonishing how little aggression this produces. It is a remarkably regulated situation, and we tried to probe the norms that keep it manageable. The best way to start was to be simple-minded and not too sophisticated, since sophistication assumes too much about the structure you wish to illuminate.

TAVRIS: What did you do?

MILGRAM: I suggested to the class that we each go up to someone on the subway and simply ask for his seat. The immediate reaction of the class was exactly the same as yours—laughter. But anxious laughter is often a sign that you are on to something important. Many members of the class felt that no one in New York would give up his seat simply because a stranger asked him to. My students did a second thing that uncovered their prejudices. They said that the person would have to justify his request by asserting illness, nausea, dizziness; they assumed that the request itself would not gain the seat. A third clue: I asked for volunteers from a class of graduate students, but they recoiled *en masse.* That's very revealing. After all, they merely had to make a trivial request. Why was it so frightening a project? In other words, the very formulation of the research question began to generate emotional clues to its answer. Finally, one brave soul, Ira Goodman, took on the heroic assignment, accompanied by a student observer. Goodman was asked to make the request courteously, and without initial justification, to 20 passengers.

TAVRIS: What happened?

MILGRAM: Within a week, rumors started to circulate at the Graduate Center. ''They're getting up! They're getting up!'' The news provoked astonishment, delight, wonder. Students made pilgrimages to Goodman as if he had uncovered a profound secret of survival in the New York subway, and at the next session of the seminar, he announced that about half of those he had asked had gotten up. He didn't even have to give a reason.

But one discrepancy struck me in Goodman's report. He had only approached 14 people instead of the hoped-for 20. Since he was normally quite conscientious, I asked why. He said: ''I just couldn't go on. It was one of the most difficult things I ever did in my life.'' Was there something idiosyncratic about Goodman, or was he telling us something profoundly revealing about social behavior generally? There was only one way to find out. Each of us would repeat the experiment, and neither I nor my colleague, Professor Irwin Katz, would be exempted.

Frankly, despite Goodman's initial experience, I assumed it would be easy. I approached a seated passenger and was about to utter the magical phrase. But the words seemed lodged in my trachea and would simply not emerge. I stood there frozen, then retreated, the mission unfulfilled. My student observer urged me to try again, but I was overwhelmed by paralyzing inhibition. I argued to myself: "What kind of craven coward are you? You told your class to do it. How can you go back to them without carrying out your own assignment?" Finally, after several unsuccessful tries, I went up to a passenger and choked out the request, "Excuse me, sir, may I have your seat?" A moment of stark anomic panic overcame me. But the man got right up and gave me the seat. A second blow was yet to come. Taking the man's seat, I was overwhelmed by the need to behave in a way that would justify my request. My head sank between my knees, and I could feel my face blanching. I was not role-playing. I actually felt as if I were going to perish. Then the third discovery: as soon as I got off the train, at the next station, all of the tension disappeared.

TAVRIS: What underlying social principles does such an experiment reveal?

MILGRAM: First, it points up the enormous inhibitory anxiety that ordinarily prevents us from breaching social norms. Asking a person for his seat is a trivial matter, yet it was extremely difficult to make the request. Second, it highlights the powerful need to justify one's request by appearing sick or exhausted. I must stress that this is not acting, but a compelled playing out of the logic of social relations. Finally, the fact that all of these intense feelings were synthesized in, and were limited to the particular situation, shows the power of immediate circumstances on feelings and behavior. I was relieved and back to normal the instant I was off the train.

TAVRIS: Your reaction sounds typical of the subjects in the obedience experiment. Many of them felt obliged to follow the experimenter's orders to shock an innocent victim, even though they felt great anxiety.

MILGRAM: Yes. The subway experience gave me a better understanding of why some subjects obeyed. I experienced the anxiety they felt as they considered repudiating the experimenter. That anxiety forms a powerful barrier that must be surmounted, whether one's action is consequential—disobeying an authority—or trivial—asking for a seat on the subway.

Do you know there are people who choose to die in a burning building rather than run outside with their pants off? Embarrassment and the fear of violating apparently trivial norms often lock us into intolerable predicaments. And these are not minor regulatory forces in social life, but basic ones.

TAVRIS: Can you recommend a similar experiment for those of us in cities without subways?

MILGRAM: If you think it is easy to violate social constraints, get onto a bus and sing out loud. Full-throated song now, no humming. Many people will say it is easy to carry out this act, but not one in a hundred will be able to do it.

The point is not to *think* about singing, but to try to *do* it. Only in action can you fully realize the forces operative in social behavior. That is why I am an experimentalist.

TAVRIS: It seems to me, though, that many experiments, while entertaining, do not take one beyond what sensitive perception and feeling would. Some people criticized the obedience work by saying, "I knew that." After all, centuries of human history amply document the excesses of following orders. What advantage derives from an experiment that confirms history?

MILGRAM: The purpose of the obedience experiment was neither to confirm nor disconfirm history, but to study the psychological function of obedience; the conditions under which it occurs, the defense mechanisms it entails, the emotional forces that keep the person obeying. The criticism you cite is akin to saying that we know people die of cancer, so why study it?

Further, it is difficult for people to sort out what they know from what they only think they know. The clearest indication of ignorance about obedience is that when psychiatrists, psychologists and others were asked to predict the performance of subjects in the experiment, they failed totally. The psychiatrists said, for example, that only one person in a thousand would administer the highest shock on the board, and they were off by a factor of 500.

Moreover, we must ask whether people really do learn the lessons of history. Isn't it always the "other guy" who shamelessly submits to authority, even in violation of elementary morality? I think it is hard for many people to accept that they themselves have the potential to yield without limit to authority. All the pedagogic means at our disposal, whether in the form of history, literature, or experiments, need to be called into service to heighten awareness of this issue.

Finally, if one group criticizes the experiments because they merely confirm history, an equally vociferous group vehemently denies that Americans are capable of the degree of obedience demonstrated in my experiment, and they consequently repudiate me and the experiment. I suggest people read my book and draw their own conclusions.

TAVRIS: Your obedience work and city work both consider the network of social rules that constrain us. In the galaxy of factors that make up a city's atmosphere, for example, which do you think are the most important?

MILGRAM: Clearly, the degree of moral and social involvement people have with each other, and the way this is limited by the objective circumstances of city life. There are so many people and events to cope with that you must simply disregard many possible inputs, just to get on.

If you live on a country road you can say hello to each of the occasional persons who passes by; but obviously you can't do this on Fifth Avenue.

As a measure of social involvement for instance, we are now studying the response to a lost child in big city and small town. A child of nine asks people to help him call his home. The graduate students report a strong difference between city and town dwellers; in the city, more people refused to extend help to the nine-year-old. I like the problem because there is no more meaningful measure of the quality of a culture than the manner in which it treats its children.

TAVRIS: But is it inevitable that big cities breed impersonal treatment of others? You don't find drunks or beggars on the streets in Chinese cities, but if you did it would be everyone's responsibility to help. The moral norms are to aid the other guy, so no one person must play lone Samaritan.

MILGRAM: I would be reluctant to compare a city such as Peking, in which the atmosphere is permeated with political doctrines and imperatives, to Western cities. Beyond that, it is true that not all large cities are alike. But the most general movement is toward an adaptation common to all cities. Paris today seems more like New York than it did 20 years ago, and 50 years from now they will be even more alike, as adaptive needs come to dominate local color. There will be some cultural differences, but these will fade, and I regard this as most unfortunate.

TAVRIS: You have just spent a year in Paris studying mental maps of the city. What are they?

MILGRAM: A mental map is the picture of the city that a person carries in his mind: the streets, neighborhoods, squares that are important to him, the way they are linked together, and the emotional charge attached to each element. The initial idea came from Kevin Lynch's book *The Image of the City*. The external city is encoded in the brain: you could say there is a city inside the mind. Even if the external city were destroyed, it could be reconstructed by reference to the mind's model of the city.

TAVRIS: What did you find out about Paris?

MILGRAM: First, that reality and mental maps are imperfectly linked. For example, the Seine may course a great arc through Paris, almost forming a half circle, but Parisians imagine it a much gentler curve, and some think the river a straight line as it flows through the city. And the pattern of known to unknown parts of the city is fascinating: there are large areas of eastern Paris that are not known to anyone but the residents of those particular neighborhoods. Old people tend to retain the map of an earlier Paris and find it hard to include newer elements, however monumental.

TAVRIS: Don't people have different maps, depending on their experience and economic status?

MILGRAM: There is both a universal mental map of Paris which all Parisians share, and there are specialized maps depending on one's personal biography and social class. We interviewed more than 200 Parisians, workers and professionals, and there were striking differences along class lines. For example, 63 percent of the professionals recognized a slide of the Place Furstenberg, an unexceptional square that professionals infuse with a kind of bourgeois sentimentality; only 15 percent of the workers could recognize it. And 84 percent of the professionals could identify the UNESCO complex at Place de Fontenoy; only 24 percent of the workers did. So there is an important class basis to the mental map.

On the other hand, as many workers as professionals recognized the Place St. Martin. And Notre Dame still represents the psychological core of the city to everyone, as it did a thousand years ago. So the maps have both universal and idiosyncratic components to them.

TAVRIS: What are mental maps good for?

MILGRAM: People make many important decisions based on their conception of a city, rather than the reality of it. That's been well demonstrated. So it is important for planners to know how the city sits in the mind. And wouldn't it be enlightening to have such mental maps for Periclean Athens, for Dickensian London? Unfortunately, there were no social psychologists to construct such maps systematically at the time, but we know better and will do our duty.

TAVRIS: I'd like to turn to another of your real-world explorations, the effects of TV violence. In eight elaborate studies you found no differences between the people who watched the antisocial show and the controls. Has the effect of television on behavior been overrated?

MILGRAM: I don't know if it's overrated, but neither I nor my colleagues were able to establish a causal relationship. My ideal experiment would have been to divide the country in half, remove all violence on television west of the Mississippi and include it east of the Mississippi, enforce laws so that no one could move from one part of the country to the other, and then see what happens over a five or ten-year period. It turned out not to be practical, so I had to work with what I had.

The approach was to take an antisocial act, write it into a real TV program (*Medical Center*), show some cities the program containing it and others the same program without it, then give everyone an opportunity to imitate the antisocial act. I thought we would detect imitation, but we didn't. You can control everything about an experiment but the outcome.

TAVRIS: But why didn't you find the link?

MILGRAM: Perhaps the antisocial act—breaking into charity boxes and stealing money—was not dramatic enough. Perhaps people have been so sated with violence in the media that one show doesn't make a difference. Perhaps there is no such link. This experiment, like most, is a chip in a complex mosaic. No one study can tell the whole story. We have not established that the portrayal of violence leads to violence, but we cannot discard that hypothesis either.

TAVRIS: Do you plan to do more research on the effects of television?

MILGRAM: I don't know. Actually, it occurs to me that perhaps it is not the content of TV but its form that constitutes the real affront to human sensibilities: I mean the constant interruption of cognitive processes every 12 minutes by irrelevant material—commercials. I wonder what decrement in appreciation and understanding comes about when children watch a show with such interruptions. I think this will be an important problem.

TAVRIS: Let's back up a moment if we may. How did you get into the field of psychology?

MILGRAM: My boyhood interests were scientific. I edited the high-school science magazine, and my first article in 1949 was on the effects of radiation on the incidence of leukemia in the Hiroshima and Nagasaki survivors. I was always doing experiments; it was as natural as breathing, and I tried to understand how everything worked.

I fell away from science in college to pursue courses in political philosophy, music and art. But I finally came to the realization that although I was interested in the questions raised by Plato, Thomas Hobbes and John Locke, I was unwilling to accept their mode of arriving at answers. I was interested in human questions that could be answered by objective methods. In the '50s the Ford Foundation had a program to move people into the behavioral sciences. It seemed like a perfect opportunity, and I shifted into social psychology at the Department of Social Relations at Harvard. Men of uncommon wisdom ran things at the time, and created a climate in which ideas and excellence found ready support and encouragement.

TAVRIS: Who were your most important influences at Harvard?

MILGRAM: Gordon Allport was my long-time mentor and friend. He was a modest man with a pink face; you felt an intense loving quality about him. Since I wasn't interested in personality theory, he did not provide a specific intellectual input, but he gave me a strong sense of my own potential. Allport was my spiritual and emotional support. He cared for people deeply.

TAVRIS: If Gordon Allport was your spiritual advisor, who was your most important intellectual influence as a student?

MILGRAM: Solomon Asch, a brilliant, creative man, who possessed great philosophic depth. He is certainly the most impressive social psychologist I have known. I was his teaching assistant when he visited Harvard, and later worked for him at the Institute for Advanced Study in Princeton. He was always very independent. I recall the day when the U.S. launched a successful space probe, after some early failures. The scientists at the Institute were visibly excited—as I was—at the prospects for space exploration. But Asch was uniquely calm, pointing out that we had enough problems on earth to solve, and he questioned the wisdom of deflecting attention to space. Of course there was enormous prescience in that view, but it wasn't recognized at the time.

TAVRIS: What about Henry Murray?

MILGRAM: A highly original man who abhorred unnecessary academic rules and regulations. But my most indelible memory of him concerns a song. In my early 20s I wrote songs as a hobby. I wrote a song for Murray that he claims got him a psychology building. They had torn down the historic old psychological clinic on Plimpton Street, and naturally everyone connected with it was very sad. Murray wanted me to write a song about it for a big dinner with President Nathan M. Pusey. At first I said no, since I was up to my ears in work. But the song more or less spontaneously materialized. After I gave Murray the song, I went off to Europe to collect data for my thesis. I didn't even turn in the paper I owed him for his course. So it was two years before I knew what had happened with the song.

TAVRIS: Which was . . .

MILGRAM: I went to find Murray to give him that long overdue paper. I was feeling enormously contrite, but the first thing he said to me was: "Stanley Milgram! You should have seen how well it went over! It was because of your song that we got this building, you know!" My song was more important to him than the late paper.

Harvard was full of lively souls like Henry Murray; some are still there. Roger Brown was a brilliant assistant professor 20 years ago and remains an inspiring scholar; Jerome Bruner was a vital and dynamic force, though he's now settled at Oxford.

TAVRIS: What would you say are the ingredients that make for a creative social psychologist?

MILGRAM: It's complicated. On the one hand, he needs to be detached and objective. On the other hand, he will never discover anything if he lacks feeling for the pulse and emotionality of social life. You know, social life is a nexus of emotional attachments that constrain, guide and support the individual. To understand why people behave as they do you have to be aware of the feelings aroused in everyday social situations.

TAVRIS: And beyond that?

MILGRAM: Out of your perception of such feelings, insights may arise. They may take the form of explicit principles of social behavior. But, more often, they express themselves in symbolic form, and the experiment is the symbol. I mean, just as a playwright's understanding of the human situation reveals itself in his own mind in dramaturgical form, so for the creative investigator, intuition translates directly into an experimental format that permits him both to express his intuition and critically examine it.

TAVRIS: Are there any ideas you had that you now especially wish you had carried out?

MILGRAM: Only one, really. The idea started in the summer of 1960, when some friends and I decided to improvise some street-theater scenes. We stopped at restaurants along the Massachusetts Turnpike, and enacted common human situations: irate wife discovers her husband with another woman and rages at him in an incomprehensible mock-foreign language. What impressed me was that despite the extreme emotion in the encounter, onlookers conspicuously avoided involvement, even when the husband shook and slapped his "wife" in retaliation.

When I returned to my room at Harvard, I reviewed the reaction of the patrons, and wrote out a set of experiments in which the subjects were to be exposed to people who needed help. Subjects would sit in a waiting room; through a closed door they overhear an argument between a man and a woman; the man would become increasingly aggressive, in gradual steps, and finally the woman would cry out for help. I planned to study when people would intervene, and under what conditions. I designed a timer into the connecting door, so I'd know exactly how long people delayed before helping.

TAVRIS: The bystander problem.

MILGRAM: Yes, although then I called it the problem of "social intrusion." A month after seeking out those experiments, I began to teach at Yale and work on the obedience experiments. I didn't have time to study social intrusion too, but once a year I issued to each class a solemn prophesy that if they worked on the bystander problem they would be making an important contribution to social psychology. Every year highly intelligent graduate students would listen with interest, and every year they would go off and study attitude change, which was fashionable at Yale then.

TAVRIS: When did they begin to see the error of their ways?

MILGRAM: With the Kitty Genovese murder, and the 38 silent witnesses. The matter attracted nationwide interest and finally social scientists attempted experimental formulations of the problem. My graduate students carried out an unpublished field study in which a supposed drunk abused a woman in a laundromat. She called for help, and the question was how long it would be before she got it. The class found the experiment fascinating. But the *Zeitgeist* was about to catch up with us. Soon many other studies of this sort were being carried out. The best work was done by Bibb Latané and John M. Darley, then at Columbia and New York University. They chose the right variables, related them to the Genovese case, applied technical ingenuity, and reported their work in clear English. Appropriately, they won the AAS prize. And the field of bystander research is still blooming.

TAVRIS: How did that make you feel?

MILGRAM: The only satisfactions I derived from all this were of two sorts: first, what I regarded as a highly important sociopsychological question was now coming under examination; and second, a kind of prophetic function was fulfilled by my own experimental analysis of this type of situation, an analysis that preceded the Kitty Genovese case by three years, yet prophesied it in many ways.

The common view is that social psychologists derive their experiments from life, and there is an important measure of truth in this. But it's also true that events, such as the Genovese case, are the inevitable unfolding of forces that experimental analysis will frequently pinpoint first. Underlying the silly incident in the restaurant was an important principle of social behavior; by focusing on that latent principle, and extending it through to a concrete dramatized experiment, one could foresee certain inevitable results of such a principle. The Genovese case was merely one publicized expression of that principle. So analysis, combined with a certain imagined dramatic extension, will often prefigure events by years and decades.

TAVRIS: You generate a lot of ideas. What happens to them?

MILGRAM: Some of these ideas are realized; others filter into the atmosphere and they stimulate others to carry them out. Some are expressed through students. Some just fade. But Leo Szilard was certainly right when he said it is not the ideas you have, but those you act on that determine your character as a scientist. Every imaginative scientist dies with a host of good ideas that never make it into print.

TAVRIS: How did you come up with the idea for the obedience experiment?

MILGRAM: I was trying to think of a way to make Asch's conformity experiment more humanly significant. I was dissatisfied that the test of conformity was judgments about *lines*. I wondered whether groups could pressure a person into performing an act whose human import was more readily apparent, perhaps behaving aggressively toward another person, say by administering increasingly severe shocks to him. But to study the group effect you would also need an experimental control; you'd have to know how the subject performed without any group pressure. At that instant, my thought shifted, zeroing in on this experimental control. Just how far *would* a person go under the experimenter's orders? It was an incandescent moment, the fusion of a general idea on obedience with a specific technical procedure. Within a few minutes, dozens of ideas on relevant variables emerged, and the only problem was to get them all down on paper.

But many years after I had completed the obedience experiments, I realized that my concerns about submission to authority had been incubating since I was a first-year graduate student.

TAVRIS: How so?

MILGRAM: For one, the central issues were symbolically expressed in a story I had concocted. Briefly, the story was about two men who agreed to accompany a clerk into an old shabby office. One of the men was informed by the clerk that his death had been scheduled for that day and that he had a choice of two possible methods of execution. The man immediately objected that neither method was suitable in his case, and after a lot of bickering, persuaded the clerk to execute him more humanely. And he was done in.

The second person, however, who was also brought into this bizarre situation, had quietly left the room. Nothing happened to him. When the clerk noticed that he had gone, he simply closed the office, glad he could quit work early that day.

The story was quite macabre, but gave me insight into certain extraordinary features of social behavior. And it contains many of the elements that later appear in the obedience experiment, in particular the way the man accepted the alternatives that were presented to him. He failed to question the legitimacy of the entire context; he became preoccupied with choices as defined by the clerk and not with the larger issue of whether he should be there at all. He forgot that he could simply leave, as his friend did.

In just this way, our experimental subjects would temporize or get too technical or worry about details, trying to find the formula that would end their conflict. They did not see the larger framework of the situation, and consequently they couldn't see how to break out of it. The ability to see the larger context is precisely what we need to liberate ourselves.

TAVRIS: What then is the solution to the problem of the good man who is "only following orders?"

MILGRAM: The first thing to realize is that there are no easy solutions. In order to have civilization you must have some degree of authority. Once that authority is established, it doesn't matter much whether the system is called a democracy or a dictatorship: the common man responds to government policies with expected obedience, whether in Nazi Germany or democratic America.

TAVRIS: Then you do not think there is much variation in the extent of obedience that governments demand, or rather in the extent of disobedience they tolerate?

MILGRAM: Every society must have a structure of authority but this doesn't mean that the range of freedom is the same in every country. And of course it is true that Germany's destruction of millions of innocent men, women and children in concentration camps demonstrated the worst excess of obedience we've seen. But American democracy also has instituted policies that were severe and inhumane: the destruction of American Indians, the enslavement of blacks, the incarceration of the Japanese during the Second World War, Vietnam. There are always people who obey, who carry out the policies. When authority goes awry, individuals do not seem to have enough resources to put on the brakes.

But the problem is complicated. Individual standards of conscience are themselves generated from a matrix of authority relationships. Morality, as well as blind obedience, comes from authority. For every person who performs an immoral act on account of authority there is another who is restrained from doing so.

TAVRIS: Then how do we guard against authority's excesses?

MILGRAM: First, we need to be aware of the problem of indiscriminate submission to authority. And I have tried to foster that awareness with my work. It is a first step. Second, since we know men will comply, even with the most malevolent authorities, we have a special obligation to place in positions of authority those most likely to be humane and wise. But there is a long-range source of hope, too. People are inventive, and the variety of political forms we have seen in the last 5000 years does not exhaust all possibilities. Perhaps the challenge is to invent the political structure that will give conscience a better chance against errant authority.

The Individual in a Social World

ESSAYS AND EXPERIMENTS

PART 1

--- ❖ ---

The Individual in the City

The argument for studying the effect of the city on the individual seems self-evident: It is the fate of many of us to live in cities, and we ought to understand how this social fact shapes feeling, action, and thought. By the mid-sixties, social psychology had studied interaction within smaller units, but it had not yet examined how the person is affected by the extended urban environment. Urban questions had a well-entrenched tradition in sociology, but for some reason the social psychologist had preferred to examine small-scale social relationships—the dyad, the small group, or in his most expansive moments, intergroup relations. Yet the city itself remained immune to sociopsychological inquiry.

Many sides to the psychological effect of city life awaited examination. There was, first, the texture of everyday experience in the urban setting. How could it be described, and what precise features contribute to the differing tone of life in cities and small towns? Everyone who visits New York City feels its frenetic pace, and some complain of the abrasiveness of its inhabitants, but it remains for the social psychologist to determine if these constitute actual or merely alleged features of the social environment, and to demonstrate this by applying objective techniques of measurement. Would it be possible to measure the "ambience" of a city as we measure the temperature of the ocean with a thermometer? The purpose of such measurement is, first, to sift objective fact from prevailing fiction, second, to allow

1

for more sensitive and valid comparisons among different settings, and finally, to stimulate us to explain such differences that we find.

An interest in such questions is most likely to arise in people who have not only felt the quality of city life, but who have a number of contrasting experiences which show them that the frenetic pace and the abrasiveness are not as invariable features of life as the law of gravity, but are variables which alter in strength in different settings.

For many years I lived in New York, Boston, and Paris. The contrast between life in these cities and my experiences in small towns doubtless stimulated my interest in this topic. This biographic accident provided a rich background of detail and experience from which a scientific exploration could be safely launched. The subjective emphasis is reflected in the first article, "The Experience of Living in Cities." The article does not start from very abstract considerations, but from the predicament of the single individual and the way in which the city constitutes a set of social facts that continuously impinge on him.

Beneath the questions raised in "The Experience of Living in Cities" is a deeper skepticism of whether differences between urban and rural persons exist at all, or whether they simply reflect prejudices and social myths. Sometimes in the midst of a lecture on urban differences I am afflicted with the painful thought that I am talking nonsense, simply perpetuating prejudices of rural folk against the city. In such moments, it is best to withdraw from academic abstraction and try to imagine the implications of such statements in concrete and measurable terms.

The required strategy is to find some simple act, embedded in the flux of daily life, that will tap a significant feature of the urban milieu. For example, in one seminar we discussed the presumed indifference of the urban dweller to the problems of his coinhabitants. Then the students and I devised a concrete situation in which children who claimed to be lost asked pedestrians for aid in downtown areas of New York City and several small towns. The initial results showed a higher likelihood of aid in the small towns. The students, David Lucido and Harold Takooshian, subsequently carried the experiments to Boston and Philadelphia and invariably found that a "lost child" is more likely to be helped in a small town than in a large city.

In all cases, the findings are actuarial. That is, the proportion of individuals who help changes from town to city, but there are always people in both settings who deny or extend help to the children. But this shift in proportion is sufficient to establish the tone of different communities, to create a distinctive ambience.

Experiments in social psychology often arise out of personal experiences. On a recent trip to Amherst, Massachusetts, I walked into a stationery store. The clerk beamed a broad smile, which immediately prompted me to believe that we were acquaintances. I rummaged my mind for the person's name, but finally apologized that I had forgotten it.

The situation rapidly deteriorated into general confusion, since the clerk was perplexed by my apology. He could not understand why I assumed that we knew each other.

The misunderstanding arose because in the urban milieu in which I live, people do not smile at one another unless they are acquainted. For the rural clerk it was natural to smile at everyone, even a stranger. Once again, the reality of rural-urban differences was asserted. I related this incident to students in my seminar. But of course, the anecdotal method rarely proves anything. Members of the class contributed countervailing anecdotes of their own implying opposite conclusions.

It was clear that only a *systematic* examination of the issue would advance us beyond an exchange of anecdotes. To carry out a systematic study we would need, at the very least, a clearly measurable act that would in some sense signify a readiness to be friendly, at least superficially friendly. I suggested we approach strangers on the street and, without explanation, extend our hands in a friendly manner, as if to shake. Would the person reciprocate and shake hands? What could be a simpler or more symbolically pregnant measure of "friendliness" than this unreflective response?

Thirteen student experimenters went into the streets of mid-town New York City, hands outstretched, then into small towns in New Jersey, Long Island, and Westchester County, forever extending their hands. The results showed a highly significant difference in the readiness of town and city dwellers to reciprocate the gesture (see Table I.1). Of the city dwellers, 38.5 percent reciprocated, but 66.7 percent of the town dwellers consumated the handshake. Although the behavior in question is simple, it is symbolically rich, and it is highly responsive to such variables as age, sex, and race. Table I.2 shows that almost three times as many women shook hands in the small towns as in the city. This is a small fact, but it is reliably gleaned and gives us a further measure of the reality of urban-town differences.

The myriad details which distinguish cities from small towns need to

TABLE I.1 INCIDENCE OF RECIPROCATED HANDSHAKING IN TOWNS AND CITY (ALL SUBJECTS)

	Towns	City	
Yes	62	40	102
	66.7%	38.5%	
No	31	64	95
	33.3%	61.5%	
	93	104	197

TABLE I.2 INCIDENCE OF
RECIPROCATED
HANDSHAKING BY WOMEN
SUBJECTS IN TOWNS AND
CITY

	Towns	City	
Yes	25	8	33
	56.8%	19.0%	
No	19	34	53
	43.2%	80.1%	
	44	42	86

Chi-square = 11.415
$p < 0.001$

be brought under the discipline of a theoretical framework. I attempted to do this in "The Experience of Living in Cities" by invoking the concept of "overload," and showing how it is produced by the demographic exigencies of urban life.

In addition to all the phenomena of the large city, resulting from density, homogeneity, and large numbers, there is a stage beyond: *the great city effect*. This refers to the special excitement of New York, Paris, London, and a few other urban agglomerations whose spirit and excitement seem to transcend the negative effects of overload.

BYSTANDER INTERVENTION

Sometimes a dramatic event will jolt ordinary people into thinking about the deeper issues of social life. It was not the murder of Kitty Genovese, but the failure of numerous neighbors to come to her aid while she was being killed that aroused consternation. Is indifference an inevitable consequence of urban life? Carey McWilliams, editor of *The Nation*, asked me to write an article about the incident. I agreed without hesitation because the Genovese case had given me an uncanny sensation of *déjà vu*. A few years earlier, in 1960, I had devised an experiment which prefigured the Genovese case in its essential details. In this experiment, a man appeared to assault a woman in the presence of a group of casual bystanders. I suspected that there would be strong inhibitions against bystander intervention: I wanted to study the exact conditions that would determine whether or not people would be motivated to intervene. I did not carry out the experiment at the time, and soon, in the Genovese affair, urban reality was to catch up and overtake experimental imagination. And in the Genovese case, a true-to-life incident rather than an experimentally contrived situation needed to be analyzed. My friend Paul

Studies in Social Intrusion

Experiments in Social Psychology: Other People's Business.

Social Involvement

The Problem: Under what circumstances do other peoples business become our own. Under what conditions do we implicate ourselves in it.

Every group of two people, circulating in the larger society, have a kind of protective social membrane around them that isolates them from the larger society. Thus, others will not interfere with their discussion, if they donot know between the two.

But, under certain circumstances, the general outsider will intrude. If for example, a man is beating his girl friend, their will be intrusion. If a person in harming another, there will be intrusion.

To undertake a series of experiments, in a naturalistic social settings, to understand some of the bases of social intrusion.

Very interesting theoretical concepts. Social privacy. Acceptable intrusions. Inviolable social fields. There are definitely forces that keep people from interfering or becoming implicated in the discussion of others. Might work with a standard intrusion situation.

Some questions: Will people more likely intrude when women are the insiders, when me are the insiders, or when insiders are mixed.
1)Relationship between side of insider group and intrusion tendency for intrusion. etc.

Aug 20 1960

Social Intrusion

The experiments could be undertaken first in a laboratory setting, and with relative ease. One could announce an experiment in perception. Several subjects would be seated in a dim room for dark adaptation to occur. It would be in that setting that the eliciting predicament would be staged. (Eventually, some of the predicaments could be moved to a more naturalistic setting).

Eliciting progression and response progression.

Eliciting progression: The staged scene could be carefully rehearsed and preplanned so that it induces more and more the likelihood of intrusion. It could go through carefully shaped stages. For example:
joking stage
light argument stage
heavier argument
girl slaps man
man slaps girl
man twist arm of girl
girl calls for help (or simply shrieks, then calls for help).

On the response progression, we can measure various degrees of intrusion. Remarks to someone else; light remarks to social couple; admonition; threat; physical intervention.

Question: why use this particular model for intrusion. Wouldn't simple joking also elicit it? Yes, in the laboratory, but certainly not in the field situation.

Devices to prevent intrusion upon first intrusion--if man speaks to neighbor--might about it, neighbor says: why don't you mind your own business? Might reinforce this with others.

FIGURE I.1
The author's notes for studies in "social intrusion" presaged the Kitty Genovese incident by several years.

Hollander, the sociologist, collaborated with me in an analysis written for *The Nation* (p. 31). A fundamental viewpoint is expressed in the article: The question of bystander intervention has a moral component to it—that is what makes it interesting. But the social psychologist needs to see beyond the moral judgment to the analyzable causes of bystander response. Whether a person intervened or not is not only an expression of personal morality, but also depends on the exact way in which numerous variables of the situation fall into place.

Generally, we think about the Genovese case from the morally superior assumption that we would do better. Here we confuse our self-perception, generally skewed in a favorable direction, with an understanding of the actual causes of behavior. We may think ill of the Kew Gardens residents, but how often has each of us averted our eyes or walked away from the scene of a confrontation where one individual was obviously in need of help?

Social psychology has no monopoly in the understanding of bystander behavior. Startling insights into the bystander phenomenon are provided by anthropological examination of life in circumstances different from our own. Colin Turnbull's monograph, *The Mountain People,* describes the life of the Ik, an African tribe which lives under such impoverished conditions that it has turned into a society where every person is concerned only with personal survival. The uniform response to another person's distress is amusement or indifference. The picture portrayed by Turnbull is dreadful and depressing, but it serves to remind us that social behavior is always responsive to the material conditions of our existence, and that social norms will change in response to altered circumstances. Even the degree of helpfulness and compassion we now display to one another is precarious, dependent upon the larger social and environmental structures that support our present mode of life.

MENTAL REPRESENTATION OF THE CITY

If the individual is to function in the city, he must have some mental representation of it, and this phenomenon is addressed in the papers on mental maps. The work was stimulated by the thinking of Kevin Lynch. His 1960 book, *The Image of the City,* sparked research on urban imagability, which by now must contain a bibliography of several hundred contributions. Parallel developments were underway in departments of geography, where cartography had long been an established specialty, and which has recently extended its mapmaking to include not merely what the geographic environment is like, but what people *think* it is like.

We can assume that individuals have at least fragmentary mental maps of the city; the scientific problem is to learn how to measure the maps and how to express generalizations on the basis of the maps of many individuals. The methods used in this type of research were quite variable, and my hope was to give it a precision, and perhaps elegance, beyond existing studies. In "A Psychological Map of New York City" (p. 72), my collaborators and I conceived of the city as an infinite number of viewing points, and we wondered to what extent each of these points communicates a sense of location to the inhabitants.

But for all of its rigor, this study was too limited in scope. The effort to photograph the 150 viewing points and to obtain recognition judgments for each of them was substantial, but the resultant findings were thin and barely scratched the surface of how individuals mentally encode a city. Recognition of scenes, after all, is but a small part of the process. I wanted a set of maps—perhaps an atlas—that captured richer aspects of the individual's mental map of a city. A Guggenheim Fellowship in 1972–1973 permitted me to go to Paris to extend the work on psychological representation.

"Psychological Maps of Paris" represents a multidimensional approach to cognitive mapping. Of all the studies reported in this book, it was the most difficult to carry out. This may seem surprising in view of its modest scope, particularly in comparison with the complex logistics of, say, the study of television violence (p. 287). But the difficulty of carrying out a study is not a fixed quantity, but a relationship between the work to be done and the resources available to do the job. In Paris I had the generous cooperation of Professor Serge Moscovici, Director of the Laboratory of Social Psychology, and the expert collaboration of Mme. Denise Jodelet. But there were almost no funds, and French subjects are more difficult to obtain than Americans, especially when their selection must conform to rigid constraints of sampling.

As I went on, the task became virtually a cottage industry, with my children pasting stamps on envelopes, my wife typing names and addresses from French phone books, and I assuming the lowly task of errand boy, messenger, and general factotum. The environment cannot help but influence the style and texture of the actual execution of research: About one-quarter of the subjects were interviewed in a Parisian restaurant. In the end, a useful surprise: The French government gave the project a grant of 35,000 francs, permitting me to employ a French survey organization to reach uncompleted cells in our sample, particularly among lower-class Parisians. The analysis of data was substantially accomplished in France, and I was impressed by the extent to which computer technology is readily available in western Europe. The results of the inquiry were summarized in "Psychological Maps of Paris"; a more extensive exhibit on the work was displayed in the Piltzer Gallery in Paris, where it appears that materials I assumed to be social psychology were construed by others as a species of conceptual art.

Space limitations in the Paris article did not then permit me to cite a 1973 study written by Pailhous describing the manner in which French

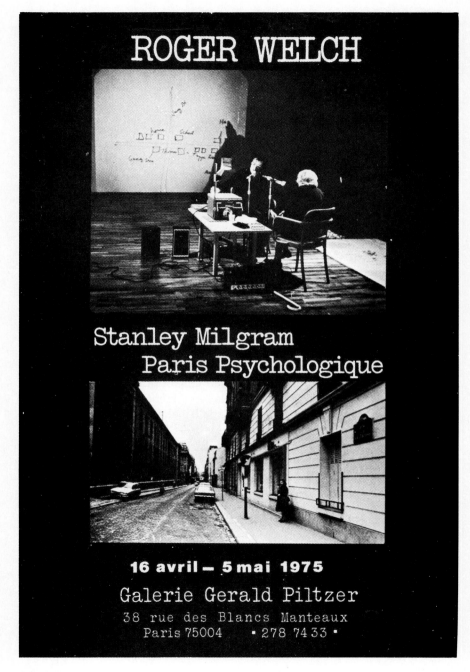

FIGURE I.2
". . . materials I assumed to be social psychology were construed by others as a species of conceptual art." (Poster designed by conceptual artist Roger Welch.)

taxi drivers learn to orient themselves in the city. Pailhous points out that drivers first develop a knowledge of a primary network of streets. This network is almost universally known. They then develop secondary networks of a more idiosyncratic nature that are linked to the primary network. The street patterns of Parisian *patés* (blocks) are highly irregular, often forming irregular polygons. But Pailhous notes that when taxi drivers are asked to draw them, they often regularize the patterns, turning a trapezoid, for instance, into a rectangle and following other gestalt principles of good form.

"Paris is a non-Euclidean city." This remark was first made by my nephew, Dr. Joseph Gerver, who was completing his dissertation in mathematics and was visiting us in Paris. His observation corresponded to my own experience. Streets one assumes to be parallel may eventually intersect. If you miss an intersection and attempt to loop back at the next, you may find yourself in a completely unfamiliar neighborhood, unable to return to your starting point. Parisian street patterns defy the Euclidean mind; they are best embodied in some abstruse Riemannian geometry.

A pleasant career could be made of mapping the world's great capitals. But I am sure the next important step is to develop an adequate theory of mental maps, one that cogently accounts for the transformation of geographic information into its psychological form. The mental map is different from the geographic reality, yet it is sufficiently veridical to be useful. What set of transforms is needed to convert the geographic city into a city of the mind?

REFERENCES

LYNCH, K., 1960. *The Image of the City.* Cambridge, Mass.: MIT and Harvard University Press.

PAILHOUS, J., 1970. *La Representation de l'Espace Urbain: L'Exemple du Chauffeur de Taxi.* Paris: Presses Universitaires de France.

TURNBULL, C., 1973. *The Mountain People.* New York: Simon & Schuster.

1

The Experience of Living in Cities

❖

When I first came to New York it seemed like a nightmare. As soon as I got off the train at Grand Central I was caught up in pushing, shoving crowds on 42nd Street. Sometimes people bumped into me without apology; what really frightened me was to see two people literally engaged in combat for possession of a cab. Why were they so rushed? Even drunks on the street were bypassed without a glance. People didn't seem to care about each other at all.

This statement represents a common reaction to a great city, but it does not tell the whole story. Obviously, cities have great appeal because of their variety, eventfulness, possibility of choice, and the stimulation of an intense atmosphere that many individuals find a desirable background to their lives. Where face-to-face contacts are important, the city offers unparalleled possibilities. It has been calculated by the Regional Plan Association[1] that in Nassau County, a suburb of New York City, an individual can meet 11,000 others within a 10-minute radius of his office by foot or car. In Newark, a moderate-sized city, he can meet more than 20,000 persons within this radius. But in midtown Manhattan he can meet fully 220,000. So there is an order-of-magnitude increment in the communication possibilities offered by a great city. That is one of the bases of its

This paper was first published in *Science*, Vol. 167 (March 13, 1970), pp. 1461–1468. The paper was based on an address given by the author on September 2, 1969 at the 77th annual meeting of the American Psychological Association in Washington, D.C. Copyright © 1970 by the American Association for the Advancement of Science. Reprinted by permission.

appeal and, indeed, of its functional necessity. The city provides options that no other social arrangement permits. But there is a negative side also, as we shall see.

Granted that cities are indispensable in complex society, we may still ask what contribution psychology can make to understanding the experience of living in them. What theories are relevant? How can we extend our knowledge of the psychological aspects of life in cities through empirical inquiry? If empirical inquiry is possible, along what lines should it proceed? In short, where do we start in constructing urban theory and in laying out lines of research?

Observation is the indispensable starting point. Any observer in the streets of midtown Manhattan will see (1) large numbers of people, (2) a high population density, and (3) heterogeneity of population. These three factors need to be at the root of any sociopsychological theory of city life, for they condition all aspects of our experience in the metropolis. Louis Wirth,[2] if not the first to point to these factors, is nonetheless the sociologist who relied most heavily on them in his analysis of the city. Yet, for a psychologist, there is something unsatisfactory about Wirth's theoretical variables. Numbers, density, and heterogeneity are demographic facts but they are not yet psychological facts. They are external to the individual. Psychology needs an idea that links the individual's *experience* to the demographic circumstances of urban life.

One link is provided by the concept of overload. This term, drawn from systems analysis, refers to a system's inability to process inputs from the environment because there are too many inputs for the system to cope with, or because successive inputs come so fast that input A cannot be processed when input B is presented. When overload is present, adaptations occur. The system must set priorities and make choices. A may be processed first while B is kept in abeyance, or one input may be sacrificed altogether. City life, as we experience it, constitutes a continuous set of encounters with overload, and of resultant adaptations. Overload characteristically deforms daily life on several levels, impinging on role performance, the evolution of social norms, cognitive functioning, and the use of facilities.

The concept has been implicit in several theories of urban experience. In 1903 Georg Simmel[3] pointed out that, since urban dwellers come into contact with vast numbers of people each day, they conserve psychic energy by becoming acquainted with a far smaller proportion of people than their rural counterparts do, and by maintaining more superficial relationships even with these acquaintances. Wirth[2] points specifically to "the superficiality, the anonymity, and the transitory character of urban social relations."

One adaptive response to overload, therefore, is the allocation of less time to each input. A second adaptive mechanism is disregard of low-priority inputs. Principles of selectivity are formulated such that investment of time and energy are reserved for carefully defined inputs (the urbanite disregards the drunk sick on the street as he purposefully navigates through the crowd). Third, boundaries are redrawn in certain social transactions so that the overloaded system can shift the burden to the other party in the exchange; thus, harried New York bus drivers once made change for customers, but now this responsibility has been shifted to the client, who must have the exact fare ready. Fourth, reception is blocked off prior to entrance into a system; city dwellers increasingly use unlisted telephone numbers to prevent individuals from calling them, and a small but growing number resort to keeping the telephone off the hook to prevent incoming calls. More subtly, a city dweller blocks inputs by assuming an unfriendly countenance, which discourages others from initiating contact. Additionally, social screening devices are interposed between the individual and environmental inputs (in a town of 5000 anyone can drop in to chat with the mayor, but in the metropolis organizational screening devices deflect inputs to other destinations). Fifth, the intensity of inputs is diminished by filtering devices, so that only weak and relatively superficial forms of involvement with others are allowed. Sixth, specialized institutions are created to absorb inputs that would otherwise swamp the individual (welfare departments handle the financial needs of a million individuals in New York City, who would otherwise create an army of mendicants continuously importuning the pedestrian). The interposition of institutions between the individual and the social world, a characteristic of all modern society, and most notably of the large metropolis, has its negative side. It deprives the individual of a sense of direct contact and spontaneous integration in the life around him. It simultaneously protects and estranges the individual from his social environment.

Many of these adaptive mechanisms apply not only to individuals but to institutional systems as well, as Meier[4] has so brilliantly shown in connection with the library and the stock exchange.

In sum, the observed behavior of the urbanite in a wide range of situations appears to be determined largely by a variety of adaptations to overload. I now deal with several specific consequences of responses to overload, which make for differences in the tone of city and town.

SOCIAL RESPONSIBILITY

The principal point of interest for a social psychology of the city is that moral and social involvement with individuals is necessarily restricted. This is a direct and necessary function of excess of input over capacity to process. Such restriction of involvement runs a broad spectrum from refusal to become involved in the needs of another person, even when the person desperately needs assistance, through refusal to do favors, to the simple withdrawal of courtesies (such as offering a lady a seat, or saying "sorry" when a pedestrian collision occurs). In any transaction more and more details need to be dropped as the total number of units to be processed increases and assaults an instrument of limited processing capacity.

The ultimate adaptation to an overloaded social environment is to totally disregard the needs, interests, and demands of those whom one does not define as relevant to the satisfaction of personal needs, and to develop highly efficient perceptual means of determining whether an individual falls into the category of friend or stranger. The disparity in the treatment of friends and strangers ought to be greater in cities than in towns; the time allotment and willingness to become involved with those who have no personal claim on one's time is likely to be less in cities than in towns.

Bystander Intervention in Crises

The most striking deficiencies in social responsibility in cities occur in crisis situations, such as the Genovese murder in Queens. In 1964, Catherine Genovese, coming home from a night job in the early hours of an April morning, was stabbed repeatedly, over an extended period of time. Thirty-eight residents of a respectable New York City neighborhood admit to having witnessed at least a part of the attack, but none went to her aid or called the police until after she was dead. Milgram and Hollander, writing in *The Nation*,[5] analyzed the event in these terms:

> Urban friendships and associations are not primarily formed on the basis of physical proximity. A person with numerous close friends in different parts of the city may not know the occupant of an adjacent apartment. This does not mean that a city dweller has fewer friends than does a villager, or knows fewer persons who will come to his aid; however, it does mean that his allies are not constantly at hand. Miss Genovese required immediate aid from those physically present. There is no evidence that the city had deprived Miss Genovese of human associations, but the friends who might have rushed to her side were miles from the scene of her tragedy.
>
> Further, it is known that her cries for help were not directed to a specific person; they were general. But only individuals can act, and as the cries were not specifically directed, no particular person felt a special responsibility. The crime and the failure of community response seem absurd to us. At the time, it may well have seemed equally absurd to the Kew Gardens residents that not one of the neighbors would have called the police. A collective paralysis may have developed from the belief of each of the witnesses that someone else must surely have taken that obvious step.

Latané and Darley[6] have reported laboratory approaches to the study of bystander intervention and have established experimentally the following principle: the larger the number of bystanders, the less the likelihood that any one of them will intervene in an emergency. Gaertner and Bickman[7] of The City University of New York have extended the by-stander studies to an examination of help across ethnic lines. Blacks and whites, with clearly identifiable accents, called strangers (through what the caller represented as an error in telephone dialing), gave them a plausible story of being stranded on an outlying highway without more dimes, and asked the stranger to call a garage. The experimenters found that the white callers had a significantly better chance of obtaining assistance than the black callers. This suggests that ethnic allegiance may well be another means of coping with overload: the city dweller can reduce excessive demands and screen out urban heterogeneity by re-sponding along ethnic lines; overload is made more manageable by limiting the "span of sympathy."

In any quantitative characterization of the social texture of city life, a necessary first step is the application of such experimental methods as these to field situations in large cities and small towns. Theorists argue that the indifference shown in the Genovese case would not be found in a small town, but in the absence of solid experimental evidence the question remains an open one.

More than just callousness prevents bystanders from participating in altercations between people. A rule of urban life is respect for other people's emotional and social privacy, perhaps because physical privacy is so hard to achieve. And in situations for which the standards are heterogeneous, it is much harder to know whether taking an active role is unwarranted meddling or an appropriate response to a critical situation. If a husband and wife are quarreling in public, at what point should a bystander step in? On the one hand, the heterogeneity of the city produces substantially greater tolerance about behavior, dress, and codes of ethics than is generally found in the small town, but this diversity also encour-ages people to withhold aid for fear of antagonizing the participants or crossing an inappropriate and difficult-to-define line.

Moreover, the frequency of demands present in the city gives rise to norms of noninvolvement. There are practical limitations to the Samaritan impulse in a major city. If a citizen attended to every needy person, if he were sensitive to and acted on every altruistic impulse that was evoked in the city, he could scarcely keep his own affairs in order.

Willingness to Trust and Assist Strangers

We now move away from crisis situations to less urgent examples of social responsibility. For it is not only in situations of dramatic need but in the ordinary, everyday willingness to lend a hand that the city dweller is said to be deficient relative to his small-town cousin. The comparative method must be used in any empirical examination of this question. A commonplace social situation is staged in an urban setting and in a small town—a situation to which a subject can respond by either extending help or withholding it. The responses in town and city are compared.

One factor in the purported unwillingness of urbanites to be helpful to strangers may well be their heightened sense of physical (and emotional) vulnerability—a feeling that is supported by urban crime statistics. A key test for distinguishing between city and town behavior, therefore, is determining how city dwellers compare with town dwellers in offering aid that increases their personal vulnerability and requires some trust of strangers. Altman, Levine, Nadien, and Villena[8] of The City University of New York devised a study to compare the behaviors of city and town dwellers in this respect. The criterion used in this study was the willingness of householders to allow strangers to enter their home to use the telephone. The student investigators individually rang doorbells, explained that they had misplaced the address of a friend nearby, and asked to use the phone. The investigators (two males and two females) made 100 requests for entry into homes in the city and 60 requests in the small towns. The results for middle-income housing developments in Manhattan were compared with data for several small towns (Stony Point, Spring Valley, Ramapo, Nyack, New City, and West Clarkstown) in Rockland County, outside of New York City. As Table 1.1 shows, in all cases there was a sharp increase in the proportion of entries achieved by an experimenter when he moved from the city to a small town. In the most extreme case the experimenter was five times as likely to gain admission to homes in a small town as to homes in Manhattan. Although the female experimenters had notably greater success both in cities and in towns than the male experimenters had, each of the four students did at least twice as well in towns as in cities. This suggests that the city-town distinction overrides even the predictably greater fear of male strangers than of female ones.

The lower level of helpfulness by city dwellers seems due in part to recognition of the dangers of living in Manhattan, rather than to mere indifference or coldness. It is significant that 75 percent of all the city respondents received and answered messages by shouting through closed doors and by peering out through peepholes; in the towns, by contrast, about 75 percent of the respondents opened the door.

Supporting the experimenters' quantitative results was their general observation that the town dwellers were noticeably more friendly and less suspicious than the city dwellers. In seeking to explain the reasons for the greater sense of psychological vulnerability city dwellers feel, above and beyond the differences in crime statistics, Villena[8] points out that, if a crime is committed in a village, a resident of a neighboring village may not perceive the crime as personally relevant, though the geographic distance may be small, whereas a criminal act committed anywhere in the

TABLE 1.1 PERCENTS OF
ENTRIES ACHIEVED BY
INVESTIGATORS FOR CITY AND
TOWN DWELLINGS (SEE TEXT)

	Entries achieved (%)	
Experimenter	City*	Small town†
Male		
No. 1	16	40
No. 2	12	60
Female		
No. 3	40	87
No. 4	40	100

*Number of requests for entry, 100.
†Number of requests for entry, 60.

city, though miles from the city dweller's home is still verbally located within the city; thus, Villena says, "the inhabitant of the city possesses a larger vulnerable space."

Civilities

Even at the most superficial level of involvement—the exercise of every-day civilities—urbanites are reputedly deficient. People bump into each other and often do not apologize. They knock over another person's packages and, as often as not, proceed on their way with a grumpy exclamation instead of an offer of assistance. Such behavior, which many visitors to great cities find distasteful, is less common, we are told, in smaller communities, where traditional courtesies are more likely to be observed.

In some instances it is not simply that, in the city, traditional courtesies are violated; rather, the cities develop new norms of non-involvement. These are so well defined and so deeply a part of city life that *they* constitute the norms people are reluctant to violate. Men are actually embarrassed to give up a seat on the subway to an old woman; they mumble, "I was getting off anyway," instead of making the gesture in a straightforward and gracious way. These norms develop because everyone realizes that, in situations of high population density, people cannot implicate themselves in each others' affairs, for to do so would create conditions of continual distraction which would frustrate purposeful action.

In discussing the effects of overload I do not imply that at every instant the city dweller is bombarded with an unmanageable number of inputs, and that his responses are determined by the excess of input at any given instant. Rather, adaptation occurs in the form of gradual evolution of norms of behavior. Norms are evolved in response to frequent discrete experiences of overload; they persist and become generalized modes of responding.

Overload on Cognitive Capacities: Anonymity

That we respond differently toward those whom we know and those who are strangers to us is a truism. An eager patron aggressively cuts in front of someone in a long movie line to save time only to confront a friend; he then behaves sheepishly. A man is involved in an automobile accident caused by another driver, emerges from his car shouting in rage, then moderates his behavior on discovering a friend driving the other car. The city dweller, when walking through the midtown streets, is in a state of continual anonymity vis-à-vis the other pedestrians.

Anonymity is part of a continuous spectrum ranging from total anonymity to full acquaintance, and it may well be that measurement of the precise degrees of anonymity in cities and towns would help to explain important distinctions between the quality of life in each. Conditions of full acquaintance, for example, offer security and familiarity, but they may also be stifling, because the individual is caught in a web of established relationships. Conditions of complete anonymity, by contrast, provide freedom from routinized social ties, but they may also create feelings of alienation and detachment.

Empirically one could investigate the proportion of activities in which the city dweller or the town dweller is known by others at given times in his daily life, and the proportion of activities in the course of which he interacts with individuals who know him. At his job, for instance, the city dweller may be known to as many people as his rural counterpart. However, when he is not fulfilling his occupational role—say, when merely traveling about the city—the urbanite is doubtless more anonymous than his rural counterpart.

Limited empirical work on anonymity has begun. Zimbardo[9] has tested whether the social anonymity and impersonality of the big city encourage greater vandalism than do small towns. Zimbardo arranged for one automobile to be left for 64 hours near the Bronx campus of New York University and for a counterpart to be left for the same number of hours near Stanford University in Palo Alto. The license plates on the two cars were removed and the hoods were opened, to provide "releaser cues" for potential vandals. The New York car was stripped of all movable parts within the first 24 hours, and by the end of 3 days was only a hunk of metal rubble. Unexpectedly, however, most of the destruction occurred during daylight hours, usually under the scrutiny of observers, and the leaders in the vandalism were well-dressed, white adults. The Palo Alto car was left untouched.

Zimbardo attributes the difference in the treatment accorded the two cars to the "acquired feelings of social anonymity provided by life in a city like New York," and he supports his conclusions with several other anecdotes illustrating casual, wanton vandalism in the city. In any comparative study of the effects of anonymity in city and town, however, there must be satisfactory control for other confounding factors: the large number of drug addicts in a city like New York; the higher proportion of slum-dwellers in the city; and so on.

Another direction for empirical study is investigation of the beneficial effects of anonymity. The impersonality of city life breeds its own tolerance for the private lives of the inhabitants. Individuality and even eccentricity, we may assume, can flourish more readily in the metropolis than in the small town. Stigmatized persons may find it easier to lead comfortable lives in the city, free of the constant scrutiny of neighbors. To what degree can this assumed difference between city and town be shown empirically? Judith Waters,[10] at The City University of New York, hypothesized that avowed homosexuals would be more likely to be accepted as tenants in a large city than in small towns, and she dispatched letters from homosexuals and from normal individuals to real estate agents in cities and towns across the country. The results of her study were inconclusive. But the general idea of examining the protective benefits of city life to the stigmatized ought to be pursued.

Role Behavior in Cities and Towns

Another product of urban overload is the adjustment in roles made by urbanites in daily interactions. As Wirth[2] has said: "Urbanites meet one another in highly segmental roles. . . . They are less dependent upon particular persons, and their dependence upon others is confined to a highly fractionalized aspect of the other's round of activity." This tendency is particularly noticeable in transactions between customers and individuals offering professional or sales services. The owner of a country store has time to become well acquainted with his dozen-or-so daily customers, but the girl at the checkout counter of a busy A & P, serving hundreds of customers a day, barely has time to toss the plaid stamps into one customer's shopping bag before the next customer confronts her with his pile of groceries.

Meier, in his stimulating analysis of the city,[4] discusses several adaptations a system may make when confronted by inputs that exceed its capacity to process them. Meier argues that, according to the principle of competition for scarce resources, the scope and time of the transaction shrink as customer volume and daily turnover rise. This, in fact, is what is meant by the "brusque" quality of city life. New standards have developed in cities concerning what levels of services are appropriate in business transactions (see Fig. 1.1).

McKenna and Morgenthau,[11] in a seminar at The City University of New York, devised a study (1) to compare the willingness of city dwellers and small-town dwellers to do favors for strangers that entailed expenditure of a small amount of time and slight inconvenience but no personal vulnerability, and (2) to determine whether the more compartmentalized, transitory relationships of the city would make urban salesgirls less likely than small-town salesgirls to carry out, for strangers, tasks not related to their customary roles.

To test for differences between city dwellers and small-town dwellers, a simple experiment was devised in which persons from both settings were asked (by telephone) to perform increasingly onerous favors for anonymous strangers.

Within the cities (Chicago, New York, and Philadelphia), half the calls were to housewives and the other half to salesgirls in women's apparel shops; the division was the same for the 37 small towns of the study, which were in the same states as the cities. Each experimenter represented

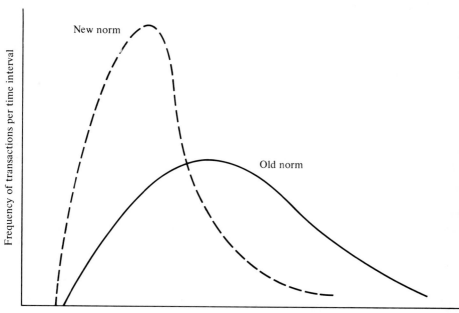

FIGURE 1.1
Changes in the demand for time for a given task when the overall transaction frequency increases in a social system. (Reprinted with permission from R. L. Meier, *A Communications Theory of Urban Growth*, 1962. Copyrighted by MIT Press, 1962.)

herself as a long-distance caller who had, through error, been connected with the respondent by the operator. The experimenter began by asking for simple information about the weather for purposes of travel. Next the experimenter excused herself on some pretext (asking the respondent to "please hold on"), put the phone down for almost a full minute, and then picked it up again and asked the respondent to provide the phone number of a hotel or motel in her vicinity at which the experimenter might stay during a forthcoming visit. Scores were assigned the subjects on the basis of how helpful they had been. McKenna summarizes her results in this manner:

> People in the city, whether they are engaged in a specific job or not, are less helpful and informative than people in small towns; . . . People at home, regardless of where they live, are less helpful and informative than people working in shops.

However, the absolute level of cooperativeness for urban subjects was found to be quite high, and does not accord with the stereotype of the urbanite as aloof, self-centered, and unwilling to help strangers. The quantitative differences obtained by McKenna and Morgenthau are less great than one might have expected. This again points up the need for extensive empirical research in rural-urban differences, research that goes far beyond that provided in the few illustrative pilot studies presented here. At this point we have very limited objective evidence on differences in the quality of social encounters in city and small town.

But the research needs to be guided by unifying theoretical concepts. As I have tried to demonstrate, the concept of overload helps to explain a wide variety of contrasts between city behavior and town behavior: (1) the differences in role enactment (the tendency of urban dwellers to deal with one another in highly segmented, functional terms, and of urban sales personnel to devote limited time and attention to their customers); (2) the evolution of urban norms quite different from traditional town values (such as the acceptance of noninvolvement, impersonality, and aloofness in urban life); (3) the adaptation of the urban dweller's cognitive processes (his inability to identify most of the people he sees daily, his screening of sensory stimuli, his development of blasé attitudes toward deviant or bizarre behavior, and his selectivity in responding to human demands); and (4) the competition for scarce facilities in the city (the subway rush; the fight for taxis; traffic jams; standing in line to await services). I suggest that contrasts between city and rural behavior probably reflect the responses of similar people to very different situations, rather than intrinsic differences in the personalities of rural and city dwellers. The city is a situation to which individuals respond adaptively.

*F*URTHER ASPECTS OF URBAN EXPERIENCE

Some features of urban experience do not fit neatly into the system of analysis presented thus far. They are no less important for that reason. The issues raised next are difficult to treat in quantitative fashion. Yet I prefer discussing them in a loose way to excluding them because appropriate language and data have not yet been developed. My aim is to suggest how phenomena such as "urban atmosphere" can be pinned down through techniques of measurement.

The "Atmosphere" of Great Cities

The contrast in the behavior of city and town dwellers has been a natural starting point for urban social scientists. But even among great cities there are marked differences in "atmosphere." The tone, pacing, and texture of social encounters are different in London and New York, and many persons willingly make financial sacrifices for the privilege of living within a specific urban atmosphere which they find pleasing or stimulating. A second perspective in the study of cities, therefore, is to define exactly what is meant by the atmosphere of a city and to pinpoint the factors that give rise to it. It may seem that urban atmosphere is too evanescent a quality to be reduced to a set of measurable variables, but I do not believe the matter can be judged before substantial effort has been made in this direction. It is obvious that any such approach must be comparative. It makes no sense at all to say that New York is "vibrant" and "frenetic" unless one has some specific city in mind as a basis of comparison.

In an undergraduate tutorial that I conducted at Harvard University some years ago, New York, London, and Paris were selected as reference points for attempts to measure urban atmosphere. We began with a simple question: Does any consensus exist about the qualities that typify given cities? To answer this question one could undertake a content analysis of travelbook, literary, and journalistic accounts of cities. A second approach, which we adopted, is to ask people to characterize (with descriptive terms and accounts of typical experiences) cities they have lived in or visited. In advertisements placed in the *New York Times* and the *Harvard Crimson* we asked people to give us accounts of specific incidents in London, Paris, or New York that best illuminated the character of that particular city. Questionnaires were then developed, and administered to persons who were familiar with at least two of the three cities.

Some distinctive patterns emerged.[12] The distinguishing themes concerning New York, for example, dealt with its diversity, its great size, its pace and level of activity, its cultural and entertainment opportunities, and the heterogeneity and segmentation ("ghettoization") of its population. New York elicited more descriptions in terms of physical qualities, pace, and emotional impact than Paris or London did, a fact which suggests that these are particularly important aspects of New York's ambience.

A contrasting profile emerges for London; in this case respondents placed far greater emphasis on their interactions with the inhabitants than on physical surroundings. There was near unanimity on certain themes: those dealing with the tolerance and courtesy of London's inhabitants. One respondent said:

> When I was 12, my grandfather took me to the British Museum . . . one day by tube and recited the *Aeneid* in Latin for my benefit. . . . He is rather deaf, speaks very loudly and it embarrassed the hell out of me, until I realized that nobody was paying any attention. Londoners are extremely worldly and tolerant.

In contrast, respondents who described New Yorkers as aloof, cold, and rude referred to such incidents as the following:

> I saw a boy of 19 passing out anti-war leaflets to passersby. When he stopped at a corner, a man dressed in a business suit walked by him at a brisk pace, hit the boy's arm, and scattered the leaflets all over the street. The man kept walking at the same pace down the block.

We need to obtain many more such descriptions of incidents, using careful methods of sampling. By the application of factor-analytic techniques, relevant dimensions for each city can be discerned.

The responses for Paris were about equally divided between responses concerning its inhabitants and those regarding its physical and sensory attributes. Cafés and parks were often mentioned as contributing to the sense that Paris is a city of amenities, but many respondents complained that Parisians were inhospitable, nasty, and cold.

We cannot be certain, of course, to what degree these statements reflect actual characteristics of the cities in question and to what degree they simply tap the respondents' knowledge of widely held preconceptions. Indeed, one may point to three factors, apart from the actual atmospheres of the cities, that determine the subjects' responses.

1. A person's impression of a given city depends on his implicit standard of comparison. A New Yorker who visits Paris may well describe that city as "leisurely," whereas a compatriot from Richmond, Virginia, may consider Paris too "hectic." Obtaining reciprocal judgment, in which New Yorkers judge Londoners, and Londoners judge New Yorkers, seems a useful way to take into account not only the city being judged but also the home city that serves as the visitor's base line.

2. Perceptions of a city are also affected by whether the observer is a tourist, a newcomer, or a longer-term resident. First, a tourist will be exposed to features of the city different from those familiar to a long-time resident. Second, a prerequisite for adapting to continuing life in a given city seems to be the filtering out of many observations about the city that the newcomer or tourist finds particularly arresting; this selective process seems to be part of the long-term resident's mechanism for coping with overload. In the interest of psychic economy, the resident simply learns to tune out many aspects of daily life. One method for studying the specific impact of adaptation on perception of the city is to ask several pairs of newcomers and old-timers (one newcomer and one old-timer to a pair) to walk down certain city blocks and then report separately what each has observed.

Additionally, many persons have noted that when travelers return to New York from an extended sojourn abroad they often feel themselves confronted with "brutal ugliness"[13] and a distinctive, frenetic atmosphere whose contributing details are, for a few hours or days, remarkably sharp and clear. This period of fresh perception should receive special attention in the study of city atmosphere. For, in a few days, details which are initially arresting become less easy to specify. They are assimilated into an increasingly familiar background atmosphere which, though important in setting the tone of things, is difficult to analyze. There is no better point at which to begin the study of city atmosphere than at the moment when a traveler returns from abroad.

3. The popular myths and expectations each visitor brings to the city will also affect the way in which he perceives it.[14] Sometimes a person's preconceptions about a city are relatively accurate distillations of its character, but preconceptions may also reinforce myths by filtering the visitor's perceptions to conform with his expectations. Preconceptions affect not only a person's perceptions of a city but what he reports about it.

The influence of a person's urban base line on his perceptions of a given city, the differences between the observations of the long-time inhabitant and those of the newcomer, and the filtering effect of personal expectations and stereotypes raise serious questions about the validity of travelers' reports. Moreover, no social psychologist wants to rely exclusively on verbal accounts if he is attempting to obtain an accurate and objective description of the cities' social texture, pace, and general atmosphere. What he needs to do is to devise means of embedding objective experimental measures in the daily flux of city life, measures that can accurately index the qualities of a given urban atmosphere.

EXPERIMENTAL COMPARISONS OF BEHAVIOR

Roy Feldman[15] incorporated these principles in a comparative study of behavior toward compatriots and foreigners in Paris, Athens, and Boston. Feldman wanted to see (1) whether absolute levels and patterns of helpfulness varied significantly from city to city, and (2) whether inhabitants in each city tended to treat compatriots differently from foreigners. He examined five concrete behavioral episodes, each carried out by a team of native experimenters and a team of American experimenters in the three cities. The episodes involved (1) asking natives of the city for street directions; (2) asking natives to mail a letter for the experimenter; (3) asking natives if they had just dropped a dollar bill (or the Greek or French equivalent) when the money actually belonged to the experimenter himself; (4) deliberately overpaying for goods in a store to see if the cashier would correct the mistake and return the excess money; and (5) determining whether taxicab drivers overcharged strangers and whether they took the most direct route available.

Feldman's results suggest some interesting contrasts in the profiles of the three cities. In Paris, for instance, certain stereotypes were borne out. Parisian cab drivers overcharged foreigners significantly more often than they overcharged compatriots. But other aspects of the Parisians' behavior were not in accord with American preconceptions: in mailing a letter for a stranger, Parisians treated foreigners significantly better than Athenians or Bostonians did, and, when asked to mail letters that were already stamped, Parisians actually treated foreigners better than they treated compatriots. Similarly, Parisians were significantly more honest than Athenians or Bostonians in resisting the temptation to claim money that was not theirs, and Parisians were the only citizens who were more honest with foreigners than with compatriots in this experiment.

Feldman's studies not only begin to quantify some of the variables that give a city its distinctive texture but they also provide a methodological model for other comparative research. His most important contribution is his successful application of objective, experimental measures to everyday situations, a mode of study which provides conclusions about urban life that are more pertinent than those achieved through laboratory experiments.

TEMPO AND PACE

Another important component of a city's atmosphere is its tempo or pace, an attribute frequently remarked on but less often studied. Does a city have a frenetic, hectic quality, or is it easygoing and leisurely? In any empirical treatment of this question, it is best to start in a very simple way. Walking speeds of pedestrians in different cities and in cities and towns should be measured and compared. William Berkowitz[16] of Lafayette College has undertaken an extensive series of studies of walking speeds in Philadelphia, New York, and Boston, as well as in small and moderate-sized towns. Berkowitz writes that "there does appear to be a significant linear relation between walking speed and size of municipality, but the absolute size of the difference varies by less than ten percent."

Perhaps the feeling of rapid tempo is due not so much to absolute pedestrian speeds as to the constant need to dodge others in a large city to avoid collisions with other pedestrians. (One basis for computing the adjustments needed to avoid collisions is to hypothesize a set of mechanical manikins sent walking along a city street and to calculate the number of collisions when no adjustments are made. Clearly, the higher the density of manikins the greater the number of collisions per unit of time, or, conversely, the greater the frequency of adjustments needed in higher population densities to avoid collisions.)

Patterns of automobile traffic contribute to a city's tempo. Driving an automobile provides a direct means of translating feelings about tempo into measurable acceleration, and a city's pace should be particularly evident in vehicular velocities, patterns of acceleration, and latency of response to traffic signals. The inexorable tempo of New York is expressed, further, in the manner in which pedestrians stand at busy intersections, impatiently awaiting a change in traffic light, making tentative excursions into the intersection, and frequently surging into the street even before the green light appears.

VISUAL COMPONENTS

Hall has remarked[17] that the physical layout of the city also affects its atmosphere. A gridiron pattern of streets gives the visitor a feeling of rationality, orderliness, and predictability but is sometimes monotonous. Winding lanes or streets branching off at strange angles, with many forks (as in Paris or Greenwich Village), create feelings of surprise and esthetic pleasure, while forcing greater decision-making in plotting one's course. Some would argue that the visual component is all-important—that the "look" of Paris or New York can almost be equated with its atmosphere. To investigate this hypothesis, we might conduct studies in which only blind, or at least blindfolded, respondents were used. We would no doubt discover that each city has a distinctive texture even when the visual component is eliminated.

SOURCES OF AMBIENCE

Thus far we have tried to pinpoint and measure some of the factors that contribute to the distinctive atmosphere of a great city. But we may also ask, Why do differences in urban atmosphere exist? How did they come about, and are they in any way related to the factors of density, large numbers, and heterogeneity discussed above?

First, there is the obvious factor that, even among great cities, populations and densities differ. The metropolitan areas of New York, London, and Paris, for example, contain 15 million, 12 million, and 8 million persons, respectively. London has average densities of 43 persons per acre, while Paris is more congested, with average densities of 114 persons per acre.[18] Whatever characteristics are specifically attributable to density are more likely to be pronounced in Paris than in London.

A second factor affecting the atmosphere of cities is the source from which the populations are drawn.[19] It is a characteristic of great cities that they do not reproduce their own populations, but that their numbers are constantly maintained and augmented by the influx of residents from other parts of the country. This can have a determining effect on the city's atmosphere. For example, Oslo is a city in which almost all of the residents are only one or two generations removed from a purely rural existence, and this contributes to its almost agricultural norms.

A third source of atmosphere is the general national culture. Paris combines adaptations to the demography of cities *and* certain values specific to French culture. New York is an admixture of American values and values that arise as a result of extraordinarily high density and large population.

Finally, one could speculate that the atmosphere of a great city is traceable to the specific historical conditions under which adaptations to urban overload occurred. For example, a city which acquired its mass and density during a period of commercial expansion will respond to new demographic conditions by adaptations designed to serve purely commercial needs. Thus, Chicago, which grew and became a great city under a purely commercial stimulus, adapted in a manner that emphasizes business needs. European capitals, on the other hand, incorporate many of the adaptations which were appropriate to the period of their increasing numbers and density. Because aristocratic values were prevalent at the time of the growth of these cities, the mechanisms developed for coping with overload were based on considerations other than pure efficiency. Thus, the manners, norms, and facilities of Paris and Vienna continue to reflect esthetic values and the idealization of leisure.

COGNITIVE MAPS OF CITIES

When we speak of "behavioral comparisons" among cities, we must specify which parts of the city are most relevant for sampling purposes. In a sampling of "New Yorkers," should we include residents of Bay Ridge or Flatbush as well as inhabitants of Manhattan? And, if so, how should we weight our sample distribution? One approach to defining relevant boundaries in sampling is to determine which areas form the psychological or cognitive core of the city. We weight our samples most heavily in the areas considered by most people to represent the "essence" of the city.

The psychologist is less interested in the geographic layout of a city or in its political boundaries than in the cognitive representation of the city. Hans Blumenfeld[20] points out that the perceptual structure of a modern city can be expressed by the "silhouette" of the group of skyscrapers at its center and that of smaller groups of office buildings at its "subcenters" but that urban areas can no longer, because of their vast extent, be experienced as fully articulated sets of streets, squares, and space.

In *The Image of the City*,[21] Kevin Lynch created a cognitive map of Boston by interviewing Bostonians. Perhaps his most significant finding was that, while certain landmarks, such as Paul Revere's house and the Boston Common, as well as the paths linking them, are known to almost all Bostonians, vast areas of the city are simply unknown to its inhabitants.

Using Lynch's technique, Donald Hooper[22] created a psychological map of New York from the answers to the study questionnaire on Paris, London, and New York. Hooper's results were similar to those of Lynch: New York appears to have a dense core of well-known landmarks in midtown Manhattan, surrounded by the vast unknown reaches of Queens, Brooklyn, and the Bronx. Times Square, Rockefeller Center, and the Fifth Avenue department stores alone comprise half the places specifically cited by respondents as the haunts in which they spent most of their time. However, outside the midtown area, only scattered landmarks were recognized. Another interesting pattern is evident: even the best-known symbols of New York are relatively self-contained, and the pathways joining them appear to be insignificant on the map.

The psychological map can be used for more than just sampling techniques. Lynch[21] argues, for instance, that a good city is highly "imageable," having many known symbols joined by widely known pathways, whereas dull cities are gray and nondescript. We might test the relative "imagibility" of several cities by determining the proportion of residents who recognize sampled geographic points and their accompanying pathways.

If we wanted to be even more precise we could construct a cognitive map that would not only show the symbols of the city but would measure the precise degree of cognitive significance of any given point in the city relative to any other. By applying a pattern of points to a map of New York City, for example, and taking photographs from each point, we could determine what proportion of a sample of the city's inhabitants could identify the locale specified by each point (see Fig. 1.2). We might even take the subjects blindfolded to a point represented on the map, then remove the blindfold and ask them to identify their location from the view around them.

One might also use psychological maps to gain insight into the differing perceptions of a given city that are held by members of its cultural subgroups, and into the manner in which their perceptions may change. In the earlier stages of life, whites and blacks alike probably have only a limited view of the city, centering on the immediate neighborhood in which they are raised. In adolescence, however, the field of knowledge of the white teen-ager probably undergoes rapid enlargement: he learns of opportunities in midtown and outlying sections and comes to see himself as functioning in a larger urban field. But the process of ghettoization, to which the black teen-ager is subjected, may well hamper the expansion of his sense of the city. These are speculative notions, but they are readily subject to precise test.

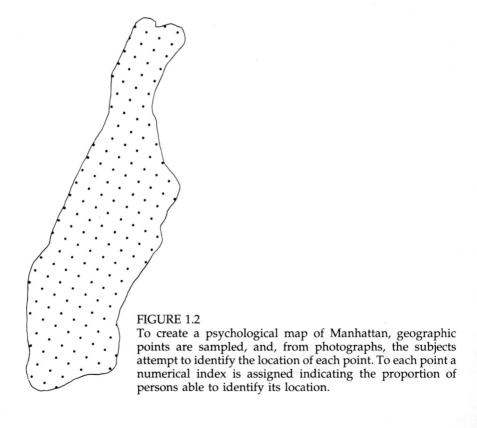

FIGURE 1.2
To create a psychological map of Manhattan, geographic points are sampled, and, from photographs, the subjects attempt to identify the location of each point. To each point a numerical index is assigned indicating the proportion of persons able to identify its location.

CONCLUSION

I have tried to indicate some organizing theory that starts with the basic facts of city life: large numbers, density, and heterogeneity. These are external to the individual. He experiences these factors as overloads at the level of roles, norms, cognitive functions, and facilities. These overloads lead to adaptive mechanisms which create the distinctive tone and behaviors of city life. These notions, of course, need to be examined by objective comparative studies of cities and towns.

A second perspective concerns the differing atmosphere of great cities, such as Paris, London, and New York. Each has a distinctive flavor, offering a differentiable quality of experience. More precise knowledge of urban atmosphere seems attainable through application of the tools of experimental inquiry.[23]

NOTES

1. *New York Times* (15 June 1969).
2. L. Wirth, *Amer. J. Soc.* **44,** 1 (1938). Wirth's ideas have come under heavy criticism by contemporary city planners, who point out that the city is broken down into neighborhoods, which fulfill many of the functions of small towns. See, for example, H. J. Gans, *People and Plans: Essays on Urban Problems and Solutions* (Basic Books, New York, 1968); J. Jacobs, *The Death and Life of Great American Cities* (Random House, New York, 1961); G. D. Suttles, *The Social Order of the Slum* (Univ. of Chicago Press, Chicago, 1968).
3. G. Simmel, *The Sociology of Georg Simmel*, K. H. Wolff, ed. (Macmillan, New York, 1950) [English translation of G. Simmel, *Die Grossstadte und das Geistesleben Die Grossstadt* (Jansch, Dresden, 1903)].
4. R. L. Meier, *A Communications Theory of Urban Growth* (MIT Press, Cambridge, Mass., 1962).
5. S. Milgram and P. Hollander, *Nation* **25,** 602 (1964).
6. B. Latané and J. Darley, *Amer. Sci.* **57,** 244 (1969).
7. S. Gaertner and L. Bickman (Graduate Center, The City University of New York), unpublished research.
8. D. Altman, M. Levine, M. Nadien, J. Villena (Graduate Center, The City University of New York), unpublished research.
9. P. G. Zimbardo, paper presented at the Nebraska Symposium on Motivation (1969).
10. J. Waters (Graduate Center, The City University of New York), unpublished research.
11. W. McKenna and S. Morgenthau (Graduate Center, The City University of New York), unpublished research.
12. N. Abuza (Harvard University), "The Paris-London-New York Questionnaires," unpublished.
13. P. Abelson, *Science* **165,** 853 (1969).

14. A. L. Strauss, ed., *The American City: A Sourcebook of Urban Imagery* (Aldine, Chicago, 1968).

15. R. E. Feldman, *J. Personality Soc. Psychol.* **10,** 202 (1968).

16. W. Berkowitz, personal communication.

17. E. T. Hall, *The Hidden Dimension* (Doubleday, New York, 1966).

18. P. Hall, *The World Cities* (McGraw-Hill, New York, 1966).

19. R. E. Park, E. W. Burgess, R. D. McKenzie, *The City* (Univ. of Chicago Press, Chicago, 1967), pp. 1–45.

20. H. Blumenfeld, in *The Quality of Urban Life* (Sage, Beverly Hills, Calif., 1969).

21. K. Lynch, *The Image of the City* (MIT and Harvard Univ. Press, Cambridge, Mass., 1960).

22. D. Hooper (Harvard University), unpublished.

23. Barbara Bengen worked closely with me in preparing an earlier version of this article. I thank Dr. Gary Winkel, editor of *Environment and Behavior,* for useful suggestions and advice.

2

The Urban Bystander

❖

Catherine Genovese, coming home from a night job in the early hours of an April morning, was stabbed repeatedly and over an extended period of time. Thirty-eight residents of a respectable New York City neighborhood admitted to having witnessed at least a part of the attack, but not one of them went to her aid or even so much as called the police until after she was dead.

We are all certain that we would have done better. Our indignation toward the residents of Kew Gardens swells to a sense of outrage. The crime, or more precisely, the lack of civic response to it, was so vile that Senator Russell of Georgia read the *New York Times* account of it into the *Congressional Record*. The fact that it *was* Senator Russell is an indication of the complex social reactions touched off by this neighborhood tragedy.

It is noteworthy, first, that anger is directed, not toward the crime, nor the criminal, but toward those who failed to halt the criminal's actions. It is a curious shift, reminiscent of recent trends in moralizing about the Nazi era. Writers once focused on the sins of the Nazis; it is now more fashionable to discuss the complicity of their victims. The event is significant, also, for the way it is being exploited. Senator Russell is but one case in point. In his home state, several brutal murders of Negroes have taken place before large crowds of unprotesting white onlookers, but the Senator has never felt called upon to insert reports of *these* brutalities into the *Record*. The crime against Miss Genovese no longer exists in and of itself. It is rapidly being assimilated to the uses and ideologies of the day.

For example, the Kew Gardens incident has become the occasion for a general attack on the city. It is portrayed as callous, cruel, indifferent to the needs of the people, and wholly inferior to the small town in the quality of its personal

This paper was written in collaboration with Paul Hollander and was first published under the title "The Murder They Heard," *The Nation*, Vol. 198, No. 25 (1964), pp. 602–604. Reprinted by permission of *The Nation*.

relationships. The abrasiveness of urban life cannot be argued; it is not true, however, that personal relationships are necessarily inferior in the city. They are merely organized on a different principle. Urban friendships and associations are not primarily formed on the basis of physical proximity. A person with numerous close friends in different parts of the city may not know the occupant of an adjacent apartment. Some hold this to be an advantage of the city; men and women can conduct lives unmonitored by the constant scrutiny of neighbors. This does not mean that a city dweller has fewer friends than does a villager, or knows fewer persons who will come to his aid; however, it does mean that his allies are not constantly at hand. Miss Genovese required immediate aid from those physically present; her predicament was desperate and not typical of the occasions when we look for the support of friends. There is no evidence that the city had deprived Miss Genovese of human associations, but the friends who might have rushed to her side were miles from the scene of her tragedy.

A truly extraordinary aspect of the case is the general readiness to forget the man who committed a very foul crime. This is typical of social reactions in present-day America. It begins to seem that everyone, having absorbed a smattering of sociology, looks at once beyond the concrete case in an eager quest for high-sounding generalizations that imply an enlightened social vista. What gets lost in many of these discussions—and what needs at least a partial restoration—is the notion that people may occasionally be responsible for what they do, even if their acts are criminal. In our righteous denunciation of the thirty-eight witnesses we should not forget that they did not commit the murder; they merely failed to prevent it. It is no more than clear thinking to bear in mind the moral difference.

A related and equally confusing error is to infer ethical values from the actual behavior of people in concrete situations. For example, in the case of Miss Genovese we must ask: did the witnesses remain passive because they thought it was the right thing to do, or did they refrain from action *despite* what they thought or felt they should do? We cannot take it for granted that people always do what they consider right. It would be more fruitful to inquire why, in general and in this particular case, there is so marked a discrepancy between values and behavior. What makes people choose a course of action that probably shames them in retrospect? How do they become reduced to resignation, acquiescence, and helplessness?

Those who vilify the residents of Kew Gardens measure them against the standard of their own ability to formulate high-minded moral prescriptions. But that is hardly a fair standard. It is entirely likely that many of the witnesses, at the level of stated opinion, feel quite as strongly as any of us about the moral requirement of aiding a helpless victim. They too, in general terms, know what *ought* to be done, and can state their values when the occasion arises. This has little, if anything, to do with actual behavior under the press of circumstances.

Furthermore, we must distinguish between the facts of the murder as finally known and reported in the press, and the events of the evening as they were experienced by the Kew Gardens residents. We can now say that if the police had been called after the first attack, the woman's life might have been saved, and we tend to judge the inaction of the Kew Gardens residents in the light of this lost possibility. That is natural, perhaps, but it is unrealistic. If those men and women had had as clear a grasp of the situation as we have now, the chances are that many of them would have acted to save Miss Genovese's life. What they had, instead, were fragments of an ambiguous, confusing, and doubtless frightening episode—one, moreover, that seemed totally incongruous in a respectable neighborhood. The very lack of correspondence between the violence of the crime and the character of the neighborhood must have created a sense of unreality which inhibited rational action. A lesser crime, one more in character with the locale—say, after-hours rowdiness from a group of college students—might have led more readily to a call for the police.

The incongruity, the sheer improbability of the event predisposed many to reject the most extreme interpretation: that a young woman was in fact being murdered outside the window. How much more probable, not to say more consoling, was the interpretation that a drunken party was sounding off, that two lovers were quarreling, or that youths were playing a nasty prank. Bruno Bettleheim, in *The Informed Heart*, describes how resistant many German Jews were to the signs around them of impending disaster. Given any possibility for fitting events into an acceptable order of things, men are quick to seize it. It takes courage to perceive clearly and without distortion. We cannot justly condemn all the Kew Gardens residents in the light of a horrible outcome which only the most perspicacious could have foreseen.

Why didn't the group of onlookers band together, run out into the street and subdue the assailant? Aside from the fact that such organization takes time, and that the onlookers were not in communication (who in such a community knows his neighbor's phone number?), there is another factor that would render such action almost impossible. Despite our current fears about the contagion of violence in the mass media, the fact remains that the middle-class person is totally unequipped to deal with its actual occurrence. More especially, he is unable to use personal violence, either singly or collectively, even when it is required for productive and socially valued ends.

More generally, modern societies are so organized as to discourage even the most beneficial, spontaneous group action. This applies with particular sharpness to the law-abiding, respectable segments of the population—such as the people of Kew Gardens—who have most thoroughly accepted the admonition: "do not take the law into your own hands." In a highly specialized society such people take it for granted that certain functions and activities—from garbage collection to fire protection; from meat certification to the control of criminals—are taken care of by specially trained people. The puzzle in the case under consideration is the reluctance to supply to the police even the barest information which it was essential they have if they were to fulfill their acknowledged functions.

Many facts of the case have not been made public, such as the quality of the relationship between Miss Genovese and the community, the extent to which she was recognized that night, and the number of persons who knew her. It is known that her cries for help were not directed to a specific person: they were general. But only individuals can act, and as the cries were not specifically directed, no particular person felt a special responsibility. The crime and the failure of community response seem absurd to us. At the time, it may well have seemed equally absurd to the Kew Gardens residents that not one of the neighbors would have called the police. A collective paralysis may have developed from the belief of each of the witnesses that someone else must surely have taken that obvious step.

If we ask why they did not call the police, we should also ask what were the alternatives. To be sure, phoning from within an apartment was the most prudent course of action, one involving the minimum of both physical inconvenience and personal involvement with a violent criminal. And yet, one has to assume that in the minds of many there lurked the alternative of going down to the street and defending the helpless woman. This, indeed, might have been felt as the ideal response. By comparison, a mere phone call from the safety of home may have seemed a cowardly compromise with what should be done. As often happens, the ideal solution was difficult, probably dangerous; but, as also happens, the practical, safe alternative may have seemed distasteful in the light of the ideal. Awareness of an ideal response often paralyzes a move toward the less than ideal alternative. Rather than accept the belittling second-best, the person so beset prefers to blot out the whole issue. Therefore, he pretends that there is nothing to get upset about. Probably it was only a drunken brawl.

The symbolic significance of "the street" for the middle-class mentality may have some relevance to the case. Although it cannot explain in full the failure to grab the telephone and call the police, it may account in part for the inertia and indifference. For the middle-class resident of a big city the street and what happens on the street are often symbolic of all that is vulgar and perilous in life. The street is the antithesis of privacy, security, and the support one derives from contemplating and living amidst prized personal possessions. The street represents the world of pushing and shoving crowds, potentially hostile strangers, sweat, dust, and noise.

Those who spend much time on the street have nothing better to do and nowhere better to go: the poor, the foot-loose, the drifters, juvenile delinquents. Therefore, the middle-class person seeks almost automatically to disengage himself from the life of the street; he is on it only from necessity, rarely for pleasure. Such considerations help explain the genesis of attitudes that prevented the witnesses from making the crucial phone call. The tragic drama was taking place on the street, hence hardly relevant to their lives; in fact, in some ways radically opposed to their outlook and concerns.

In an effort to make the strongest possible case against the Kew Gardens citizens, the press has ignored actual dangers of involvement, even at the level of calling the police. They have treated the "fears" of the residents as foolish rationalizations, utterly without basis. In doing so they have conveniently forgotten instances in which such involvement did not turn out well for the hero. One spectacular case in the early fifties, amply publicized by the press, concerned the misfortune of Arnold Schuster. While riding in the subway this young Brooklyn man spotted Willie Sutton, an escaped criminal. He reported this information to the police, and it led to Sutton's arrest. Schuster was proclaimed a hero, but before a month was up Schuster was dead—murdered in reprisal for his part in Sutton's recapture. Schuster had done nothing more than phone the police.

The fact is that there *are* risks even in minimal forms of involvement, and it is dishonest to ignore them. One becomes involved with the police, with the general agents of publicity that swarm to such events, and possibly with the criminal. If the criminal is not caught immediately, there is the chance that he will learn who called the police (which apartment did they enter first, whose pictures are in the papers, etc.) and may fear that the caller can identify him. The caller, then, is of special concern to the criminal. If a trial is held, the person who telephoned is likely to be a witness. Even if he is jailed, the criminal may have underworld friends who will act to avenge him. One is a responsible citizen and a worthy human being, not because of the absence of risk but because one acts in the face of it.

In seeking explanations for their inaction, we have not intended to defend, certainly not to excuse, Kew Gardens' passive witnesses. We have sought, rather, to put ourselves in their place, to try to understand their response. The causes we have suggested are in no way sufficient reason for inaction. Perhaps we should have started with a more fundamental question: Why should anyone have gone to the aid of the victim? Why should anyone have taken the trouble to call the police? The answer must be that it is a matter of common decency to help those who are in distress. It is a humane and compassionate requirement in the relations between people. Yet how generally is it observed? In New York City it is not at all unusual to see a man, sick with alcohol, lying in a doorway; he does not command the least attention or interest from those who pass by. The trouble here, as in Kew Gardens, is that the individual does not perceive that his interests are identified with others or with the community at large. And is such a perception possible? What evidence is there in the American community that collective interests have priority over personal advantage?

There are, of course, practical limitations to the Samaritan impulse in a major city. If a citizen attended to every needy person, if he were sensitive to and acted on every altruistic impulse that was evoked in the city, he could scarcely keep his own affairs in order. A calculated and strategic indifference is an unavoidable part of life in our cities, and it must be faced without sentimentality or rage. At most, each of us can resolve to extend the range of his responsibilities in some perceptible degree, to rise a little more adequately to moral obligations. City life is harsh; still, we owe it to ourselves and our fellows to resolve that it be no more harsh than is inevitable.

3

On Maintaining Social Norms: A Field Experiment in the Subway

❖

The general question that motivated this research was: How are social norms maintained? Our focus was on the type of norm described by Garfinkel (1964) as "routine grounds of everyday activity," norms which regulate everyday activity and which are neither made explicit nor codified. Scheff (1960) refers to this class of norms as "residual rules," residual in the sense that they are the restraints on behavior that persist after the formal social norms have been sorted out of the analysis. Scheff isolates these rules on the basis of two criteria: (1) people must be in substantial agreement about them; and (2) they are not noticed until a violation occurs. These rules have been likened to the rules of grammar in that one can follow them without an explicit knowledge of their content and yet notice a violation immediately.

The fact that these residual rules are usually unexpressed creates a serious obstacle to their study: We are virtually inarticulate about them. When compared with formal laws, for example, which have been explicitly codified, residual rules have been left unarticulated by the culture.

An important distinction between these residual rules and laws can be drawn in terms of enforcement. The mechanism for the maintenance of laws is obvious.

This article was written in collaboration with John Sabini and first appeared in A. Baum, J. E. Singer, and S. Valins (eds.) (1978), *Advances in Environmental Psychology*, 1, *The Urban Environment*, Lawrence Erlbaum Associates, Hillsdale, New Jersey. Reprinted by permission.

The entire law enforcement establishment is charged with the responsibility of keeping behavior within the law. Society is quite explicit about the consequences of breaking the law and about who should administer punishment. But who is charged with maintaining residual rules? What consequences should the residual rule breaker expect? Scheff posits a negative feedback system through which the rule breaker is returned to the straight and narrow, but he does not elaborate on the feedback process itself. Scott (1971), in an analysis of social norms from the point of view of the operant conditioning paradigm, defines social norms as "patterns of sanctions" and sanctions as the "reinforcing effect of interaction. (p. 85)" In this formulation, norms are maintained by the negative consequences of the violation. If this is the case, it should be possible to identify the negative consequences that are supposed to befall the violator. This, then, determined our strategy: we would violate a residual rule and observe the consequences to the violator.

The idea of studying this class of norms by their violation was introduced by Garfinkel (1964); his accounts contain qualitative evidence about the consequences of norm violation. The present research goes further in measuring the effects of violating a residual norm; it centers on a discrete and measurable response to the rule-breaker's action. We are thus able to quantify how people react to violated norms and by systematically changing features of the encounter, to treat the matter experimentally.

The residual rule selected for study was a rule of social behavior on the New York City subway system. The requirements of appropriate social behavior on the subway are, on the face of it, simple. People get on the subway for a very clear and specific reason: to get from one place to another in a brief period of time. The amount of interaction among the riders required for this purpose is minimal and the rules governing this interaction are widely adhered to. One rule of subway behavior is that seats are filled on a first-come, first-served basis. Another implicit rule is one that discourages passengers from talking to one another. Even though riders are often squeezed into very close proximity, they are rarely observed to converse. The experimenters in this study violated these rules by asking people for their seats. This procedure allowed for discrete, measurable responses: people could either give up their seats or refuse to do so.

Several notions about the outcome of such a request may be formulated:

1. Scott's analysis predicts that such a violation would result in "negative consequences."

2. Scheff suggests that a possible outcome of a residual rule violation is a process of "normalization." Normalization is the attribution

of a meaning to the violation that would make it seem not to be a violation at all. The attribution—"the experimenter is asking because he is sick"—would be such a "normalization."

3. Most of the experimenters expected not only refusal but some form of active rebuke.

4. Common sense suggests that it is impossible to obtain a seat on the subway simply by asking for it.

Harold Takooshian obtained data on this last point. He asked 16 people to predict what percentage of requests would result in the offer of a seat. Answers ranged from 1% to 55%; the median prediction was that 14% of those who were asked would give up their seats.

Before we describe the experimental procedure, it is worth pointing out some things that the procedure was *not*. The procedure was not an attempt to obtain seats by demanding that riders give them up. Experimenters were instructed to be sure to phrase their questions as requests, not as demands. The procedure was not designed to question the subjects' right to their seats. The subjects' right to their seats was affirmed in the request; you do not request things from people which they do not rightfully possess. The procedure does *not* involve some momentous or unreasonable request. Nothing of any great or lasting value was requested from the subjects. It is, in fact, the observation that this request is so reasonable and yet so rare that suggests the operation of some strong inhibitory social force.

*P*ROCEDURE

The experimenters were six male and four female graduate students. One woman was black; the other experimenters were white. Experimenters worked in pairs; as one performed the manipulation, the other recorded the data and observations.

The passengers on several mid-town routes of the New York City subway system formed the subject pool for the experiment. Experimenters were free to select their own subjects under the following constraints: Each experimenter asked one passenger from each of the following categories: man under 40 (by experimenter's approximation), woman under 40, man over 40, woman over 40. One member of each category was approached by each experimenter in each of the three conditions described in the following. Experimenters approached members of their own race only.

1. In the first condition (no justification), the experimenter approached a seated subject and said, "Excuse me. May I have your

seat?" The observer recorded the age and sex of the subject, whether or not the subject gave up the seat, and other reactions of the subjects and other passengers. Information about the time of day, subway line, and nearest station was also recorded.

As Table 3.1 shows, 56% of the subjects got up and offered their seats to the experimenters. An additional 12.3% of the subjects slid over to make room for the experimenter. (Experimenters had been instructed to ask for seats only if all of the seats in a car were taken, but it sometimes occurred that, although there did not appear to be any seats, room could be generated if the passengers squeezed together.) If these two responses are combined, we see that 68.3% of the subjects obtained seats by asking for them.

2. A second condition tested the hypothesis that subjects gave up their seats because they assumed the experimenters had some important reason for requesting it. In order to rule out this assumption, experimenters were instructed to say "Excuse me. May I have your seat? I can't read my book standing up." The

TABLE 3.1 SUBWAY EXPERIMENTS: RESPONSES IN EACH EXPERIMENTAL CONDITION[a]

No Justification Condition $n = 41$	
Subjects who gave up their seats	56.0%
Subjects who slid over to make room for E	12.3%
Subjects who did not give up their seats	31.7%
Trivial Justification Condition $n = 43$	
Subjects who gave up their seats	37.2%
Subjects who slid over to make room for E	4.7%[b]
Subjects who did not give up their seats	58.1%
Overheard Condition $n = 41$	
Subjects who gave up their seats	26.8%
Subjects who slid over to make room for E	9.8%[c]
Subjects who did not give up their seats	63.4%
Written Condition $n = 20$	
Subjects who gave up their seats	50.0%
Subjects who slid over to make room for E	0.0%[d]
Subjects who did not give up their seats	50.0%

[a]Overall Chi square for four conditions collapsing subjects who gave up their seats with those who slid over = 9.44, $df = 3$, $p < .05$.
[b]Z test between No Justification and Trivial Justification conditions (collapsing as above): $Z = 2.3$, $p < .05$.
[c]Z test between No Justification and Overheard conditions (collapsing as above): $Z = 2.7$, $p < .05$.
[d]Z test between No Justification condition and Written condition (collapsing as above): not significant.

experimenter stood holding a paperback mystery. It was expected that by supplying this trivial reason, experimenters would receive fewer seats. The expectation was confirmed; experimenters received significantly fewer seats (41.9% of the requests, $z = 2.3$, $p < .05$). In Scheff's terms, the trivial justification prevented the process of normalization; subjects could not as easily create some adequate justification for the request.

3. A third condition was included because we believed that subjects might have been so startled by the request that they didn't have time to formulate an adequate reply.[1] It seemed that they might have surrendered their seats because it was easier to do so than to figure out how to refuse in the brief time allowed. This condition was, therefore, designed to allow more time to formulate a reply.

    To do this, it was necessary to alert the passenger that a seat might be requested. An experimenter and confederate entered the subway car from different doors and converged in front of the subject. They then engaged in the following conversation, while giving the impression that they were strangers: E to confederate, "Excuse me. Do you think it would be alright if I asked someone for a seat?" The confederate replied "What?" E repeated, "Do you think it would be alright if I asked someone for a seat?" The confederate replied, noncommittally, "I don't know."

    This conversation was enacted in a sufficiently loud voice so that the passengers seated in front of the pair would definitely overhear it. The seated passengers would be alerted to the possibility that one of them might be approached with a request to surrender his or her seat. It gave the seated passengers time to formulate a response to the request, eliminating the startle component of the earlier conditions.

    Thus, after acting out the foregoing exchange, the experimenter paused for approximately 10 seconds, then turned to the nearest seated passenger, and requested his or her seat. In this condition, experimenters received seats only 36.5% of the time, compared to 68.3% in Condition 1. The additional time between the overhearing of the conversation and the direct request was used to advantage. Subjects were better prepared to turn down the request.

4. Finally, we wished to separate the content of the request from the oral manner in which it was delivered. An orally delivered question directed to a person seems to demand an immediate oral response. We wondered whether a written message would reduce the demand for an immediate and obliging response. Accordingly, in this condition, the experimenter stood in front of the subject and wrote the following message on a sheet of notebook

paper: "Excuse me. May I have your seat? I'd like very much to sit down. Thank you." The experimenter then passed the message to the subject, saying, "Excuse me." We expected fewer seats than in the basic variant, as the request on paper seemed less direct and somewhat more distant, especially since the subject was not forced to engage the experimenter in eye contact as he formulated a reply. Our expectation was wrong. Experimenters received seats 50.0% of the time, a nonsignificant decrease from the initial condition. (Each experimenter carried out this procedure twice rather than four times; the overall n equaled 20.) The reason for this result is not clear. This method seemed to add a touch of the bizarre to the procedure, perhaps adding to the subject's eagerness to end the whole interaction by simply giving up his seat.

Observers also recorded other aspects of the subjects' reactions. Subjects often had a vacant and bewildered facial expression. Of the subjects who gave up their seats in the initial condition, 70% did so without asking, "Why?"[2] Other subjects responded by simply saying, "No." Some subjects didn't seem to be distressed at all. Subjects who attributed sickness to the experimenter were often very concerned and comforting.

Information was also gathered about the reactions of other passengers who witnessed the incident. On a few occasions, other passengers openly chided a subject who had given up a seat. A more common reaction was for one rider to turn to another and say something such as, "Did you see that? He asked for a seat!" Such a comment points to the abnormal nature of the event and invites criticism of it. Witnesses to the exchange often turned and stared at the experimenter as he or she left the car.

The effects of the sex and age of experimenters and subjects are noted in Tables 3.2 and 3.3. Although these variables yield substantial differences in results, they are somewhat tangential to our main thesis and are not discussed in detail here.

An important aspect of the maintenance of social norms is revealed in the emotional reaction of the experimenters. Most students reported extreme difficulty in carrying out the assignment. Students reported that when standing in front of a subject, they felt anxious, tense, and embarrassed. Frequently, they were unable to vocalize the request for a seat and had to withdraw. They sometimes feared that they were the center of attention of the car and were often unable to look directly at the subject. Once having made the request and received a seat, they sometimes felt a need to enact behavior that would make the request appear justified (e.g., mimicking illness; some even felt faint).

We introduced our study partly in terms of the operant conditioning paradigm proposed by Scott as a framework for the understanding of social norms. What implications do our results have for this position? The

TABLE 3.2 EFFECT OF SEX OF EXPERIMENTER AND SUBJECT ON
ACCEDING TO REQUEST (FOR ALL CONDITIONS)

Sex of experimenter	Sex of subject	No. of subjects (n)	Responses		
			Got up (% of n)	Didn't get up (% of n)	Slid over (% of n)
M	M	45	40.0	53.3	6.7
	F	40	30.0	65.0	5.0
Total	(M + F)	85	35.3	58.8	5.9
F	M	30	66.7	26.7	6.7
	F	29	34.5	51.7	13.8
Total	(M + F)	59	50.8	39.0	10.2

TABLE 3.3 EFFECT OF EXPERIMENTER SEX AND SUBJECT AGE ON
ACCEDING TO REQUEST (FOR ALL CONDITIONS)

Age of of subject	Sex of experimenter	No. of subjects (n)	Responses		
			Got up (% of n)	Didn't get up (% of n)	Slid over (% of n)
Under 40	M	42	54.7	42.8	2.5
	F	30	63.3	30.0	6.7
Total	(M + F)	72	58.3	37.5	4.2
Over 40	M	43	27.9	62.9	9.2
	F	29	37.9	48.2	13.9
Total	(M + F)	72	31.9	57.0	11.1

answer depends on how one interprets "patterns of sanctions" which
Scott holds maintain social norms. If this phrase is interpreted in its most
simple and direct sense, and in a way consistent with the operant paradigm, it means the objectively specifiable response of the social environment to the violation. If we use this interpretation, the operant analysis
does not work. The response on the part of others to a request for a seat is
usually to grant the request. The 68.3% rate with which experimenters
received seats corresponds to a variable ratio schedule of positive rein-
forcement (VR2). Skinner (1953) has found that behavior reinforced under
this schedule is enhanced rather than discouraged. If we take "patterns of
sanctions" to include the internal, emotional effects of the request which
are not produced by the environment but which are direct accompaniments of the experimenters' behavior, the analysis has some merit, but it
leads directly to the question: Why does the act of making this simple
request cause such an acute emotional response?[3]

One might approach this question by focusing on the content of the request; after all, the experimenters did ask for a seat from someone when they had no clear right to do so. But this focus on the seat seems misguided. The intensity of the emotion the experimenters experienced is incommensurate with the small cost involved in the subjects' giving up their seats. The significance of the request lies not in the seat (that is not the heart of the matter), but in the redefinition of the immediate relationship between experimenters and subjects that the request involves. Since it is this disruption of relationships that constitutes the essence of the violation, it can better be understood as a breach of a structure of social interaction than as merely a violation of rules of equity in interaction.

One analysis of the structure of social interaction that may help us to understand the sources of this effect has been provided by Goffman (1959). His description of the breakdown of interaction that results when an actor discredits his role fits well the description our experimenters gave of their experiences:

> At such moments the individual whose presentation has been discredited may feel ashamed while the others present may feel hostile, and all the participants may come to feel ill at ease, nonplussed, out of countenance, embarrassed, experiencing the kind of anomy that is generated when the minute social system of face-to-face interaction breaks down (p. 12).

One might argue with some cogency that the experimenters were playing a social role, that of a subway rider, and that they discredited it by asking for the seat. But this use of "role" and "discrediting" seems strained and forced. Our results indicate, rather, that this "anomy" is a more general phenomenon resulting directly from doing something that "just isn't done" in a particular setting, whether it is related to the performance of any important social role or not.

This interpretation is consistent with Berger and Luckmann's argument (1967, cf. pp. 53–67) that the primary and essential means of social control is the sheer objectivity of the social world. They argue that it is the immediate and unreflective perception by actors of "the way things are done" which stabilizes individual conduct and *ipso facto* the social order. Under this perspective, both the sanctions that Scott considers and the discrediting of identity that Goffman has explored are secondary; that is, they are derivative of this basic means of control.

To be sure the concept of "those things that just aren't done" is itself a complex one, containing both a statistical proposition (such actions *do not* occur) and a normative proposition (such actions *ought not* to occur). Moreover, there remains the problem of specifying the precise content of those things that "just aren't done," a discussion we shall not develop here.

The results of our experience in doing something that "just isn't done" suggest that knowledge of the objective social order controls behavior not only cognitively (people may simply never have thought of asking for a seat), but emotionally: actions outside of understood routine paths appropriate to the social setting, at least in this case, give rise to an intense, immediate, inhibitory emotion. This emotion[4] restricts individual action to the routine patterns that constitute the stable background of everyday life.[5]

*N*OTES

1. Although it might seem to be a simple matter to say "No" to the request, as Goffman (1971) points out, requests demand either compliance or an "accounted denial." That is, one does not merely say "no" to a polite request, one gives a justification for saying "no." It takes time to realize that a justification is not required in this case or to construct one. Many subjects may have given up their seats simply because they didn't know how *not* to.

2. If subjects asked, "Why?", experimenters were instructed to respond, "I'm very tired." If the subject proposed a reason. "Are you sick?", the experimenter was to agree.

3. Even if we allow this more liberal interpretation of "patterns of sanctions" (more liberal, probably, than Scott intended), an operant analysis of the problem is not without its problems. Such an analysis would be required to argue either that all of our experimenters had been severely traumatized by asking for a seat in the subway in the past (an improbable assumption, especially for those experimenters new to the city), or that the emotion results from "stimulus generalization" from similar experiences. This notion of generalization is both vague and, as Chomsky (1959) has pointed out, mentalistic.

4. The exact nature of this inhibitory emotion is open to further inquiry. It might be argued that the affect produced was *guilt* over either taking the seat or bothering the passenger. But the seat is not a very important matter, nor were the riders lastingly disturbed. Further, the emotion was confined to the subway car itself. As soon as experimenters left the car they felt thoroughly at ease. This emotion, rooted in the situation, seems closer to embarrassment than guilt.

    Harold Takooshian (1972) has proposed an empirical test. He has suggested that the procedure be changed such that an experimenter stands before a confederate (preferably an older woman) and bluntly ask her for her seat, which she reluctantly surrenders. She is then to stand in front of the experimenter as he makes himself comfortable in her seat. The question is whether the experimenter would feel great tension even though there is absolutely no reason for him to feel guilt. The experimenter may find himself feeling embarrassed nonetheless sitting there in the sight of the other passengers.

5. A question remains as to whether this inhibition against substantial interaction among riders is functional. On the one hand, this inhibition simplifies the situation considerably for users of the subway. Since it is common knowledge that everyone minds his own business on the subway, a rider is free to assume a passive posture with regard to other riders. He need not be prepared to respond to demands from all those who surround him either for his attention or for more substantial involvement. On the other hand, daily contact with the by

now clichéd "faceless masses" of fellow riders may contribute to the alienation and anonymity often associated with urban life.

REFERENCES

BERGER, P., and LUCKMANN, T. (1967). *The Social Construction of Reality*, Doubleday Anchor, New York.

CHOMSKY, N. (1959). Review of *Verbal Behavior, Language,* Jan.–Mar., **35,** 26–58.

GARFINKEL, H. (1964). Studies of the routine grounds of everyday activity, *Social Problems,* Winter, **11,** (3), 225–250.

GOFFMAN, E. (1959). *The Presentation of Self in Everyday Life,* Anchor Doubleday, New York.

GOFFMAN, E. (1971). *Relations in Public,* Harper, New York.

SCHEFF, T. (1960). *Being Mentally Ill: A Sociological Theory,* Aldine, Chicago.

SCOTT, J. F. (1971). *Internalization of Norms,* Prentice-Hall, Englewood Cliffs, N.J.

SKINNER, B. F. (1953). *Science and Human Behavior.* Macmillan, New York.

TAKOOSHIAN, H. (1972). Report on a Class Field Experiment, Unpublished manuscript.

4

$\mathcal{R}$esponse to $\mathcal{I}$ntrusion into $\mathcal{W}$aiting $\mathcal{L}$ines

❖

I t is generally agreed that the queue constitutes a small scale social system that possesses three distinguishing features: first, its function is to regulate the sequence in which people gain access to goods or services; second, the ordering is given a distinctive spatial form; and third, maintenance of the line depends on a shared knowledge of the standards of behavior appropriate to this situation (Cooley, 1902/1964; Mann, 1970; Mann & Taylor, 1967; Milgram & Toch, 1969; Moles & Rohmer, 1976; Schwartz, 1975).

Liebowitz (1968) offered one analysis of why queues develop. Consider the situation where there is a commodity in unlimited supply. If customers were to arrive at the service point (e.g., ticket window) at equal intervals, and the transaction period was fixed, no queue would evolve as long the service interval (i.e., transaction time) did not exceed the arrival rate.

But the arrival patterns of clients are seldom fixed; customers often reach the service point in a random manner, and, as a consequence, individuals encroach upon the service time of others. In addition to the sporadic nature of new arrivals, service time is not always uniform. The combination of these two factors obliges the new arrivals to wait. Queues constitute an organization of waiting on an egalitarian principle. The only means by which queues can be eliminated from these situations is by significantly increasing the number of service personnel.

This chapter was written in collaboration with Hilary James Liberty, Raymond Toledo, and Joyce Wackenhut. Reprinted from *Journal of Personality and Social Psychology*, Vol. 5, No. 4 (1986), pp. 683–689. Copyright © 1986 the American Psychological Association. Reprinted by permission.

This solution is economically unsound because it requires a large service staff on a continuous standby basis in order to cope with occasional overload.

From a formal point of view, a person does not have to stand in line to be part of a queue (Liebowitz, 1968; Saaty, 1961). Any ordering of people's access to a point of service, whether through numerical assignment (as in stores where patrons take numbers) or appointment (as at restaurants, doctors' waiting rooms, etc.), constitutes a formal queue. But the waiting line is of particular interest to social psychologists for two reasons: It is the type of the queue we encounter most often in everyday life; and beyond this, it is more than an abstract ordering—it is a social occasion and, thus, governed by general sociopsychological rules.

If we probe more deeply into the psychological response to a queue, we observe that it contains two contradictory elements. On the one hand, the queue is an impediment to individuals who wish immediate satisfaction of goals. They cannot buy tickets, pies, or sausage because others stand between them and the service point. On the other hand, it is a social mechanism that protects individuals from those who arrive later. As in the case of most social arrangements, people defer to the restraints of the form, but they are also its beneficiary. The queue thus constitutes a classic illustration of how individuals create social order, on the basis of a rudimentary principle of equity, in a situation that could otherwise degenerate into chaos.

As with any social arrangement, the queue has a potential to break down. This may result from pressures that arise from within the waiting line or outside it. Here we shall concentrate on the latter. People arriving with urgent time pressure may choose to violate the queue by rushing up to the service window or inserting themselves at midqueue. What prevents this from happening? Sources of control inhere at the levels of facilities, roles, and norms. First, physical barriers to intrusion, such as rails or ropes, force people to line up one behind the other and constitute impediments to intrusion. Schwartz (1975, p. 99) termed such facilities *ecological supports.* At the level of roles, specific personnel (e.g., a bank guard or usher) may be designated to enforce observance of the queue's rules. At the normative level, two factors operate: People may not break into a queue because they feel it is wrong to do so; they have internalized the norms appropriate to this social form. Normative control implies its usual complementary side: Those already standing in line may play a role in enforcing the norm.

Charles Cooley highlighted the normative character of the queue when he wrote in 1902:

> Suppose one had to stand in line at the post office with a crowd of other people, waiting to get his mail. There are delay and discomfort to be borne; but these he will take with composure because he sees that they are part of the

necessary conditions of the situation, which all submit to alike. Suppose, however, that while patiently waiting his turn he notices someone else, who has come in later, edging into the line ahead of him. Then he will certainly be angry. The delay threatened is only a matter of a few seconds; but here is a question of justice, a case for indignation, a chance for anger to come forth. (pp. 281–282)

Cooley thus implied that it is not only the loss of position and time that inspires wrath among orderly queuers, but the violation of the rule, in and of itself, that is sufficient cause for angry feelings. In this article we shall examine experimentally the response by those standing in line to intruders.

Among the first to conduct empirical studies of waiting lines, Mann and Taylor (1967) made three observations on the problem of intrusion: The first was that the queue will seldom unite in any coordinated manner in order to dislodge a queue jumper. Second, although others may indicate disapproval, the responsibility for expelling an intruder falls on the person who stands just behind the intrusion point (Mann, 1970, p. 392); third, those individuals who precede the intrusion point are the ones least likely to object to a queue violation.

These observations, yet to be tested experimentally, point to the need for a deeper empirical and theoretical analysis of the queue. Theoretically, we must relate the defense of the queue to its most distinctive feature, namely the linear spatial disposition of its members. How does this unique spatial configuration affect the way in which the line defends its integrity?

In many social systems, the violation of norms is covert and cannot be easily observed. One of the attractive features of the queue, from a methodological standpoint, is that the propagation of effects is reduced to a highly visible, linear dimension, thus simplifying its description and measurement (in comparison with the occurrence of such effects in more inchoate social aggregates). The present study examines the response of the queue to intruders by having confederates break into naturally formed lines and noting how the lines respond to them. We shall then try to describe the underlying psychological structure that generates the results.

METHOD

Experimental Conditions

In the experiments described below, we studied intrusions into a total of 129 waiting lines that had spontaneously formed at railroad ticket counters, betting parlors, and other New York City locations. The lines had an average length of 6 persons, excluding experimental personnel.

Nature of the intrusions.   A confederate calmly approached a point between the third and fourth persons in line and said in a neutral tone, "Excuse me, I'd like to get in here." Before any responses could be made, the intruder injected himself (or herself) into the line and faced forward. If the experimental intruder was explicitly admonished to leave the line, he or she did so. Otherwise the intruder remained in the line for one minute before departing. Three female and 2 male graduate students served as intruders. An observer was stationed nearby to record physical, verbal, and nonverbal reactions to the intrusion.

Number of intruders.   We reasoned that a greater number of intruders would impose greater temporal costs on those waiting in line and thus would elicit a greater number of objections. Accordingly, we introduced an experimental variation in which two intruders simultaneously broke into a waiting line.

The role of buffers.   The buffer was a confederate who passively occupied a position between the point of intrusion and the next naive queuer. Use of buffers enabled us to determine if responsibility for objecting to the intruder would be displaced from the person immediately behind the point of intrusion to others in the line. In some experimental conditions, two buffers were used, standing behind each other immediately after the point of intrusion. (In conditions requiring buffers, the buffer[s] joined the tail end of the line, and intrusion was postponed until buffers moved up just behind the intended entry position.)

Summary of experimental conditions.   The experimental design thus used two independent variables: number of intruders (one or two) and number of buffers (zero, one, or two) yielding a complete crossing of variables by level, resulting in six experimental conditions, as shown in Table 4.1.

TABLE 4.1 OBJECTIONS TO INTRUSIONS IN SIX EXPERIMENTAL CONDITIONS

Condition	No. of lines	No. of intruders	No. of buffers	No. of lines in which objections occurred	% of lines in which objections occurred
1	22	1	0	12	54.0
2	24	1	1	6	25.0
3	20	1	2	1	5.0
4	23	2	0	21	91.3
5	20	2	1	5	25.0
6	20	2	2	6	30.0

Dependent Measures

For purposes of analysis the position of each person in line in relation to the point of intrusion was of primary interest. We designated the intrusion point as 0 (zero), with the persons following this point designated +1, +2, +3 . . . +n, whereas those preceding the point of intrusion were, with each remove from the intrusion point, designated −1, −2, −3, . . . −n, as shown below:

$$\text{Head} \quad -2 \;\; -1 \;\; 0 \;\; +1 \;\; +2 \;\; +3 \;\; +4 \;\; +5 \quad \text{End}$$

Intrusion
point

Following completion of our experiment, we learned of a study by Harris (1974) on the frustration-aggression hypothesis (Dollard, Doob, Miller, Mowrer, & Sears, 1939) that used experimental techniques similar to our own. In Harris's study the waiting line was the locus but not the object of study and, therefore, was geared toward different theoretical aims. Pertinent aspects of Harris's study will be taken up later.

RESULTS

Qualitative Components

The responses of those standing in line ranged from physical ejection of the intruder to total indifference. A behavior coding scheme that encompassed the observed responses was prepared:

Physical action. Physical action against the intruder occurred in 10.1% of the lines. We counted any physical laying on of hands in this category. This included tugging at the sleeve or tapping the shoulder of the intruder or, in a few cases, pushing the intruder firmly out of the line. This type of response normally originated in the person standing immediately behind the intruder.

Verbal objections. Attempts to expel the intruder by verbal means were the most common form of reaction against the intruder. The comments ranged from the polite to the hostile, but all demanded that the intruder get out of the line or go to the back of the line. Typical statements included the following:

"Excuse me, you have to go to the back of the line."
"Hey buddy, we've been waiting. Get off the line and go to the back."

"No way! The line's back there. We've all been waiting and have trains to catch."

Generalized expressions of verbal disapproval (which did not, however, contain a specific statement that the intruder should leave the line) were also coded as verbal objections to the intruder. These expressions of disapproval were more tentative than those described above. Typical remarks were:

"Are you making a line here?"

"Excuse me, it's a line."

"Um . . . are you waiting to buy a ticket?"

Together, these two types of verbal objection to the intruder occurred in 21.7% of the lines.

Nonverbal objections.   Nonverbal objections to the intruder consisted of dirty looks, hostile stares, and gestures to the intruder to get to the end of the line. They occurred in 14.7% of the lines.

For purposes of analysis, each of the above types of response was regarded as an attempt to expel the intruder and was consolidated into a single measure, which we termed *objections* to the intruder.

Quantitative Results

Objection rates had a very wide range, varying from a low of 5.0% in the condition in which there were two buffers and only one intruder to a high of 91.3% where there were two intruders and no buffers, as Table 4.1 shows.

The number of persons objecting to the intruder(s) according to the queuer's position in line is shown in Table 4.2. Of the 302 persons who occupied the four positions following the intrusion point, 18.2% exhibited some form of direct objection to the intruder compared with 8.0% of the 250 persons who occupied the two positions immediately in front of the intruder. These two percentages were significantly different by a chi-square test, indicating that those following the point of intrusion were more likely to object than those standing in front of the intrusion point (M = 12.69, $p < .01$), as Figure 4.1 shows.

To further examine the effects of the number of intruders and buffers on objection rates, logit models using number of intruders (one or two) and number of buffers (zero, one, or two) as independent variables and number of objections as the dependent variable were set up.

The application of logit models involves testing a series or hierarchy of models to determine which independent variables (or combinations or levels of these independent variables) significantly affect the dependent variable (i.e., number of objections or number of lines in which objections occurred).

TABLE 4.2 SPATIAL DISTRIBUTION OF RESPONSES TO INTRUSIONS: PERCENTAGE AND NUMBER OF PERSONS OBJECTING ACCORDING TO POSITION IN LINE

				Position in line			
Condition	% − 2	% − 1	I	% + 1	% + 2	% + 3	% + 4
1	4.5 (1/22)	22.7 (5/22)		36.4 (8/22)	14.3 (2/14)	0.0 (0/9)	0.0 (0/7)
2	0.0 (0/22)	12.5 (3/24)		Buf	16.7 (4/24)	0.0 (0/15)	0.0 (0/9)
3	0.0 (0/18)	5.0 (1/20)		Buf	Buf	0.0 (0/20)	0.0 (0/18)
4	4.3 (1/23)	21.7 (5/23)		86.9 (20/23)	43.5 (10/23)	9.1 (2/22)	0.0 (0/20)
5	0.0 (0/18)	10.0 (2/20)		Buf	20.0 (4/20)	0.0 (0/15)	0.0 (0/4)
6	0.0 (0/18)	10.0 (2/20)		Buf	Buf	15.0 (3/20)	11.8 (2/17)
Total	1.7 (2/121)	14.0 (18/129)		62.2 (28/45)	24.7 (20/81)	5.0 (5/101)	2.7 (2/75)

Note. The figures in parentheses show the exact number of persons for each position on which the percentage figures are based. I = intrusion point. Buf = buffer (a confederate who passively occupied a position between the point of intrusion and the next naive queuer).

The hierarchy of models is constructed so as to start with the simplest model (no effects) and end with the most complicated one (all independent variables and all interaction effects). At each step of the hierarchy an additional term is included. The model *accepted* is the first one (i.e., the simplest) that cannot be rejected by use of a chi-square likelihood ratio test.

The results for the possible logit models of the present study are given in Tables 4.3 and 4.4. Table 4.3 provides models for the number of persons who objected; Table 4.4 gives models for the overall number of lines in which objections occurred.

Examining the results for Hierarchy 1 in Table 4.3, we observe that the first model that cannot be rejected is Model 3 ($p = .24$, *ns*). This model contains one buffer (B1) and one intruder (I) (entered in the previous model, Model 2), which means that the number of intruders (one vs. two) and the presence of a buffer (vs. no buffer) significantly affect the objection rate. According to this model, the presence of two buffers (vs. one) had no effect and no interaction effects between buffers and intruders.

Observing the results for Hierarchy 2, the first model that cannot be rejected is Model 9 ($p = .19$, *ns*). This model specifies the significance of

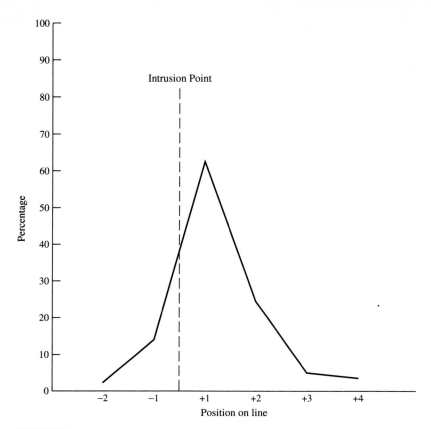

FIGURE 4.1
Percentage of persons objecting according to position in line.

number of intruders (one vs. two) and number of buffers (zero vs. one and also one vs. two). Because Model 3 is more parsimonious (e.g., contains one less term) than Model 9, we accepted Model 3 over Model 9.

The results for total number of lines in which objections occurred, given in Table 4.4, are the same as those for the overall objection rate. Model 13, the simplest model accepted from Hierarchy 1, is chosen over Model 19, the one accepted from Hierarchy 2, because of its greater parsimony. This model once again specifies the significance of the number of intruders (one vs. two) and the presence of a buffer (vs. no buffer), this time on the total number of lines where objections occurred.

In sum, objections occurred more often in lines with two intruders than in lines with one intruder. Objections were more frequent when there were no buffers than when there was either one or two buffers. And there was no interaction between number of buffers and number of intruders.

TABLE 4.3 LOGIT MODELS FITTED TO CROSS-CLASSIFICATION OF RATE OF OBJECTION OF PERSONS IN LINE

Model	Likelihood ratio statistic	df	p
	Hierarchy 1		
1. E	43.257	5	.0000
2. I	33.937	4	.0000
3. B1	4.164	3	.2443
4. B2	3.333	2	.1889
5. IB1	3.332	1	.0680
	Hierarchy 2		
6. E	43.257	5	.0000
7. B1	10.491	4	.0330
8. B2	9.784	3	.0205
9. I	3.333	2	.1889
10. IB1	3.332	1	.0680

Note. E = equiprobability model. I = intruders (one vs. two). B1 = buffers (none vs. one). B2 = buffers (one vs. two). IB1 = interaction term of intruders (one vs. two) and buffers (zero vs. one).

Reactions of the Experimental Intruders

The several experimental confederates reported highly negative affect associated with the task of intruding into lines. Before each trial, many of the confederates procrastinated at length, often pacing nervously near the target area, spending as much as a half hour working up the "nerve" to intrude. For some, the anticipation of intruding was so unpleasant that physical symptoms, such as pallor and nausea, accompanied intrusions. Reactions of this type have been reported previously by Garfinkel (1964) and Milgram and Sabini (this volume, Chapter 3). They constitute the "inhibitory anxiety that ordinarily prevents individuals from breaching social norms" (this volume, page xxvi), and indicate that the internal restraints against intruding into lines play a significant role in assuring the integrity of the line.

TABLE 4.4 LOGIT MODELS FITTED
TO CROSS-CLASSIFICATION OF
RATE OF OBJECTION OF LINES

Model	Likelihood ratio statistic	df	p
	Hierarchy 1		
11. E	47.372	5	.0000
12. I	40.785	4	.0000
13. B1	6.056	3	.1089
14. B2	5.124	2	.0772
15. IB1	2.924	1	.0873
	Hierarchy 2		
16. E	47.372	5	.0000
17. B1	13.714	4	.0083
18. B2	13.009	3	.0046
19. I	5.124	2	.0772
20. IB1	2.924	1	.0873

Note. E = Equiprobability model. I = in-truders (one vs. two). B1 = buffers (none vs. one). B2 = buffers (one vs. two). IB1 = interaction term of intruders (one vs. two) and buffers (zero vs. one).

DISCUSSION

Cost Versus Moral Outrage

Cooley (1902) has indicated that it is not mainly the loss of position and time that angers the orderly queuers, but the violation of the social order that they have observed. Mann (1970), Moles and Rohmer (1976), and Schwartz (1978) emphasized the cost to the queuer.

Comparison of the responses of queuers standing behind the point of intrusion with those of queuers standing in front of the intrusion point bears directly on this issue, for only those standing behind the intruder are displaced by the action and incur a cost. The results indicate that whereas 73.3% of all objections came from those standing behind the point of intrusion, only 26.6% came from those in front. Thus the cost factor, emphasized by Mann and others, played a larger role than sheer moral indignation in stimulating objections to the interloper. The condition that used two intruders further underscores the role of cost in stimulating objections. Two intruders double the delay for those standing behind them and also provoke twice as many attempts at expulsion as a single intruder.

Yet, Cooley's observation cannot be dismissed, for the data indicate that a small but measurable proportion of those in front of the intrusion point object to the intruder. Moreover, the fact that those standing behind the intruder incur a cost does not mean that they are not also responding in terms of their anger at a moral transgression, amplified by the fact that they suffer its consequences.

There is an additional, perceptual factor that may influence the greater volume of objections after the intrusion point: Those behind the intruder face the locus of the intrusion, whereas those preceding the intrusion point have their backs to the scene and, therefore, are less likely to notice the violation.

Beyond the Cost Factor

Thus far we have focused on differential rates of objection before and after the intrusion point. But even those standing behind the intrusion point did not all object. The volume of objection dropped off sharply with each remove from the intrusion point. Cost cannot explain this result. Every person behind the intrusion point incurs the same cost; each is equally displaced by an intruder. One might assume, therefore, that they would all have the same desire to remove the violator and would respond accordingly. But the results show this is not the case. Why did individuals beyond the +1 position so rarely object?

It is clear that the general reluctance to enter into a confrontation with another person, with its attendant risks, potential for embarrassment, and disruption of an orderly social scene (Goffman, 1959, 1963), although it undoubtedly plays a general inhibitory role, cannot account for the differential participation of those closer or further from the intrusion point.

We have found it useful to analyze the problem from the standpoint of the Latané and Darley (1970) bystander intervention paradigm. The intrusion situation has two things in common with the bystander situation: First, some incident has occurred that calls for some sort of intervention. Second, the intervention is frequently not forthcoming, especially from those standing beyond the +1 position. We shall now focus on their situation.

First, following the Latané and Darley model, the individual must notice the incident. Those in the +1 position are in a better position to notice the intrusion than those further back in the line.

Once the person has observed the incident, he or she proceeds to the second level of the Latané-Darley paradigm, namely, interpreting whether the event is one that requires intervention. When a queuer sees someone entering the line, he or she must define it as an illicit intrusion before taking action. Unless the individual is physically close to the intrusion point, it may be difficult to distinguish between a *blatant intrusion* and the somewhat more legitimate practice of *placekeeping* (Mann, 1970). This ambiguity can lead to inaction. Thus in the present study, when those closest to the point of intrusion did not signal that something was wrong, those further down the line may have interpreted this as evidence of a legitimate entry.

Once having noticed the incident and decided it is illicit, the queuer must next, according to this model, decide whether he or she is responsible for taking action. Action is frequently inhibited, according to Latané and Darley, because of the diffusion of responsibility. On the queue, responsibility in the line is not so much diffused as focused on the person closest to the intruder. As in the subway research described by Piliavin, Rodin, and Piliavin (1969), those closest to the disruptive event are felt to have a special obligation to deal with it. There may be reluctance on the part of people further back in line to do someone else's duty.

This analysis shows that cost alone cannot account for all our results; there is an underlying structure to the situation, linked to the linear spatial configuration of the queue. The experimental conditions using buffers further illuminate this point. Buffers were introduced to see if responsibility for removing the intruder(s) would be assumed by someone else in line in the event that the person immediately following the intruder failed to object. We found no such tendency. When a buffer (i.e., a passive confederate) occupied the +1 position, the objection rate of those in the +2 position was not higher than when this position was preceded by a naive queuer (indeed it tended to be lower). A similar effect was observed for those individuals in position +3, when two buffers were used. In other words, there was no displacement of the defensive response if it did not occur at the point of intrusion.

An alternative explanation offered by Harris (1974) is that the diminishing level of "aggression" to intruders in a line is due to a goal gradient effect. Her findings indicate that an intruder butting in closer to the service point evoked more aggression than one butting in further down the line. A general goal gradient effect may well be at work, but in our study the sharp increase in objections immediately after the intrusion point introduced a striking discontinuity in response that must be accounted for in its own right.

Harris's findings raise the question of goal gradient effects in interpreting the results of buffers. Our buffers did displace the subject one or two positions further from the goal. However, this displacement was minimal compared with the contrast points used by Harris (3rd vs. 12th position). Moreover, in our study the dampening effect of a single buffer was substantial, but did not differ significantly when an additional displacement was caused by a second buffer, thus pointing to the limited value of a goal gradient explanation within the range examined.

Limitations in the Results

There are two important limitations in the present data. First as a matter of experimental procedure, the intruder left the line whenever he or she was directly challenged for improper entry. We chose this procedure to avoid any serious conflicts that might have resulted if the intruder failed to comply with an explicit demand to leave the line. As a consequence, however, we do not know what would have occurred if the intruder had insisted on remaining in line. Perhaps others in the line would have joined in the attempt to remove the intruder.

A second limitation on the data concerns the nature of the item distributed at the service point. Several distinctions need to be made: The item distributed at the service point may be in limited or unlimited supply. If the item is scarce, the intruder may deny it to those behind him or her. Sometimes, there is no limitation in the supply of the item, but time may be in short supply, as at an airport. By encroaching on priority the intruder may cause a person to lose critical time and, thereby, miss his or her plane. People stand in lines to attain items and services that range from the trivial to the vital. Those standing in a food distribution line during periods of famine may display far less tolerance for intruders than our typical subjects in Grand Central Station. Thus, replication of the experiment for lines of widely varying utilities would provide a broader picture of the response to intruders.

CONCLUSION: THE PSYCHOLOGICAL STRUCTURE OF THE QUEUE

We have referred to the line as a *social system*, and more needs to be said in justifying this designation. A line is a social system in that there is a shared set of beliefs governing the behavior of the individual participants, so that they no longer act in terms of purely personal wishes but instead, by reference to a common social representation. The force of this representation varies from one culture to the next; for example, travelers often report on the readiness of the English to form queues, in contrast with the peculiar resistance to queue formation in Latin cultures (Hall, 1959; Lee, 1966).

Any social system requires a means of defense, and in this study we deliberately initiated intrusions into the queue to observe how the queue protects its integrity. The type of defense we observed both results from the underlying psychological structure of the queue and gives us a clue as to the nature of that structure.

That each spatial arrangement has consequences for the resulting psychological structure is, of course, no surprise to social psychologists ever since Bavelas (1948) and Leavitt (1951) showed us the consequences for leadership, efficiency, and satisfaction in their analysis of artificially generated communication structures. Indeed, their analysis is applicable to an understanding of the queue, in that they demonstrated that in linear structures communication is most likely between those in adjacent positions, and this type of structure works against the emergence of centralized coordination. Thus, the fact that the intruder in our studies was addressed principally by those adjacent to him is consonant with a general theory of communication structures.

There are, additionally, several features particular to the waiting line that work against concerted action:

1. There is no prior history of communication among those standing in line. Indeed, the very spatial disposition of persons, in which no individual faces anyone else, discourages such group formation. Thus, when an attack on the line occurs, there is no previous group experience to draw upon. We may hypothesize that a line consisting of persons already known to each other (such as a group of classmates) would be more likely to act in concert against an interloper.

2. One of the difficulties in mounting a systemic attack on the intruder is that to do so requires that people lose their place in the line, and thus it disrupts the very form they are attempting to defend.

3. Moreover, a system's resilience depends not only on its capacity to defend against disturbances, but also its capacity to ignore, adjust to, and tolerate them. Although confrontation with the intruder would serve to maintain the physical order of the line, it may risk the escalation of a localized incident into a general fracas, threatening the disintegration of the entire system. By not challenging the intruder, the queue may protect the system against the appearance of disorder. As Schwartz has written, "the chaotic dissolution of the queue can be forestalled not only by the default of deviance but also by its contingent toleration" (1975, p. 96).

4. Allowing the intruder to remain in line serves the system in another way, namely co-opting those who are a threat to its survival: Once an intruder is part of the line, she or he has an investment in its continued existence.

In addition to the forces that restrain individuals from objecting to violations of the norm of first come, first served, other factors are at play that determine how the queue is defended. We will now examine the precise nature of this defense.

First, we note that the defensive responses are primarily of a normative character: Appropriate standards are enunciated for the intruder as a means of reasserting the socially sanctioned character of the queue. Sometimes the assertions simply point to the social representation: "This is a line, here." At other times, they address the intruder's transgression: "No breaking in here." Or they may specify the appropriate action: "Get to the end of the line."

The second characteristic of the defensive response is that it is local rather than systemic. That is, the response occurs at the point of intrusion and diminishes rapidly with each remove from that point. The line as a whole does not respond to the intruder in a coordinated fashion. What is the significance of this datum? Quite clearly, it signals the character of the queue's underlying structure. A system will respond to threat in a coordinated fashion when it possesses a relatively high degree of system integration with centralized control of its disparate parts. Purely local defense, such as we have observed in the queue, signifies relatively weak integration of parts with an absence of differentiated functions or central coordination.

Indeed, we would argue that this is precisely the situation that obtains in the queue. What is the main bonding mechanism of the queue? It resides in replicated segments. The principal focus for each person in line is the space between himself or herself and the person standing just in front. This is the space the queuer will defend most vigorously, if the queuer is to defend the line at all. A willingness to object to intrusions quickly attentuates with positions further down the line. The queue will hold together if each member defends the space immediately in front, which the queuer often experiences as a zone of special responsibility.

The queue is thus articulated through a series of overlapping zones, each centering on the individual standing in line and extending a few removes forward and a remove behind. The queue is segmental in structure, as often occurs in systems of linear composition. Segmental structures are particularly likely to arise in short-lived systems formed through accretion of their constituent units, as in the case of waiting lines. With this analysis, we hope we have achieved one of our principal theoretical objectives; namely, to relate the type of defense observed in the queue to the unique spatial configuration of this social form.

REFERENCES

BAVELAS, A. (1948). A mathematical model for group structures. *Applied Anthropology, 7,* 16–30.

COOLEY, C. H. (1964). *Human nature and the social order.* New York: Schocken Brooks. (Original work published 1902)

DOLLARD, J., DOOB, L. W., MILLER, N. E., MOWRER, O. H., & SEARS, R. R. (1939). *Frustration and aggression.* New Haven, CT: Yale University Press.

GARFINKEL, H. (1964). Studies of the routine grounds of everyday activities. *Social Problems, 11,* 225–250.

GOFFMAN, E. (1959). *The presentation of self in everyday life.* Garden City, NY: Doubleday.

GOFFMAN, E. (1963). *Behavior in public places: Notes on the social organization of gatherings.* New York: Macmillan.

HALL, E. T. (1959). *The silent language.* Greenwich, CT: Fawcett Publications.

HARRIS, M. B. (1974). Mediators between frustration and aggression in a field experiment. *Journal of Experimental Social Psychology, 10,* 561–571.

LEE, A. M. (1966). *Applied queuing theory.* London: Macmillan.

LATANÉ, B., & DARLEY, J. M. (1970). *The unresponsive bystander: Why doesn't he help?* New York: Appleton.

LEAVITT, H. J. (1951). Some effects of certain communication patterns on group performance. *Journal of Abnormal and Social Psychology, 46,* 38–50.

LIEBOWITZ, M. A. (1968). Queues. *Scientific American, 219,* 96–103.

MANN, L. (1969). Queue culture: The waiting line as a social system. *American Journal of Sociology, 75,* 340–354.

MANN, L. (1970). The social psychology of waiting lines. *American Scientist, 58,* 390–398.

MANN, L., & TAYLOR, K. R. (1969). Queue counting: The effect of motives upon estimates of numbers in waiting lines. *Journal of Personality and Social Psychology, 12,* 95–103.

MILGRAM, S., & TOCH, H. (1969). Collective behavior: Crowds and social movements. In G. Lindzey & E. Aronson (Eds.), *The handbook of social psychology* (2nd ed., Vol. 4, pp. 507–610). Reading, MA: Addison-Wesley.

MOLES, A., & ROHMER, E. (1976). *Micropsychologie et vie quotidienne* [Micropsychology and daily life]. Paris: Denoel/Gonthier.

PILIAVIN, I. M., RODIN, J., & PILIAVIN, J. A. (1969). Good samaritanism: An underground phenomenon? *Journal of Personality and Social Psychology, 13,* 289–299.

SAATY, T. L. (1961). *Elements of queuing theory.* New York: McGraw-Hill.

SCHWARTZ, B. (1975). *Queuing and waiting: Studies in the social organization of access and delay.* Chicago: University of Chicago Press.

SCHWARTZ, B. (1978). Queues, priorities, and social process. *Journal of Personality and Social Psychology, 41,* 3–12.

5

The Idea of Neighborhood

❖

To understand the problem a sociologist has in handling the concept of neighborhood, the reader must retrieve the cognitive maps of childhood. If you grew up in a large city, you knew best those living on your own block. Awareness of the city radiated outward, with the density of information diminishing rapidly with the distance from home. Beyond a few blocks on either side, street names grew vague and faces unfamiliar. The area of comfortable familiarity constituted the experience of neighborhood. (For those raised in Brooklyn or the Bronx, psychological boundaries were set at 5 ± 2 streets from one's home stoop.)

Yet we know that cities do not consist of an indefinitely large number of neighborhoods each centering on one of millions of inhabitants only a slight spatial remove from his fellows. Rather there is a small number of social labels applied to definable geographic areas. Because population characteristics of a city are continuously variable, with no clear demarcation between one side of the street and the other, society imposes categorical labels on specific geographic realms. Neighborhood categories are not simply found in nature, but are consensually imposed definitions. This is the first sense in which communities are socially constructed according to Suttles's analysis.

A neighborhood label, once affixed, has real consequences, Suttles points out. For outsiders it reduces decision-making to more manageable terms. Instead of dealing with the variegated reality of numerous city streets, the resident can form a set of attitudes about a limited number of social categories and act accordingly. Thus a mother will instruct her child to stay out of Harlem, or judge that a boy who lives in Riverdale is probably acceptable for her daughter. Newcomers may be attracted or repelled by areas defined with a high or a low prestige label. For

This paper was a review of *The Social Construction of Communities*, by Gerald D. Suttles, Chicago: University of Chicago Press, 1972. It was first published in *Science* **178** (November 1, 1972), pp. 494–495. Copyright © 1972 by the American Association for the Advancement of Science. Reprinted by permission.

those who live within it, the neighborhood defines areas relatively free of intruders, identifies where potential friends are to be found or where they are to be cultivated, minimizes the prospects of status insult, and simplifies innumerable daily decisions dealing with spatial activities. Thus the mental map of neighborhoods is not superfluous cognitive baggage, but performs important psychological and social functions.

But what sets the boundaries on neighborhoods: ethnic homogeneity, physical barriers, economic characteristics? All of these play a part, but in the final analysis it is a creative social construction. Most often the neighborhood boundary is an arbitrary street or intersection, rather than a physical barrier. Thus, in New York City, Harlem "begins" on the north side of 96th Street. The demographic approach, which equates neighborhoods with particular concentrations of ethnic or racial types, is less interesting for Suttles than the question "How are varying proportions of racial, ethnic, and income groups selectively highlighted in the reputation of local communities?"

If the neighborhood exists first as a creative social construction, it nonetheless possesses a number of important properties. First, it becomes a component of an individual's identity, "a stable judgmental reference against which people are assessed. . . ." (That is why when you ask a person what city he comes from he will tell you without blush, but when you ask about his neighborhood the question may be considered too personal for casual conversation; for the neighborhood is a status-differentiating component.) A neighborhood may derive its reputation from several sources: first, from the master identity of the area of which it is a part (Yorkville is part of the fashionable East Side); second, through comparison and contrast with adjacent communities; and third, from historic claims, a game, Suttles points out, in which all communities can win, since the new community offers the image of an area unshackled by tradition, and the older community takes pride in its association with the past. The best time to capture the "meaning" of a neighborhood, it occurs to this reviewer, is on moving day, when two sets of pertinent associations are revealed: those generated by people moving in, and those disclosed by people moving out.

Readers will also recognize that neighborhoods deemed "desirable" need not always have the best physical features. Consider the upper East Side in New York City. Unless an apartment overlooks Central Park, it is an area devoid of breathing space, consisting of stone towers built on acres of unrelieved pavement. Park Avenue is a fuming canyon of hydrocarbons. It is a wonder not only that people will pay exorbitant Park Avenue rents and maintenance charges but that they are willing to live there at all. Note that Harlem, which in popular imagery possesses only rat-infested slums, actually contains a considerable amount of attractive housing. But none of this figures in the public image of these two areas.

The images are social constructions linked to but not wholly identifiable with the facts.

We define urban communities, therefore, because the concept simplifies the complicated and inchoate qualities of the city, dividing it into differentiable segments and thereby rendering it cognitively manageable.

What then of the idea of a community as first and foremost a group of people bound together by common sentiments, a primordial solidarity? In Suttles's eyes, the view is poorly realized in fact and represents an overromanticized view of social life. Communities do lead to social control, they do "segregate people to avoid danger, insult, and status claims"; but whatever sentiments are engendered by neighborhoods are strictly tied to functional realities and can in no sense be treated as gratuitous expressive solidarity. Moreover, the notion of a closely interdependent, self-contained community, having its prototype in the rural village, was never an appropriate model for urban living. Of greater pertinence to an analysis of urban life are the *multiple* levels of community organization in which the resident participates.

The smallest of these units is the "face block." For children it is the prescribed social world carved out by parents. It is here that face-to-face relations are most likely, and the resulting institutional form is the block association. Next, in Suttles's typology, is the "defended neighborhood," which is the smallest segment of the city recognized by both residents and outsiders as having some corporate identity, and possessing many of the facilities needed to carry out the daily routine of life. The defended neighborhood frequently lacks official recognition, and its boundaries, because they have no legal status, are often precarious. Street gangs arise which protect it from unwanted incursions by outsiders.

The urban resident also participates in the "community of limited liability," a larger realm possessing an institutionally secure name and boundaries. The concept, originally developed by Morris Janowitz, emphasizes the "intentional, voluntary, and especially the partial and differential involvement of residents in their local communities." Frequently an external agent, such as a community newspaper, is the most important guardian of a community's sense of boundaries, purposes, and integrity. A single individual may be defined as living in several such communities. The multiple claims on the person may limit and even paralyze active involvement in any of them.

Even larger segments of the city, such as an entire East Side area, may also take shape in response to environmental pressures, creating an "expanded community of limited liability." Thus an individual may find himself picketing to keep a highway not just out of his neighborhood, but out of the entire South Side.

Thus what Suttles teaches us is that the concept of neighborhood is not adequate to handle the multiple levels of urban organization in which the individual participates. Varied levels of community organization are created as responses to the larger social environment. Neighborhoods cannot be seen as a society in microcosm. They never were, and never can be. The urban community is a form of social differentiation within a total society.

Does Suttles's analysis have a bearing on the contemporary issue of "community control"? It suggests, first, that the fully self-contained community within the city is a fiction. The urban community can be a differentiated but never a fully autonomous unit within the larger urban context. Second, Suttles points out that the idea of a centralized government is not incompatible with a well-served local community. "One of the sources of community weakness in most American cities is that many mayors are responsible to local communities but have little direct recourse to the federal levels at which major power and resources are located." In Sweden, in contrast, the mayors of certain local communities are appointed by the central government but this strengthens rather than weakens the resources available to the community.

It is a central theme of Suttles's analysis that "total societies are not made up from a series of communities, but communities are areas which come into being through their recognition by the wider society." Suttles overstates the case. Sometimes cities do develop through the coalescing of smaller communities, which continue to maintain their identity. London is a good example. To some extent it depends on the phase of a city's development under discussion. In later stages of development, when a city's origins are no longer relevant to its functioning, the social-constructive approach may well constitute the dominant mode of defining neighborhoods. More important, is the point really worth a great deal of theoretical fuss?

The book has other faults: It is repetitious and disjointed, with a number of essays only tangentially related to the main theme. Yet these flaws are unimportant alongside the book's considerable achievements. First, it helps break away from the limiting view of Park, Burgess, and others that "a city consists of a mosaic of little worlds which touch but do not interpenetrate." The urban community is a form of social differentiation within a total society. Second, Suttles teaches us that the concept of neighborhood is not adequate to handle the multiple levels of urban organization in which the individual participates. Participation ranges from the face block to larger segments of the city. Third, Suttles shows that there is no necessary discontinuity between how we experience neighborhoods, communities, cities, and so on and the sociological concepts needed to describe them. Neighborhoods are not primarily segments of real estate but collective representations existing in the minds of inhabitants, and attaining reality through social consensus. This is a stimulating viewpoint of great heuristic value. Fourth, he demonstrates that the phenomenon of mental maps, developed by Kevin Lynch and others, is not a disembodied esthetic or cognitive phenomenon but is part of the ongoing life of individuals, with practical meaning and significance. Fifth, Suttles translates the concept of territoriality, so foolishly caricatured in the work of Ardrey, Morris, and others, into its proper human context. He recognizes the importance of territoriality in human life, without equating it with its animal expression. Finally, his book is a work of considerable originality and insight; the author is a keen observer, bringing the same order of sensitivity to urban analysis that Erving Goffman has applied to the study of small-scale social interaction. And in both cases, we emerge with a sense of clarified perception.

6

The Familiar Stranger: An Aspect of Urban Anonymity

❖

Nothing is more characteristic of urban life than the fact that we often gain extreme familiarity with the faces of a number of persons, yet never interact with them. At my railroad station, for example, I have stood at a commuter station for several years, often in the company of people whom I have never gotten to know. The faces and the people are treated as part of the environment, equivalent to the scenery, rather than persons with whom one talks, exchanges greetings.

Harry From, one of my students, wrote that the familiar stranger is the end product of a process, which like friendship, takes time. Moreover, it is a covert process and often leads to a frozen relationship. To become a familiar stranger a person (1) has to be observed, (2) repeatedly for a certain time period, and (3) without any interaction.

There is a powerful rule at work among familiar strangers; the further away from the scene of their routine encounter, the more likely they will interact with each other. Thus if they encounter each other in a faraway country, they are most likely to acknowledge each other, engage in conversation, and even experience a warm surge of familiarity and friendship. Why is it that people who have not in

This paper was first published in the *Division 8 Newsletter*, Division of Personality and Social Psychology, Washington: American Psychological Association, July 1972. Copyright © 1972 by the American Psychological Association. Reprinted by permission.

several years spoken to each other, while standing in each other's presence, are in a distant setting moved to address each other as persons?

Barriers build up between familiar strangers which become difficult to surmount, so that when the familiar stranger needs to make a request, he prefers to make it to a total stranger rather than a familiar though hitherto unacknowledged face.

Extraordinary incidents, such as a flood, help move people out of their impersonal relations. The incident itself is temporary, and thus involves not an extended commitment, but only one that lasts as long as the temporary disruption of routine.

A few years ago several students at The City University of New York attempted to study the phenomenon of the familiar stranger. They got up early in the morning, and went out to the commuter stations that feed into New York City. They photographed large clusters of commuters, many standing back to back at the station, or staring straight ahead (see Figure 6.1). Each figure in the photograph was numbered, the photographs were duplicated, and the students returned the next week distributing the photographs to the commuters, with a cover letter explaining our purposes, and a questionnaire dealing with the phenomenon of the familiar stranger. We found that 89.5 percent of those questioned reported at least one familiar stranger. The average commuter claimed 4.0 individuals at the station whom he recognized but never spoke to, compared to a mean of 1.5 individuals with whom he conversed. Some familiar strangers turn out to be "socio-metric stars" in that they are recognized by a large proportion of commuters at their station, even if never spoken to.

Many passengers told us they often think about their fellow commuters, trying to figure out what kind of lives they lead, what their jobs are like, etc. They have a fantasy relationship to familiar strangers that may never eventuate in action. But it is a real relationship, in which both parties have agreed to mutually ignore each other, without any implication of hostility. Indeed, sometimes only the right circumstance is needed to change the relationship. Consider this: A woman collapsed on the streets of Brooklyn, not far from her apartment house. She had been a familiar stranger to another resident of the street for years. The resident immediately took responsibility for the unconscious woman, not only calling an ambulance, but riding with her to the hospital to make certain she was treated properly, and to assure that her possessions were not stolen by ambulance attendants. She said later that she had felt a special responsibility for the woman, because they had seen each other for years, even if they had never spoken. The familiar stranger status is not the absence of a relationship, but a special form of relationship, that has properties and consequences of its own.

Why do familiar strangers exist? It is a response to overload: in order to handle all the possible inputs from the environment we filter out inputs so that we allow only diluted forms of interaction. In the case of the

(a)

(b)

FIGURE 6.1
Typical photographs distributed to commuters, used in the study of the familiar
stranger.

familiar stranger, we permit a person to impinge on us perceptually, but close off any further interaction. In part this is because perceptual processing of a person takes considerably less time than social processing. We can see a person at a glance, but it takes more time to sustain social involvement. If the temporal relations were reversed, that is, if perception took a longer amount of time than social communication, a quite different phenomenon would result: We would typically talk with people whom we did not have time to visually perceive.

7

A Psychological Map of New York City[1]

❖

A city consists of streets, squares and buildings that exist in objective, geographic space. But there is also a psychological representation of the city that each inhabitant carries around in his head. When a man comes to a strange city, at first he does not know his way around. He sticks close to a few known reference points, such as his hotel or the main shopping street, and quickly feels disoriented if he strays from these few familiar paths. With increasing experience, he begins to build up a picture in his mind of how the streets connect with one another, the relationship among paths, and specific turns he must take to move from one point to another. He acquires a representation of the city which we may call a psychological map. A psychological map is the city as mirrored in the mind of an individual. The acquisition of an adequate representation of the city may be a slow process, filled with confusion, and inevitably only partial in its achievement. Very few individuals, if any, have a total grasp of all of the streets and intersections of a major metropolis, but each of us holds at least the fragment of such a map.

In this paper, we shall describe a psychological map of New York City constructed by our research team. But before going further, I would like to raise some general questions about psychological maps and review some of the work that has been carried out in this field. We start with the notion that the person has a psychological representation of some features of the environment. The first

This paper was written in collaboration with Judith Greenwald, Suzanne Kessler, Wendy McKenna, and Judith Waters. It was first published in *American Scientist*, Vol. 60, No. 2 (March–April 1972), pp. 194–200. Reprinted by permission, *American Scientist*, Journal of Sigma Chi, The Scientific Research Society of North America.

question, then, in constructing a mental map, concerns the units of the environment that are to be mapped. In previous research, the scale of maps has varied from those of small campuses to the maps people have in their head of the entire world (Saarinen, 1971; Hooper, 1970; Stea, 1969; Gould, 1967). There is an important difference, of course, in acquiring a mental map of one's campus and that of the world. The campus map is mediated by direct experience, moving about the university buildings and piecing scenes together into some cognitive structure. The image of the world is learned not from direct exposure, but through formal schemata of it as represented in maps and atlases.

Once we have decided what units of geography are to be mapped, we need to decide which psychological features are of greatest interest. The most basic question is whether a given geographical entity exists at all in a person's cognitive repertory. If asked to draw a map of Central America, does he include Costa Rica and El Salvador? If asked about New York City neighborhoods, is the subject aware of the existence of Chelsea and Morningside Heights? And beyond the identification of an element lies the question of whether he knows the geographic position of one entity in relation to another. (He may be able to name Chelsea, but not know its position in relation to other neighborhoods.) In addition to these purely cognitive features, the individual may possess a set of attitudes or feelings toward different parts of the region or city. In principle, it is possible to map an entire city, block by block, in terms of *any* definable psychological dimension (e.g., perceived level of safety-danger). Gould (1967) has mapped the geography of England in terms of the residential desirability of its varying regions.

The major methodological problem in all this is how to externalize the mental map, that is, how to get it out of the individual's subjective experience and onto paper for public scrutiny. One simple method is to ask a person to draw a map of the area in question, say a city, showing all of the streets he knows, and indicating all of the neighborhoods and landmarks he can think of. A decade ago, Kevin Lynch (1960), at MIT, asked a group of Bostonians to do this. While certain landmarks, such as Paul Revere's house and the Boston Common, as well as paths linking them, turned out to be widely known, large areas of the city were not represented in typical mental representations. Certain neighborhoods hardly existed at all in the minds of Bostonians. This again highlights the difference between the cartographer's map and the psychological map. Donald Hooper (1970) informally applied this cognitive mapping technique to New York City with similar results. The psychological representation of New York was found to be localized in downtown landmarks, with much of the city having no cognitive representation at all.

Once the map of a single individual has been externalized, the next problem is that of aggregating the individual maps so as to be able to draw some general conclusion. The problem is that unique configurations

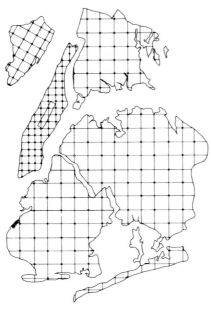

FIGURE 7.1
The stylized map of the five boroughs on page 81 shows the percentage of correct placements in neighborhoods of 152 viewing points in the city. The map to the left shows the grid that formed the basis of selection of the viewing points. Photographs taken at some of the grid intersections are shown on the following pages.

FIGURE 7.2
Queens (Q-7), Woodside houses between Broadway and 31st Avenue. The percentages of subjects who correctly identified this view are: borough: 22 percent; neighborhood, 3 percent; street, 0.9 percent.

are always difficult to aggregate in any meaningful fashion. One is reminded of the work of a nineteenth-century criminologist who attempted to find the average criminal type by superimposing the photographed faces of many criminals onto a single photographic plate, using the resulting portrait as an ideal or average type. Unfortunately, the resulting face was virtually nondescript and resembled no one, criminal or otherwise.

However, the problem of aggregation can be reduced by imposing appropriate constraints. The greater the number of constraints imposed on the subject in externalizing his map, the more readily the production of several individuals can be combined. The psychological map devised by our team is heavily constrained. Subjects are asked to make a simple unidimensional judgment (i.e., whether they can or cannot recognize several scenes of New York). The results of all subjects are then combined without difficulty. This procedure generates a second general type of psychological map, one which takes for granted an objective geographic map, and attempts to plot psychological characteristics onto it. It parallels the approach of a meteorologist mapping weather. In a weather map variables such as temperature, barometric pressure, and wind direction are made at various points and are plotted onto a preexisting map of the region. Similarly, our psychological map attempts to plot a psychological variable onto the geography of New York City.

Psychologists have not been the only persons interested in psychological maps. Geographers such as David Stea (1969), Peter Gould (1967), and Thomas Saarinen (1971) have tried not merely to describe cognitive representations but also to develop concepts for analyzing such maps. Stea asks: "What are the elements out of which people mentally organize large geographic spaces?" and concludes that people think in terms of *points* (New York, Chicago, Canada, etc.). Further, he concludes that these points may be arranged in some *hierarchy* (some are larger, more important, desirable, etc.); that the areas are *bounded* with clear or fuzzy lines of demarcation; that people think in terms of *paths* connecting different points and whether *barriers* block any pair of points. Stea says that "it matters not a whit that we cannot directly observe a mental map. . . . If a subject behaves as if such a map existed, it is sufficient justification for the model."

In typical studies employing these concepts, subjects are asked to make distance, direction, or size estimates of geographic points. Average results are then compared to the objective reality, the point of interest being the type of deviation from reality contained in the mental images. Thus Griffin (1948) argues that the relative areas ascribed to various regions reflect the importance individuals assigned to them. We have all seen the map of the "New Yorker's idea of the United States," in which the city occupies a vast area of the country, and the Midwest is shrunk to a fraction of its actual size.

A final question concerns the manner in which individuals use mental maps in everyday life to locate themselves in the environment or navigate from one point to another. The question of orientation was raised as early as 1913 by Trowbridge, and continues as a lively issue. Stea suggests that two very different mental approaches may be used in moving from one point to another. In one case, the person proceeds on the basis of a set of specific operations, so that the map consists less of an overall image than a sequence of directional instructions tied to specific cues. The person starts off in an initial direction until he comes to cue_1, such as a building or landmark, at which point he turns right or left until he gets to cue_2, and so forth, until his destination is reached. In a second strategy, the individual proceeds not in terms of a sequence of operations but through a generalized image of the city. Through successive approximations, he zeroes in on the target, constantly referring his position to his knowledge of the city's structure. This second strategy allows for the use of alternative routes, whereas the former method does not. Moreover, Stea points out that in the specific sequence method, "if you miss a cue [choice point], you're lost."

The capacity to form such a representation of the overall structure of the city depends not only on the individual but on the city as well, and the degree to which it is imagible. A highly imagible city does not mean that every point is equally identifiable. Rather, there are clearly identifiable focal points throughout the city which are interconnected and thus form a coherent picture. Lynch, in his seminal work, *The Image of the City* (1960), argues that high imagibility is a crucial condition for a livable and enjoyable social setting. Moreover, imagibility is crucial in orienting an individual in a city, in communicating a sense of place to him that immediately informs him of location, direction, etc. The total absence of such orienting features is an unnerving experience. It is interesting that the anxiety inherent in such disorientation is most acutely expressed in nightmares in which an individual wanders aimlessly in vaguely familiar but elusively unidentifiable streets.

The imagibility of different parts of the city is interesting for another reason. It allows us to define the psychological boundaries of a city, which need not, of course, coincide with its political boundaries. The methods used by Lynch and others are natural starting points in the assessment of a city's imagibility. But the next step, we felt, should be in the direction of precision by constructing a map that goes beyond landmark specification to the measurement of the exact degree of cognitive significance of any one point in the city relative to any other point. The remainder of this paper describes the method we employed in obtaining a cognitive map of New York City. The key paradigm underlying the psychological map presented here takes the form: If an individual is placed at random at a point in the city, how likely is he to know where he is?

FIGURE 7.3
Manhattan (M-26), the entrance to Central Park at West 72nd Street (the Dakota).
The percentages who correctly identified this view are: borough, 90 percent;
neighborhood, 59 percent; street, 39 percent.

In order for a person to know his location three requirements must be
met: First, the scene he confronts needs to be differentiable in some respect
from other scenes in the city. If all buildings look exactly the same, a
person cannot know where he is. Second, he must match the unique input
against some memory of it. The memory may have been acquired through
direct exposure, or indirectly through the study of photographs, maps, or
hearsay. Third, even if an individual can recognize a scene, he cannot
necessarily place it in relation to other parts of the city. ("This street is
terribly familiar, but I don't have the slightest idea where we are.")
Placing the scene in the larger framework is a final requirement if we are
to say that the subject knows where he is.

Our main goal, then, was to make a precise assessment of just which
parts of New York City are easiest to recognize and which are most
difficult. Our problem was to devise methods that would uncover, in an
objective and reliable fashion, the mental representations of New York
City held by its residents.

SAMPLING AND PROCEDURE

Only by applying an objective method of scene sampling can assertions drawn from a limited number of cases be applied to the phenomenon as a whole. To illustrate this point, consider the case of a casual investigator who wants to know whether Manhattan or Brooklyn is more recognizable.

He shows a group of people a picture of the Empire State Building to represent Manhattan and his uncle's garage to represent Brooklyn. He would find, no doubt, that more people could recognize the Empire State Building in Manhattan than his uncle's garage in Brooklyn. But that would hardly be an objective basis for asserting that Manhattan was more recognizable than Brooklyn. In one case, he deliberately chose a well-known landmark, and in the other, an insignificant structure. A Brooklyn lover could as easily bias his photographs in the opposite way, photographing the Brooklyn Academy of Music and an insignificant hot dog stand in Manhattan. The only way to control this kind of bias is to introduce an objective method of geographic sampling that could be readily applied not only in New York but in any city in the world (should comparative studies be attempted).

There are many objective ways to choose a set of viewing points. We decided to take advantage of the fact that the entire world is mapped on a coordinate system, lines of latitude and longitude, and that they form regular intersections, so that any point on earth can be specified in terms of these coordinates. While the lines of latitude and longitude appear very far apart on the usual maps, it is possible to obtain maps that carry the system down to a very fine coordinate system. We selected a grid system based on the 1000-meter Universal Transverse Mercator grid ticks shown in U.S. Geological Survey maps of New York City. Wherever a 1000-meter line of latitude intersected a 1000-meter line of longitude, we took a viewing point for our study.

For economy, we systematically thinned out the viewing points in the Bronx, Brooklyn, Queens, and Staten Island, and the final pattern of viewing points is shown in Fig. 7.1. We ended up with 25 viewing points in the Bronx, 22 in Brooklyn, 31 in Queens, 20 in Staten Island, and 54 in Manhattan. Since we wanted to use a large number of subjects, we could not take the subjects to each location, and instead we showed them color slides and asked them to identify the location pictured. A professional photographer was instructed to take a picture that would give the most information to the viewer (e.g., a building rather than an empty lot).

Since familiarity with different parts of the city probably depends on place of residence, we needed a representative sample of all New Yorkers. Thus the most important variable on which our 200 subjects differed was place of residence: they were geographically representative of the population distribution by borough, based on the 1960 census. Subjects were recruited with an advertisement in *New York Magazine,* whose readers, we assumed, would be interested in the city and thus motivated to participate. The total sample represented a particular segment of the New York population. Though some were in their teens and some in their sixties, the majority of the subjects were young adults in their twenties, with a mean age of 28.9. The sex distribution paralleled the city's, with a slight majority of women. According to the Hollingshead scale of social position (1957), the median subject held a job at the minor professional level and had completed college. The median subject had lived in his neighborhood five to ten years and in New York City over 20 years.

Subjects were assembled in groups in a large lecture room with a screen in front. Upon arrival, each was given an answer booklet and a neighborhood map and told to become familiar with the map, which was divided into 54 neighborhoods. They were informed that the main purpose of the study was to discover how well people can recognize various parts of the city. The color slides were then projected onto the screen, and the subjects were asked to imagine that they were viewing these scenes from the window of a bus that was touring the city. The subjects were then asked to indicate in the answer booklet which of the five boroughs they believed the scene was located in. They were also called upon to identify the scene in terms of more exacting criteria—in what neighborhood the scene was to be found and, beyond that, on which precise street. The entire procedure took about ninety minutes.

RELATIVE RECOGNIZABILITY

Based on the proportion of subjects who were able to place each of the 152 scenes in (a) its correct borough, (b) its correct neighborhood, and (c) its exact street location, we may now ask a series of questions concerning the relative recognizability of each of the five boroughs. (It is possible that the figures are somewhat inflated by the fact that if a person took a guess he would be correct 20 percent of the time in any case.)

What proportion of the scenes from each borough were correctly attributed to that borough? By summing the percentage of correct responses for all points in the borough and dividing this figure by the number of points, we arrive at the overall characterization of the borough in terms of an arithmetic mean:

Bronx	25.96%
Brooklyn	35.79
Manhattan	64.12
Queens	39.64
Staten Island	26.00

Clearly, Manhattan emerges as the most recognizable of the five boroughs, with about twice as many correct placements as the others.

There is another way to look at the data. Of the 26 viewing points that were placed in the correct borough by at least 75 percent of the participants, 23 viewing points fall in Manhattan. This certainly corresponds to our generally held notion that Manhattan is better known than other parts of the city.

However, our data tell us more than this, for we may now adopt a more stringent criterion of recognition and ask: What proportion of the scenes in each borough were placed in their correct *neighborhood*? Another way of formulating this is to ask to what degree a street scene communicates to the person the neighborhood he is in. Examining the information on neighborhood placement, we find very substantial differences according to borough:

Bronx	5.85%
Brooklyn	11.42
Manhattan	31.98
Queens	10.76
Staten Island	5.40

A randomly selected scene in Manhattan is five times more likely to be placed in its correct neighborhood than a randomly selected scene in the Bronx; Manhattan scenes do almost three times as well as scenes in Brooklyn and Queens. The superior information value of Manhattan becomes even more pronounced when a more exacting criterion of recognition is applied. When we ask subjects to identify each scene in terms of *street location*, we find the following distribution of accurate guesses:

Bronx	2.56%
Brooklyn	2.83
Manhattan	15.52
Queens	2.21
Staten Island	0.6

The reader must again be reminded that these scenes were not selected because of the likelihood they would be recognized, but were mechanically sampled completely independent of their scenic value.

This overall picture holds true no matter which borough the person comes from. A resident of Queens is four times more likely to identify a street location in Manhattan than in his own borough (3.76 percent for his home borough of Queens vs. 15 percent for Manhattan). Areas of Queens

FIGURE 7.4
This stylized map of New York City shows the correct placement of scenes at 152 viewing points in the city, placed according to neighborhood.

FIGURE 7.5
Manhattan (M-13), 125th Street between 7th and 8th Avenues. The percentages of subjects who correctly identified this view are: borough, 86 percent; neighborhood, 78 percent; street, 49 percent.

have often been accused of being nondescript, and taxi drivers are reputed to fear entering Queens lest they never find their way out. And with good reason, when even the people who live in Queens are lost in their home borough compared with the sense of place they experience in Manhattan! Thus it is correct to say that New York City is not merely culturally but also imagistically rooted in Manhattan.

Aside from Manhattan, residents recognize their own borough better than they recognize any other, and they are better at recognizing their own borough than people from any of the others. But these results are overshadowed by the pre-eminence of Manhattan in the psychological map of all New Yorkers, irrespective of where they live (see Table 7.1).

We have been interested not only in the correct guesses made by subjects but also in the kinds of errors they made. When a subject misclassified a scene from the Bronx, where did he tend to place it? Table 7.2 presents a matrix which indicates not only the percentage of subjects who accurately guessed the correct borough but also the percentage of subjects who erred, broken down according to the boroughs which are mistakenly guessed. It appears that, while Manhattan is rarely confused with any other borough, the Bronx, Brooklyn, and Staten Island are often

FIGURE 7.6
Manhattan (M-8), 147th Street between Riverside Drive and Broadway. The percentages of subjects who correctly identified this view are: borough, 50 percent; neighborhood, 18 percent; street, 9 percent.

thought to be Queens. It is as though subjects said to themselves: "Well, I don't really know where that was taken, but it looks as if it might be Queens." One could refer to the phenomenon as a Queens response bias. While the largest percentage of subjects either guessed the correct borough or answered "Don't know" (in the case of the Bronx and Staten Island), the second largest percentage of subjects guessed Queens.

Finally, we may ask whether the residents of any one borough are better at recognizing the city as a whole than the residents of any other borough. As shown in Table 7.3, the differences among residents of the five boroughs are not very large on any of the categories. In other words, there is no evidence that residents of any particular borough are more accurate at recognizing the city as a whole than residents of any other borough.

What general principles account for the major findings of the study? First, an area can only be recognized if people are exposed to it. As we might expect, Manhattan's high index of recognizability is due, in important measure, to the fact that, as the cultural and entertainment core, it attracts persons from all over the city. Even a highly distinctive architec-

TABLE 7.1 PERCENT OF CORRECT BOROUGH, NEIGHBORHOOD, AND STREET PLACEMENT BY BOROUGH OF RESIDENCE

Borough of residence	Bronx			Brooklyn			Manhattan			Queens			Staten Island		
	B	N	S*	B	N	S	B	N	S	B	N	S	B	N	S
Bronx	40.94	14.40	6.58	21.99	5.78	0.69	69.93	34.77	18.24	33.66	7.72	1.51	18.88	4.44	0.28
Brooklyn	18.63	2.27	1.32	49.19	19.89	5.37	67.41	26.18	11.57	37.15	8.70	1.46	28.87	5.32	0.32
Manhattan	25.58	5.55	2.19	28.97	7.95	2.46	65.09	38.03	21.04	34.71	8.81	2.48	27.95	5.00	0.91
Queens	25.67	5.18	2.52	34.50	8.50	1.17	66.43	31.71	15.00	54.54	15.15	3.76	20.00	2.40	0.20
Staten Island	12.04	0.92	0.0	36.46	9.62	3.85	59.38	24.11	8.93	18.18	3.79	1.52	61.25	30.00	3.75

*B = borough; N = neighborhood; S = street.

TABLE 7.2 MATRIX OF CLASSIFICATIONS SHOWING CORRECT
PERCENTAGES AS WELL AS MISCLASSIFICATIONS, BY BOROUGH

When the borough was:	*Percent of subjects who identified scenes as:*					*Combined errors*	*Don't know*
	Bx	*B*	*M*	*Q*	*S.I.*		
Bronx	**25.96**	14.89	6.92	17.33	3.48	42.62	31.51
Brooklyn	10.33	**35.79**	8.08	18.17	2.94	39.12	25.00
Manhattan	7.81	8.17	**64.12**	3.44	0.49	19.88	15.89
Queens	8.82	14.76	2.94	**39.64**	4.94	31.46	28.52
Staten Island	11.45	10.15	1.50	21.70	**26.00**	44.80	29.05

tural display will not be widely recognized if it is too far off the beaten path; centrality in relation to major population flow is crucial.

The second major factor seems to be the overall architectural or social distinctiveness of the area. Columbus Circle and Rockefeller Center impress themselves because of their unique configuration of spaces and buildings. Chinatown and Little Italy communicate themselves through cultural and racial features of their respective neighborhoods. The degree to which a scene in the city will be recognized can be summarized by the formula

$$R = f(C \times D)$$

in which R is recognition, C stands for centrality to population flow, and D represents social or architectural distinctiveness.

We have seen that New York City, as a psychological space, is very uneven. It is not at all clear that such world cities as London, Paris, Tokyo, and Moscow have comparably uneven psychological textures. It would be extremely interesting to construct a similar psychological map of other

TABLE 7.3 AVERAGE PERCENT CORRECT
(OVER ALL BOROUGHS) ACCORDING TO
WHERE SUBJECT LIVES

Borough of residence	Borough	Neighborhood	Street
Bronx	37.08	13.42	5.46
Brooklyn	40.25	12.47	4.01
Manhattan	36.46	13.07	5.82
Queens	40.23	12.59	4.53
Staten Island	37.46	13.69	3.61
All subjects combined	38.30	13.08	4.64

FIGURE 7.7
Brooklyn (B-3), Adelphi Street between Fulton Street and Atlantic Avenue. The percentages of subjects who correctly identified this view are: borough, 48 percent; neighborhood, 27 percent; street, 2 percent.

major cities of the world to determine how successfully each city, in all its parts, communicates to the resident a specific sense of place which locates him in the city, assuages the panic of disorientation, and allows him to build up an articulated image of the city as a whole. Contours could be drawn around the psychological core of the city to show whether it is compressed or coextensive with the city around it. My guess is that Paris holds together better than New York because it has focal points that are more successfully distributed throughout the city. In addition, if only out of a sense of scientific duty, we ought to take the psychological map to the drearier cities of the world. It would probably turn out that their index of recognizability is about on a par with that of Queens or the Bronx. The deeper misfortune of their inhabitants is that they cannot take a subway into a vibrant and highly imagible core.

There is a moral here for the outlying boroughs. The construction of identifiable monuments in their neighborhoods, the addition of distinctive decorative touches to their houses, and emphasis on local color would help them emerge from the gray, nondescript character they now possess into more vivid and exciting locales.

NOTE

1. This research would not have been possible without the public-spirited assistance of *New York Magazine* and its executive editor, Sheldon Zalaznick. Over a thousand volunteers were recruited through its advertising pages. Thanks are also due to Pacy Markman for his talent in recruiting subjects and to Lynne Goodstein for assistance in graphics.

REFERENCES

EMERSON, W., 1969, "A review of geographic and psychologic research into the structure of environmental images," University of Minnesota, unpublished.

GOULD, P., 1967. "Structuring information on spacio-temporal preferences," *J. Regional Science*, Vol. 7, No. 2 (supplement).

GRIFFIN, D., 1948, "Topographical orientation," *Foundations of Psychology*. New York: J. Wiley.

HOOPER, D., reported in S. Milgram, 1970, "The experience of living in cities," *Science*, Vol. 167.

LYNCH, K., 1960, *The Image of the City*. Cambridge, Mass.: MIT and Harvard University Press.

MILGRAM, S., 1970, "The experience of living in cities," *Science*, Vol. 167.

SAARINEN, T., 1971, "The use of projective techniques in geographic research," mimeo.

STEA, D., 1969, "Environment perception and cognition: Toward a model for mental maps," Student Publication of the North Carolina State University School of Design, Vol. 18.

STEA, D., 1969, "The measurement of mental maps: An experimental model for studying conceptual spaces," Studies in Geography #17: Behavioral Problems in Geography: A Symposium, Northwestern University.

TROWBRIDGE, C. C., 1913, "On fundamental methods of orientation and imaginary maps," *Science*, Vol. 38.

8

Psychological Maps of Paris[1]

❖

In this report we shall explore the way in which Parisians mentally represent their city. It is not an examination of Paris as a geographic reality, but rather of the way that reality is mirrored in the minds of its inhabitants. And the first principle is that reality and image are imperfectly linked. The Seine may course a great arc in Paris, almost forming a half circle, but Parisians imagine it a much gentler curve, and some think the river a straight line as it flows through the city.

Paris, the city of stone, is the template from which the mental map draws its structure, but it is not the same as the map. The person harboring a mental model of Paris may die, but the city endures. The city may vanish through flood or nuclear holocaust, but the maps encoded in millions of human brains are not thereby destroyed.

The main problem in investigating a mental entity is to learn how to render it observable. The person's mental image of Paris is not like his driver's license, something he can pull out for inspection. Rather, we shall have to tease the information from the subject, using whatever means psychology can offer to inspect the contents of the mind (Downs and Stea, 1973).

It is not quite as easy as simply asking the person. First, many of the concepts people have about cities are nonverbal, spatial ideas. They are not easily translated into words, particularly on the part of subjects of limited education. Moreover,

This paper was written in collaboration with Mme. Denise Jodelet. The research was supported by a fellowship to the senior author from the John Simon Guggenheim Memorial Foundation, and by a grant from the Délégation Générale à la Recherche Scientifique, an agency of the French Government. It was first published in *Environmental Psychology: People and Their Physical Settings* (second edition), H. M. Proshansky, W. H. Ittelson, and L. G. Rivlin (eds.), New York: Holt, Rinehart and Winston, 1976. Reprinted by permission of Alexandra Milgram.

Parisians are all exposed to stereotypes about their city, readily available clichés, which do not so much tap their personal ideas of the city, as their immersion in a world of prepackaged platitudes. We want to get at something more personal and more closely tied to direct experience.

HANDDRAWN MAPS

To begin, our 218 subjects, drawn from each of the 20 arrondissements (i.e., administrative sectors) of Paris in proportion to their numbers, were asked to draw a map of Paris in which they were to mention all of the elements of the city that came to mind; they could illustrate their maps with monuments, squares, neighborhoods, streets, or whatever elements spontaneously occurred to them. They were told further that their sketch should not resemble a tourist map of Paris, but ought to express their personal view. Let us now consider the maps of some of the subjects:

Map 108   (Fig. 8.1). The subject is a 25-year-old commercial agent, with university degrees in physical chemistry. His first entries on the map were Boulevard St. Germain and St. Michel, then the Faculté des Sciences at Jussieu, suggesting that his student experience remains dominant. The modern structures of the Zamanski Tower at the Faculté des Sciences and the 50-story Maine-Montparnasse office tower are prominently shown. Youthful subjects, more often than their elders, include these contemporary elements as if the mental maps of the old were internalized a long time ago and cannot admit these recent additions. Rising in the northwest, the massive office complex, La Défense, is given an almost projective significance, as it hovers menacingly alongside the city. The map expresses the central dilemma of contemporary Paris: how can it preserve its distinctive character, formed in earlier centuries, while coming to grips with modernity?

Map 070   (Fig. 8.2). Map 070 is drawn by a 50-year-old woman who, at the time of the interview, lived in the 12th arrondissement; however, for 15 years she had resided in the 4th, which she maps with scrupulous detail, even to the point of indicating the one-way street directions for automobiles. She centers her map not on Paris as a whole, but on a segment of it that has special meaning to her. Yet she is able to link her personal experience to highly public landmarks such as the Louvre and the Palais Royale. Perhaps it is characteristic of Paris that one can readily fuse private and public aspects of life through the network of streets and landmarks.

Map 215   (Fig. 8.3). This subject is a 33-year-old butcher who lives in the 11th arrondissement. At first the map looks confusing, but we begin to discern the elements of a set of life circumstances when we examine it closely. He does not forget to include his home arrondissement, which is something of a hidden one to most subjects. Nor does he neglect La

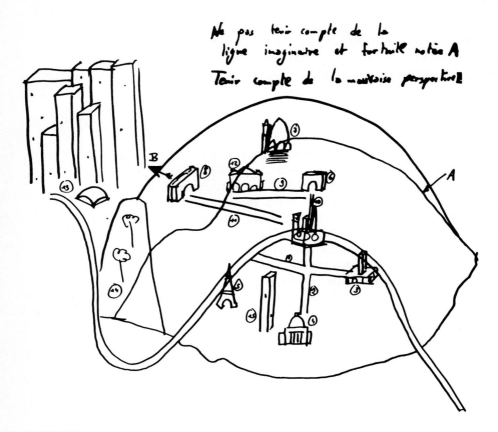

FIGURE 8.1
Map 108.

Villette, where the major stockyards and slaughterhouses of Paris are to be found. One can imagine his visits to the great exposition hall at the Porte de Versailles, to see displays of meat cutting equipment, motorcycles, and perhaps automobiles. Faubourg St. Antoine, of revolutionary significance, is placed on the Left Bank, where it would seem to belong politically.

We are most confused, perhaps, by the inverted curvature he has given to the Seine; the disposition of elements along the river seem all out of line with reality. Yet if Etoile, Maison de la Radio, and the Porte de St. Cloud deviate from their true spatial coordinates, they do preserve a meaningful topological sequence.

Map 037   (Fig. 8.4). A mental map is not limited to reality, but may incorporate visions of how a city ought to be. This subject, an architect, organizes the city around the Place de la Concorde. He envisages a major avenue stretching south from the Place, over the Seine, piercing the

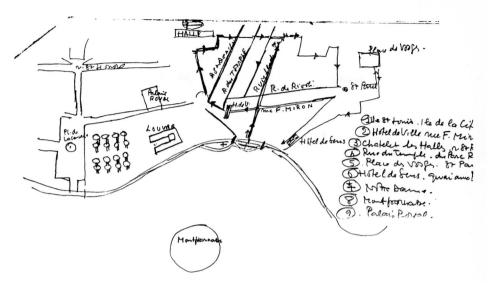

FIGURE 8.2
Map 070.

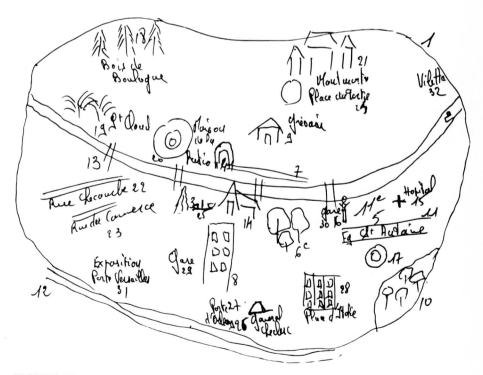

FIGURE 8.3
Map 215.

Chambre des Députés, and continuing south into the heart of the Left Bank, terminating in an impressive structure (as yet unrealized). From that point, a broad avenue would sweep northwest to reveal the Eiffel Tower, and another northeast leading to the colonnade of Madeleine (displaced from its present location). Such mental maps are fanciful. Yet Paris as it exists was born first as a set of ideas, and the Paris to come is also germinating in the minds of architects and city planners. The subject's concern with problems of automobile traffic represents a realistic attention to the city's most severe environmental problem.

It is clear the subjects did not merely derive their maps from personal, direct experience with the city. They learned them, in part, from other maps. Street maps of Paris, prepared by technically skilled cartographers, are an inherent part of contemporary Parisian culture. Probably not a single subject could have generated a map of the city accurately showing its form and basic structure without reference in his own mind to maps he has already seen. But through processes of selectivity, emphasis, and distortion, the maps become projections of life styles, and express emotional cathexes of the participants.

Second, neither the city, nor the mental maps of the city, are simple agglomerations of elements; they are structures. It is the essence of

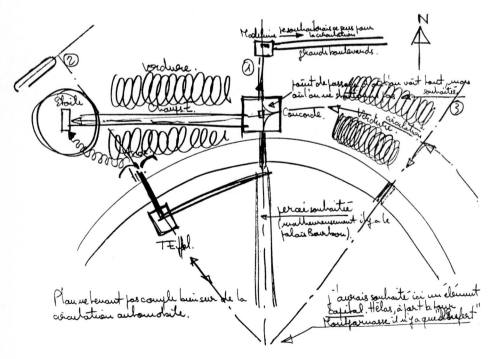

FIGURE 8.4
Map 037.

structure that displacement of one element is not an isolated event, but has consequences for the other elements with which it is linked.

Finally, a map that a person draws of his city is not his mental map, but is only a clue to it. He may not be able to draw very well; he may have images in his mind which he cannot put on paper. He may make errors in his initial strokes that complicate his later completion of the map. But still, the sketch is an opening into his conception of the city.

*P*ARIS AS A COLLECTIVE REPRESENTATION

A city is a social fact. We would all agree to that. But we need to add an important corollary: the perception of a city is also a social fact, and as such needs to be studied in its collective as well as its individual aspect. It is not only what *exists* but what is *highlighted* by the community that acquires salience in the mind of the person. A city is as much a collective representation as it is an assemblage of streets, squares, and buildings. We discern the major ingredients of that representation by studying not only the mental map in a specific individual, but by seeing what is shared among individuals. Toward this end, we turn from the clinical use of individual maps to an actuarial analysis of the entire group of maps provided by the subjects.

*E*MERGING ELEMENTS

The sequence that spontaneously emerges as subjects sketch their maps of Paris may tell us what is uppermost in their minds when they think of the city. What is most salient is probably what comes out first. With this point in mind, from the outset we had asked our subjects to number each element as they drew it, emphasizing that the numbering process is to accompany their process of drawing, and not be applied afterward.

Most subjects begin their maps of Paris by drawing a rough ellipse designating the city limits. Unlike many cities in the United States, such as Los Angeles, which do not possess a strong form and whose boundaries bleed off into surrounding areas, Paris possesses a clear boundary and its form impresses itself on the inhabitants. The boundary is sharply etched by the *périphérique*, a highway wrapped around the city, separating the city from the densely populated suburbs, and providing a contemporary moat-in-motion to replace the historic walls.

Within the city there are almost a thousand different elements included in the maps of our subjects, but only one feature is the first entry of a large number of participants, the Seine. After the city limits are sketched, it is the element that far and away is drawn first. It is not only a basic geographic fact of the city, but its most salient psychological fact as well, and much of the subjects' subsequent mapmaking is organized around it.

But there is a serious distortion in the way the Seine is represented. In reality the path of the Seine resembles a wave that enters Paris at the Quai Bercy, rises sharply northward, tapers slightly as it flows into separate streams around the islands, initiates its flat northernmost segment at the Place de la Concorde, then turns sharply in a great 60° bend at the Place d'Alma to flow out of the southwestern tip of the city. But in their drawings, 91.6 percent of the subjects understated the river's degree of curvature. Several subjects pulled it through the city as a straight line, and the typical subject represented the Seine as a gentle arc of slight but uniform curvature.

Because the course of the river is made to resemble an arc of gentle convexity, some subjects find it necessary to force the river through the Bois de Boulogne, and there is no space for the Auteuil and Passy districts. Accordingly, these districts are eliminated or displaced to the Left Bank.

Figure 8.5 compares the actual course of the Seine to the average curvature imparted by the subjects.

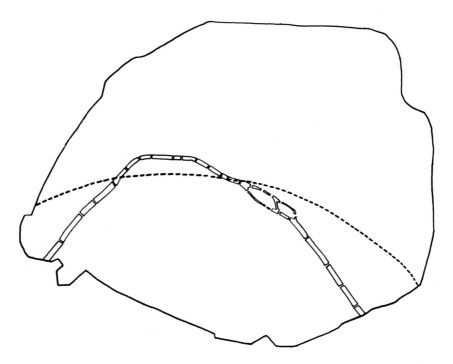

FIGURE 8.5
Perceived curvature of the Seine. The dotted line represents the median curvature imparted to the Seine in the subject's handdrawn maps. It is superimposed on the actual course of the river.

Why does this systematic distortion occur? Quite clearly it reflects the subjects' experience. Although the Alma bend of the Seine is apparent in high aerial views of the city, it is not experienced as a sharp curve in the ordinary walk or drive through the city. The curve is extended over a sufficient distance so that the pronounced turn of the river is obscured. Such long, slow curves have, in almost all studies of orientation in cities, proved to be the most confusing, and difficult to reconstruct (Lynch, 1960).

We return now to the general question of the sequence with which the elements are set down. After the Seine, Notre Dame and Île de la Cité are set down most often as the first entries. The three elements of the Seine, Île de la Cité, and Notre Dame are at the very heart of the idea of Paris. Lutèce was born on the Île de la Cité; Notre Dame was constructed there 800 years ago. The sequence with which subjects enter their elements in the handdrawn maps recapitulates this history.

Unlike a city such as New York, whose psychological core has shifted continuously northward (and now focuses on the area between 34th and 86th Streets), the psychological center of Paris has remained true to its origins, building outward from the Seine, never shifting its center away from its historic root. The remarkable stability of the "heart of Paris" confers a dimension of permanence to the city's psychological structure.

*T*HE MAJOR ELEMENTS

Altogether our subjects entered 4,132 elements in their maps, an average of 19 for each subject. If the city did not impress on its inhabitants a sense of its structure, its highlights and nodes, we would find little agreement among the subjects. But, in fact, time and again we find the same locations, showing up in the handdrawn maps. Indeed, about half of all the 4,132 elements are accounted for by only 26 locations.

We need to translate the frequency of information into cartographic form. Perhaps we can take a cue from Rand McNally. When the population of a city is large, Rand McNally translates this information into **BOLD TYPOGRAPHY,** and the population of a small city is expressed by smaller print. In Fig. 8.6 we have shown the names of the locales, streets, and monuments in a size proportional to the number of people who cited them; that is, in proportion to their salience to the Parisians.

Parisians like to say that there is a tourist Paris, but the real Paris is something quite apart. But if we examine the maps produced by the subjects, we see that time and again tourist Paris—the famous monuments and landmarks—reappears as the basic structuring devices in their own productions of the city. Paris is integral, and it is not possible to efface l'Etoile, the Louvre, and others from any intelligent representation of the city.

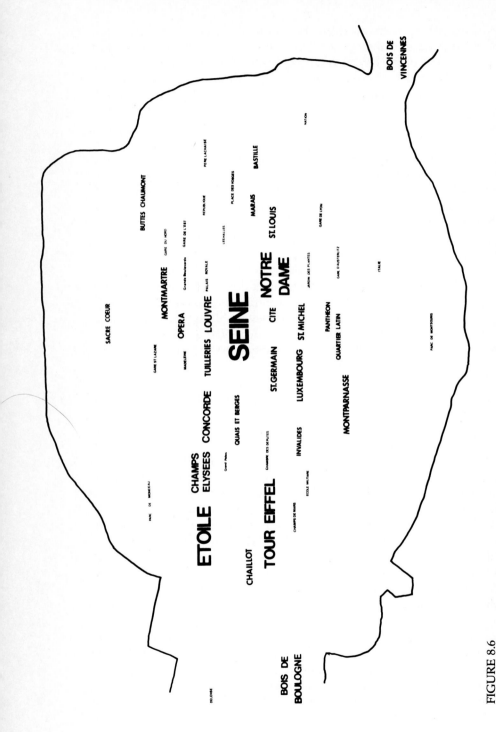

FIGURE 8.6
The 50 most frequently cited elements. The name of each locale is shown in a size proportional to the number of subjects who included it in their handdrawn maps of Paris.

In scoffing at tourist Paris, Parisians imply they have access to a much deeper treasure, and choose to dissociate themselves from the city's public aspect. But, of course, the very greatness of Paris and its attraction to millions reside in its very availability as a city.

In Table 8.1 we have listed by rank, and irrespective of when the items appeared in the subject's map, the fifty elements of the Paris cityscape listed most frequently by the subjects.

TABLE 8.1 THE FIFTY ELEMENTS MOST FREQUENTLY INCLUDED IN THE HANDDRAWN MAPS OF PARIS

Rank	Name of element	Percent of maps in which this element appears	Rank	Name of element	Percent of maps in which this element appears
1.	Seine	84.3	26.	Bastille	22.1
2.	Limites de Paris	81.5	27.	Quartier Latin	20.7
3.	Etoile, Arc de Triomphe	61.9	28.	Panthéon	20.7
			29.	Place des Vosges	18.4
4.	Notre Dame	55.5	30.	Gare de Lyon	18.4
5.	Tour Eiffel	54.6	31.	Champ de Mars	17.9
6.	Bois de Boulogne	49.1	32.	Madeleine	17.9
7.	Louvre	45.4	33.	Parc Monceau	17.0
8.	Concorde	45.4	34.	Parc de Montsouris	16.6
9.	Champs Elysées	40.4	35.	Gare St. Lazare	16.6
10.	Jardin du Luxembourg	38.5	36.	Jardin des Plantes	16.1
11.	Bois de Vincennes	38.1	37.	Gare de l'Est	15.6
12.	Gare et Tour Montp.	35.3	38.	Palais Royale	15.2
13.	Île de la Cité	33.9	39.	Gare du Nord	14.7
14.	Tuileries	33.5	40.	Place de la République	14.3
15.	Butte Montmartre	32.1	41.	Gare d'Austerlitz	13.8
16.	Chaillot, Trocadero	32.1	42.	Père Lachaise	12.9
17.	Île de St. Louis	31.7	43.	Porte, Place d'Italie	12.4
18.	St. Germain	31.2	44.	Place de la Nation	12.0
19.	Opéra	30.7	45.	Chambre des Députés	11.5
20.	Boulevard St. Michel	30.1	46.	École Militaire	11.5
21.	Invalides	29.8	47.	Les Halles	10.1
22.	Marais	26.2	48.	Grand, Petit Palais	9.7
23.	Buttes Chaumont	24.4	49.	La Défense	9.7
24.	Sacre Coeur	23.4	50.	Grands Boulevards	9.2
25.	Quais, Berges	22.5			

No city consists of a set of isolated elements floating in an urban vacuum, but some cities possess a dense set of pathways tying its varied monuments and squares together. A city is either barren or fertile, depending on the degree to which its varied elements are woven into an interconnected web. The sum becomes greater than the parts by virtue of their relationship to each other. To uncover the associational structures of Paris, we posed the following problem to our subjects:

> We shall name an element in the Paris scene, then we would like you to wander with the mind's eye to the next specific element in your own mental imagery, which we would then like you to write down. For example, if we say "Tour Eiffel" you might summon up the scene in your mental imagery, probe around mentally, and say "Palais de Chaillot" or "Pont d'Iéna," or you might think of the Champ de Mars. Whatever comes to mind as forming a natural connection is what interests us.

In this way we hoped to see how the varied elements in the subject's mental structure of Paris were held together. The 20 stimulus locales that we provided the subjects are listed in Table 8.2.

In Column *A* we have indicated the number of links forged between each stimulus location and some other location by at least 10 percent of the subjects. For example, there are six such links for the Arc de Triomphe, five links for the Tour Eiffel, and so on. There is a great difference in the degree to which the different stimulus locales are embedded in a context of mental associations. Among the most richly embedded sites are Arc de Triomphe, l'Opéra, Notre Dame de Paris, and Panthéon. The most weakly embedded are Buttes Chaumont and Père Lachaise.

The structure of associations for two of the stimulus locales is shown in the "molecules" in Fig. 8.7.

By linking up the separate molecules at points of overlap, one may map the entire network of associations for the city, the reticulate structure of its images.

A related measure of the "embeddedness" is the proportion of subjects who are unable to give any association whatsoever to a stimulus location. As Column *B* of Table 8.2 shows, this varies greatly from one location to the next. Fewer than one percent of the subjects were unable to provide an association to the Arc de Triomphe, while 34 percent were unable to provide any association for the Parc de Montsouris. The former is a well-embedded element, while the latter is poorly articulated with the main structure of the city.

Although we asked our subjects to concentrate on geographic, visual elements, they often included purely social or historical features such as "La Guillotine" or "clochards," as if these elements could simply not be excluded from the meaning of a particular locale. We used this informa-

TABLE 8.2 MENTAL LINKS TO TWENTY STIMULUS LOCALES

Stimulus locales	A Number of locales with which stimulus locale is linked by 10 percent of the subjects or more	B Percent of subjects who fail to link stimulus locale with any other locale
Arc de Triomphe	6	.5
Notre Dame	6	1.8
Place de la Concorde	6	1.8
L'Opéra	6	2.3
Sacre Coeur	2	2.3
Le Louvre	4	3.7
Tour Eiffel	5	5.1
Gare St. Lazare	1	5.5
Bois de Vincennes	3	6.9
Porte St. Martin	2	11.0
Le Panthéon	6	11.5
Tour St. Jacques	4	12.4
Place de la Nation	2	13.3
École Militaire	3	13.8
Place de la République	2	16.1
Lion de Belfort	3	18.4
Parc des Buttes Chaumont	0	20.2
Place d'Italie	3	22.5
Père Lachaise	0	27.0
Parc de Montsouris	1	34.0

tion to create an additional map (Fig. 8.8); one in which each locale is surrounded by the verbal associations it stimulated.

RECOGNITION OF PARISIAN SCENES

There are numerous representations of things that a person cannot externalize through drawing or verbal recall. He may be able to see a loved one's face in his mind's eye without being able to draw it. But he is likely to recognize it if shown a photograph. And the same is true of cities. A person may have encoded visual aspects of the city that can be most sensitively uncovered through recognition, that is by seeing if the person can match an external stimulus to some memory of it. Accordingly, to supplement the method of "free recall" used in drawing maps of the city, we presented subjects with 40 photographed scenes of Paris, which they were asked to identify. Correct recognition shows that a scene is an active

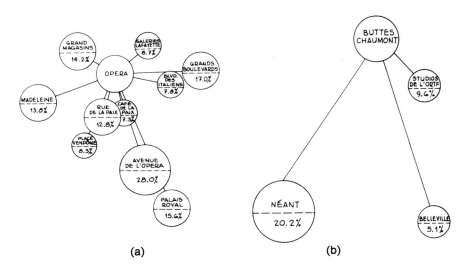

(a)   (b)

FIGURE 8.7
(a) Association to Opéra. Shows all associations to the stimulus locale Opéra made by at least 5 percent of the subjects. (b) Associations to Buttes Chaumont. Shows all associations to the stimulus locale Buttes Chaumont made by at least 50 percent of the subjects.

part of the subject's representation of the city, even if he did not spontaneously include it in his map.

We scored recognition by noting the percentage of subjects who correctly identified the scene, and as Table 8.3 shows, this ranged from 100 percent for Etoile to under 5 percent for Rue de Cambrai and Place d'Israël. We may touch briefly on four aspects of the recognition data: *icons of the city, confusions, class differences,* and *paradoxical unknowns* (see Fig. 8.9).

Icons of the City

All of the groups shown the photographs, whether professionals or workers, recognized the same four scenes with the greatest degree of accuracy: Etoile, Notre Dame, Place de la Concorde, and the Palais de Chaillot. What distinguishes these scenes is not so much their beauty, as their monumentality, special historic significance, and scenic grandeur. (To this group one could, without doubt, add the Eiffel Tower and Sacre Coeur (Sondages, 1951).) Each of these scenes has come to be indelibly associated with Paris, not merely within the city, but abroad as well. One might conclude, therefore, that those sites which are universally identifiable among residents serve as internationally circulated symbols of the

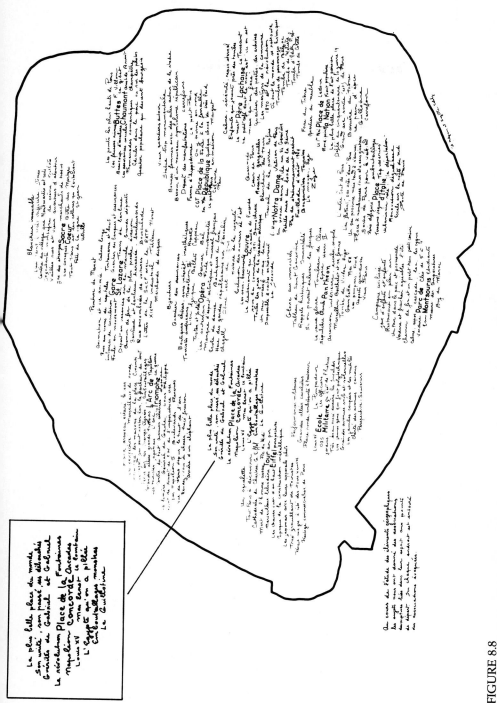

FIGURE 8.8
Ideational associations to several stimulus locales.

TABLE 8.3 RECOGNITION OF PARISIAN SCENES

Scenes shown to group I*	Percent of S's who correctly identified scene	Scenes shown to group II*	Percent of S's who correctly identified scene
Etoile	100.0	Place Denfert	
Notre Dame	98.5	Rochereau	94.4
Place de la Concorde	97.0	Place Vendôme	90.8
Palais de Chaillot	93.3	Place de la République	81.6
Mosque	82.8	Parc Monceau	80.5
Louvre (Porte la Tremoille)	79.0	Place du Tertre	79.3
Places des Vosges	70.1	Porte de St. Cloud	61.0
Porte St. Martin	67.0	Square du Vert Galant	59.8
UNESCO (Place Fontenoy)	52.0	École des Beaux Arts	58.7
Musée des Arts		Place des Victoires	56.3
Africains	46.4	Arène de Lutèce	55.2
Place Furstenberg	44.8	Fontaine Molière	55.2
Parc de Montsouris	44.8	Eglise d'Alésia	54.0
Eglise Orthodox	44.8	Fontaine des Innocents	49.4
Place Félix Eboué	39.6	Place St. André des Arts	31.0
Avenue d'Italie	36.6	Mémorial du Martyr Juif	23.0
Monument de la		Passage Dellesert	20.7
Déportation	30.6	Avenue Clichy	16.1
Fontaine Cuvier	37.7	Place Rodin	12.6
Avenue des Gobelins	7.5	Pont Bir Hakeim	12.6
Place d'Israël	4.5	Place de Santiago	6.9
Rue de Cambrai	4.5		

*Twenty scenes were shown to each of two groups of subjects, studied at different times.

city. This formula is, however, too simple: Denfert Rochereau, with its imposing Lion de Belfort, though recognized by 94 percent of the subjects, in no way functions as an international symbol. (This raises questions of urban iconography too complex to discuss here. We may also ponder why Paris is so richly endowed with exportable symbols, while such great urban centers as São Paulo and Chicago lack them entirely.)

Confusions

In the mental representation of a city, two quite separate geographic locales may be collapsed into a single imagined site. Thus, many Parisians mentally combined the nonsectarian Monument de la Déportation (located on the Île de la Cité) and the Mémorial du Martyr Juif (located in St. Paul) into a single locale, believing there is only one such monument, rather than the two that actually exist. Porte St. Martin was frequently

Icon: *Etoile, 100 percent correct identification.*

Confusion: *Porte St. Martin, 67.0 percent identification. Often misidentified as Porte St. Denis.*

Class differences: *UNESCO at Place Fontenoy, 52 percent correct overall. Professionals, 67 percent; workers, 24 percent.*

Unknown: *Place D'Israël, identified by 4.5 percent of the subjects.*

FIGURE 8.9
Representative photographs used in the recognition text.

misidentified as Porte St. Denis, highlighting the psychologically interchangeable character of the two arches.

Class Differences

Class factors shape the maps of the subjects by segregating rich and poor residentially, and also by transmitting a class-linked culture to various segments of the population. Thus, Place Furstenberg is recognized by 59 percent of the professional subjects, but only 17 percent of the workers; UNESCO headquarters by 67 percent versus 24 percent. The icons of the city, however, are recognized equally by all groups, serving as integrative elements in the urban culture.

Paradoxical Unknowns

When a city is deficient in fine squares and architecture, mediocre locales may be widely publicized because they are the best of what is available. But in Paris, a surfeit of riches creates an opposite situation. Competition for a place in the mind is fierce; many worthy locales are excluded. Thus Place Felix Eboué, which displays an impressive and monumental fountain, is recognized by less than half of the Parisians, while 87 percent of the subjects cannot identify Place Rodin. Place d'Israël, which could serve as an architectural showpiece, sinks to virtual obscurity—identified by only 4.47 percent of the subjects. Locational factors play some part. But more critically, the data highlight how the mental maps which Parisians internalize are not only individual products, but are in an important degree social constructions. Any one of these last scenes possesses sufficient aesthetic value to serve as a widely known feature of the Parisian environment. If society chose to publicize Place Rodin, the square could become as famous as (God forbid) the urinating statue of Brussels. Social definition determines, through selectivity and reiteration, which features of the city acquire salience in the mental maps of the inhabitants.

PARIS, KNOWN AND UNKNOWN

The photographic recognition test tells us about the knowledge of specific landmarks, but we wanted a more general picture of the known and unknown parts of the city. Accordingly, we provided each subject with an illustrated map of the city, which we overprinted with the boundaries of the 80 administrative districts (quartiers). We asked each subject to study his map and indicate the ten quartiers with which he was most familiar, and those that were least familiar to him. By combining the response for all subjects, we generate a gradient of asserted familiarity across the entire city.

The five most familiar quartiers are contiguous and center on the Quartier Latin and Île de la Cité. The next five choices accrete to this cluster, but also extend to the Champs Elysées and Etoile. When subjects are asked to list the quartier they know least well, we find a striking movement away from the center of Paris to the peripheral arrondissements.

Figure 8.10 shows how these data, translated into respective arrondissements, delineate a ring of unknown areas around the core of Paris. Curiously, in this map the boundary between known and unknown parts of the city retraces part of the route of the last wall of Paris, the Férmiers Généraux. Although the wall was torn down in 1859 its effects endure in the mental maps of contemporary Parisians, with the least familiar parts of the city lying outside the boundary where the wall once stood.

The residential patterns of Paris create a class basis to known and unknown parts of the city. Generally speaking, the wealthier segments of the population live in the western part of the city, and the poorer classes

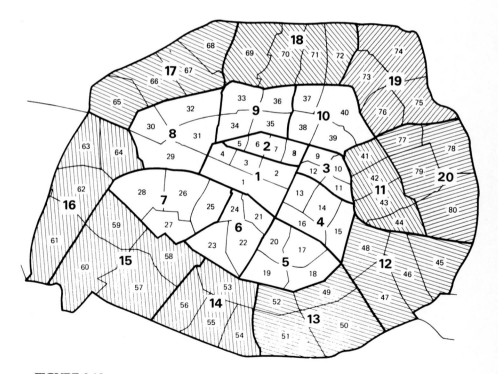

FIGURE 8.10
Least known areas of Paris, by arrondissement. The shaded portion of the map indicates the ten arrondissements that contain areas subjects indicate they know least well.

TABLE 8.4 LEAST FAMILIAR ARRONDISSEMENTS BY SOCIAL CLASS

Rank	Arrond.	Percent of S's indicating a quartier in this arrondissement to be among the least familiar	Arrond.	Percent of S's indicating a quartier in this arrondissement to be among the least familiar
1	20	69.3	15	61.0
2	19	68.2	13	58.5
3	12	62.5	17	53.7
4	18	61.4	16	51.2

live in the east. It is not surprising, therefore, that the areas least known to the working-class subjects should differ from those of the middle-class professionals, as Table 8.4 shows. While all of the least-known arrondissements are on the periphery of Paris, there is no overlap between the class-linked perceptions. It is only a knowledge of the central arrondissements of Paris that is claimed by both groups.

SOCIAL PERCEPTIONS

While ethnic turfs have a salient place in the representation of New York, with exception of the North African districts, and the Jewish quarter around St. Paul, they do not figure greatly in the mental maps of Paris. The city does not have the multiple ethnic concentrations found in New York, and areas are not selectively highlighted and affixed with an ethnic label, a process Suttles (1972) has shown to be important in the definition of ethnic neighborhoods. In pre-World War II Paris, areas of the city were rich in residents from particular provinces, and subjects continue to identify the quartiers around Gare de Montparnasse as *Paris des Bretons*. On the other hand, the Chinese community that once flourished behind the Gare de Lyon receives no representation in the maps of contemporary Parisians.

Subjects locate the very poor in the northeastern districts; while the wealthy are overwhelmingly situated in the 16th arrondissement, at the western edge of the city (Table 8.5). This is a sharply differentiated perception, with no geographic overlap between the two groups. The criminally dangerous areas of Paris are identified with the 18th and 19th arrondissements, with the greatest threat to personal safety ascribed to the Goutte d'Or quartier, which houses many North African immigrants.

The responses to several purely personal questions appear to derive from this rough socioeconomic map. When subjects are asked if there is a quartier they would refuse to live in under any circumstances, they cite the quartiers around Goutte d'Or (quartiers 71, 72, 73, 74).

TABLE 8.5 QUALITIES ASCRIBED TO DIFFERENT AREAS OF PARIS

| Qualities | The arrondissements in which the quality on the left is most frequently located, ranked 1–4, and the percentage of all subjects locating the quality within this arrondissement.* (N = 218) | | | |
	1	2	3	4
Paris of the rich	16 87.6%	17 20.6%	8 18.3%	7 17.0%
Paris of the poor	18 38.5%	19 31.7%	20 29.8%	13 11.0%
Dangerous Paris	18 38.5%	9 31.7%	10 29.8%	19 11.0%
Areas you like best	6 70.6%	4 65.1%	1 57.8%	5 51.4%
Areas in which you would refuse to live under any circumstances	18 37.2%	19 27.1%	10 18.3%	8 17.0%
Areas you know best	6 73.9%	1 61.5%	5 58.3%	8 57.8%
Areas you know least well	20 60.1%	13 58.7%	19 57.3%	18 55.0%
Snobbish Paris	16 49.1%	6 15.1%	8 14.7%	17 9.6%
"Paris des Bretons"	15 50.0%	4 34.9%	6 23.4%	—
Where you would move if you became wealthy	6 33.9%	4 31.2%	7 24.8%	16 21.6%
Friendlier, more relaxed atmosphere	6 30.3%	5 22.5%	4 18.3%	7 14.7%
Greatest loss of pleasant qualities because of urban renewal	15 43.1%	1 14.2%	13 13.8%	6 10.1%

*Subjects were instructed to give all responses in terms of quartiers and not arrondissements. (There are four quartiers in each arrondissement.) But we have integrated the results and presented them in terms of arrondissements for ease of comprehension, particularly for those familiar with the city.

The deepest affection for the city is reserved for its central historic areas, with the best-liked quartiers falling out in the 6th, followed by 4th, 1st, and 5th arrondissements. Along related lines, subjects were asked to engage in a pleasant financial fantasy: *Suppose you came into a great deal of money, and could afford to live anywhere in Paris. Where would you move to?* The arrondissements exerting the greatest residential attraction are, in order of popularity, 6th, 4th, 7th, and 16th. The single most desired location is the Île de St. Louis. Popular with all groups, and particularly so with younger Parisians, 36.2 percent of those under 30 speculated that if they had a financial windfall they would move there, to the island in the middle of Paris, but removed from the bustle.

The subjects' attachment to "le vieux Paris" is expressed in a somewhat different form when they responded to the following hypothetical problem: *Suppose you were about to go into exile, and had a chance to take only one last walk through the city. What would be your itinerary?* Each subject was given an unmarked street map and was asked to trace a final itinerary of not more than three kilometers. Many idiosyncratic routes appeared as subjects traced paths through childhood neighborhoods, sites of romantic encounters, and so on. But when we focus on the commonly selected paths (any street segment transversed by at least five of the subjects) a definite pattern is revealed (Fig. 8.13). The densest network of walks are along the quais of the Seine, on the Île de la Cité and the Quartier Latin. (Smaller numbers of subjects chose to stroll through Place des Vosges, Palais Royale, and Montmartre.) And a considerable group chose to walk along the Champ Elysées. Paris contains more than 3500 streets within its

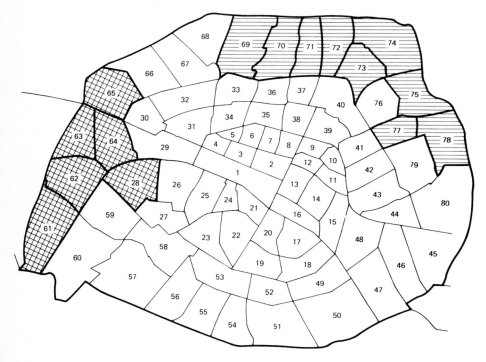

FIGURE 8.11
Perception of rich and poor areas. Shows all quartiers which at least 10 percent of the subjects indicated as among the right (grating) or poor (striped) areas of Paris.

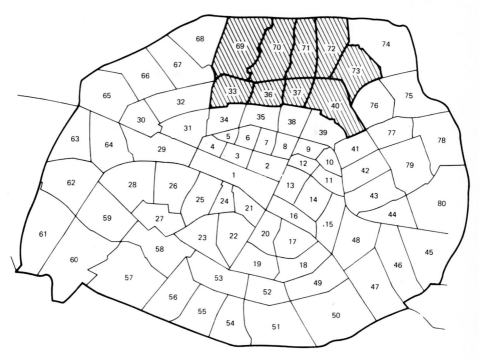

FIGURE 8.12
Paris dangereux. Indicates the quartiers perceived as being the most dangerous, from the standpoint of criminal activity.

limits (Hillairet, 1964), but the concentration of choices on only a score of these reveals the few which have a shared emotional significance.

*I*NTUITIONS AND SECRETS

Before drawing the report to a close, we wish to make a few additional observations about Paris and the processes of its mental representation. A person may know many things about a city while not being aware that he possesses such knowledge; and such implicit knowledge may be widely shared. Consider the following hypothetical situation we presented to the subjects:

> Suppose you were to meet someone in Paris, a person whom you had never met before, and you knew the exact date and time of the meeting, but not the place. Assume the person you were to meet operated under the similar handicap of not knowing where you would wait for him. Where in Paris would you wait so as to maximize the chances of encountering the person?

Subjects were encouraged to use their intuition in answering the

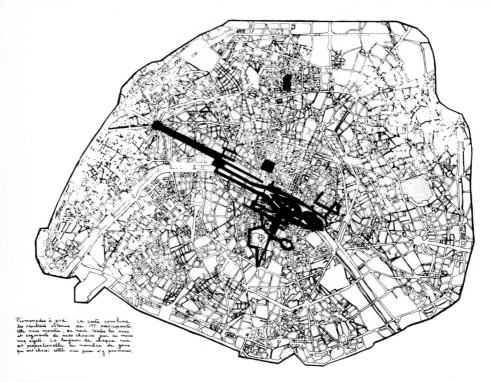

FIGURE 8.13
Last walks before going into exile. The black paths indicate all street segments
chosen by at least five subjects. The width of each segment is proportional to the
number of subjects who traverse segment during their last walk.

question, but this did not prevent many of them from denouncing the
question as illogical, stupid, and unanswerable. But those who responded
($N = 188$) demonstrated that a set of appropriate—even intelligent—
responses was possible. (An answer to this question may be considered
"appropriate" if it is selected by a large number of other respondents, and
thus represents a shared intuition of where others are likely to wait.) Two
principles governed the choice of locales: (a) some subjects selected a
location that was unequivocally representative of the city, (b) other
subjects chose locales that by custom and practice had become institution-
alized waiting places (much as the clock at Grand Central Station in New
York serves this function).

Six locations accounted for more than 50 percent of all answers, as
Table 8.6 shows. The largest number of Parisians indicated they would
wait by the Eiffel Tower, the preeminent symbol of Paris in modern times.
(What would the dominant response have been prior to its construction in
1889? We have no psychological maps to tell us.) The second most
popular choice was the Monument des Morts at the Gare St. Lazare. The

TABLE 8.6 MEETING PLACES CHOSEN TO MAXIMIZE ENCOUNTER

Location	Percent of subjects selecting this location (N = 188)
Tour Eiffel	16.5
Monument des Morts (Gare St. Lazare)	8.0
Etoile	7.4
Opéra	7.4
Blvd. St. Germain	6.9
Notre Dame	6.9
Blvd., Pl. St. Michel	6.9

consensus generated by this question shows that the inhabitants share an implicit, intuitive knowledge of the city that can be crystalized given the proper stimulus.

A second observation is that even poorly known areas of a city may exercise a fascination for the inhabitant: thus, three-fourths of the subjects answered affirmatively when asked if there was any part of Paris they did not know well but were attracted to. (The most popular choice was *le Marais,* a once unfashionable area that has recently experienced a renaissance.) And subjects generated the names of 155 different locales when asked if they had come across any places of particular beauty or interest that were unknown to the general public. Among their responses were: quaint provincial streets off the Parc de Montsouris; Villa Montmorency, a rustic residential enclave of several acres into which the noise of the surrounding streets scarcely penetrates; the courtyards off the Rue de Sèvres, which represent the inner folds of the convoluted brain of Paris, providing a great deal more surface area than a mere skimming of the surface would suggest; Canal St. Martin; Place des Peupliers; Cour du Rohan, and numerous others. Many of the so-called "places of beauty" were actually cited by a large number of subjects, yet more important is the subject's attitude that the city yields some secrets to him alone, and that Paris is intricate, variegated, and inexhaustible in its offerings.

But it is false to end this report as a panegyric. For many Parisians assert that the city is declining in quality, succumbing to vehicular pollution, noise, and the flight of artisans from the city; they assert that urban renewal is destroying a good deal of the beauty of Paris, and they locate its worst effects in the 15th, 1st, and 13th arrondissements, where modern apartment buildings and office towers have replaced the greater charm, but also the greater decrepitude, of the older structures.

The problem for modern Paris, then, is to learn something about the transmutation of charm into its contemporary forms, and to learn it quickly, before the old is brutally replaced by the new, and only the street patterns remain.

SUMMARY

In this paper we described a number of psychological maps of Paris generated by its inhabitants, detailed representations of the city expressed in cartographic form, rather than as simple opinions, attitudes, and words. The peculiar value of such mental maps is that they tease out the person's view of a city in a way that permits a ready comparison with the reality. They allow a treatment of the city's spatial character in a way that words frequently avoid. And they show how urban space is encoded, distorted, and selectively represented, while yet retaining its usefulness to the person. For the image of the city is not just extra mental baggage; it is the necessary accompaniment to living in a complex and highly variegated environment.

Such maps are multi-dimensional. They contain cognitive and also emotional and intuitive components, and a variety of procedures is needed to bring them to light. The maps are not only individual products; they are shaped by social factors, and therefore acquire the status of collective representations—that is, symbolic configurations of belief and knowledge promoted and disseminated by the culture.

NOTE

1. Grateful acknowledgment is made to Professor Serge Moscovici for his generous aid, and to Anne André, Ben Zion Chanowitz, Alexandra Milgram, and Judith Waters for research assistance. The services of the Institut Français d'Opinion Publique were employed in interviewing the working-class segment of our sample and in computer analyzing the data from all subjects. The assistance of Paris MENSA is gratefully acknowledged.

REFERENCES

DOWNS, R. M., AND STEA, D., *Image and Environment: Cognitive Mapping and Spatial Behavior.* Chicago: Aldine, 1973.

GOULD, P., AND WHITE, R., *Mental Maps.* Baltimore: Penguin Books, 1974.

HILLAIRET, J., *Dictionnaire Historique des Rues de Paris.* Paris: Les Editions de Minuits, 1964.

LYNCH, K., *The Image of the City.* Cambridge, Mass.: The MIT Press, 1960.

APPENDIX DISTRIBUTION OF SUBJECTS BY SEX AND ARRONDISSE-
MENT

	Percent of subjects in study (N = 218)			*Percent distribution according to*
Arrondissement	*Men*	*Women*	*Total*	*1968 census*
1	1.6	2.2	1.8	1.3
2	0.8	2.2	1.4	1.4
3	3.2	1.1	2.3	2.2
4	4.8	1.1	3.2	2.2
5	4.0	4.3	4.1	3.2
6	2.4	1.1	1.8	2.7
7	4.8	2.2	3.7	3.4
8	2.4	3.3	2.8	2.7
9	2.4	5.4	3.7	3.4
10	4.8	4.3	4.6	4.5
11	6.3	4.3	5.5	7.0
12	8.7	4.3	6.9	6.1
13	4.0	4.3	4.1	5.8
14	7.1	6.5	6.9	6.2
15	8.7	12.0	10.1	9.1
16	8.7	5.4	7.3	8.4
17	7.1	8.7	7.8	8.3
18	7.1	14.1	10.1	9.4
19	6.3	5.4	6.0	5.5
20	4.8	7.6	6.0	7.2

Sondages: Revue Française de l'Opinion Publique, 1951, No. 2, pp. 1–41. ''Paris, une enquête psychosociale.'' Anonymous.

SUTTLES, G., *The Social Construction of Communities.* Chicago: University of Chicago Press, 1972.

9

The Vertical City

———— ❖ ————

Cities have risen. Only a hundred years ago it was unusual to find buildings in the city rising higher than six or seven stories. It is only in our own century that the metropolitan towers have soared. Skyscrapers began in America, but throughout the world their numbers have increased. São Paulo and Mexico City grow them in dense concentration. Even Paris is flirting with them.

The vitality of the modern city is expressed in the growth of its skyscrapers: Cities build higher as a sign of economic preeminence. We know that Houston and Seattle have become important places by their ascending skylines. The skyscraper forces itself upon the landscape as a central point of perceptual attention, seen from all over the city. But one tall building does not make a vertical city. Only the dense packing of skyscrapers into a town center produces the critical effect. The imposing structures symbolize the dominant role of the city in the larger geographic landscape.

We can tell a lot about a society by knowing who occupies its tallest buildings. In the Middle Ages, the dominant institutions of the era commanded attention by building higher than all the others. In the secular domain the castle was built on the high ground, and rising above the roofs of the town were the soaring spires of the cathedral.

We need to ask, therefore, what institution announces itself these days through our tallest buildings. Why naturally, the dominant institution of our society—business. Indeed, many of the tallest buildings take their names from the companies they house. One thinks of the RCA, Citicorp, and Chrysler Buildings in New York, or Sears Tower in Chicago. These buildings dominate the urban skyline of contemporary America in proportion to the significance of these firms in the economy.

This paper first appeared in the *CUNY Graduate School Magazine*, Spring/Summer 1984, 3, 1, 9–13. Reprinted by permission of Alexandra Milgram.

114

The modern skyscraper houses a particular kind of activity, one that meets the needs of our present stage of economic and technical development. Rarely are industrial goods manufactured in skyscrapers. Rather, these structures are reserved for bureaucratic and administrative functions, a point stressed by Jean Gottmann, in his perspective analysis, "Why the Skyscraper?" In these buildings, people push paper or computer keyboards, consult with one another, and have ready access to expertise and the views of others. They often serve as the headquarters of major companies, i.e., as the locus of their brains, rather than their brawn. They are ideal for information processing, bringing individuals into convenient proximity.

But does the vertical growth of the city alter the way we think and act? Before addressing this question, let us recall that a related issue has concerned social scientists for many years.

RURAL-URBAN COMPARISONS

At the turn of the century, Georg Simmel wrote on the differences in mental organization of those who lived in the city and those who lived in the small town. The city people used their minds, and the country folk their hearts. The city people were exposed to intense stimulation which altered their inner life, and they adopted an objective, rational way of looking at things. According to Simmel, cities such as Vienna, Berlin, and London gave rise to a different mental outlook than the traditional small community.

In the 1930s the great urban sociologist, Louis Wirth, compared the burgeoning metropolis with the small town and rural community. He found many differences in tone and behavior arising from the great increase in numbers, density, and heterogeneity of the metropolis.

THE VERTICAL CITY VS. THE FLAT CITY

Today we need to compare the vertical city to the flat city. What difference does it make that we live in a place with tall buildings? How does it alter our thinking and behavior? Or does it make a difference at all? Perhaps the most important question concerns the effect of verticality on human relationships.

Here we need to distinguish between two sets of effects: Those that occur within the skyscraper itself, and those that affect the part of the city in which the skyscraper is located. For the neighborhood in which it is situated, the skyscraper has obvious physical consequences, such as blocking out the sky and sunlight. In some cities, such as Tokyo, people are financially compensated for the loss of views and sunlight, but in New York we think of it as tough luck.

The main effect of the skyscraper on its neighborhood is to spew enormous numbers of people onto the street. The throngs that surge in and out of the office towers create the crowded dynamic, elbow-to-elbow character of the city's downtown streets. It is precisely this concentration of people that permits the vast increase in face-to-face communication in downtown areas. It has been calculated by the regional Plan Association that in suburban Nassau County an individual can meet 11,000 others within a 10 minute radius of his office by foot or car, but in mid-town Manhattan, he can meet fully 220,000. So there is an order-of-magnitude increment in the communication possibilities offered by the vertical city.

This possibility for more intensive and varied social contacts is perhaps the principal benefit of stacking people up in office towers. Businessmen, lawyers, and entrepreneurs can all get together within a few minutes of their offices. Many of the social contacts occur at the street level, as in a restaurant. This serves as common ground among those who come from competing firms, and where neither party has the conspicuous advantage of owning the turf.

The network of adjacent streets in a flat city creates neighborhoods, that is, extended areas which one can walk through, which have a distinctive tone and character. Shop owners are very concerned about the type of shop that opens next to them or down the block. For they all contribute to the neighborhood's ambience. In contrast, within the skyscraper, one is scarcely aware of what transpires on the floor above or the floor below. Those who work on another floor are of another world, another universe. The addition of a third dimension thus laminates activity, and those in different dimensions are considered irrelevant to each other.

If we work in a large one-story room, as we find in suburban shopping malls, we may see someone a hundred feet from us, and wave to the person or at least keep the person in visual contact. But if the person is on another floor, though in measured distance he may be only ten or twelve feet away, he is no longer in our field of awareness, since we cannot see through the materials that comprise our floors and ceilings. Thus, unless such floors are constructed of transparent materials, verticality visually segments our experience into noncommunicating strata.

All features of the environment are given social meaning. If we look at the power, prestige, and wealth of those who work in an office tower, we find a strong correlation between these features and how high up the person's office is located. People work their way up to the top both figuratively and in terms of measured inches. Those of lowly status almost never occupy the high floors of the skyscraper, unless they are servants of the wealthy and powerful.

FIGURE 9.1

"We sit at a desk in an office tower peering across to an adjacent skyscraper. Behind its glass windows we dimly perceive another office worker immersed in the daily routine. The worker moves silently in a self-contained universe, very remote. The visual sighting is as if from another galaxy."

SOME PSYCHOLOGICAL EFFECTS OF HEIGHT

In the 19th century the height of a building could be related to the height of a man or woman. It was possible for a person walking through the city streets to calculate, even if unconsciously, that it would take a certain number of men standing on each other's shoulders to reach a rooftop. The skyscraper introduced a radical change of scale, so that the person became miniscule in comparison with it, and all sense of the human scale was lost.

From the skyscraper we look down on the pedestrians in the street below, and they are reduced to the appearance of insects, or more abstractly, points moving along the walkways. We look down as if from that throne once assigned to the Deity. Yet, on the same day into our office come ordinary people whom we deal with face to face. Just as the city, with its heterogeneous population, forces upon us multiple cultural perspectives, the skyscraper forces us into multiple perceptual perspectives on a daily basis. We see people face to face, and by looking down from our windows, as abstracted points in motion, creating a relativism of viewpoint characteristic of the urban setting. The person in the skyscraper is also exposed to a broader vista of the city. Whether this leads to a stronger identification with what he surveys, or merely a sense that he owns and can exploit this broader realm, is dependent upon his character and general orientation to life.

Each office structure, although surrounded by other tall buildings, possesses a self-contained character. We sit at a desk in an office tower peering across to an adjacent skyscraper. Behind its glass windows we dimly perceive another office worker immersed in the daily routine. The worker moves silently in a self-contained universe, very remote. The visual sighting is as if from another galaxy.

THE ELEVATOR

The elevator is to the vertical city what the automobile is to a sprawling metropolis such as Los Angeles. The rise of cities awaited such a device, and Elisha G. Otis provided the needed equipment.

The rider of the elevator is forced into contact with others whom he does not know, in conditions of extreme proximity; few elevators are half as large as a bedroom. The other patrons exercise a form of control which differs from the subway, with its predesignated stops.

Where the elevator stops is determined by other users. They enforce a burden of waiting and interruption that is beyond a passenger's control. Sometimes the rider, in a moment of pique, feels that other riders are infringing on his "rights" when they have the temerity to interrupt his transit, not once, but twice as they both enter and leave on floors sandwiched between his starting point and destination.

Talking in a crowded elevator almost always has an awkward and attention getting quality. When we see a pair of friends board an elevator and engage in conversation we are often bemused, embarrassed, and nonplussed by being forced to overhear their exchange. They know we are listening to them, we know it, we all pretend otherwise. It forces us to be eavesdroppers.

The elevator, in its most usual form, is the only transportation device which does not offer a view, except episodically, as the door opens, and we briefly catch sight of a floor. This "glimpsed experience" is characteristic of perception in the city; we see many people in our everyday rounds for a few seconds and they vanish.

Before the invention of the elevator, a premium was placed on housing which was on the ground floor, so that it was not necessary to walk many stairs to get to one's dwelling. With the perfection of the elevator, height was converted into an asset. The ground floor has lost much of its appeal, because of its vulnerability to crime.

The elevator pushes the abstracted and alienated quality of urban experience to its limit. Buses give visible access to the passing scene. But in the elevator, we stand in the most intimate proximity to strangers, often facing the backs of their heads, but focus on the flashing numbers that signal our transit.

Although the price we pay for all other means of transportation has risen sharply in recent years, the elevator remains a free ride, for reasons that are more traditional than absolutely necessary. The elevator distance traversed in, say, one of the taller skyscrapers, may be greater than that between several bus stops, but no fee is charged for such a ride. (There is an exception—elevators that take people to observation decks, such as the one on top of the Empire State Building. But here it may be argued, one is paying for the view rather than the ride.)

RESEARCH

There has always been a certain amount of research in social psychology that touches on the question of verticality, mainly in connection with residential housing. Early research by Festinger, Schachter, and Back in a university housing project showed that people did not form friendships as readily if they lived on different floors of the project. Rather, friendships were much more likely to form among those who lived on the same floor. David Glass and Jerome Singer studied children who lived on upper and lower floors of apartments over the access roads to the George Washington Bridge. They found that the children living on lower floors suffered more from the noise and noxious emissions of the automobile traffic. Height served to protect residents on the higher floors from environmental pollutants. Communication figures as a key factor in Oscar Newman's

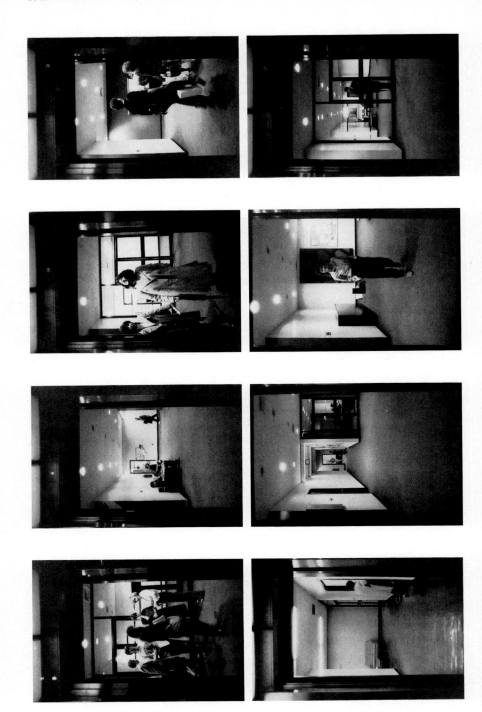

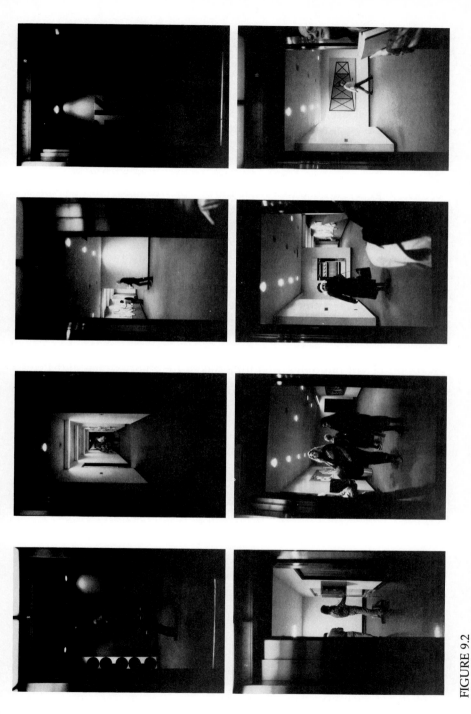

FIGURE 9.2
The Glimpsed Experience: A ride up the 18-story route of the Graduate Center elevator offers passengers the "glimpsed experience."

assertion that building height affects crime. For example, when families live above a certain height, parents can no longer keep an eye on their children playing down below, and thus the playing space becomes more vulnerable to crime.

In one of the more morbid investigations on verticality, social psychologist Leon Mann examined the situation of persons threatening to commit suicide by jumping from the ledge of buildings. In some cases the street crowd that had gathered below taunted and encouraged the person to jump, while in other cases the crowds did not. Mann found that taunting was less likely to occur if the person stood on a ledge more than six stories high. He argued that when the person was higher, it was harder for the crowd to communicate with the suicidee.

The Human Response to Tall Buildings is a convenient collection of articles dealing with the considerable amount of research that has appeared during the last decade. Among the investigations are: the negative effects of office towers, such as blocking sunlight, obstructing views, and oversized scale; the problem of evacuating people from high rises; and the relationship between floor of residence and satisfaction. In high-rise apartment houses the higher up people live, the more satisfied they are with their apartments.

In my seminar on urban psychology, a most interesting study of the perception of tall buildings was undertaken by Stuart Green and Peter Dan. Through photomontage, they displaced major landmark skyscrapers from their actual locations in the city to completely unrealistic ones. For example, in one scene they placed the Empire State Building directly behind the Metropolitan Opera House, while in another slide, they displaced the Citicorp building southward. A majority of New York City residents failed to notice the alterations in skyline that the student experiments created. Although skyscrapers are a clear and significant feature of the urban scene, they create a somewhat random pattern in people's minds, and their spatial relationship to each other is not well remembered.

*L*IMITS TO THE VERTICAL CITY

The soaring skyscraper differs from the cathedral in an important respect. The cathedral was substantially hollow, so that when you entered it, you confronted an interior space as impressive in its height from the inside as it was from the outside. You looked up to see magnificent soaring columns and arches. But if you look up when you enter the lobby of a skyscraper such as the Chrysler Builder, you see only the ceiling of the next floor, and not the interior space tapering to a needle. To assuage this disappointment, architects are beginning to scoop out tall spaces inside

FIGURE 9.3
Photomontages by doctoral students Stuart Green and Peter Dan were used in experiments testing people's perceptions of tall buildings. People did not notice that the Empire State Building was displaced from its normal location (in top photo). Below, the experimenters combined vertical elements from New York and Paris in a single montage.

the skyscraper in the form of atriums which sustain the feeling of interior height.

For those who walk around at ground level, there is a problem with viewing skyscrapers. Surrounded as they are by other buildings, sky-scrapers are very hard to see in their entirety. Pedestrians circulate in the urban canyons, scarcely aware of anything above the street level. Only the tourists crane their necks upward. Indeed, modern city architecture has never faced up to one of its most obvious problems: Most skyscrapers only look like coherent structures in the architect's drawings. People rarely have the space or vista needed to encompass a view of the building, particularly when, in a city such as New York, it is set in a narrow street.

If the skyscrapers lord it over the city, and give their occupants the satisfaction of broad vistas, they are in the long run self-defeating. For there is always a danger of obstruction by new and competing buildings. Instead of a cherished view extending to the horizon, the dismayed executive may see only another businessman looking back. "Of course," the thought may occur to him, "it is always possible to build higher." Thus, the competetiveness of the business world finds a new battleground in the placement and height of its citadels.

*F*URTHER READING

Donald J. Conway. (Ed.) *Human Response to Tall Buildings.* Stroudsburg, Pa.: Dowden, Hutchinson & Ross, 1977.

Paul Goldberger. *The Skyscraper.* New York: Alfred A. Knopf, 1982.

Jean Gottmann. *"Why the Skyscraper?"* in *Taming Megapolis* (Edited by H. Wentworth Eldredge). New York: Doubleday, 1967.

PART 2

————— ❖ —————

The Individual and Authority

A n experimental paradigm is a plan for exploration. It does not guarantee what will be found, nor what the ultimate cost of the undertaking will be, but it creates a point of entry into an uncharted domain. Since World War II, three important human conflicts have been explored through the experimental paradigms of social psychology. Each exposes the individual to a dilemma, and allows the individual to resolve it in a way consistent with or in opposition to moral values. The first is the dilemma of truth versus conformity examined in Asch's experiment on group pressure. The second is the conflict between altruism and self-interest systematically examined in the work of Latané and Darley. And the third is the conflict between authority and conscience dealt with in my experiment on obedience.

Each paradigm poses a problem for the individual: Should I tell the truth or go along with the group? Should I involve myself in other people's troubles or remain aloof? Should I hurt an innocent person or disobey authority? These problems were not invented by social psychologists. They are inevitable dilemmas of the human condition. Every person must confront them simply by being a member of society.

The experiments share an important technical feature. The dependent measure in each case is a morally significant act. Thus the experiments acquire a *prima facie* interest, because they show what variables increase or decrease the performance of acts which are not only concrete and measurable, but speak to significant human values. Yet in the final analysis, the contribution of social psychology is an intellectual rather than a moral contribution. It shows that the course of action in each situation cannot be explained by a simple moral judgment, but resides in an analysis of the situational components of each dilemma.

The origins of the obedience study as a laboratory paradigm are described in detail later in this chapter (p. 127). But the laboratory paradigm merely gave scientific expression to a more general concern about authority, a concern forced upon members of my generation, in particular upon Jews such as myself, by the atrocities of World War II. Susan Sontag, the social critic, described her reaction upon first seeing photographs of the death camps:

> . . . One's first encounter with the photographic inventory of ultimate horror is a kind of revelation, perhaps the only revelation people are granted now, a negative epiphany. For me, it was photographs of Bergen–Belsen and Dachau which I came across by chance in a bookstore in Santa Monica in July, 1945. Nothing I have seen—in photographs or in real life—ever cut me as sharply, deeply, instantaneously. Ever since then, it has seemed plausible to me to think of my life as being divided into two parts: before I saw those photographs (I was twelve) and after. My life was changed by them, though not until several years later did I understand what they were about.

The impact of the holocaust on my own psyche energized my interest in obedience and shaped the particular form in which it was examined.

"Some Conditions of Obedience and Disobedience to Authority" presents a survey of the obedience experiments, and prior to publication of my book[1] was the most comprehensive description of the research. The article first appeared in *Human Relations* in 1956, then was reprinted in *The American Journal of Psychiatry*, followed by a critique of Martin Orne and Charles Holland. They applied a "demand characteristic" analysis to the obedience studies. Shortly afterward, I was invited to give a colloquium at the University of Pennsylvania. I suggested that this be in the form of a debate between myself and Professor Orne. Dr. Orne graciously consented, and we were perhaps both astonished to see an auditorium filled with several hundred spectators eager for gladiatorial combat. It was a good debate, conducted on a high level, and ultimately productive of deeper understanding. "Interpreting Obedience: Error and Evidence," which appeared in 1972, summarizes my views on this matter.

A stinging and unexpected challenge to the obedience experiment appeared in the form of an ethical criticism by Dr. Diana Baumrind. "Ethical Issues in the Study of Obedience" constitutes my reply to Dr. Baumrind; it spells out my views on the ethical aspects of the investigation. There is one point, however, that should have received greater emphasis. The central moral justification for allowing my experiment is that it was judged acceptable by those who took part in it. Criticism of the experiment that does not take account of the tolerant reaction of the participants has always seemed to me hollow. This applies particularly to criticism centering on the use of technical illusion (or "deception," as the critics prefer to say) that fails to relate this detail to the central fact that subjects find the device acceptable. The participant, rather than the external critic, must be the ultimate source of judgment in these matters.

Acts of obedience and disobedience may be examined in the laboratory, but their most crucial expression occurs in the real world. The experiments were begun in 1960. Five years later the nation was deeply involved in an unpopular war in southeast Asia, and thousands of young men fled to Canada to avoid the draft, while others declared themselves war resisters and went to prison. During the Vietnam War, psychiatrist Willard Gaylin interviewed a number of these resisters, and I was asked to review his book, *War Resisters in Prison,* for *The Nation* (p. 191).

Social psychology is a cumulative discipline. Investigators with greater or lesser creativity build on the contributions of those who precede them. In a recent interview,[2] Dr. Richard Evans asked about the experimental antecedents of the obedience studies, then moved on to a discussion of the ethical and social implications of these investigations. The following is a portion of that interview, the conversational syntax and tone of which I have made no attempt to formalize.

EVANS: . . . One of your experiments has received wide attention. It was a kind of outgrowth of the group pressure study, testing just exactly what people will do under pressure from an experimenter, a scientist in a kind of laboratory setting. How did you happen to begin thinking in terms of this type of experiment? Maybe you would describe it briefly for us.

MILGRAM: Very often, when there's an idea, there are several points of origin to it. It doesn't necessarily develop in linear fashion from what one has been working on previously. I was working for Asch in Princeton, New Jersey, in 1959–1960. I was thinking about his group pressure experiment. One of the criticisms that had been made of his experiments is that they lack a surface significance, because, after all, an experiment with people making judgments of lines has a manifestly trivial content. So the question I asked myself is: How can this be made a more humanly significant experiment?

It seemed to me that if, instead of having a group exerting pressure on the judgments about lines, the group could somehow induce something more significant from the person, then that might be a step in giving a greater face significance to the behavior induced by the group. Could a group, I asked myself, induce a person to act with severity against another person? . . . I envisioned a situation very much like Asch's experiment in which there would be a number of confederates and one naive subject, and instead of confronting the lines on a card, each one of them would have a shock generator. In other words, I transformed Asch's experiment into one in which the group would administer increasingly higher levels of shock to a person, and the question would be to what degree an individual would follow along with the group. That's not yet the obedience experiment, but it's a mental step in that direction.

Then I wondered how one would actually set it up. What would constitute the experimental control in this situation? In Asch's experiment, there is a control—the proportion of correct judgments the person makes in the absence of group pressure. So I said to myself, "Well, I guess I would have to study a person in this situation in the absence of any group pressure. But then, how would one get the person to increase the shocks? I mean, what would be the force that would get him to increase the shocks?" And then the thought occurred, "Well, I guess the experimenter would have to tell him to give higher and higher shocks. Just how far will a person go when an experimenter instructs him to give increasingly severe shocks?" Immediately I knew that that was the problem I would investigate. It was a very excited moment for me, because I realized that although it was a very simple question, it was one that would admit itself to measurement, precise investigation. One could immediately see the variables to be studied, with the dependent measure being how far a person would go in administering shocks.

EVANS: Well, let's be a little bit more specific. We could talk about authority in the form of the experimenter, or we could talk about group pressure, acquiescence to the group. There's a very interesting distinction here.

MILGRAM: There are both features in common and features that are different. What we have in common is, in both instances, the abdication of individual judgment in the face of some external social pressure. But there are also factors that are quite different. I would like to call what happens to Asch's subjects "conformity," and I would like to call what happens in my experiment "obedience." In conformity, as illustrated by Asch's experiment, there is no explicit requirement on the part of the group members that a person go along with them. Indeed, the presence of an explicit requirement might even eliminate the person's yielding. The individual members of Asch's group give their judgments; there's a felt pressure to comply with them, but there's no explicit demand to do so. In the obedience situation, the experimenter explicitly prescribes certain behavior. That's one difference.

A second very important difference is that in conformity, as illustrated in Asch's experiment, you're dealing basically with a process of which the end product is the homogenization of behavior. The pressure is not that you be better than me, or worse than me, but that you be the same as me. Obedience arises out of differentiation of social structure. You don't start from the assumption that we are the same; one person starts with a higher status. You don't repeat his action; you execute his order.

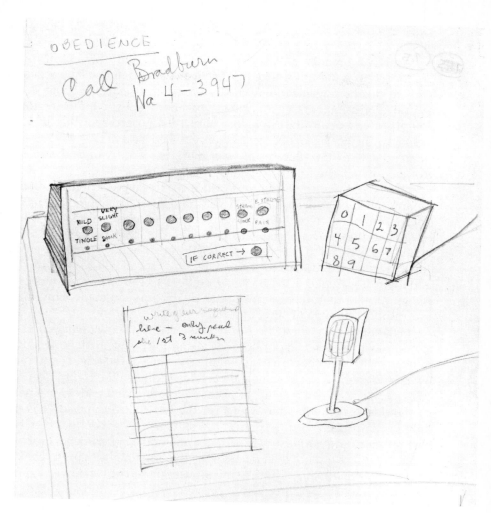

FIGURE II.3
Early sketch of the simulated shock generator used in the obedience studies.
(Princeton, Spring 1960.)

And it doesn't lead to homogenization of behavior, but rather to some
kind of division of labor.

There's another distinction that's quite important psychologically.
After subjects have been in Asch's experiment and they are questioned by
the experimenter, they almost invariably deny that they gave in to the
group. Even if errors in judgment are pointed out, they will tend to ascribe
them to their own deficiencies. But in the obedience experiment, the result
is the opposite. The subjects disclaim any responsibility for their action. So
I think there are factors in common, certainly. We're dealing in both cases
with what I would call the abdication of individual initiative in the face of

some external social pressure. But there are also these distinguishing aspects to it.

And in a broader philosophic way they're quite different also. . . . Conformity is a natural source of social control in democracy, because it leads to this homogenization. But obedience in its extreme forms is the natural expression of fascistic systems, because it starts with the assumption of differences in the rights of people. It's no accident that in Nazi Germany, the virtues of obedience were extolled, and at the same time an inherent part of the philosophy was the idea of inferior and superior groups; I mean, the two go together.

EVANS: As an example, let me just take a current piece of research that we are involved in dealing with a very fascinating phenomenon in our culture—smoking. Now we have some pretty good evidence, and this is one of the things we're going to be looking at, that perhaps smoking begins as a reaction to peer pressure. On the other hand, we have the very interesting fact that authority stresses that this type of behavior is going to lead to cardiovascular disease, cancer, etc., etc. Here you have at once peer and authority pressure. In terms of this distinction you made, how could you resolve this type of situation?

MILGRAM: I'll try. First, the word "authority" is used in many different ways. When we talk about a medical authority, we're talking about someone with expertise. That's not quite the same as the kind of authority I was studying, which is someone perceived to have the right to control one's behavior. When a teenager hears an authority on television saying he shouldn't smoke, he doesn't accept the fact that that person has the right to control behavior. Secondly, you still have these conflicts between peer pressure and authority pressure. In one of the experiments I carried out, it was shown that when peers in my experimental situation rebelled against the experimenter, they tremendously undercut his power. I think the same thing is operating here; you have pressures from an authority, but you have pressures from peers which sometimes neutralize this. It's only when you have, as you have in my experiment, an authority who in the basic experiment operates in a free field without countervailing pressures other than the victim's protests that you get the purest response to authority. In real life, of course, you're confronted with a great many countervailing pressures that cancel each other out.

EVANS: One of the things, of course, that you're acutely aware of is that partly because of Congressional pressure, partly because of some—what would we say—some second looks at our consciences in the behavioral sciences, we are beginning to get increasingly concerned now about the whole matter of what rights we have with respect to our subjects. When you were doing that earlier obedience to authority study, it's very clear that you were operating completely within the ethical framework of psychologists in those days. You debriefed the subjects, and there was really no harm done to the victims, and so on. However, in the present utilization of subjects, we are very hung up on the phrase, "informed consent," and this raises a very tough problem for the investigator. For example, do you think you could have done that experiment if you followed the present ethical standards of "informed consent"? Let's say that you were about to engage in an experiment where the subjects were going to be exposed to a certain amount of stress. One type of stress might be the fact that you're going to be ordering somebody to get shocked.

MILGRAM: Well first of all, before you do the experiment, you don't know there will be stress.

EVANS: All right, that's a good point.

MILGRAM: The subject must make a decision, but we don't know if it's going to be accompanied by stress. Many of the most interesting things we find out in experimentation you don't learn until you carry it out. So to talk about "informed consent" presumes that you know the fundamental consequences of your experiment, and that just isn't the case for my investigations. That's one aspect of the problem; it's not the entire problem, however. There is the fact that misinformation is used in these experiments, that illusions are used. For example, in my obedience experiment, the victim does not actually *get* the shocks; although the subject is *told* he is getting the shocks. Furthermore, it's an experiment on obedience, in which the subject is the focus of the experiment rather than the other person, but a cover story attempts to deflect attention from that. Now could the experiment be run if we told people beforehand that this was going to be the case? Not in its particulars. It is possible that one could develop a system whereby people are told generally that they're asked to be in a psychology experiment, and that in psychology experiments illusions are sometimes used. Sometimes stress arises. Perhaps a subject pool of such persons who are not necessarily used immediately could be created. They would then be invited to an experiment, having been given the general instruction that these things may but don't necessarily happen in psychological experimentation. That would be one way of handling the problem. . . .

EVANS: Of course one of the points made about informed consent is that after all we're dealing, often, with a purely phenomenological situation. How can you give informed consent in advance as a human subject in an experiment when the total mass of feelings and experiences and sensitivities, even pain, cannot really be verbalized?

MILGRAM: Well, I think to some extent that's true, added to the fact that one is very often ignorant of what will happen before an experiment. Reactions to such situations can be diverse. Ninety percent of the subjects can react in a perfectly calm way; others can become agitated. But then we must know whether psychology is excluding stress and agitation from its domain of study. Do we really want to say that any of these aversive emotions are to be excluded from psychological inquiry? I think that's a question that's yet to be resolved, but my personal vote is "no." At the same time I don't want to be put in the position of saying that I'm *for any kind* of experimentation.

EVANS: Were you surprised by the reaction to your obedience experiment?

MILGRAM: I must say that I was totally astonished by the criticism that my experiment engendered. I thought what I was doing was posing a very legitimate question. How far would people proceed if they were asked to give increasingly severe shocks to another person? I thought that the decision rested with the subject. Perhaps that was too naive an assumption from which to start an investigation.

It is true that technical illusions were used in the experiment. I would not call them deceptions, because that already implies some base motivation. After all, the major illusion used was that the person did not receive shocks. One might have imitated the investigators who have done studies in traumatic avoidance conditioning where human beings are, in fact, shocked to near-tetanizing levels. I chose not to. I thought that the illusion was used for a benign purpose.

I'm convinced that much of the criticism, whether people know it or not, stems from the results of the experiment. If everyone had broken off at slight shock or moderate shock, this would be a very reassuring finding and who would protest? Indeed, I would say that there's a tendency these days to make inferences about the experimenter's pernicious tendency. Personally, and even professionally, I would have been very pleased if people had broken off at mild shock.

EVANS: Were you surprised that they went so far?

MILGRAM: I was, but if they had not been so obedient, it would not have prevented my research program. I would simply have studied the variables leading to an increase or diminution in the amount of obedience. And in fact, one could say that the results that I got threw a wrench into the program in that many variables were washed out because too many people obeyed. One didn't have that distribution of responses—that bell-shaped distribution—that would have been most convenient for studying the effects of specific variables.

EVANS: There have been statements made by people about both the work of Zimbardo and yourself which I think it's only fair to hear you react to. Some people have suggested, some journalists particularly, that both you and Dr. Zimbardo got involved in experiments that were exciting, interesting, unique, and that because of the uproar about the ethics, you have begun to rationalize, by trying to extrapolate from your findings something relating to a bigger picture. For example, in the case of Zimbardo, he has now become a strong advocate for prison reform, arguing that this little experiment will teach mankind how horrible prisons are. In your case, you have, more or less, extrapolated the whole question of the dangers of authoritarian rule in American culture. In your book, *Obedience to Authority*, you go into this. Now, Dr. Zimbardo is not here to speak for himself, but what about your reaction to this?

MILGRAM: The very first article that I wrote on obedience ["Behavioral Study of Obedience"], before anyone had really reacted to the experiments, discussed the societal problem. So it's not true that trying to find the larger application of the issue is motivated by ethical criticism. Beyond that, what disturbs me somewhat is the absence of any assumption of good will and good faith. I believe that a certain amount of good will is necessary on the part of society for the conduct of any enterprise. Criticisms of that sort seem to me to start from some assumption of bad faith on the part of the investigators, which I don't believe, in my case or the Zimbardo case, has anything to do with the truth.

EVANS: Were there any criticisms of this particular effort that have troubled you that perhaps we haven't mentioned?

MILGRAM: Well, I think the question of the limits of experimentation is a real one. I believe that there are many experiments that should not be carried out. I don't oppose criticism, because I think there's a societal function served by it. The investigator wants to study things. Society, in the form of certain critics, will establish limits. I think the net outcome will be a kind of equilibrium between scientific values and other values, but I don't believe that most investigators, certainly myself, are limited to scientific values. There are thousands of experiments that could be very useful from the standpoint of increasing knowledge that one would never carry out, because in one's own estimation, they would violate moral principles. It doesn't mean that one doesn't think of them. For example, an experiment in which neonates are deposited onto a deserted island, and one watches their development over three generations, assuming they survive, would be stupendously informative, but grossly immoral.

EVANS: Well now, moving to another area of your work that is extremely intriguing, we have the research dealing with the experience of living in cities. While in your earlier experiment you were studying obedience to authority and the resulting cruelty, at the same time, beginning to become noticeable, were cases like the famous Kitty Genovese case, where we had another kind of, shall we say, horrendous reaction to a fellow man. But in this case, rather than the administering of shock under experimental conditions, the apathy was what was cruel. The work of Darley and Latané (1970), and a great deal of subsequent work, has gone very carefully into trying to understand something about the nature of this so-called bystander apathy, also asking: Is there any real altruism in man? The findings of this line of research suggest that there's some cause for optimism. It seems to me that in your analysis of living in the cities (Milgram, 1970), in a very broad and fascinating way, you extend some of these interpretations, and so it might be kind of interesting to hear what led you in this particular direction.

MILGRAM: May I, before doing that, try to draw some connections between the bystander work and the work on authority?

EVANS: Oh yes, certainly.

MILGRAM: To some extent, a lot of bystander work shows that when society becomes complicated, there are specialized organizations set up, such as the police, which have authority in particular domains, and then people abdicate responsibility to them. After all, in the Genovese case, people thought it was not their responsibility; it was the responsibility of those in authority—that is, the police—to do something about this matter. The particular tragedy in the Genovese case was that no one even notified the police. There's another thing that comes out in some of the other Latané and Darley studies—I'm thinking particularly of the smoke experiment. They've shown that a group of people is less likely to respond to an emergency than a single individual. That really shows how ineffectively people function in the absence of authority. When there's no group structure, when there's no predesignated leadership, it can lead to enormous inefficiency. You see, none of these issues is really one-sided. Under certain circumstances, authority is very useful. It wouldn't exist in human society, I assure you, if it did not serve important adaptive functions.

NOTES

1. S. Milgram, *Obedience to Authority: An Experimental View* (New York: Harper & Row, 1974).
2. R. Evans (ed.), *The Making of Social Psychology*. (New York: Gardner, 1980). Reprinted by permission of the editor.

REFERENCES

ASCH, S., 1958. "Effects of group pressure upon modification and distortion of judgments." In *Readings in Social Psychology*, 3rd ed., eds. E. E. Maccoby, T. M. Newcomb, and E. L. Hartley. New York: Holt.

KORTE, C., and MILGRAM, S., 1970. "Acquaintance networks between racial groups: application of the small world method." *J. Pers. Soc. Psychol.* 15:(2) 101–8.

LATANÉ, B., and DARLEY, J., 1970. *The Unresponsive Bystander: Why Doesn't He Help?* New York: Appleton.

LYNCH, K., 1960. *The Image of the City*. Cambridge, Mass.: M.I.T. Press and Harvard University Press.

MILGRAM, S., 1963. "Behavioral study of obedience." *J. Abnorm. Soc. Psychol.* 67:371–78.

———, 1965, "Some conditions to obedience and disobedience to authority." *Hum. Rel.* 18:(1) 57–76.

———, 1967. "The small world problem." *Psychol. Today* 1:(1) 60–67.

———, 1970a. "The experience of living in cities." *Science* 167:146–168.

————, 1970b. "The experience of living in cities: a psychological analysis." In *Psychology and the Problems of Society*, eds. F. F. Korten, S. W. Cook, and J. I. Lacey. Washington, D.C.: American Psychological Association.

————, 1972. "Interpreting obedience." In *The Social Psychology of Psychological Research*, ed. A. Miller. New York: Free Press.

————, 1974a. *Obedience to Authority*. New York: Harper & Row.

————, 1974b. "The city and the self." Time-Life Films: Time-Life Building, Rockefeller Center, New York, N.Y. 10020.

TRAVERS, J., and MILGRAM, S., 1969. "An experimental study of the small world problem." *Sociometry* 32:(4) 425–43.

ZIMBARDO, P., ET AL., 1973. "The mind is a formidable jailer: a Pirandellian prison." *The New York Times*, p. 38, April 8, 1973.

10

Some Conditions of Obedience and Disobedience to Authority[1]

❖

The situation in which one agent commands another to hurt a third turns up time and again as a significant theme in human relations. It is powerfully expressed in the story of Abraham, who is commanded by God to kill his son. It is no accident that Kierkegaard, seeking to orient his thought to the central themes of human experience, chose Abraham's conflict as the springboard to his philosophy.

War too moves forward on the triad of an authority which commands a person to destroy the enemy, and perhaps all organized hostility may be viewed as a theme and variation on the three elements of authority, executant, and victim.[2] We describe an experimental program, recently concluded at Yale University, in which a particular expression of this conflict is studied by experimental means.

In its most general form the problem may be defined thus: if X tells Y to hurt Z, under what conditions will Y carry out the command of X and under what conditions will he refuse. In the more limited form possible in laboratory research, the question becomes: If an experimenter tells a subject to hurt another person, under what conditions will the subject go along with this instruction, and under what conditions will he refuse to obey. The laboratory problem is not so much a

This paper was first published in *Human Relations*, Vol. 18, No. 1 (1965), pp. 57–75. The research was supported by grants from the National Science Foundation and from a small grant from the Higgins Fund of Yale University. Reprinted by permission of Alexandra Milgram.

dilution of the general statement as one concrete expression of the many particular forms this question may assume.

One aim of the research was to study behavior in a strong situation of deep consequence to the participants, for the psychological forces operative in powerful and lifelike forms of the conflict may not be brought into play under diluted conditions.

This approach meant, first, that we had a special obligation to protect the welfare and dignity of the persons who took part in the study; subjects were, of necessity, placed in a difficult predicament, and steps had to be taken to ensure their wellbeing before they were discharged from the laboratory. Toward this end, a careful post-experimental treatment was devised and has been carried through for subjects in all conditions.[3]

TERMINOLOGY

If Y follows the command of X we shall say that he has obeyed X; if he fails to carry out the command of X, we shall say that he has disobeyed X. The terms to *obey* and to *disobey*, as used here, refer to the subject's overt action only, and carry no implication for the motive or experiential states accompanying the action.[4]

To be sure, the everyday use of the word *obedience* is not entirely free from complexities. It refers to action within widely varying situations, and connotes diverse motives within those situations: a child's obedience differs from a soldier's obedience, or the love, honor, and *obey* of the marriage vow. However, a consistent behavioral relationship is indicated in most uses of the term: in the act of obeying, a person does what another person tells him to do. Y obeys X if he carries out the prescription for action which X has addressed to him; the term suggests, moreover, that some form of dominance-subordination, or hierarchical element, is part of the situation in which the transaction between X and Y occurs.

A subject who complies with the entire series of experimental commands will be termed an *obedient* subject; one who at any point in the command series defies the experimenter will be called a *disobedient* or *defiant* subject. As used in this report the terms refer only to the subject's performance in the experiment, and do not necessarily imply a general personality disposition to submit to or reject authority.

SUBJECT POPULATION

The subjects used in all experimental conditions were male adults, residing in the greater New Haven and Bridgeport areas, aged 20 to 50 years, and engaged in a wide variety of occupations. Each experimental condition described in this report employed 40 fresh subjects and was carefully balanced for age and occupational types. The occupational composition for each experiment was: workers, skilled and unskilled: 40 percent; white collar, sales, business: 40 percent; professionals: 20 percent. The occupations were intersected with three age categories (subjects in 20's, 30's, and 40's, assigned to each condition in the proportions of 20, 40, and 40 percent, respectively).

THE GENERAL LABORATORY PROCEDURE[5]

The focus of the study concerns the amount of electric shock a subject is willing to administer to another person when ordered by an experimenter to give the "victim" increasingly more severe punishment. The act of administering shock is set in the context of a learning experiment, ostensibly designed to study the effect of punishment on memory. Aside from the experimenter, one naïve subject and one accomplice perform in each session. On arrival each subject is paid $4.50. After a general talk by the experimenter, telling how little scientists know about the effect of punishment on memory, subjects are informed that one member of the pair will serve as teacher and one as learner. A rigged drawing is held so that the naïve subject is always the teacher, and the accomplice becomes the learner. The learner is taken to an adjacent room and strapped into an "electric chair."

The naïve subject is told that it is his task to teach the learner a list of paired associates, to test him on the list, and to administer punishment whenever the learner errs in the test. Punishment takes the form of electric shock, delivered to the learner by means of a shock generator controlled by the naïve subject. The teacher is instructed to increase the intensity of electric shock one step on the generator on each error. The learner, according to plan, provides many wrong answers, so that before long the naïve subject must give him the strongest shock on the generator. Increases in shock level are met by increasingly insistent demands from the learner that the experiment be stopped because of the growing discomfort to him. However, in clear terms the experimenter orders the teacher to continue with the procedure in disregard of the learner's protests. *Thus, the naïve subject must resolve a conflict between two mutually incompatible demands from the social field. He may continue to follow the orders of the experimenter and shock the learner with increasing severity, or he may refuse to follow the orders of the experimenter and heed the learner's pleas. The experimenter's authority operates not in a free field, but against ever-mounting countervailing pressure from the person being punished.*

A few technical points need to be considered before the findings of the study are described. For the purpose of delivering shock, a simulated shock generator is used, with 30 clearly marked voltage levels that range from 15 to 450 volts. (Each level is activated by one of 30 individual lever switches set in a horizontal line.) The naïve subject is given a sample shock of 45 volts to convince him of the authenticity of the instrument. The generator bears verbal designations that range from "Slight Shock" to "Danger: Severe Shock."

The responses of the victim are standardized on tape, and each protest is coordinated to a particular voltage level on the shock generator. Starting with 75 volts the learner begins to grunt and moan. At 150 volts he demands to be let out of the experiment. At 180 volts he cries out that he can no longer stand the pain. At 300 volts he refuses to provide any more answers to the memory test, insisting that he is no longer a participant in the experiment and must be freed. In response to this last tactic, the experimenter instructs the naïve subject to treat the absence of an answer as equivalent to a wrong answer, and to follow the usual shock procedure. The experimenter reinforces his demand with the statement: "You have no other choice, you must go on!" (This imperative is used whenever the naïve subject tries to break off the experiment.) If the subject refuses to give the next higher level of shock, the experiment is considered at an end. A quantitative value is assigned to the subject's performance based on the maximum-intensity shock he administered before breaking off. Thus any subject's score may range from zero (for a subject unwilling to administer the first shock level) to 30 (for a subject who proceeds to the highest voltage level on the board). For any particular subject and for any particular experimental condition, the degree to which participants have followed the experimenter's orders may be specified with a numerical value, corresponding to the metric on the shock generator.

This laboratory situation gives us a framework in which to study the subject's reactions to the principal conflict of the experiment. Again, this conflict is between the experimenter's demands that he continue to administer the electric shock, and the learner's demands, which become increasingly more insistent, that the experiment be stopped. The crux of the study is to vary systematically the factors believed to alter the degree of obedience to the experimental commands, to learn under what conditions submission to authority is most probable and under what conditions defiance is brought to the fore.

PILOT STUDIES

Pilot studies for the present research were completed in the winter of 1960; they differed from the regular experiments in a few details: for one, the victim was placed behind a silvered glass, with the light balance on the glass such that the victim could be dimly perceived by the subject (Milgram, 1961).

Though essentially qualitative in treatment, these studies pointed to several significant features of the experimental situation. At first no vocal feedback was used from the victim. It was thought that the verbal and voltage designations on the control panel would create sufficient pressure to curtail the subject's obedience. However, this was not the case. In the absence of protests from the learner, virtually all subjects, once commanded, went blithely to the end of the board, seemingly indifferent to the verbal designations ("Extreme Shock" and "Danger: Severe Shock"). This deprived us of an adequate basis for scaling obedient tendencies. A force had to be introduced that would strengthen the subject's resistance to the experimenter's commands, and reveal individual differences in terms of a distribution of break-off points.

This force took the form of protests from the victim. Initially, mild protests were used, but proved inadequate. Subsequently, more vehement protests were inserted into the experimental procedure. To our consternation, even the strongest protests from the victim did not prevent all subjects from administering the harshest punishment ordered by the experimenter; but the protests did lower the mean maximum shock somewhat and created some spread in the subject's performance; therefore, the victim's cries were standardized on tape and incorporated into the regular experimental procedure.

The situation did more than highlight the technical difficulties of finding a workable experimental procedure: It indicated that subjects would obey authority to a greater extent than we had supposed. It also pointed to the importance of feedback from the victim in controlling the subject's behavior.

One further aspect of the pilot study was that subjects frequently averted their eyes from the person they were shocking, often turning their heads in an awkward and conspicuous manner. One subject explained: "I didn't want to see the consequences of what I had done." Observers wrote:

> . . . subjects showed a reluctance to look at the victim, whom they could see through the glass in front of them. When this fact was brought to their attention they indicated that it caused them discomfort to see the victim in agony. We note, however, that although the subject refuses to look at the victim, he continues to administer shocks.

This suggested that the salience of the victim may have, in some degree, regulated the subject's performance. If, in obeying the experimenter, the subject found it necessary to avoid scrutiny of the victim, would the converse be true? If the victim were rendered increasingly more salient to the subject, would obedience diminish? The first set of regular experiments was designed to answer this question.

*I*MMEDIACY OF THE VICTIM

This series consisted of four experimental conditions. In each condition the victim was brought "psychologically" closer to the subject giving him shocks.

In the first condition (Remote Feedback) the victim was placed in another room and could not be heard or seen by the subject, except that, at 300 volts, he pounded on the wall in protest. After 315 volts he no longer answered or was heard from.

The second condition (Voice Feedback) was identical to the first except that voice protests were introduced. As in the first condition the victim was placed in an adjacent room, but his complaints could be heard clearly through a door left slightly ajar and through the walls of the laboratory.[6]

The third experimental condition (Proximity) was similar to the second, except that the victim was now placed in the same room as the subject, and 1½ feet from him. Thus he was visible as well as audible, and voice cues were provided.

The fourth, and final, condition of this series (Touch-Proximity) was identical to the third, with this exception: The victim received a shock only when his hand rested on a shockplate. At the 150-volt level the victim again demanded to be let free and, in this condition, refused to place his hand on the shockplate. The experimenter ordered the naïve subject to force the victim's hand onto the plate. Thus obedience in this condition required that the subject have physical contact with the victim in order to give him punishment beyond the 150-volt level.

Forty adult subjects were studied in each condition. The data revealed that obedience was significantly reduced as the victim was rendered more immediate to the subject. The mean maximum shock for the conditions is shown in Fig. 10.1.

Expressed in terms of the proportion of obedient to defiant subjects, the findings are that 34 percent of the subjects defied the experimenter in the Remote condition, 37.5 percent in Voice Feedback, 60 percent in Proximity, and 70 percent in Touch-Proximity.

How are we to account for this effect? A first conjecture might be that as the victim was brought closer the subject became more aware of the intensity of his suffering and regulated his behavior accordingly. This makes sense, but our evidence does not support the interpretation. There are no consistent differences in the attributed level of pain across the four conditions (i.e. the amount of pain experienced by the victim as estimated by the subject and expressed on a 14-point scale). But it is easy to speculate about alternative mechanisms:

    Empathic cues.   In the Remote and to a lesser extent the Voice Feedback conditions, the victim's suffering possesses an abstract,

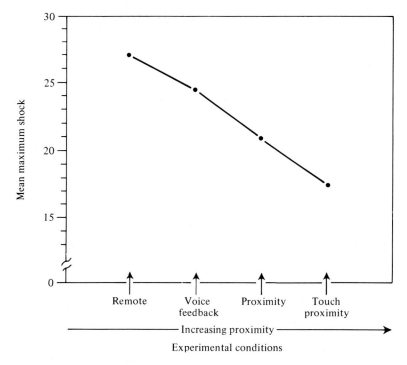

FIGURE 10.1
Mean maxima in proximity series.

remote quality for the subject. He is aware, but only in a conceptual sense, that his actions cause pain to another person; the fact is
apprehended, but not felt. The phenomenon is common enough.
The bombardier can reasonably suppose that his weapons will
inflict suffering and death, yet this knowledge is divested of affect
and does not move him to a felt, emotional response to the
suffering resulting from his actions. Similar observations have been
made in wartime. It is possible that the visual cues associated with
the victim's suffering trigger empathic responses in the subject and
provide him with a more complete grasp of the victim's experience.
Or it is possible that the empathic responses are themselves
unpleasant, possessing drive properties which cause the subject to
terminate the arousal situation. Diminishing obedience, then,
would be explained by the enrichment of empathic cues in the
successive experimental conditions.

Denial and narrowing of the cognitive field.   The Remote condition
allows a narrowing of the cognitive field so that the victim is put
out of mind. The subject no longer considers the act of depressing a

lever relevant to moral judgment, for it is no longer associated with the victim's suffering. When the victim is close it is more difficult to exclude him phenomenologically. He necessarily intrudes on the subject's awareness since he is continuously visible. In the Remote condition his existence and reactions are made known only after the shock has been administered. The auditory feedback is sporadic and discontinuous. In the Proximity conditions his inclusion in the immediate visual field renders him a continuously salient element for the subject. The mechanism of denial can no longer be brought into play. One subject in the Remote condition said: "It's funny how you really begin to forget that there's a guy out there, even though you can hear him. For a long time I just concentrated on pressing the switches and reading the words."

Reciprocal fields.   If in the Proximity condition the subject is in an improved position to observe the victim, the reverse is also true. The actions of the subject now come under proximal scrutiny by the victim. Possibly, it is easier to harm a person when he is unable to observe our actions than when he can see what we are doing. His surveillance of the action directed against him may give rise to shame, or guilt, which may then serve to curtail the action. Many expressions of language refer to the discomfort or inhibitions that arise in face-to-face confrontation. It is often said that it is easier to criticize a man "behind his back" than to "attack him to his face." If we are in the process of lying to a person it is reputedly difficult to "stare him in the eye." We "turn away from others in shame" or in "embarrassment" and this action serves to reduce our discomfort. The manifest function of allowing the victim of a firing squad to be blindfolded is to make the occasion less stressful for him, but it may also serve a latent function of reducing the stress of the executioner. In short, in the Proximity conditions, the subject may sense that he has become more salient in the victim's field of awareness. Possibly he becomes more self-conscious, embarrassed, and inhibited in his punishment of the victim.

Phenomenal unity of act.   In the Remote condition it is more difficult for the subject to gain a sense of *relatedness* between his own actions and the consequences of these actions for the victim. There is a physical and spatial separation of the act and its consequences. The subject depresses a lever in one room, and protests and cries are heard from another. The two events are in correlation, yet they lack a compelling phenomenological unity. The structure of a meaningful act—*I am hurting a man*—breaks down because of the spatial arrangements, in a manner somewhat analogous to the disappearance of phi phenomena when the blinking lights are spaced too far apart. The unity is more fully achieved in the Proximity condition as the victim is brought closer to the action that causes him pain. It is rendered complete in Touch-Proximity.

Incipient group formation.   Placing the victim in another room not only takes him further from the subject, but the subject and the experimenter are drawn relatively closer. There is incipient group formation between the experimenter and the subject, from which the victim is excluded. The wall between the victim and the others deprives him of an intimacy which the experimenter and subject feel. In the Remote condition, the victim is truly an outsider, who stands alone, physically and psychologically.

When the victim is placed close to the subject, it becomes easier to form an alliance with him against the experimenter. Subjects no longer have to face the experimenter alone. They have an ally who is close at hand and eager to collaborate in a revolt against the experimenter. Thus, the changing set of spatial relations leads to a potentially shifting set of alliances over the several experimental conditions.

Acquired behavior dispositions.   It is commonly observed that laboratory mice will rarely fight with their litter mates. Scott (1958) explains this in terms of passive inhibition. He writes: "By doing nothing under . . . circumstances [the animal] learns to do nothing, and this may be spoken of as passive inhibition . . . this principle has great importance in teaching an individual to be peaceful, for it means that he can learn not to fight simply by not fighting." Similarly, we may learn not to harm others simply by not harming them in everyday life. Yet this learning occurs in a context of proximal relations with others, and may not be generalized to that situation in which the person is physically removed from us. Or possibly, in the past, aggressive actions against others who were physically close resulted in retaliatory punishment which extinguished the original form of response. In contrast, aggression against others at a distance may have only sporadically led to retaliation. Thus the organism learns that it is safer to be aggressive toward others at a distance, and precarious to be so when the parties are within arm's reach. Through a pattern of rewards and punishments, he acquires a disposition to avoid aggression at close quarters, a disposition which does not extend to harming others at a distance. And this may account for experimental findings in the remote and proximal experiments.

Proximity as a variable in psychological research has received far less attention than it deserves. If men were sessile it would be easy to understand this neglect. But we move about; our spatial relations shift from one situation to the next, and the fact that we are near or remote may have a powerful effect on the psychological processes that mediate our behavior toward others. In the present situation, as the victim is brought closer to the subject ordered to give him shocks, increasing numbers of subjects break off the experiment, refusing to obey. The concrete, visible, and proximal presence of the victim acts in an important way to counteract the experimenter's power to generate disobedience.[7]

CLOSENESS OF AUTHORITY

If the spatial relationship of the subject and victim is relevant to the degree of obedience, would not the relationship of subject to experimenter also play a part?

There are reasons to feel that, on arrival, the subject is oriented primarily to the experimenter rather than to the victim. He has come to the laboratory to fit into the structure that the experimenter—not the victim— would provide. He has come less to understand his behavior than to *reveal* that behavior to a competent scientist, and he is willing to display himself as the scientist's purposes require. Most subjects seem quite concerned about the appearance they are making before the experimenter, and one could argue that this preoccupation in a relatively new and strange setting makes the subject somewhat insensitive to the triadic nature of the social situation. In other words, the subject is so concerned about the show he is putting on for the experimenter that influences from other parts of the social field do not receive as much weight as they ordinarily would. This overdetermined orientation to the experimenter would account for the relative insensitivity of the subject to the victim, and would also lead us to believe that alterations in the relationship between subject and experimenter would have important consequences for obedience.

In a series of experiments we varied the physical closeness and degree of surveillance of the experimenter. In one condition the experimenter sat just a few feet away from the subject. In a second condition, after giving initial instructions, the experimenter left the laboratory and gave his orders by telephone. In still a third condition the experimenter was never seen, providing instructions by means of a tape recording activated when the subjects entered the laboratory.

Obedience dropped sharply as the experimenter was physically removed from the laboratory. The number of obedient subjects in the first condition (Experimenter Present) was almost three times as great as in the second, where the experimenter gave his orders by telephone. Twenty-six subjects were fully obedient in the first condition, and only nine in the second (Chi square obedient *vs.* defiant in the two conditions, df = 14.7; $p < 0.001$). Subjects seemed able to take a far stronger stand against the experimenter when they did not have to encounter him face to face, and the experimenter's power over the subject was severely curtailed.[8]

(a) Shock generator used in the experiments. Fifteen of the 30 switches have already been depressed.

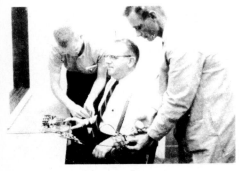

(b) The learner is strapped into a chair and electrodes are attached to his wrist. Electrode paste is applied by the experimenter. The learner provides answers by depressing switches that light up numbers on an answer box.

(c) The subject receives a sample shock from the generator.

(d) The subject breaks off the experiment. On the right, an event recorder wired into the generator automatically records the switches used by the subject. (From the film Obedience, distributed by the Penn State Audio-Visual Services.)

FIGURE 10.2
Photographs of the obedience experiments.

Moreover, when the experimenter was absent, subjects displayed an interesting form of behavior that had not occurred under his surveillance. Though continuing with the experiment, several subjects administered lower shocks than were required and never informed the experimenter of their deviation from the correct procedure. (Unknown to the subjects, shock levels were automatically recorded by an Esterline-Angus event recorder wired directly into the shock generator; the instrument provided us with an objective record of the subjects' performance.) Indeed, in telephone conversations some subjects specifically assured the experimenter that they were raising the shock level according to instruction, whereas in fact they were repeatedly using the lowest shock on the board. This form of behavior is particularly interesting: although these subjects acted in a way that clearly undermined the avowed purposes of the experiment, they found it easier to handle the conflict in this manner than to precipitate an open break with authority.

Other conditions were completed in which the experimenter was absent during the first segment of the experiment, but reappeared at the point that the subject definitely refused to give higher shocks when commanded by telephone. Although he had exhausted his power via telephone, the experimenter could frequently force further obedience when he reappeared in the laboratory.

Experiments in this series show that the *physical presence* of an authority is an important force contributing to the subject's obedience of defiance. Taken together with the first experimental series on the proximity of the victim, it would appear that something akin to fields of force, diminishing in effectiveness with increasing psychological distance from their source, have a controlling effect on the subject's performance. As the victim is brought closer, the subject finds it harder to administer shocks to him. When the victim's position is held constant relative to the subject, and the authority is made more remote, the subject finds it easier to break off the experiment. This effect is substantial in both cases, but manipulation of the experimenter's position yielded the more powerful results. Obedience to destructive commands is highly dependent on the proximal relations between authority and subject.

*T*ENSIONS

The description of final scores does not fully convey the character of the subjects' performance, and it would be useful to interrupt our reporting of quantitative relationships to remark on the subjects' general reaction to the situation.

One might suppose that a subject would simply break off or continue as his conscience and temperament dictated. Yet this is very far from what happened. These were powerful reactions of tension and emotional strain in a substantial proportion of the participants. Persons were observed to sweat, tremble, stutter, bite their lips, and groan as they found themselves increasingly implicated in the experimental conflict. Some sense of the subjects' mood can be found in a transcript of their remarks at break-off point. Here are the remarks of two defiant subjects:

> Is he banging? . . . Is he hurt out there? Well, I don't want to be responsible for anything that happens to him. No, I can't go on with it. I don't know whether he's all right or not. I mean he may have a heart condition or something; I wouldn't feel right doing it. He's banging for help. He's evidently in trouble or he wouldn't bang . . . I don't see any sense to this—to knocking him out or something. I just can't see it.
> *[Subject refuses to administer shocks]*   *[Subject 0108]*

> The man is banging. He wants to get out . . . I'm sorry. If the man wants to get out I'd just as soon stop . . . I don't want to administer any more [extremely excited] . . . I will gladly refund the check, but I will not harm this man . . . I'm sorry, I will not give him any more if he obviously wants to get out. There is no money in the world that will make me hurt another individual.
> *[Subject 010X]*

And here is a transcript from an obedient subject. He began the experiment calmly, but became increasingly tense as the experiment proceeded. After administering the 150-volt shock, he began to address the experimenter in agitated tones:

> *150 volts delivered.* You want me to keep going?
> *165 volts delivered.* That guy is hollering in there. There's a lot of them here. He's liable to have heart condition. You want me to go?
> *180 volts delivered.* He can't stand it! I'm not going to kill that man in there! You hear him hollering? He's hollering. He can't stand it. What if something happens to him?. . . I'm not going to get that man sick in there. He's hollering in there. You know what I mean? I mean I refuse to take responsibility. He's getting hurt in there. He's in there hollering. Too many left here. Geez, if he gets them wrong. There's too many of them left. I mean who is going to take responsibility if anything happens to that gentleman?
> *[The experimenter accepts responsibility.]* All right.
> *195 volts delivered.* You see he's hollering. Hear that. Gee, I don't know.
> *[The experimenter says: 'The experiment requires that you go on.']*—I know it does, sir, but I mean—hugh—he don't know what he's in for. He's up to 195 volts.
> *210 volts delivered.*
> *225 volts delivered.*
> *240 volts delivered.* Aw, no. You mean I've got to keep going up with the scale? No sir. I'm not going to kill that man! I'm not going to give him 450 volts!
> *[The experimenter says: 'The experiment requires that you go on.']*—I know it does, but that man is hollering there, sir . . .

Despite his numerous, agitated objections, which were constant accompaniments to his actions, the subject unfailingly obeyed the experimenter, proceeding to the highest shock level on the generator. He displayed a curious dissociation between word and action. Although at the verbal level he had resolved not to go on, his actions were fully in accord with the experimenter's commands. This subject did not want to shock the victim, and he found it an extremely disagreeable task, but he was unable to invent a response that would free him from E's authority. Many subjects cannot find the specific verbal formula that would enable them to reject the role assigned to them by the experimenter. Perhaps our culture does not provide adequate models for disobedience.

One puzzling sign of tension was the regular occurrence of nervous laughing fits. In the first four conditions 71 of the 160 subjects showed definite signs of nervous laughter and smiling. The laughter seemed entirely out of place, even bizarre. Full-blown, uncontrollable seizures were observed for 15 of these subjects. On one occasion we observed a seizure so violently convulsive that it was necessary to call a halt to the experiment. In the post-experimental interviews subjects took pains to point out that they were not sadistic types and that the laughter did not mean they enjoyed shocking the victim.

In the interview following the experiment subjects were asked to indicate on a 14-point scale just how nervous or tense they felt at the point of maximum tension (Fig. 10.3). The scale ranged from "not at all tense and nervous" to "extremely tense and nervous." Self-reports of this sort are of limited precision and at best provide only a rough indication of the subject's emotional response. Still, taking the reports for what they are worth, it can be seen that the distribution of responses spans the entire range of the scale, with the majority of subjects concentrated at the center and upper extreme. A further breakdown showed that obedient subjects reported themselves as having been slightly more tense and nervous than the defiant subjects at the point of maximum tension.

How is the occurrence of tension to be interpreted? First, it points to the presence of conflict. If a tendency to comply with authority were the only psychological force operating in the situation, all subjects would have continued to the end and there would have been no tension. Tension, it is assumed, results from the simultaneous presence of two or more incompatible response tendencies (Miller, 1944). If sympathetic concern for the victim were the exclusive force, all subjects would have calmly defied the experimenter. Instead, there were both obedient and defiant outcomes, frequently accompanied by extreme tension. A conflict develops between the deeply ingrained disposition not to harm others and the equally compelling tendency to obey others who are in authority. The subject is quickly drawn into a dilemma of a deeply dynamic character, and the presence of high tension points to the considerable strength of each of the antagonistic vectors.

Moreover, tension defines the strength of the aversive state from which the subject is unable to escape through disobedience. When a person is uncomfortable, tense, or stressed, he tries to take some action

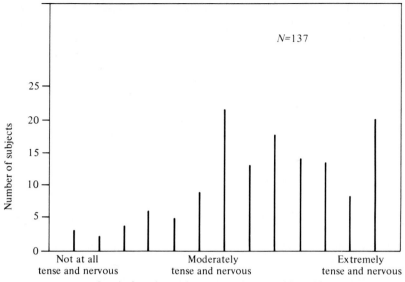

FIGURE 10.3
Level of tension and nervousness: the self-reports on "tension and nervousness" for 137 subjects in the Proximity experiments. Subjects were given a scale with 14 values ranging from "not at all tense and nervous" to "extremely tense and nervous." They were instructed: "Thinking back to that point in the experiment when you felt the most tense and nervous, indicate just how you felt by placing an X at the appropriate point on the scale." The results are shown in terms of midpoint values.

that will allow him to terminate this unpleasant state. Thus tension may serve as a drive that leads to escape behavior. But in the present situation, even where tension is extreme, many subjects are unable to perform the response that will bring about relief. Therefore there must be a competing drive, tendency, or inhibition that precludes activation of the disobedient response. The strength of this inhibiting factor must be of greater magnitude than the stress experienced, or else the terminating act would occur. Every evidence of extreme tension is at the same time an indication of the strength of the forces that keep the subject in the situation.

Finally, tension may be taken as evidence of the reality of the situations for the subjects. Normal subjects do not tremble and sweat unless they are implicated in a deep and genuinely felt predicament.

BACKGROUND AUTHORITY

In psychophysics, animal learning, and other branches of psychology, the fact that measures are obtained at one institution rather than another is irrelevant to the interpretation of the findings, so long as the technical facilities for measurement are adequate and the operations are carried out with competence.

But it cannot be assumed that this holds true for the present study. The effectiveness of the experimenter's commands may depend in an important way on the larger institutional context in which they are issued. The experiments described thus far were conducted at Yale University, an organization which most subjects regarded with respect and sometimes awe. In post-experimental interviews several participants remarked that the locale and sponsorship of the study gave them confidence in the integrity, competence, and benign purposes of the personnel; many indicated that they would not have shocked the learner if the experiments had been done elsewhere.

This issue of background authority seemed to us important for an interpretation of the results that had been obtained thus far; moreover it is highly relevant to any comprehensive theory of human obedience. Consider, for example, how closely our compliance with the imperatives of others is tied to particular institutions and locales in our day-to-day activities. On request, we expose our throats to a man with a razor blade in the barber shop, but would not do so in a shoe store; in the latter setting we willingly follow the clerk's request to stand in our stockinged feet, but resist the command in a bank. In the laboratory of a great university, subjects may comply with a set of commands that would be resisted if given elsewhere. *One must always question the relationship of obedience to a person's sense of the context in which he is operating.*

To explore the problem we moved our apparatus to an office building in industrial Bridgeport and replicated experimental conditions, without any visible tie to the university.

Bridgeport subjects were invited to the experiment through a mail circular similar to the one used in the Yale study, with appropriate changes in letterhead, etc. As in the earlier study, subjects were paid $4.50 for coming to the laboratory. The same age and occupational distributions used at Yale and the identical personnel were employed.

The purpose in relocating in Bridgeport was to assure a complete dissociation from Yale, and in this regard we were fully successful. On the surface, the study appeared to be conducted by Research Associates of Bridgeport, an organization of unknown character (the title had been concocted exclusively for use in this study).

The experiments were conducted in a three-room office suite in a somewhat run-down commercial building located in the downtown shopping area. The laboratory was sparsely furnished, though clean, and marginally respectable in appearance. When subjects inquired about professional affiliations, they were informed only that we were a private firm conducting research for industry.

Some subjects displayed skepticism concerning the motives of the Bridgeport experimenter. One gentleman gave us a written account of the thoughts he experienced at the control board:

> . . . Should I quit this damn test? Maybe he passed out? What dopes we were not to check up on this deal. How do we know that these guys are legit? No furniture, bare walls, no telephone. We could of called the Police up or the Better Business Bureau. I learned a lesson tonight. How do I know that Mr. Williams [the experimenter] is telling the truth . . . I wish I knew how many volts a person could take before lapsing into unconsciousness . . .
>
> [Subject 2414]

Another subject stated:

> I questioned on my arrival my own judgment [about coming]. I had doubts as to the legitimacy of the operation and the consequences of participation. I felt it was a heartless way to conduct memory or learning processes on human beings and certainly dangerous without the presence of a medical doctor.
>
> [Subject 2440V]

There was no noticeable reduction in tension for the Bridgeport subjects. And the subjects' estimation of the amount of pain felt by the victim was slightly, though not significantly, higher than in the Yale study.

A failure to obtain complete obedience in Bridgeport would indicate that the extreme compliance found in New Haven subjects was tied closely to the background authority of Yale University; if a large proportion of the subjects remained fully obedient, very different conclusions would be called for.

As it turned out, the level of obedience in Bridgeport, although somewhat reduced, was not significantly lower than that obtained at Yale. A large proportion of the Bridgeport subjects were fully obedient to the experimenter's commands (48 percent of the Bridgeport subjects delivered the maximum shock versus 65 percent in the corresponding condition at Yale).

How are these findings to be interpreted? It is possible that if commands of a potentially harmful or destructive sort are to be perceived as legitimate they must occur within some sort of institutional structure. But it is clear from the study that it need not be a particularly reputable or distinguished institution. The Bridgeport experiments were conducted by an unimpressive firm lacking any credentials; the laboratory was set up in a respectable office building with title listed in the building directory. Beyond that, there was no evidence of benevolence or competence. It is possible that the *category* of institution, judged according to its professed function, rather than its qualitative position within that category, wins our compliance. Persons deposit money in elegant, but also in seedy-looking banks, without giving much thought to the differences in security they offer. Similarly, our subjects may consider one laboratory to be as competent as another, so long as it is a scientific laboratory.

It would be valuable to study the subjects' performance in other contexts which go even further than the Bridgeport study in denying institutional support to the experimenter. It is possible that, beyond a certain point, obedience disappears completely. But that point had not been reached in the Bridgeport office: almost half the subjects obeyed the experimenter fully.

*F*URTHER EXPERIMENTS

We may mention briefly some additional experiments undertaken in the Yale series. A considerable amount of obedience and defiance in everyday life occurs in connection with groups. And we had reason to feel in light of the many group studies already done in psychology that group forces would have a profound effect on reactions to authority. A series of experiments was run to examine these effects. In all cases only one naïve subject was studied per hour, but he performed in the midst of actors who, unknown to him, were employed by the experimenter. In one experiment (Groups for Disobedience) two actors broke off in the middle of the experiment. When this happened 90 percent of the subjects followed suit and defied the experimenter. In another condition the actors followed the orders obediently; this strengthened the experimenter's power only slightly. In still a third experiment the job of pushing the switch to shock the learner was given to one of the actors, while the naïve subject performed a subsidiary act. We wanted to see how the teacher would respond if he were involved in the situation but did not actually give the shocks. In this situation only three subjects out of forty broke off. In a final group experiment the subjects themselves determined the shock level they were going to use. Two actors suggested higher and higher shock levels; some subjects insisted, despite group pressure, that the shock level be kept low; others followed along with the group.

Further experiments were completed using women as subjects, as well as a set dealing with the effects of dual, unsanctioned, and conflicting authority. A final experiment concerned the personal relationship between victim and subject. These will have to be described elsewhere, lest the present report be extended to monographic length.

It goes without saying that future research can proceed in many different directions. What kinds of response from the victim are most effective in causing disobedience in the subject? Perhaps passive resistance is more effective than vehement protest. What conditions of entry into an authority system lead to greater or lesser obedience? What is the effect of anonymity and masking on the subject's behavior? What conditions lead to the subject's perception of responsibility for his own actions? Each of these could be a major research topic in itself, and can readily be incorporated into the general experimental procedure described here.

LEVELS OF OBEDIENCE AND DEFIANCE

One general finding that merits attention is the high level of obedience manifested in the experimental situation. Subjects often expressed deep disapproval of shocking a man in the face of his objections, and others denounced it as senseless and stupid. Yet many subjects complied even while they protested. The proportion of obedient subjects greatly exceeded the expectations of the experimenter and his colleagues. At the outset, we had conjectured that subjects would not, in general, go above the level of "Strong Shock." In practice, many subjects were willing to administer the most extreme shocks available when commanded by the experimenter. For some subjects the experiment provided an occasion for aggressive release. And for others it demonstrated the extent to which obedient dispositions are deeply ingrained and engaged, irrespective of their consequences for others. Yet this is not the whole story. Somehow, the subject becomes implicated in a situation from which he cannot disengage himself.

The departure of the experimental results from intelligent expectation, to some extent, has been formalized. The procedure was to describe the experimental situation in concrete detail to a group of competent persons, and to ask them to predict the performance of 100 hypothetical subjects. For purposes of indicating the distribution of break-off points, judges were provided with a diagram of the shock generator and recorded their predictions before being informed of the actual results. Judges typically underestimated the amount of obedience demonstrated by subjects.

In Fig. 10.4, we compare the predictions of forty psychiatrists at a leading medical school with the actual performance of subjects in the experiment. The psychiatrists predicted that most subjects would not go beyond the tenth shock level (150 volts; at this point the victim makes his first explicit demand to be freed). They further predicted that by the twentieth shock level (300 volts; the victim refuses to answer) 3.73 percent of the subjects would still be obedient; and that only a little over one-tenth of one percent of the subjects would administer the highest shock on the board. But, as the graph indicates, the obtained behavior was very different. Sixty-two percent of the subjects obeyed the experimenter's commands fully. Between expectation and occurrence there is a whopping discrepancy.

Why did the psychiatrists underestimate the level of obedience?

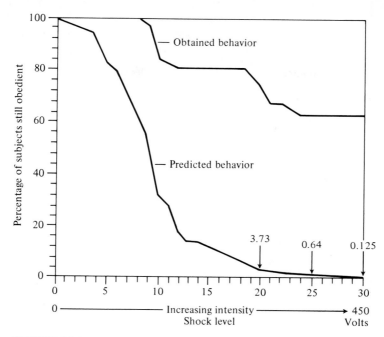

FIGURE 10.4
Predicted and obtained behavior in voice feedback.

Possibly, because their predictions were based on an inadequate conception of the determinants of human action, a conception that focuses on motives *in vacuo*. This orientation may be entirely adequate for the repair of bruised impulses as revealed on the psychiatrist's couch, but as soon as our interest turns to action in larger settings, attention must be paid to the situations in which motives are expressed. A situation exerts an important press on the individual. It exercises constraints and may provide push. In certain circumstances it is not so much the kind of person a man is, as the kind of situation in which he is placed, that determines his actions.

Many people, not knowing much about the experiment, claim that subjects who go to the end of the board are sadistic. Nothing could be more foolish than an overall characterization of these persons. It is like saying that a person thrown into a swift-flowing stream is necessarily a fast swimmer, or that he has great stamina because he moves so rapidly relative to the bank. The context of action must always be considered. The individual, upon entering the laboratory, becomes integrated into a situation that carries its own momentum. The subject's problem then is how to become disengaged from a situation which is moving in an altogether ugly direction.

The fact that disengagement is so difficult testifies to the potency of the forces that keep the subject at the control board. Are these forces to be conceptualized as individual motives and expressed in the language of personality dynamics, or are they to be seen as the effects of social structure and pressures arising from the situation field?

A full understanding of the subject's action will, I feel, require that both perspectives be adopted. The person brings to the laboratory enduring dispositions toward authority and aggression, and at the same time he becomes enmeshed in a social structure that is no less an objective fact of the case. From the standpoint of personality theory one may ask: What mechanisms of personality enable a person to transfer responsibility to authority? What are the motives underlying obedient and disobedient performance? Does orientation to authority lead to a short-circuiting of the shame-guilt system? What cognitive and emotional defenses are brought into play in the case of obedient and defiant subjects?

The present experiments are not, however, directed toward an exploration of the motives engaged when the subject obeys the experimenter's commands. Instead, they examine the situational variables responsible for the elicitation of obedience. Elsewhere, we have attempted to spell out some of the structural properties of the experimental situation that account for high obedience, and this analysis need not be repeated here (Milgram, 1963). The experimental variations themselves represent our attempt to probe that structure, by systematically changing it and noting the consequences for behavior. It is clear that some situations produce greater compliance with the experimenter's commands than others. However, this does not necessarily imply an increase or decrease in the strength of any single definable motive. Situations producing the greatest obedience could do so by triggering the most powerful, yet perhaps the most idiosyncratic, of motives in each subject confronted by the setting. Or they may simply recruit a greater number and variety of motives in their service. But whatever the motives involved—and it is far from certain that they can ever be known—action may be studied as a direct function of the situation in which it occurs. This has been the approach of the present study, where we sought to plot behavioral regularities against manipulated properties of the social field. Ultimately, social psychology would like to have a compelling *theory of situations* which will, first, present a language in terms of which situations can be defined; proceed to a typology of situations; and then point to the manner in which definable properties of situations are transformed into psychological forces in the individual.[9]

POSTSCRIPT

Almost a thousand adults were individually studied in the obedience research, and there were many specific conclusions regarding the variables that control obedience and disobedience to authority. Some of these have been discussed briefly in the preceding sections, and more detailed reports will be released subsequently.

There are now some other generalizations I should like to make, which do not derive in any strictly logical fashion from the experiments as carried out, but which, I feel, ought to be made. They are formulations of an intuitive sort that have been forced on me by observation of many subjects responding to the pressures of authority. The assertions represent a painful alteration in my own thinking; and since they were acquired only under the repeated impact of direct observation, I have no illusion that they will be generally accepted by persons who have not had the same experience.

With numbing regularity good people were seen to knuckle under the demands of authority and perform actions that were callous and severe. Men who are in everyday life responsible and decent were seduced by the trappings of authority, by the control of their perceptions, and by the uncritical acceptance of the experimenter's definition of the situation, into performing harsh acts.

What is the limit of such obedience? At many points we attempted to establish a boundary. Cries from the victim were inserted; not good enough. The victim claimed heart trouble; subjects still shocked him on command. The victim pleaded that he be let free, and his answers no longer registered on the signal box; subjects continued to shock him. At the outset we had not conceived that such drastic procedures would be needed to generate disobedience, and each step was added only as the ineffectiveness of the earlier techniques became clear. The final effort to establish a limit was the Touch-Proximity condition. But the very first subject in this condition subdued the victim on command, and proceeded to the highest shock level. A quarter of the subjects in this condition performed similarly.

The results, as seen and felt in the laboratory, are to this author disturbing. They raise the possibility that human nature or, more specifically, the kind of character produced in American democratic society cannot be counted on to insulate its citizens from brutality and inhumane treatment at the direction of malevolent authority. A substantial proportion of people do what they are told to do, irrespective of the content of the act and without limitations of conscience, so long as they perceive that the command comes from a legitimate authority. If in this study an anonymous experimenter could successfully command adults to subdue a fifty-year-old man and force on him painful electric shocks against his protests, one can only wonder what government, with its vastly greater authority and prestige, can command of its subjects. There is, of course, the extremely important question of whether malevolent political institutions could or would arise in American society. The present research contributes nothing to this issue.

In an article titled "The Dangers of Obedience," Harold J. Laski wrote:

> . . . civilization means, above all, an unwillingness to inflict unnecessary pain. Within the ambit of that definition, those of us who heedlessly accept the commands of authority cannot yet claim to be civilized men.
>
> . . . Our business, if we desire to live a life, not utterly devoid of meaning and significance, is to accept nothing which contradicts our basic experience merely because it comes to us from tradition or convention or authority. It may well be that we shall be wrong; but our self-expression is thwarted at the root unless the certainties we are asked to accept coincide with the certainties we experience. That is why the condition of freedom in any state is always a widespread and consistent skepticism of the canons upon which power insists.

NOTES

1. This research was supported by two grants from the National Science Foundation: NSF G-17916 and NSF G-24152. Exploratory studies carried out in 1960 were financed by a grant from the Higgins Funds of Yale University. I am grateful to John T. Williams, James J. McDonough, and Emil Elges for the important part they played in the project. Thanks are due also to Alan Elms, James Miller, Taketo Murata, and Stephen Stier for their aid as graduate assistants. My wife, Sasha, performed many valuable services. Finally, I owe a profound debt to the many persons in New Haven and Bridgeport who served as subjects.

2. Consider, for example, J. P. Scott's analysis of war in his monograph on aggression:

> . . . while the actions of key individuals in a war may be explained in terms of direct stimulation to aggression, vast numbers of other people are involved simply by being part of an organized society.
>
> . . . For example, at the beginning of World War I an Austrian archduke was assassinated in Sarajevo. A few days later soldiers from all over Europe were marching toward each other, not because they were stimulated by the archduke's misfortune, but because they had been trained to obey orders. (Slightly rearranged from Scott (1958), *Aggression*, p. 103.)

3. It consisted of an extended discussion with the experimenter and, of equal importance, a friendly reconciliation with the victim. It is made clear that the victim did *not* receive painful electric shocks. After the completion of the experimental series, subjects were sent a detailed report of the results and full purposes of the experimental program. A formal assessment of this procedure points to its overall effectiveness. Of the subjects, 83.7 percent indicated that they were glad to have taken part in the study; 15.1 percent reported neutral

feelings; and 1.3 percent stated that they were sorry to have participated. A large number of subjects spontaneously requested that they be used in further experimentation. Four-fifths of the subjects felt that more experiments of this sort should be carried out, and 74 percent indicated that they had learned something of personal importance as a result of being in the study. Furthermore, a university psychiatrist, experienced in outpatient treatment, interviewed a sample of experimental subjects with the aim of uncovering possible injurious effects resulting from participation. No such effects were in evidence. Indeed, subjects typically felt that their participation was instructive and enriching. A more detailed discussion of this question can be found in Milgram (1964).

4. *To obey* and *to disobey* are not the only terms one could use in describing the critical action of Y. One could say that Y is cooperating with X, or displays conformity with regard to X's commands. However, *cooperation* suggests that X agrees with Y's ends, and understands the relationship between his own behavior and the attainment of those ends. (But the experimental procedure, and, in particular, the experimenter's command that the subject shock the victim even in the absence of a response from the victim, preclude such understanding.) Moreover, cooperation implies status parity for the co-acting agents, and neglects the asymmetrical, dominance-subordination element prominent in the laboratory relationship between experimenter and subject. *Conformity* has been used in other important contexts in social psychology, and most frequently refers to imitating the judgments or actions of others when no explicit requirement for imitation has been made. Furthermore, in the present study there are two sources of social pressure; pressure from the experimenter issuing the commands, and pressure from the victim to stop the punishment. It is the pitting of a common man (the victim) against an authority (the experimenter) that is the distinctive feature of the conflict. At a point in the experiment the victim demands that he be let free. The experimenter insists that the subject continue to administer shocks. Which act of the subject can be interpreted as conformity? The subject may conform to the wishes of his peer or to the wishes of the experimenter, and conformity in one direction means the absence of conformity in the other. Thus the word has no useful reference in this setting, for the dual and conflicting social pressures cancel out its meaning.

In the final analysis, the linguistic symbol representing the subject's action must take its meaning from the concrete context in which the action occurs; and there is probably no word in everyday language that covers the experimental situation exactly, without omissions or irrelevant connotations. It is partly for convenience, therefore, that the terms *obey* and *disobey* are used to describe the subject's actions. At the same time, our use of the words is highly congruent with dictionary meaning.

5. A more detailed account of the laboratory procedure can be found in Milgram (1963). A similar and independently evolved experimental procedure, employing a shock generator, victim, and learning task, was reported by Buss (1961). Buss used the technique for studying aggression, not obedience, and did not make use of the fundamental measure employed in the present study: break-off points.

6. It is difficult to convey on the printed page the full tenor of the victim's responses, for we have no adequate notation for vocal intensity, timing, and

general qualities of delivery. Yet these features are crucial to producing the effect of an increasingly severe reaction to mounting voltage levels. (They can be communicated fully only by sending interested parties the recorded tapes.) In general terms, however, the victim indicates no discomfort until the 75-volt shock is administered, at which time there is a light grunt in response to the punishment. Similar reactions follow the 90- and 105-volt shocks, and at 120 volts the victim shouts to the experimenter that the shocks are becoming painful. Painful groans are heard on administration of the 135-volt shock, and at 150 volts the victim cries out, "Experimenter, get me out of here! I won't be in the experiment any more! I refuse to go on!" Cries of this type continue with generally rising intensity, so that at 180 volts the victim cries out, "I can't stand the pain," and by 270 volts his response to the shock is definitely an agonized scream. Throughout, he insists that he be let out of the experiment. At 300 volts the victim shouts in desperation that he will no longer provide answers to the memory test; and at 315 volts, after a violent scream, he reaffirms with vehemence that he is no longer a participant. From this point on, he provides no answers, but shrieks in agony whenever a shock is administered; this continues through 450 volts. Of course, many subjects will have broken off before this point.

A revised and stronger set of protests was used in all experiments outside the Proximity series. Naturally, new baseline measures were established for all comparisons using the new set of protests.

There is overwhelming evidence that the great majority of subjects, both obedient and defiant, accepted the victims' reactions as genuine. The evidence takes the form of: (a) tension created in the subjects (see discussion of tension); (b) scores on "estimated-pain" scales filled out by subjects immediately after the experiment; (c) subjects' accounts of their feelings in post-experimental interviews; and (d) quantifiable responses to questionnaires distributed to subjects several months after their participation in the experiments. This matter will be treated fully in a forthcoming monograph.

(The procedure in all experimental conditions was to have the naïve subject announce the voltage level before administering each shock, so that— independently of the victim's responses—he was continually reminded of delivering punishment of ever-increasing severity.)

7. Admittedly, the terms *proximity, immediacy, closeness,* and *salience-of-the-victim* are used in a loose sense, and the experiments themselves represent a very coarse treatment of the variable. Further experiments are needed to refine the notion and tease out such diverse factors as spatial distance, visibility, audibility, barrier interposition, etc.

    The Proximity and Touch-Proximity experiments were the only conditions where we were unable to use taped feedback from the victim. Instead, the victim was trained to respond in these conditions as he had in Experiment 2 (which employed taped feedback). Some improvement is possible here, for it should be technically feasible to do a Proximity series using taped feedback.

8. The third condition also led to significantly lower obedience than this first situation, in which the experimenter was present, but it contains technical difficulties that require extensive discussion.

9. My thanks to Professor Howard Leventhal of Yale for strengthening the writing in this paragraph.

REFERENCES

Buss, Arnold H., 1961. *The Psychology of Aggression.* New York and London: John Wiley.

Kierkegaard, S., 1843. *Fear and Trembling.* English edition. Princeton: Princeton University Press, 1941.

Laski, Harold J., 1929. "The dangers of obedience." *Harper's Monthly Magazine* **159,** June, 1–10.

Milgram, S., 1961. "Dynamics of obedience: experiments in social psychology." Mimeographed report, *National Science Foundation,* January 25.

——, 1963. "Behavioral study of obedience." *J. Abnorm. Soc. Psychol.* **67,** 371–378.

——, 1964. "Issues in the study of obedience: a reply to Baumrind." *Amer. Psychol.* **19,** 848–852.

Miller, N. E., 1944. "Experimental studies of conflict." In J. McV. Hunt (ed.), *Personality and the Behavior Disorders.* New York: Ronald Press.

Scott, J. P. 1958. *Aggression.* Chicago: University of Chicago Press.

11

Interpreting Obedience: Error and Evidence[1]

❖

Thus far we have been singularly unsuccessful in finding an experimental task which
would be discontinued, or indeed refused by subjects in an experimental situation . . .

(M. Orne, 1962)

In the October 1968 issue of the *International Journal of Psychiatry*, Orne and
Holland sought to reinterpret the findings of my experimental studies of
obedience and disobedience to authority. In this paper, I shall discuss their
comments and, beyond this, address myself to some of the related questions that
have formed part of Orne's thinking, and which have found their way into his
critique.[2]

To begin, I note that Orne does not question the behavioral outcomes obtained
in the obedience experiments, but focuses on the psychological meaning behind
them. This point of agreement on behavior is important. First, it gives us a
common empirical starting point for our discussion. Second, it places a burden on
the critic. Let us leave open for the moment whether the subject's state of mind is
characterized by the suspiciousness and disbelief that Orne postulates, assuming
only that the subject complies outwardly with the experimenter. The critic must
still ask *why* subjects respond with a show of outward compliance. The forces in a

This paper was first published in *The Social Psychology of Psychological Research*, Arthur G. Miller (ed.),
New York: The Free Press, 1972, pp. 139–154. Reprinted by permission of Alexandra Milgram.

situation that constrain a person to adhere to required external forms cannot be dismissed as inconsequential. Nor in my view is such compliance most profitably seen as a methodological wrinkle but rather as a social fact of interest in its own right. An orientation in terms of demand characteristics, then, is questionable on two counts: (1) it treats compliance merely as if it were an impediment to research, thereby deflecting attention from the substantive issues underlying such compliance; and (2) it is presented as an explanation while it functions mainly as a depreciatory label.

There is a further implication in the locus of Orne's criticism. It is certainly legitimate to accept the behavioral facts and carry out arguments in regard to the psychological attitudes that lie behind them. However, a warning is in order: namely, this shift in no way diminishes the need for evidence in support of argumentation. I am afraid Orne has assumed that once he has moved the argument off the level of behavioral evidence, he is free to proceed on the basis of speculation and anecdote. In this he is quite wrong. Systematic evidence is of decisive importance and must be brought to bear on the argument.

II

What characterizes Orne's piece is gross overstatement of a point that has an element of validity, is corrected for with relative ease by control procedures, and ought to be seen in its proper place. Orne's first major argument is that subjects do not accept the experimental situation at face value. To make matters perfectly clear, let us state explicitly what subjects may fail to believe: (1) they may not believe the experiment is about memory and learning; (2) they may not believe the learner is getting painful shocks; (3) they may not believe the learner is the focus of experiment. Only the second of these points is critical, for as long as the subject believes he is transmitting painful shocks to the learner on command of the experimenter, the essential manipulatory intent of the experiment is achieved. The fact is that most subjects do believe that the shocks are painful, some subjects are unsure about it, and a few subjects do not believe it. This has been assessed at points during the experiment, immediately after the experiment, and in questionnaire and interview studies a year after the experiment. Orne asserts that no evidence has been presented on this question. This is false. The first published report states:

> With few exceptions subjects were convinced of the reality of the experimental situation, that they were administering shocks to another person, and the most potent shocks were extremely painful. In the post-experimental interview subjects were asked: "How painful to the learner were the last few shocks that you administered to him?" Subjects were instructed to indicate

their answers on a printed 14-point scale, ranging from "Not at all painful" to "Extremely painful." The modal response was 14 (Extremely painful) with the mean at 13.42 [1963, p. 375].

Moreover, the occurrence of tension provided striking evidence of the subject's genuine involvement in the experimental conflict, and this has been observed and reported throughout in the form of representative transcripts (1963), scale data (1965b), and filmed accounts (1965a). In the course of a recent debate with Orne (1969), a member of the audience pointed out that he would be willing to consider Orne's interpretation a possibility if, indeed, subjects gave evidence of a wry, tongue-in-check attitude, but that Orne's view was untenable in view of the formidable tension and strain observed. Orne's suggestion that the subjects only *feigned* sweating, trembling, and stuttering to please the experimenter is pathetically detached from reality, equivalent to the statement that hemophiliacs bleed to keep their physicians busy. To be sure, I could certainly improve my image with D. Baumrind (1964), and others who have criticized the experiment because of the tension it induced, constructing a defense on Orne's interpretation, but this would be utterly false, for the conflict *was* present, intensely experienced, and cannot be wished or theorized away.

In all experimental conditions the level of pain was interpreted as very high, bordering on the upper extreme. In condition (02), Voice Feedback (when the victim is audible but not visible), the mean on the 14-point scale for obedient subjects is 11.36 and falls within the "extremely painful" zone of the scale. More than half the obedient subjects use the extreme upper point on the scale, and at least one subject indicated by a + sign that "extremely painful" was not a strong enough designation. Of the 40 subjects in this condition, two indicated on the scale (with scores of 1 and 3) that they did not think the victim received painful shocks, and both

TABLE 11.1 SUBJECTS' ESTIMATE OF PAIN FELT BY VICTIM

	Obedient S's		Defiant S's		
Condition	$\bar{x}$	n	$\bar{x}$	n	$\bar{x}$
Remote victim	13.50	(20)	13.27	(11)	13.42
Voice feedback	11.36	(25)	11.80	(15)	11.53
Proximity	12.69	(16)	11.79	(24)	12.15
Touch proximity	12.25	(28)	11.17	(12)	11.93
Coronary tape(a)	11.40	(26)	12.25	(14)	11.70
Coronary tape(b)	11.98	(20)	12.05	(20)	12.02
Bridgeport replication	11.79	(19)	11.81	(18)	11.80
Women as subjects	12.88	(26)	12.07	(14)	12.60
Experimenter departs	11.67	(31)	12.39	(9)	11.83

TABLE 11.2 RESPONSE TO QUESTION ON BELIEF IN FOLLOW-UP QUESTIONNAIRE

During the experiment	Defiant	Obedient	All subjects
1. I fully believed the learner was getting painful shocks.	62.5% (230)	47.9% (139)	56.1% (369)
2. Although I had some doubts, I believed the learner was *probably* getting the shocks.	22.6% (83)	25.9% (75)	24.0% (158)
3. I just wasn't sure whether the learner was getting the shocks or not.	6.0% (22)	6.2% (18)	6.1% (40)
4. Although I had some doubts, I thought the learner was probably not getting the shocks.	7.6% (28)	16.2% (47)	11.4% (75)
5. I was certain the learner was not getting the shocks.	1.4% (5)	3.8% (11)	2.4% (16)

subjects were obedient. These subjects, it would appear, were not successfully exposed to the manipulatory intent of the experimenter. But even this is not so simple, since denial of an unpleasant action can serve a defensive function, and some subjects come to view their performance in a favorable light only by reconstructing what their state of mind was when they were administering shocks. The question is: Did they hold their disbelief as a firm hypothesis or as a fleeting notion among many other notions?

The broad quantitative picture of subjects' testimony on belief can be examined, among other ways, by scrutinizing responses to a follow-up questionnaire distributed about a year after subjects participated in the study. Item 4 of the questionnaire is reprinted above, along with the distribution of responses to it.

There are several ways to describe the results. Emphasizing the positive side, one could say that only 4 percent of the subjects were certain the learner was *not* getting any shocks, while 96 percent, in some degree or other, felt the learner was receiving the shocks. Or one could put the most negative interpretation possible on the results by asserting that only half of the subjects fully accepted the experimental deception. But the fairest treatment of the data is to say that three-quarters of the subjects (the first two categories), by their own testimony, acted under the belief that they were administering painful shocks. It would have been an easy out at this point to have denied that the hoax had been accepted. But only a fifth of the group indicated having had serious doubts.

David Rosenhan of Swarthmore College carried out a replication of the obedience experiment in order to obtain a base measure for further studies of his own. He took elaborate interviewing steps. Among other things, he established the interviewer as a person independent of the experiment, who demands a detailed account of the subject's experience and probes the issue of belief even to the point of asking, "You really mean you didn't catch on to the experiment?" On the basis of highly stringent criteria of full acceptance, Rosenhan reports that (according to the determination of independent judges), 68.9 percent of the subjects thoroughly accepted the authenticity of the experiment. Examining the performance of these subjects, he reports that 85 percent were fully obedient. (Rosenhan, it must be pointed out, employed a subject population that was younger than that used in the original experiments, and this, I believe, accounts for the higher level of obedience.[3])

When my experimental findings are subjected to a comparable type of analysis, they are not altered in any substantial manner. For example, in condition (02), Voice Feedback, of those subjects who indicated acceptance of the deception (categories 1 and 2), 58 percent were obedient; of those who indicated category 1, 60 percent were obedient. Over all experimental conditions this manner of controlling the data slightly reduced the proportion of obedient-to-defiant subjects. The changes leave the relations among conditions intact and are inconsequential for interpreting the meaning or import of the findings.

In sum, the majority of subjects accept the experimental situation as genuine; a few do not. Within each experimental condition it was my estimate that two to four subjects did not think they were administering painful shocks to the victim, but I adopted a general rule that no subject be removed from the data, because selective removal of subjects on somewhat inprecise criteria is the quickest way to inadvertently shape hypotheses. Even now I am not willing to dismiss those subjects, because it is not clear that their rejection of the technical illusion was a cause of their obedience or a consequence of it. Does it not occur to Orne that cognitive processes may serve to rationalize behavior that the subject has felt compelled to carry out? It is simple indeed for a subject to explain his behavior by stating he did not believe the victim received shocks, and some subjects come to this position as a post facto explanation of their actions. The explanation has no cost to them and goes a long way toward preserving their positive self-conception. It has the additional benefit of demonstrating how astute and clever they were to penetrate a carefully laid cover story.

More important, however, is to be able to see the role of denial in the total process of obedience and disobedience, for denial is not a *deus ex machina* that descends on the laboratory and sweeps away all else. It is rather one specific cognitive adjustment of several that occur in the experiment, and needs to be properly placed in terms of its functioning in the performance of some subjects.

III

Leaving the evidential basis of this discussion, let us now consider the arguments Orne offers to support his idea that subjects see through the experimental illusions. Orne says, first, that the subjects of psychological experiments tend to "view their task as a problem-solving situation which requires them to determine the 'real' situation and respond appropriately." I do not share the belief that people by and large are suspicious, distrustful, and given to outguessing scientific authorities; nor do I think that among postal clerks, high-school teachers, salesmen, engineers, and laborers—our typical subjects—a great deal is known about psychological experiments. It is true, as Orne says, that within university circles a certain "scuttlebutt" develops about such endeavors, but it is very much a matter of local campus culture and, as Orne must surely know, not relevant to this study, which relied on a general not a campus population (1963, 1965b). Some of our subjects were highly intelligent, others of very limited intellectual ability. Very few of them approached the experiment with implicit distrust of the experimenter. Rather than trying to outwit him, subjects occasionally wanted to engage him in personal problems and probably held the idea of a psychiatric interview in their image of psychology. What kind of world does Orne postulate? It is a world populated with mutually suspicious persons, each with concealed motives and working at cross purposes. I do not believe this corresponds to reality, not even the reality of a psychological experiment. I am struck by the fact that Orne not only approaches the question of experimentation from an acutely suspicious point of view, but assumes experimental subjects possess a similar outlook. He supposes that they, too, are searching for concealed motives and hidden meanings, while, in fact, this is true for only a small fraction of subjects of characteristically paranoid outlook.

Orne contends that there are incongruities in the experimental process that give away the deception. He says that a subject would find it implausible that he be required to administer shocks to an individual to test a presumed relation between punishment and learning when the experimenter could as easily give the shocks himself. Yet Orne could determine, by reading that portion of the instructions reprinted in the initial report of the experiment (1963), that a role was assigned to the subject and a reason for his administering the shocks was given. Each subject was told:

> We don't know how much punishment is best for learning, and we don't know how much difference it makes as to who is giving the punishment, whether an adult learns best from a younger or an older person than himself, or many things of that sort. So in this study we are bringing together a number of adults of different occupations and ages. And we're asking some of them to be teachers and some of them to be learners. We want to find out just

what effect different people have on each other as teachers and learners, and also what effect punishment will have on learning in this situation.

Another source of doubt, according to Orne, is "The incongruity between the relatively trivial experiment and the imperturbability of the E on the one hand . . . and the extremity of the victim's suffering. . . ." One could argue with equal conviction that people usually do not assess the relative importance of scientific studies and that the cool, competent stance of the experimenter is the typical posture of authority in modern times, so that casting him in this role contributes to the plausibility of the situation. But the argument can only be resolved by assessment of the subject's acceptance of the situation.[4]

A major problem with the demand characteristic approach is that it is always *post facto*. Orne is quite incapable of knowing what the results of a scientific experiment will be. He only knows how to argue after the results are in. Moreover, he forgets that from the standpoint of a "demand characteristic" analysis, virtually all of the cues in the obedience experiment communicate the necessity to break off the experiment, yet many subjects are unable to do so.

Finally, at times Orne describes the experiment backwards, implying that the subject is told right off to administer dangerous shocks to a screaming person. Far from it, there is an important developmental aspect to the experiment which comes to constrain and control the subject's behavior. The early stages of the experiment are quite proper, even uneventful; it is only gradually as the shock levels intensify that conflict arises. The earlier parts of the experiment, in which any reasonable person would participate, only gradually ease the subject into a conflict; when conflict arises the subject has already routinized his behavior, committed himself to the procedure and, in consequence, is locked into the situation. The shifting, step by step, and piecemeal escalation of shocks plays an important part in exacting obedience, and, moreover, sets the experiment apart from other studies, such as the nitric acid study, which lack this temporal component.

IV

Since Orne makes frequent reference to the experiments he has carried out, some comments ought to be made about them. Many of them are not experiments at all, but only incidents involving one or two individuals. Orne rarely carries his incidents out in sufficient numbers to view the full range of responses to them. Yet they represent, relatively speaking, strong points in Orne's style of inquiry, for often he dispenses with evidence altogether and turns with an air of authority to anecdotes. The anecdotal method does not have much standing in science and has never, to my knowledge, settled anything. Nonetheless, we may critically examine some of Orne's stories, if only to expose the flawed logic with which they are applied to present issues.

Orne tells us that about eighty years ago a hypnotized woman was induced to perform many seemingly antisocial acts, such as stabbing a victim, but could not be induced to undress before an assemblage of males. Orne concludes that the woman did not believe she was inflicting stab wounds. First, this is a gratuitous assumption. Neither Orne nor I have the slightest idea of what went through this woman's mind, and there is no evidence now to help us decide.

But there is a more significant point. Orne asserts that an act such as undressing possesses an irreducible meaning that "transcends the context" [Orne, 1968, p. 228] and therefore cannot be elicited by a hypnotist. One imagines the hypnotist standing Svengali-like over the poor girl, intoning, "You are in my power: Undress! Undress!" All very fine, but it is hard to see what this has to do with the exercise of authority through ordinary channels of social structure, which is the subject matter of the experiments on obedience.

A military officer does not need to rely on animal magnetism or Svengali-like poses to exact compliance from his subordinates. The parties are embedded in a socially defined hierarchical structure and this fact dominates their behavior. Social structure is not a mysterious thing. From the standpoint of the participating subject it is the conviction that another person, by virtue of his status, has the right to prescribe behavior for him.

Let us return to undressing the girl, but now shift from the irrelevant issue of hypnotism to the pertinent question of social structure. It is well known that under a proper set of role relationships, e.g., when visiting a gynecologist, a woman not only undresses but allows her body to be thoroughly inspected. So we are left to conclude that not even hypnotism can bring about what is readily and routinely accomplished by legitimized societal roles. And that is precisely what we have investigated: our subjects are not hypnotized, but they are defined into social roles that place them in a position of subordination vis-à-vis the experimenter.

Let us note a further point. The woman taking part in her medical checkup does not deny that she is undressing before a male stranger but she defines the meaning of the act in a manner that permits it. In the experiment the subject does not deny he is shocking the victim, but he defines the meaning of his act in terms of the constructive purposes outlined by the experimenter. This is not an alternative to complying with authority, but is the typical cognitive concomitant of such compliance.[5]

Orne asserts that direct inferences about obedience in real life cannot be drawn from an experimental context. His documentation consists of a speculative anecdote that is offered as a parallel to the obedience experi-

ment, but which on analysis proves to be misleading and without pertinence.

Orne states:

> Anyone who believes direct inference about obedience in real life can be
> drawn from an experimental context should ask his secretary to type a letter
> and, after making certain there are no errors, ask her to tear it up and retype it.
> With rare exceptions, two or three such trials should be sufficient to ensure
> that the E will require a new secretary.

It is hard to see that this anecdote has anything to do with my
obedience experiment or real life. In the experiment, the act of shocking
the victim is coordinated to a set of rational purposes concerning advancement of knowledge about the effects of punishment on learning. Nor does
the anecdote have much to do with obedience in other settings. Not even
in the army are individuals ordered to perform a destructive act for its
own sake. The burning of a village containing innocent civilians is carried
out with the explanation that it is to impress the populace, or to frighten
the inhabitants into cooperating, or to enforce a system of military justice.
Were the secretary in Orne's anecdote provided a set of rational purposes
for the destructive act, Orne's story would end differently.

The criminal-act experiments on which Orne rests much of his
argument also bear little resemblance to the obedience experiment or to
life outside the laboratory. In these experiments, the subject is simply told
to stab or throw nitric acid at a human target. Orne contends that the
subject knows that no one really will be harmed and therefore obeys. It is
the same in the obedience experiment, Orne says. But it is not the same.
An important feature of the nitric acid experiment is that a meaningless
act is arbitrarily demanded of the subject. In the obedience experiments,
the act of shocking the victim is tightly embedded in a set of socially
constructive purposes, namely, the furtherance of knowledge in regard to
memory and learning processes. Obedience occurs not as an end in itself
but as an instrumental element in a situation that the subject construes as
significant and meaningful. Further, in contrast to the nitric acid study, in
the obedience experiment the experimenter explicitly denies the possibility of harm. He states, "Although the shocks can be extremely painful,
they cause no permanent tissue damage." (The subject also watches, after
the electrode is attached to the victim's wrist, the application of a paste "to
avoid blisters and burns.") The indications of harm come from other
sources, and the subject must weigh information from his own senses
against his trust in and dependence on the experimenter. Most of Orne's
analysis ignores this critical aspect of the experiment and is simply not
relevant to it.[6]

In summary, the several points on which the obedience experiment
differs from the models provided by Orne are: First, we are not dealing

with the *personal power* of the experimenter as in the case of hypnosis but, quite explicitly, with the consequence of social structure for action. A clearly defined hierarchical relationship exists between subject and authority. Second, the purposes which authority defines are not senseless and stupid (as in the nitric acid study) but are readily accepted by the subject as worthwhile. Third, the experiment has an important temporal aspect to it. It begins with the mutual consent of all parties and only gradually leads into conflict.

V

The issue of ecological validity comes down to two very different though equally important points that are not kept clearly distinct in Orne's thinking. The first question is: Within the context of a psychological experiment, will a subject accept that he is administering painful shocks to another person against his will? The question must be resolved by resorting to evidence and not simply rhetoric. The second question, which is analytically quite separate, is: Does the behavior established in the laboratory have any generality beyond the circumstances in which it was observed, or is the experimental situation so special that nothing that was observed can contribute to a general view of the functions of obedience in wider social life?

Orne observes that behavior is legitimized in the subject-experimenter relationship. He sees this only as getting in the way of establishing general truths, while in actuality, it is precisely an understanding of behavior *within* legitimized social relationships that the investigation seeks to attain. What Orne can construe only as an impediment is in fact a strategic research opportunity.

Orne wishes to show the uniqueness of the psychological experiment as a context for eliciting behavior, but his manner of supporting the view is specious. Thus he informs us that "it was essential for the subject to be in an actual subject-experimenter relationship in order to have him carry out these actions; despite repeated attempts not one of our colleagues could be induced to attempt any one of these acts." This merely says that the presence of legitimized, hierarchical role relations is needed for exacting compliance. And this is correct. But the further implication that only the subject-experimenter relationship possesses this quality is not merely gratuitous, but blind to the reality of social life, which is replete with hierarchical structures, and which in significant measure is composed of them. Orne's colleagues did not comply for the same reason, that, during a parade, when the marshal shouts "left face" the military band turns left but the onlooking pedestrians do not. One group consists of subordinates in a hierarchical structure and the other does not. We can in a despairing moment conclude that this establishes the uniqueness of a parade as a social situation, or we can see through to the deeper principle that only persons defined into a hierarchical structure will respond to it. It is precisely those situations in which a person is defined into a hierarchical structure that constitutes the subject matter of the obedience experiment.

Perhaps the main source of confusion in Orne's thinking is his failure to keep clearly in mind the distinction between social occasions that are hierarchically organized and those that are not. To move from a discussion of one into the other, without taking account of the critical change, can only lead to muddled thought.

The occasion we term a psychological experiment shares its essential structural properties with other situations composed of subordinate-superordinate roles. In all such circumstances the person responds not so much to the content of what is required but on the basis of his relationship to the person who requires it. Indeed, I am tempted to assert this principle in more drastic form: where legitimate authority is the source of action, *relationship overwhelms content*. That is what is meant by the importance of social structure and that is what is demonstrated in the present experiment.

VI

The obedience experiment makes use of a technical illusion, namely that the learner was receiving shocks, when in fact he was an actor. Orne asserts that, according to his analysis, cues in the experiment would not allow the subject to accept this illusion. In fact, observation and data show that Orne's conjecture is wrong, that most subjects do accept the illusion.

There are, to be sure, many alternative methods for accruing evidence, and if the use of a technical illusion is the stumbling block to confidence in the results, then the investigator who wishes to study obedience can do two things. First, he can study the performance of only those subjects who fully accept the illusion. We have already discussed how the data of Milgram and Rosenhan, controlled in this manner, continue to yield levels of obedience comparable to those reported in the original articles. A second approach is to study situations in which no illusion is required because the naïve subject himself serves as the victim. Even when subjects cannot possibly deny the genuineness of what they are doing, because it is happening to them, they comply in extraordinary degree. Thus Turner and Solomon (1962) and Shor (1962) have reported that subjects willingly accept near traumatizing shocks when serving in their experiments. Kudirka (1965) presents an experiment of unusual interest in which subjects were instructed to perform a highly noxious, although not dangerous, task, namely, eating bitter crackers (they were soaked in strong quinine solution). The crackers were extremely distasteful and gave rise to facial distortions, grunts, groans, and in some subjects feelings of nausea. Since in this experiment the subject is himself the victim, none of Orne's criticism relating to deception is applicable. The question is whether compliance with the experimenter will occur in any significant degree. The first finding was that the requirement of obedience was so powerful that the experiment could not be done with the experimenter present: virtually all subjects obeyed. Kudirka, therefore, consciously weakened the experimenter's authority by removing him from the laboratory. Even under these circumstances 14 of the 19 subjects continued to the end of the experiment, each one ingesting, frequently with considerable disgust, 36 quinine soaked crackers.

Orne himself (1962b) has used the example of subjects carrying out extremely boring, stupid, and meaningless tasks (such as performing endless serial additions, then tearing up answer sheets) to show the power of the experimenter to induce action in his subjects. He says that although these actions may appear stupid, subjects perform them because they occur within a psychological experiment. When Orne moves on to the obedience experiment, however, he shifts his argument. The power of the experimenter, which Orne so carefully demonstrated, suddenly evaporates. Whereas his subjects genuinely did carry out actions prescribed by the experimenter, Orne would have us believe that my subjects did not. This is, at best, twisted logic, and Orne really cannot have it both ways. On the one hand he asserts an extreme degree of control over the subject, and on the other hand he denies this control exists in the present experiment. It is far more logical to see the obedience experiment as climaxing a consistent line of research demonstrating the power of authority, a line that can be traced to Frank (1944), through Orne (1962b), and into the present research.

His argument is further weakened by his failure to come to grips with the Bridgeport variation of the experiment in which the university setting was eliminated. For years Orne has pointed to the benignity of the university and hospital setting and the manner in which these specific contexts invalidate experimental studies of antisocial behavior. Insofar as Orne's general position is concerned, the implication of the Bridgeport experiment would seem to be that the university context may be less important than thought in the elicitation of antisocial behavior and that whatever elementary social structure is required for its elicitation can function independently of established, benevolent organizations.

At the conclusion of his critical evaluation, Orne calls for "experiments that are not recognized as such by the subjects" to elucidate the true nature of man. I call his attention, then, to a study in which a group of nurses, on duty in hospital wards, were the unknowing subjects (Hofling, et al., 1966). The nurses were given over the telephone an irregular order to administer medication. The voice of the caller, purporting to be a known physician, was unfamiliar to the nurse; the medicine was not on the ward stocklist and thus unauthorized; the dose requested was double the maximum dose shown on the pill box; and the procedure of ordering medication by telephone was in violation of hospital policy. Yet of the 22 nurses tested in this fashion, 21 gave the medication as ordered. In reply to a questionnaire, a majority of a control group of nurses said that they would not have given the medication. The parallel results found in Hofling's results in a naturalistic setting and those found in my laboratory study are striking and lend support to the ecological validity of my laboratory findings.

Ecological validity refers to mapping the range of conditions under which a phenomenon will appear. If Orne is saying there are more experiments to be done, and the present experiments do not give all the answers, I entirely agree with him. But the ultimate effect of Orne's work seems to be the denial of scientific knowledge.

Orne does a disservice of his high methodological ideas when he pursues his doctrines so zealously that, in order to make them fit, he misstates the manner in which the obedience study was conducted (p. 143), or continues to insist on his presuppositions in the face of contrary evidence (p. 139). For we must then ask whether this theory is a useful scientific analysis or shades into an autistic construction in which the themes of conspiracy, distrust, contaminants, and concealed motives play a commanding part. Without question, one may legitimately ask whether the subjects believed the victim received painful shocks, but the answer resides in evidence, not the infallibility of Orne's presuppositions.

Orne's arguments, built largely on anecdotes, are slippery and shift to meet the needs of a limited intellectual orientation. Their aim seems to be to deny the reality of a phenomenon, whether it be hypnosis (1959, 1965), sensory deprivation (1964), general experimentation (1962b), or obedience (1968). Orne's doctrine begins with a population of subjects who are actively suspicious and distrustful, except when trust is the ingredient that will render the experiment invalid; then they are trustful (Orne, 1968, p. 291). Demand characteristics come next: The experimenter is not really studying what he wants to study, for the subject has thwarted the possibility of objective inquiry by giving him only what he wants to hear. Evidence for this view is nonexistent, and indeed, Sigall, Aronson, and Van Hoose (1970) have recently reported a study showing it does not hold up.

In any case, Orne realizes that the argument of the "cooperating subject" cannot invalidate the obedience experiment, since the experimenter makes quite explicit to the subject what he "wants," and the degree to which the subject gives him what he "wants" constitutes the actual experimental measure. Accordingly, Orne again shifts his argument, arguing that outward behavior is not what it seems to be, and there are hidden meanings beneath the surface. One might note that Orne's interest in the hidden meaning is pursued in disregard of the manifest meaning of the behavior and, indeed, is employed to discount what is most apparent.

Orne does not hesitate to use the obedience experiment to discredit hypnotic phenomena (1965); having done this he next turns to discredit the obedience experiment, introducing irrelevant arguments and misstatements of fact along the way. He next asserts the unqualified uniqueness of psychological experiments, so that nothing found within them has relevance to anything else. The overall pattern of this work does not point to the possibilities for studying phenomena, but only to the possibility for discrediting them. Orne does not see a possible link between the compliance found in his studies and the compliance observed in the obedience experiments, for his aim in reporting his findings of compliance is to show how impossible the experimental situation was for determining scientific truth. Finally, there is no substance in things, only methodological wrinkles. This seems to me the history of the school of social psychology which Orne has assiduously cultivated. I do not believe that, in its present one-sided form, it constitutes a contribution to our understanding of human behavior. While specific details of this viewpoint are sometimes plausible, the rigid presuppositions animating such ideology invariably deform the total picture until it no longer corresponds with reality.

Certain methodological correctives derived from this point of view can, I believe, be of value. Increased experimental sophistication in the form of careful interviewing and avoidance of obvious pitfalls (e.g., employing psychology majors as subjects) can enhance the quality of experimentation. But these steps are only helpful when detached from the tunnel vision of conspiratorial thought and applied with a sense of balance to the problem at hand.

VII

Despite the rhetorical vigor of the Orne and Holland piece, it contains a good deal of error and much that is irrelevant. Let us summarize its major deficiencies:

1. Orne's case rests on the supposition that subjects do not believe they are administering painful shocks to the learner. He builds this case not by looking at evidence, but by anecdote and by weaving a speculative analysis not based on fact. In doing so he disregards information obtained by direct observations, interviewing, quantitative scales, and questionnaire studies, all of

which indicate that most subjects accept the experiment at face value.

2. If we are uneasy about the degree to which the authenticity of the experiment was experienced by a fraction of the subjects, we may take the step of considering only those subjects for whom we are certain the manipulatory intent was most fully achieved. For the critical question is not whether some subjects disbelieved, but whether, among these who did fully believe, performance was such that the major conclusions are altered. The data of several investigators show that the phenomenon of obedience holds up for subjects who fully accepted the experiment at face value.

3. Orne mechanically applies a critique of the experiments based on his criticism of hypnotic phenomena. This is the wrong model. Obedience to authority explicitly treats of the consequences of social structure for behavior. The experimental situation is constructed of hierarchically defined role relations. All of Orne's illustrations showing the power of social structure do not, as he believes, invalidate the findings, but only serve to show how general is the phenomenon.

4. If deception is the key issue, then all that the investigator interested in obedience needs to do is to study behavior in which the subject himself is the victim, in which case Orne's criticism of plausibility cannot apply. Studies of this sort have been reported. All the evidence, including that obtained by Orne, points to the extreme compliance of subjects in obeying the experimenter and carrying out acts that are stupid, tedious, noxious, and painful. Orne himself writes he could not find any task which subjects would refuse to do. That was an insight he ought to have taken seriously and pursued to its logical conclusion.

5. Orne asserts that the university context invalidates studies of antisocial behavior, but fails to come to grips with a replication of the experiment run with no visible university affiliation.

6. The trouble with "demand characteristics" is that those who rely on the concept are incapable of predicting the results of an experiment and only know how to apply the label after the facts are in. Then, any number of "demand characteristic" analyses can be formulated. Indeed, the strongest case can be made for the view that all of the cues in the study tell the subject of the necessity to break off. Yet many of them are unable to break with authority.

7. The basic logical contradiction in Orne's argument is that at one moment he argues for the extreme compliance of subjects to experimental commands, and at the next he argues against the reality of such compliance. A set of shifting arguments is em-

ployed in the service of nihilistic outlook. With far greater logic, one can set the obedience experiment in a context of research that shows, with increasing clarity and force, the profound consequences of submission to authority, a line of research to which Orne's early work (1962b) has contributed in an important way.

NOTES

1. The author wishes to thank Barbara Kline, Mary Englander, and Lynne Steinberg for assistance in preparing this paper.
2. For brevity of reference I shall employ Orne's name exclusively in dealing with the above paper. This is not in any way meant to diminish the contribution of Dr. Holland to the paper, but rather is used to be concise and to focus my criticism on a well-known body of methodological philosophy which has appeared under Orne's name.
3. Holland's thesis (1969), though it contains many serious flaws of procedure which are fatal to the successful replication of the experiment, nonetheless offers supporting data on the issue. By Holland's own calculation, only a quarter of the subjects were successfully subjected to the manipulatory intent of the experiment. He would be perfectly correct, then, in looking at these subjects and determining the proportion of obedient subjects. It turns out that 70 percent of his "good" subjects are obedient, a figure that slightly exceeds my own figures, but is nonetheless of the same order of magnitude. Unfortunately, Holland carried out the study in 1967, and employed as his subjects students in an introductory psychology class. The author should have steered as far clear from psychology undergraduates as possible, for they would constitute the worst possible subjects for an experiment in which prior knowledge of the experiment is a fatal contaminant.
4. Recently, Ring, Wallston, and Corey (1970) carried out an obedience experiment in which the experimenter's behavior was made more animated and responsive, and this does not lead to any decrement in obedience. Instead of electric shock, the authors substituted excruciatingly painful noise fed to the subject's ear. Ninety-one percent of the subjects were maximally obedient.
5. Orne may properly pose the question: Can one devise an *experiment* in which women will undress? Of course it is possible to devise such an experiment. Naturally, the act of undressing would have to be coordinated to a set of rational purposes that the subject could accept. Indeed, an experiment has already been carried out by Masters and Johnson (1966) at Washington University in which, in the course of studies of sexual response, women—some prostitutes but others ordinary girls—not only undressed before the investigators but masturbated and engaged in coitus as well. Can we expect Orne to write an article arguing that the women did not really think they were engaging in coitus because of the imperturbable quality of the investigators?
6. Incidentally, Orne believes that if unhypnotized subjects throw nitric acid at individuals it is because they believe they will not really harm the other individual. My guess is that there is more to it than this, that in some degree they do not feel accountable for what they are doing.

REFERENCES

BAUMRIND, D., "Some thoughts on ethics of research: After reading Milgram's 'Behavioral study of obedience.'" *American Psychologist* 1964, **19**: 421–423.

FRANK, J.D., "Experimental studies of personal pressure and resistance." *Journal of General Psychology*, 1944, **30**: 23–64.

HOFLING, C. K., BROTZMAN, E., DALRYMPLE, S., GRAVES, N., AND PIERCE, C. M., "An experimental study in nurse-physician relationships." *The Journal of Nervous and Mental Disease*, 1966, **143** (2): 171–180.

HOLLAND, C. H. "Sources of variance in the experimental investigation of behavioral obedience." Unpublished doctoral dissertation, University of Connecticut, 1967.

KUDIRKA, N. K., "Defiance of authority under peer influence." Unpublished doctoral dissertation, Yale University, 1965.

MASTERS, W. H., AND JOHNSON, V. E., *Human Sexual Response*. Boston: Little, Brown and Co., 1966.

MILGRAM, S., "Behavioral study of obedience." *Journal of Abnormal and Social Psychology*, 1963, **67**: 371–378.

———, *Obedience* (a filmed experiment). Distributed by the New York University Film Library, Copyright 1965 (a).

———, "Some conditions of obedience and disobedience to authority." *Human Relations*, 1965, **18**: 57–75 (b).

ORNE, M. T., "The nature of hypnosis: Artifact and essence." *Journal of Abnormal and Social Psychology*, 1959, **58**: 277–299.

———, "Antisocial behavior and hypnosis: Problems of control and validation in empirical studies." In G. H. Estabrooks (ed.), *Hypnosis: Current problems*. New York: Harper and Row, 1962 (a).

———, "On the social psychology of the psychological experiment: With particular reference to demand characteristics and their implications." *American Psychologist*, 1962, **17** (11): 776–783 (b).

ORNE, M. T., AND Evans, F. J., "Social control in the psychological experiment: Antisocial behavior and hypnosis." *Journal of Personality and Social Psychology*, 1965, **1**, 189–200.

ORNE, M. T., AND HOLLAND, C. C., "On the ecological validity of laboratory deceptions." *International Journal of Psychiatry*, 1968, **6** (4): 282–293.

ORNE, M. T., AND MILGRAM, S., "Obedience or demand characteristics." A debate held at the University of Pennsylvania on February 19, 1969.

ORNE, M. T., AND SCHEIBE, K. E., "The contribution of nondeprivation factors in the production of sensory deprivation effects." *Journal of Abnormal and Social Psychology*, 1964, **68** (1): 3–12.

ORNE, M. T., SHEEHAN, P. W., AND EVANS, F. J., "Occurrence of post-hypnotic behavior outside the experimental setting." *Journal of Personality and Social Psychology*, 1968, **9** (2, Pt. 1): 189–196.

RING, K., WALLSTON, K. AND COREY, M., "Mode of debriefing as a factor affecting subjective reaction to a Milgram-type obedience experiment—an ethical inquiry." *Representative Research in Social Psychology*, 1970, **1** (1): 67–88.

Rosenhan, D., "Some origins of concern for others." In P. Mussen, J. Langer, and M. Covington (eds.), *Trends and Issues in Developmental Psychology.* New York: Holt, Rinehart & Winston, 1969.

———, "Obedience and rebellion: Observations on the Milgram three-party paradigm." In preparation.

Shor, R. E., "Physiological effects of painful stimulation during hypnotic analgesia under conditions designed to minimize anxiety." *International Journal of Clinical and Experimental Hypnosis,* 1962, **10**: 183–202.

Sigall, H., Aronson, E., and Van Hoose, T., "The cooperative subject: Myth or reality?" *Journal of Experimental Social Psychology,* 1970, **6**: 1–10.

Turner, L. H., and Solomon, R. L., "Human traumatic avoidance learning: Theory and experiments on the operant-respondent distinction and failures to learn." *Psychological Monographs,* 1962, **76** (40, whole no. 559).

12

Subject Reaction: The Neglected Factor in the Ethics of Experimentation

———— ❖ ————

Social psychology is concerned with the way in which individual behavior, thoughts, and action are affected by the presence of other people. Although experimentation is not the only way of garnering knowledge in the discipline, it is a major tool of inquiry. As experiments in social psychology typically involve human subjects, they necessarily raise ethical issues, some of which I will discuss here.

INFORMED CONSENT

Many regard informed consent as the cornerstone of ethical practice in experimentation with human subjects. Yet social psychology has until now been unable to assimilate this principle into its routine experimental procedures. Typically, subjects are brought into an experiment without being informed of its true purpose. Indeed, sometimes subjects are misinformed. Is such a procedure ever justifiable?

Herbert Kelman[1] has distinguished two quite different explanations for not informing the potential subject of the nature of the experiment in which he is to

This article first appeared in *The Hastings Center Report*, October 1977, pp. 19–23. © The Hastings Center, 1977. Reprinted by permission.

take part. One might term the first the motivational explanation; that is, if one told the subject what the experiment was to be like, he might refuse to participate in it. Misinforming people to gain their participation appears a serious violation of the individual's rights, and cannot routinely constitute an ethical basis for subject recruitment.

The second, more typical, reason for not informing a subject is that many experiments in social psychology cannot be carried out if the subject knows about the experiment beforehand.

Consider in this connection Solomon Asch's classic study[2] of group pressure and conformity. The subject is told that he is to take part in a study on the perception of lines. He is asked to make a judgment as to which of three lines is equivalent in length to a standard line, but he does so in the presence of other individuals who, unknown to him, are working for the experimenter and give wrong answers. The experimenter's purpose is to see whether the subject will go along with the erroneous group information or resist the group and give the correct answer.

Clearly the subject is misinformed in several respects. He is told that he is to take part in an experiment on perception rather than group pressure. He is not informed that the others present are working for the experimenter, but is led to believe that they have the same relationship to the experimenter as he. It is apparent that if a subject were informed of the true purpose before participating in the study, he could not experience the psychological conflict that is at the crux of Asch's study. The subject is not denied the information because the experimenter fears he would not participate in the study, but for strictly epistemological reasons, that is, for somewhat the same reason the author of a murder mystery does not reveal to the reader who the culprit is: to do so would undermine the psychological effects of the reading experience.

A majority of the experiments carried out in social psychology use some degree of misinformation. Such practices have been denounced as "deception" by critics, and the term "deception experiment" has come to be used routinely, particularly in the context of discussions concerning the ethics of such procedures. But in such a context, the term "deception" somewhat biases the issue. It is preferable to use morally neutral terms such as "masking, "staging," or "technical illusions" in describing such techniques, because it is not possible to make an objective ethical judgment on a practice unless it is described in terms that are not themselves condemnatory.

Is the use of technical illusions ever justified in experiments? The simplest response, and the one that is most socially and ethically comfortable, is to assert unequivocally that they are not. We all know that honesty and a fully informed relationship with the subject is highly desirable and should be implemented whenever possible. The problem is that many also believe strongly in the value of inquiry in social psychology, of its potential to enlighten us about human social behavior, and ultimately to benefit us in important ways. Admittedly, this is a faith, but one which impels us to carefully examine whether the illusions and misinformation required by experiments have any claim to legitimacy. We know that illusions are accepted in other domains without affronting our moral sensibilities. To use a simple-minded example, on radio programs, sound-effects of prancing horses are typically created by a sound-effects man who uses split coconut shells; rainfall is created by sand falling on metal sheets, and so forth. A certain number of listeners know about this, some do not; but we do not accuse such programs of deceiving their listeners. Rather we accept the fact that these are technical illusions used in support of a dramatic effort.

Most experiments in social psychology, at least the good ones, also have a dramatic component. Indeed, in the best experiments the subjects are brought into a dramaturgical situation in which the script is only partially written: it is the subject's actions that complete the script, providing the information sought by the investigator. Is the use of technical illusions to be permitted in radio programs, but not scientific inquiry?

There are many instances in everyday life in which misinformation is tolerated or regarded as legitimate. We do not cringe at the idea of giving children misinformation about Santa Claus, because we feel it is a benign illusion, and common sense tells us it is not harmful. Furthermore, the practice is legitimized by tradition. We may give someone misinformation that takes him to a surprise party. The absolutists may say that this is an immoral act, that in doing so one has lied to another person. But it is more important to focus on the person who is the recipient of this information. Does he find it a demeaning experience, or a delightful treat?

One thing is clear: masking and technical illusions ought never to be used unless they are indispensable to the conduct of an inquiry. Honesty and openness are the only desirable basis of transaction with people generally. This still leaves open the question of whether such devices are permissible when they cannot be avoided in a scientific inquiry.

There is another side to this issue. In the exercise of virtually every profession there may be some exemption from general moral practice which permits the profession to function. For example, although a citizen who has witnessed a murder has a moral obligation to come forth with this information, lawyers have a right—indeed an obligation—of "privileged communication." A lawyer may know that his client has committed a murder, and is obligated not to tell the authorities. In other words, a generally accepted moral obligation is suspended and transformed in the case of legal practice, because in the long run we consider this exemption beneficial to society.

Similarly, it is generally impermissible to examine the genitals of strange women. But it is a technical requirement for the practice of obstetrics and gynecology. Once again, for technical reasons, we suspend

The Obedience Experiments

In order to take a close look at the act of obeying, I set up a simple experiment at Yale University. Eventually, the experiment was to involve more than a thousand participants and would be repeated at several universities, but at the beginning, the conception was simple. A person comes to a psychological laboratory and is told to carry out a series of acts that come increasingly into conflict with conscience. The main question is how far the participant will comply with the experimenter's instructions before refusing to carry out the actions required of him.

But the reader needs to know a little more detail about the experiment. Two people come to a psychology laboratory to take part in a study of memory and learning. One of them is designated as a "teacher" and the other a "learner." The experimenter explains that the study is concerned with the effects of punishment on learning. The learner is conducted into a room, seated in a chair, his arms strapped to prevent excessive movement, and an electrode attached to his wrist. He is told that he is to learn a list of word pairs; whenever he makes an error, he will receive electric shocks of increasing intensity.

The real focus of the experiment is the teacher. After watching the learner being strapped into place, he is taken into the main experimental room and seated before an impressive shock generator. Its main feature is a horizontal line of thirty switches, ranging from 15 volts to 450 volts, in 15-volt increments. There are also verbal designations which range from SLIGHT SHOCK TO DANGER—SEVERE SHOCK. The teacher is told that he is to administer the learning test to the man in the other room. When the learner responds correctly, the teacher moves on to the next item; when the other man gives an incorrect answer, the teacher is to give him an electric shock. He is to start at the lowest shock level (15 volts) and to increase the level each time the man makes an error, going through 30 volts, 45 volts, and so on.

The "teacher" is a genuinely naïve subject who has come to the laboratory to participate in an experiment. The "learner," or victim, is an actor who actually receives no shock at all. The point of the experiment is to see how far a person will proceed in a concrete and measurable situation in which he is ordered to inflict increasing pain on a protesting victim. At what point will the subject refuse to obey the experimenter?

Conflict arises when the man receiving the shock begins to indicate that he is experiencing discomfort. At 75 volts, the "learner" grunts. At 120 volts he complains verbally; at 150 he demands to be released from the experiment. His protests continue as the shocks escalate, growing increasingly vehement and emotional. At 285 volts his response can only be described as an agonized scream.

Observers of the experiment agree that its gripping quality is somewhat obscured in print. For the subject, the situation is not a game; conflict is intense and obvious. On the one hand, the manifest suffering of the learner presses him to quit. On the other, the experimenter, a legitimate authority to whom the subject feels some commitment, enjoins him to continue. Each time the subject hesitates to administer shock, the experimenter orders him to continue. To extricate himself from the situation, the subject must make a clear break with authority. The aim of this investigation was to find when and how people would defy authority in the face of a clear moral imperative.

From Obedience to Authority:
An Experimental View
by Stanley Milgram
(New York: Harper & Row, 1974), pp. 3–4.

a general moral rule in the exercise of a profession, because we believe the profession is beneficial to society.

The question arises: is there any comparable exemption due the social scientist because of technical requirements in the kind of work he does, which in the long run, we believe will benefit society? It is true that most often the individual participant in an experiment is not the beneficiary. Rather it is society as a whole that benefits, or at least, that is the supposition of scientific inquiry.

Still another side to the use of staging by social psychologists is frequently overlooked. The illusions employed in most experiments are usually short-term. They are sustained only insofar as they are required for the purpose of the experiment. Typically, the subject is informed of the experiment's true character immediately after he has participated in it. If for thirty minutes the experimenter holds back on the truth, at the conclusion he reaffirms his confidence in the subject by extending his trust to him by a full revelation of the purpose and procedures of the experiment. It is odd how rarely critics of social psychology experiments mention this characteristic feature of the experimental hour.

From a formal ethical standpoint, the question of misinformation in social psychology experiments is important, because dissimulation subverts the possibility of informed consent. Indeed, the emphasis on "deception" has virtually preempted discussion of ethics among social psychologists. Some feel it is a misplaced emphasis. Support is given to this view by a recent study by Elinor Mannucci.[3] She questioned 192 laymen concerning their reaction to ethical aspects of psychology experiments, and found that they regard deception as a relatively minor issue. They were far more concerned with the quality of the experience they would undergo as subjects. For example, despite the "deceptive" elements in the Asch experiment the great majority of respondents in Mannucci's study were enthusiastic about it, and expressed admiration for its elegance and significance. Of course, the layman's view need not be the final word, but it cannot be disregarded, and my general argument is that far more attention needs to be given to the experiences and views of those who actually serve as subjects in experiments.

NEGATIVE EFFECTS

Is an experiment that produces some sort of negative, aversive, or stressful effect in the subject ever justified? In this matter, two parameters seem critical: first, the intensity of the negative experience, and second, its duration. Clearly, the discussion that follows refers to effects that do not permanently damage a subject, and which most typically do not exceed in intensity experiences which the subject might encounter in ordinary life.

One thing is clear. If we assert categorically that negative emotions can never ethically be created in the laboratory, then it follows that highly significant domains of human experience are excluded from experimental study. For example, we would never be able to study stress by experimental means; nor could we implicate human subjects in experiments involving conflict. In other words, only experiments that aroused neutral or positive emotions would be considered ethical topics for experimental investigation. Clearly, such a stricture would lead to a very lopsided psychology, one that caricatured rather than accurately reflected human experience.

Moreover, historically, among the most deeply informative experiments in social psychology are those that examine how subjects resolve conflicts, for example: Asch's study of group pressure studies the conflict between truth and conformity; Bibb Latané and John Darley's bystander studies[4] create a conflict as to whether the subject should implicate himself in other people's troubles or not get involved; my studies of obedience[5] create a conflict between conscience and authority. If the experience of conflict is categorically to be excluded from social psychology, then we are automatically denying the possibility of studying such core human issues by experimental means. I believe that this would be an irreparable loss to any science of human behavior.

My own studies of obedience were criticized because they created conflict and stress in some of the subjects. Let me make a few comments about this. First, in this experiment I was interested in seeing to what degree a person would comply with an experimental authority who gave orders to act with increasing harshness against a third person. I wanted to see when the subject would refuse to go on with the experiment. The results of the experiment showed first that it is more difficult for many people to defy the experimenter's authority than was generally supposed. The second finding is that the experiment often places a person in considerable conflict. In the course of the experiment subjects sometimes fidget, sweat, and break out in nervous fits of laughter. I have dealt with some of the ethical issues of this experiment at length elsewhere,[6] but let me make a few additional remarks here.

SUBJECT REACTION: A NEGLECTED FACTOR

To my mind, the central moral justification for allowing my experiment is that it was judged acceptable by those who took part in it. Criticism of the experiment that does not take account of the tolerant reaction of the participants has always seemed to me hollow. I collected a considerable amount of data on this issue, which shows that the great majority of subjects accept this experiment, and call for further experiments of this sort. The table on p. 186 shows the overall reaction of participants to this study, as indicated in responses to a questionnaire. On the whole, these data have been ignored by critics, or even turned against the experimenter, as when critics claim that "this is simply cognitive dissonance. The more subjects hated the experiment, the more likely they are to say they enjoyed it." It becomes a "damned-if-they-like-it and damned-if-they-don't" situation. Critics of the experiment fail to come to grips with what the subject himself says. Yet, I believe that the subject's viewpoint is of extreme importance, perhaps even paramount. Below I shall present some approaches to ethical problems that derive from this view.

Some critics assert that an experiment such as mine may inflict a negative insight on the subject. He or she may have diminished self-esteem because he has learned he is more submissive to authority than he might have believed. First, I readily agree that the investigator's responsibility is to make the laboratory session as constructive an experience as possible, and to explain the experiment to the subject in a way that allows his performance to be integrated in an insightful way. But I am not at all certain that we should hide truths from subjects, even negative truths. Moreover, this would set experimentation completely apart from other life experiences. Life itself often teaches us things that are less than pleasant, as when we fail an examination or do not succeed in a job interview. And in my judgment, participation in the obedience experiment had less effect on a participant's self-esteem than the negative emotions engendered by a routine school examination. This does not mean that the stress of taking an examination is good, any more than the negative effects of the obedience experiments are good. It does mean that these issues have to be placed in perspective.

EXCERPT FROM QUESTIONNAIRE USED IN A
FOLLOW-UP STUDY OF THE OBEDIENCE RESEARCH

Now that I have read the report, and all things considered . . .	Defiant	Obedient	All
1. I am very glad to have been in the experiment	40.0%	47.8%	43.5%
2. I am glad to have been in the experiment	43.8%	35.7%	40.2%
3. I am neither sorry nor glad to have been in the experiment	15.3%	14.8%	15.1%
4. I am sorry to have been in the experiment	0.8%	0.7%	0.8%
5. I am very sorry to have been in the experiment	0.0%	1.0%	0.5%

I believe that it is extremely important to make a distinction between biomedical interventions and those that are of a purely psychological character, particularly the type of experiment I have been discussing. Intervention at the biological level *prima facie* places a subject "at risk." The ingestion of a minute dose of a chemical or the infliction of a tiny surgical incision has the potential to traumatize a subject. In contrast, in all of the social psychology experiments that have been carried out, there is no demonstrated case of resulting trauma. And there is no evidence whatsoever that when an individual makes a choice in a laboratory situation—even the difficult choices posed by the conformity or obedience experiments—any trauma, injury, or diminution of well-being results. I once asked a government official, who favored highly restrictive measures on psychology experiments, how many cases of actual trauma or injury he had in his files that would call for such measures. He indicated that not a single such case was known to him. If this is true, then much of the discussion about the need to impose government restrictions on the conduct of psychology experiments is unrealistic.

Of course, one difficulty in dealing with negative effects is the impossibility of proving their nonexistence. This is particularly true of behavioral or psychological effects. It seems that no matter what procedures one follows—interviewing, questionnaires, or the like—there is always the possibility of unforeseen negative effects, even if these procedures do not uncover them. Therefore, in an absolute sense, one can never establish the absence of negative effects. While this is logically correct, we cannot use this as a basis for asserting that such effects necessarily follow from psychological experimentation. All we can do is rely on our best judgment and assessment procedures in trying to establish the facts, and to formulate our policies accordingly.

*I*S ROLE PLAYING A SOLUTION?

Given these problems and the particular requirements of experiments in social psychology, is there any way to resolve these issues so that the subject will be protected, while allowing experimentation to continue? A number of psychologists have suggested that role playing be substituted for any experiment that requires misinformation. Instead of bringing the subject into a situation whose true purpose and nature were kept from him, the subject would be fully informed that he was about to enter a staged situation, but he would be told to act *as if it* were real. For example, in the obedience experiment subjects would be told: "pretend you are the subject performing an experiment and you are giving shocks to another person." The subject would enter the situation knowing the "victim" was not receiving shocks, and he would go through his paces.

I do not doubt that role playing has a certain utility. Indeed, every good experimenter employs such role playing when he is first setting up his laboratory situation. He and his assistants often go through a dry run to see how the procedure flows. Thus, such simulation is not new, but now it is being asked to serve as the end point, rather than the starting point of an experimental investigation. However, there is a major scientific problem. Even after one has had a subject role play his way through an experimental procedure, we still must wonder whether the observed behavior is the same as that which a genuine subject would produce. So we must still perform the crucial experiment to determine whether role-played behavior corresponds to nonrole-played behavior.

Nor is role playing free of ethical problems. A most striking simulation in social psychology was carried out by Philip Zimbardo at Stanford University.[7] Volunteers were asked to take part in a mock prison situation. They were to simulate either the role of prisoner or guard with the roles chosen by lot. They were picked up at their homes by local police cars, and delivered to Zimbardo's mock prison. Even in the role-playing version of prison, the situation became rather ugly and unpleasant, and mock guards acted cruelly toward the mock prisoners. The investigator called off the simulation after six days, instead of the two weeks for which it had been planned. Moreover, the simulation came under very heavy ethical criticism. The ethical problems that simulation was designed to solve did not all disappear. The more closely role-playing behavior corresponds to real behavior, the more it generates real emotions, including aversive states, hostile behavior, and so on. The less real emotions are present, the less adequate the simulations. From the standpoint of the aversive emotions aroused in a successful simulation, ethical problems still exist.

Kelman aptly summarized the state of simulation research when he stated that simulation is not so useless a tool of investigation as its critics first asserted, nor as free of ethical problems as its proponents believed.[8]

PRESUMPTIVE CONSENT

Recall that the major technical problem for social psychology research is that if subjects have prior knowledge of the purposes and details of an experiment they are often, by this fact, disqualified from participating in it. Informed consent thus remains an ideal that cannot always be attained. As an alternative, some psychologists have attempted to develop the doctrine of *presumptive consent*. The procedure is to solicit the view of a large number of people on the acceptability of an experimental procedure. These respondents would not themselves serve in the experiment, having been "spoiled" in the very process of being told the details and purposes of the experiment. But we could use their expressed views about participation as evidence of how people in general would react to participation.

Assuming the experiment is deemed acceptable, new subjects would be recruited for actual participation. Of course, this is, ethically, a far weaker doctrine than that which relies on informed consent of the participant. Even if a hundred people indicate that they would be willing to take part in an experiment, the person actually chosen for participation might find it objectionable. Still, the doctrine of the "presumed consent of a reasonable person" seems to me better than no consent at all. That is, when for epistemological purposes the nature of a study cannot be revealed beforehand, one would try to determine in advance whether a reasonable person would consent to being a subject in the study and use that as a warrant either for carrying out the investigation or as a basis for modifying it

Perhaps a more promising solution is to obtain *prior general consent* from subjects in advance of their actual participation. This is a form of consent that would be based on subjects' knowing the general types of procedures used in psychological investigations, but without their knowing what specific manipulations would be employed in the particular experiment in which they would take part. The first step would be to create a pool of volunteers to serve in psychology experiments. Before volunteering to join the pool people would be told explicitly that sometimes subjects are misinformed about the purposes of an experiment, and that sometimes emotional stresses arise in the course of an experiment. They would be given a chance to exclude themselves from any study using deception or involving stress *if they so wished.* Only persons who had indicated a willingness to participate in experiments involving deception or stress would, in the course of the year, be recruited for experiments that involved these elements. Such a procedure might reconcile the technical need for misinformation with the ethical problem of informing subjects.

Finally, since I emphasize the experience of the person subjected to procedures as the ultimate basis for judging whether an experiment should continue or not, I wonder whether participants in such experiments might not routinely be given monitoring cards which they would fill out and submit to an independent monitoring source while an experiment is in progress. An appropriate monitoring source might be a special committee of the professional organization, or the human subjects' committee of the institution where the experiment is carried out. Such a procedure would have the advantage of allowing the subject to express reactions about an experiment in which he has just participated, and by his comments the subject himself would help determine whether the experiment is allowable or not. In the long run, I believe it is the subject's reaction and his experience that needs to be given its due weight in any discussion of ethics, and this mechanism will help achieve this aim.

REFERENCES

1. Herbert Kelman, "Remarks made at the American Psychological Association," New Orleans, 1974.
2. Solomon E. Asch, *Social Psychology* (New York: Prentice Hall, 1952).
3. Elinor Mannucci, *Potential Subjects View Psychology Experiments: An Ethical Inquiry*. Unpublished Doctoral Dissertation. The City University of New York, 1977.
4. Bibb Latané and John Darley, *The Unresponsive Bystander: Why Doesn't He Help?* (New York: Appleton, 1970).
5. Stanley Milgram, *Obedience to Authority: An Experimental View* (New York: Harper and Row, 1974).
6. Stanley Milgram, "Issues in the Study of Obedience: A Reply to Baumrind," *American Psychologist* 19 (1964), 848–52.
7. Philip Zimbardo, "The Mind Is a Formidable Jailer: A Pirandellian Prison," *The New York Times Magazine* (April 8, 1973), p. 38.
8. Kelman, "Remarks."

13

*D*isobedience in the *S*ixties

———— ❖ ————

Americans who are unwilling to kill for their country are thrown into jail. And our generation learns, as every generation has, that society rewards and punishes its members not in the degree to which each fulfills the dictates of individual conscience but in the degree to which the actions are perceived by authority to serve the needs of the larger social system. It has always been so. Jesus was a good man by any standard of individual morality but a threat to the structure of Roman authority. Every epoch produces its share of highly moral individuals whose very purity pushes them into conflict with the state. The task of democracy is to strive to reconcile the disparity between individual conscience and societal needs.

Resisting induction into the military is a crime only in the purely technical sense that federal statutes provide penalties for it. But the resisters are the very opposite of criminals. First, they act out of moral ideals, not in opposition to them. Second, while the criminal's actions are geared to personal profit, the resister willingly suffers loss to uphold a moral ideal. Third, while the criminal seeks to evade the law, the resister offers himself to it. Nor is the resister a revolutionary: for he accepts the legitimacy of authority without being willing to serve it in specifically immoral ways. Finally, he is not truly alienated: one who has no deep involvement with his country can depart from it without the pains of incarceration.

Willard Gaylin, a psychiatrist, sets out to examine the motives and thoughts of a group of men in prison for war resistance. He moves to a consideration of the flaws of the prison system, and ineluctably is forced to extend his concern to the idea of incarceration itself as a civilized human practice. "The more I thought of it,

This paper was a book review of *In the Service of Their Country: War Resisters in Prison*, by Willard Gaylin, New York: Viking, 1970. The review was first published in *The Nation*, Vol. 211, No. 1 (July 6, 1970). Reprinted by permission of *The Nation*/The Nation Co., Inc.

the more monstrous it seemed that anyone should have the power to deprive another human being of five years of life—merely as punishment." He is right, of course, and putting men in cages will surely come to be seen as one of the barbarisms of our age. It becomes doubly shameful when the men in jail have acted on principles of conscience.

The actual chances of landing in jail vary enormously from one person to the next, depending largely on whether the resister has the wit, cash and proper legal counsel to circumvent the law. With proper religious credentials he is more likely to be granted C.O. status. Inequity in the application of the draft laws is one of the recurrent themes in this subtle and moving account of Gaylin's research.

All of the men studied are war resisters in a special sense. When a man decides that he will not enter the armed forces, several options are open to him. He can go underground (a strategy best suited to ghetto blacks, for whom there are poor administrative records). He can flee the country, or he can attempt to circumvent induction by whispering concocted sexual secrets to the psychiatrist at the induction center. Some dedicated resisters enter the army with the aim of subverting it from within, and they, no doubt, constitute the most dangerous element from the standpoint of the military.

Gaylin's interviewees chose a different course. They refused induction and offered themselves for imprisonment. Even after imprisonment the options were not fully closed, for each man had to decide whether to continue his resistance by refusing to cooperate with prison authorities in any degree, or to serve as a model prisoner. Typically, war resisters chose the latter course, a position that is consistent with their moral stance.

Life in prison is rotten, and it becomes increasingly clear that it is not merely the time taken from normal living that counts as punishment but immersion in a kind of social hell, consisting of tedium, senseless authoritarian routine, and the need to protect oneself from depredations of fellow inmates. Gaylin became a well-liked visitor to the resisters who looked forward to a break from the routine of prison life and a sympathetic ear. The research method thus exemplifies the constructive possibilities of scientific inquiry. The very process of inquiry brought a ray of light to the men. Gaylin's own sensitivity and professional tact ensured that the men did not perceive themselves as guinea pigs. This was further assured by Gaylin's temperate use of psychiatric doctrines. In seeking to find unconscious motives, the author does not discredit conscious ones. He views psychoanalytic concepts as complementary to everyday levels of explanation, and in no way supplants them. He refuses to start with the assumption that going to jail itself constitutes a neurotic symptom.

Gaylin used as his main tool of investigation the psychoanalytic interview, adhering to Freud's doctrine that "it is only when you stop asking questions that the truth emerges." Only occasionally does he turn the subject matter in a direction of interest to him. Mostly he wants to examine the ideas and feelings that the resisters summon up.

The procedure shows the strengths and limitations of the psychiatric interview. Each life is presented vividly and makes sense in its own terms; it is difficult to find generalizations applicable to all the cases. Gaylin is sparse on interpretation, preferring that the client paint his own portrait. The most promising scientific fact deals with birth order: almost all of the war resisters are first sons, suggesting that some special relationship to authority, implicit in the role of the son-who-will-replace-the-father, is at the motivational root of the resister's act.

Gaylin's sympathies lie with the resisters, not so much, I suspect, because they resisted war in general but because they resisted involvement in a particularly odious war. The reader's sympathies will be correspondingly colored by the general antipathy to the Vietnamese adventure. It is not at all clear that the moral advantage the resisters acquire at this particular moment in American history would automatically apply to resistance to all wars at all times.

Although in some respects going to prison has the quality of an act of martyrdom, it differs in that life does not end with the act; it is only interrupted. We have yet to understand how the resister comes retrospectively to fit the experience into the broader pattern of his life. In this connection, it would be helpful to speak to those who had resisted in other wars, and who have now gained a perspective on their actions. Resistance in World War II could serve as a particularly interesting point of comparison, since refusal to serve in the armed forces was not at the time viewed sympathetically by any sizable fraction of the population.

We admire the resisters for their moral stance, but this is not to be confused with an effective political act. The resisters did not win converts in prison; their individual decisions have no effect on the efficiency of the war machine: the man who refuses to go into the army is simply replaced by the next in line. So, we confront a morally inspired, but politically ineffective act of the lone individual against the system. The burden of effective resistance is thus shifted to those willing to sacrifice individual purity for the attainment of practical political goals: evasion of prison, organized collective action, and a willingness to be personally tainted are the price of maximally effective resistance, and are exemplified in the actions of men of stature such as Willy Brandt, who fled Germany to fight Nazism in the Norwegian underground. Some Germans have never forgiven Brandt, but the nation did elect him Premier. It remains to be seen whether Americans will allow similar political opportunities to those who have taken up the battle in Canada.

Since there will always be individuals who refuse induction on moral grounds, the nation must work to eradicate deficiencies in the law. Until the recent Supreme Court decision, belief in a Supreme Being was a *sine qua non* of C.O. status. Philosophic convictions that function as a religion may now be sufficient grounds for granting exemption from military service. But the person must be opposed to all wars. This does not yet reflect the process whereby moral judgments are formed. A person may, on moral grounds, be willing to fight in one war, yet find participation in another war morally repugnant. The law must come to recognize this reality, and permit selective conscientious objection. The technical difficulty is to devise procedures for separating those objections that are rooted in morality and those that are simply self-serving. Finally, the country needs to provide war resisters not the brutal and meaningless experience of prison but constructive forms of alternative national service. The impact of Gaylin's book will help move us in this direction.

PART 3

———— ❖ ————

The Individual
and the Group

How is a group possible? Each participant in the group is a complex individual with purposes and motives of his own, and yet the group is able to function effectively, even with harmony. This must be due to the fact that each individual member adjusts his behavior with reference to the other participants; social psychologists attempt to understand the nature and extent of that adjustment. The effects of groups—small groups as well as the larger aggregation of individuals we term a crowd—are explored in the following pages.

Having made these general observations, it still becomes necessary to find a clear way to study group effects. For me, the decisive paradigm was contained in the group pressure experiments of Solomon E. Asch.

In Asch's experiments, a group of four to six subjects was shown a line of a certain length and had to say which of three lines matched it. All but one of the subjects in the group had been secretly instructed beforehand to select one of the wrong lines on each trial. The naïve subject was so placed that he heard the answers of most of the group before he had to announce his own decision. Asch found that under this form of social pressure, a large fraction of subjects went along with the group rather than accept the unmistakable evidence of their own eyes.

I had the good fortune to work for and with Professor Asch at both Harvard and Princeton. Asch was inspiring, particularly when he was not teaching formally but was simply exposing his cerebral processes in the course of conversation. He is a man of quiet intellectual brilliance.

Most of the papers in this section are variations on the theme of Asch's experiment. I mean "variations" in the musical sense of the term, the way Brahms wrote variations on Haydn. As in music, sometimes the theme of the master is clear and little adorned. Sometimes the original motif is all but obscured, as the variations take off in new directions and become virtually independent of their origins. Probably the master doesn't always like the way his themes are shifted in key and emphasis. *Tant pis.* For me, Asch's experiment rotates as a kind of permanent intellectual jewel. Focus analytic light on it, and it diffracts energy into new and interesting patterns.

Indeed, in my graduate teaching, I have often designed variations of his experiment to carry out as a class exercise, or simply as thought-experiments. The following ten such variations are among my favorites.

1   *Pro-social conformity.*   In Asch's experiment, the group is shown to limit, constrain, and distort the individual's response. One variant examined the pro-social effects of group pressure. Subjects were free to decide on an amount to contribute to a series of charities. Confederates upped the amount for each of eight charities, and, under the influence of the group, subjects donated ever-increasing amounts to the charities. "Liberating Effects of Group Pressure" (p. 231) continues this tradition of constructive conformity.

2   *Sequential influence.*   In Asch's experiments, the naïve subject faces the unanimous opinion of a simultaneously assembled group. In this variant, subjects are exposed to the unanimous opinion of several individuals, but each confederate confronts the subject individually, on different days, during the course of a week. The influence summates and approximates that of a simultaneously assembled group.

3   *Influencing the alienated.*   How would a group influence a person who was negatively oriented toward it? Students were asked to design experimental techniques for influencing the alienated. Some students believed the group can induce the behavior it wants by publicly calling for the opposite, on the assumption that the hostile person will perform contrary to what he thinks the group wants. Others emphasize that it is better to work on reducing the alienation.

4   *Action conformity.*   Asch's subjects yield in regard to a verbal judgment. But can the group induce the person to perform *actions* he would not otherwise engage in? What is the range of signifi-

cant behavior that the group can shape? (See "Group Pressure and Action against a Person," p. 219.)

5   *Enduring effects of yielding.*   In Asch's experiment, the consequence of the subject's yielding does not transcend the laboratory hour. It is a fully self-contained experience. Is this the basis of the group's power? Would a person as readily conform to the group in regard to acts that endure beyond the laboratory hour? For example, would subjects expose their foreheads to a permanent green dye if all of the confederates appeared to do so? Would a naïve subject be willing to sign a marriage certificate if the group sheepishly did so? This is a critical and as yet untested variant.

6   *The group's response to pressure.*   Asch's experiment examines how an individual responds to pressures exerted by a group. But how do *groups* respond when they are under the unanimous pressure of a larger field of groups? Asch's partnership variation touches on but does not fully develop this issue.

7   *The conformity of inaction.*   Asch's subjects are influenced by a majority that takes a positive action (making a definite judgment). But can a group induce passivity by the example of its own inaction? This shades into typical bystander experiments.

8   *Forewarned subjects.*   In this variant, we expressly informed subjects that from time to time members of the group would deliberately give incorrect answers. This changed the basic psychological character of the experience, but surprisingly, some subjects still went along with the group as a kind of reflexive imitation.

9   *Repetition of stimulus.*   Subjects in an auditory variation of the Asch experiment (subjects heard two tones and were asked to indicate which was the longer; the group gave the incorrect answer) were free to request a repetition of the stimulus before giving their judgments. Subjects were therefore free to clarify their perception, but few subjects requested a repetition of the tones. This is particularly true of those who yield to the group in their judgment of tonal lengths. Their conformity is so deep, it does not permit them to reduce uncertainty, even when they have an opportunity to do so.

10   *Black box conformity.*   In the Asch study, the subject and the group have equal access to the stimulus material. My student, Rita Dytell, carried out a "black box" variation, in which the group had access to the stimulus material but not the subject. This corresponds to the fact that we must often decide whether to accept judgments made by others on events which they have observed but which we have not.

Each variation, substantially inspired by the Asch paradigm, sheds light on a new aspect of social influence and speaks to the immense fecundity of the original experiment.

There is a progression in the several experimental papers reprinted in this section. In "Nationality and Conformity," the effect of group pressure on individual judgments is studied and is shown to vary—a little—from one national setting to the next. The purpose was to use the Asch experiment as a measuring instrument to study the level of conformity in two national cultures. As a result of this experience, I became less interested in national cultures and more interested in the effects of group pressure. Surely it is not limited to changing a person's verbal pronouncement.

The issue of verbal conformity is, of course, extremely important. The entire climate of a community comes to be determined by the freedom which individuals feel to express themselves. The capacity of groups to stultify original expression or dissenting ideas is an important fact of social life. But conformity extends beyond the merely verbal. The very deeds of the person may come to be shaped by the group, and this notion is brought within an experimental framework in "Group Pressure and Action against a Person" (p. 219).

I have explained elsewhere (p. 127) how the obedience experiments are related to Asch's experiments twice removed—first by substitution of a consequential act for a verbal judgment, and then by focusing on the authority rather than the group. In "Liberating Effects of Group Pressure," we come full circle. The group breaks the yoke of authority, and by its example restores the person's integrity against authoritarian excess.

In real life, the constructive uses of group pressure go considerably beyond this experimental demonstration. Individuals frequently seek out groups whose pressures and standards will help them develop and maintain desired ends. We may welcome the pressures to conform to a group whose values are enlightened and which strengthens our own ideals.

The themes of individual submission to group pressure, the conflict of conscience and authority, and the constructive role that groups have on the individual seem to me central to an individual's experience with the social world. The basic fact of human experience is that we are born into a social matrix, yet each of us strives to be an individual. The social matrix is indispensable to our lives, equips us with language and the habits of civilized men and women, endows us with goals, values, and the needed company of one another. Yet once the values are given to us, they become our very own and the individual must strive to maintain individual conscience, judgment, and critical intellect against the pressures of the crowd, and the assertive strength of doctrinaire authority.

What is most distinctive about people is what they have gotten from others: language, habits of rational thought, humane values. Yet to maintain what is best, an individual often needs to stand alone against the

FIGURE III.4
Norwegian subject in group pressure study. (Illustration by Roy Superior.)

crowd and against authority. A person internalizes these values and must then defend them even against the society that gave them. Though enormous pressures may bear down on a person to abandon critical intelligence, dispense with conscience, and surrender humanity, that person will often prove hardy and resilient, transcend the pressure of the moment, and reaffirm the power and integrity of one's own spirit. Well, as our experiments show, it does not always happen this way. But it remains a worthy ideal.

In addition to the experimental articles, an excerpt is reprinted from my dissertation, *Conformity in Norway and France,* completed in 1960. The excerpt on ethics (p. 215) is perhaps ironic in that the experiments on obedience were to become a few years later a focus of ethical controversy. Irrespective of the ethical status of the obedience experiment, the specific implication of some critics that I was indifferent to ethical matters is hardly borne out by this early empirical research into experimental ethics.

REFERENCES

ASCH, S. E., 1956. "Studies of independence and conformity: I. A minority of one against a unanimous majority." *Psychological Monographs,* **70** (9, Whole No. 416).

DYTELL, R., 1970. "An analysis of how people use groups as a source of information on which to base judgments." Unpublished doctoral dissertation, The City University of New York.

14

Nationality and Conformity[1]

❖

People who travel abroad seem to enjoy sending back reports on what people are like in various countries they visit. A variety of national stereotypes is part and parcel of popular knowledge. Italians are said to be "volatile," Germans "hard-working," the Dutch "clean," the Swiss "neat," the English "reserved," and so on. The habit of making generalizations about national groups is not a modern invention. Byzantine war manuals contain careful notes on the deportment of foreign populations, and Americans still recognize themselves in the brilliant national portrait drawn by Alexis de Tocqueville more than 100 years ago.

And yet the skeptical student must always come back to the question: "How do I know that what is said about a foreign group is true?" Prejudice and personal bias may color such accounts, and in the absence of objective evidence it is not easy to distinguish between fact and fiction. Thus the problem faced by the modern investigator who wishes to go beyond literary description is how to make an objective analysis of behavioral differences among national groups. By this he means simply an analysis that is not based on subjective judgments and that can be verified by any competent investigator who follows the same methods.

It is easy to show objectively that people in different countries often speak different languages, eat different foods and observe different social customs. But can one go further and show national differences in "character" or "personality"? When we turn to the more subtle dimensions of behavior, there is very little

This paper was first published in *Scientific American*, Vol. 205, No. 6 (December 1961), pp. 45–51. Reprinted by permission. Copyright © 1961 by Scientific American, Inc. All rights reserved. Illustrations are by Bernarda Bryson. Reprinted by permission.

evidence to make a case for national differences. It is not that such differences are to be denied out of hand; it is just that we lack sufficient reliable information to make a clear judgment.

Before reporting the results of my own study let me refer briefly to some earlier efforts to achieve objectivity in studying this elusive problem. One approach has been to examine the literature and other cultural products of a nation in the hope of identifying underlying psychological characteristics. For example, Donald V. McGranahan of Harvard University studied successful stage plays performed in Germany and the U.S. and concluded that German stage characters were more devoted to principles and ideological notions, whereas the Americans were more concerned with the attainment of purely personal satisfactions. The obvious limitation of such a study is that the behavior and attitudes under examination are the synthetic ones of the stage and may bear little or no resemblance to those of real life.

Another indirect approach has relied on the tools of clinical psychology. This method was pioneered by anthropologists in the study of small, primitive societies and has only recently been applied to modern urban nations. These studies rely heavily on such tests as the Rorschach ink-blot test and the thematic apperception test (TAT). In the latter the subject is shown a drawing of a situation that can be variously interpreted and is asked to make up a story about it. The major difficulty here is that the tests themselves have not been adequately validated and are basically impressionistic.

Finally, sample surveys of the type developed by Elmo Roper and George Gallup in this country have been applied to the problem. Geoffrey Gorer, an English social scientist, based his study *Exploring English Character* on a questionnaire distributed to 11,000 of his compatriots. The questions dealt with varied aspects of English life, such as courtship patterns, experiences in school and practices in the home. Unfortunately there are many reasons why an individual's answer may not correspond to the facts. He may deliberately distort his answers to produce a good impression, or he may have genuine misconceptions of his own behavior, attributable either to faulty memory or to the blindness people often exhibit toward their own actions and motivations.

These methods should not be dismissed as unimportant in the study of national characteristics. Yet in principle if one wants to know whether the people of one nation behave differently from those of another, it would seem only reasonable to examine the relevant behavior directly, and to do so under conditions of controlled observations in order to reduce the effects of personal bias and to make measurement more precise.

An important step in this direction was reported in 1954 by an international team of psychologists who worked together as the Organization for Comparative Social Research. This team studied reactions to threat and rejection among school children in seven European nations, using hypotheses advanced by Stanley Schachter of Columbia University. The inquiry was not specifically designed to study national characteristics but chiefly to see if certain concepts regarding threat and rejection would hold up when tested in different countries. In the course of the study certain differences between countries did turn up, but the investigators felt they were not necessarily genuine. Conceivably they were due to defects in the experiment or to inadequacies in the theory behind it. Although its focus was on theory validation, this study is a landmark in cross-national research. Unfortunately the Organization for Comparative Social Research halted its research program when the study was completed.

My own investigation was begun in 1957. My objective was to see if experimental techniques could be applied to the study of national characteristics, and in particular to see if one could measure conformity in two European countries: Norway and France. Conformity was chosen for several reasons. First, a national culture can be said to exist only if men adhere, or conform, to common standards of behavior; this is the psychological mechanism underlying all cultural behavior. Second, conformity has become a burning issue in much of current social criticism; critics have argued that people have become too sensitive to the opinions of others, and that this represents an unhealthy development in modern society. Finally, good experimental methods have been developed for measuring conformity.

The chief tool of investigation was a modified form of the group-pressure experiment used by Solomon E. Asch and other social psychologists. In Asch's original experiment a group of half a dozen subjects was shown a line of a certain length and asked to say which of three other lines matched it. All but one of the subjects had been secretly instructed beforehand to select one of the "wrong" lines on each trial or in a certain percentage of the trials. The naïve subject was so placed that he heard the answers of most of the group before he had to announce his own decision. Asch found that under this form of social pressure a large fraction of subjects went along with the group rather than accept the unmistakable evidence of their own eyes.

Our experiment is conducted with acoustic tones rather than with lines drawn on cards. Five of the subjects are confederates of the experimenter and conspire to put social pressure on the sixth subject. The subjects listen to two tones and are asked to say which is the longer. The five confederates answer first and their decisions are heard by the subject, who answers last. The confederates have been instructed to announce wrong answers on 16 of the 30 trials that constitute one experiment.

We elected to use tones rather than lines because they are better suited to an experimental method using "synthetic groups." Two psychologists working at Yale University, Robert Blake and Jack W. Brehm, had

FIGURE 14.1

The conformity experiment required that the subject discriminate between the lengths of two tones heard through headphones, and measured the extent to which he went along with the wrong answers given—it seemed to him—by five other subjects listening to the same tones. Actually, no other subjects were present; the illusion was created by tape recordings. The top drawing by Bernarda Bryson shows what the subject saw as he entered the experimental room. The middle drawing shows what the subject, seated in the far left-hand booth, imagined the situation to be while he was taking the test. The drawing at the bottom shows the actual situation.

discovered that group-pressure experiments can be conducted without requiring the actual presence of confederates. It is sufficient if the subject thinks they are present and hears their voices through headphones. With tape recordings it is easy to create synthetic groups. Tapes do not have to be paid by the hour and they are always available.

When the test subject entered our laboratory, he saw several coats on hangers and immediately got the impression that others were present. He was taken to one of six closed booths, where he was provided with headphones and a microphone. As he listened to the instructions through the headphones he overheard the voices of the other "subjects" and assumed that all the booths were occupied. During the actual experiment he would hear five taped answers before he was asked to give his own.

Except when we made a technical slip the subject never caught on to the trick. Most subjects became deeply involved in the situation, and strong tensions were generated when they realized they must stand alone against five unanimous opponents. This situation created a genuine and deeply felt conflict that had to be resolved either through independence or conformity.

Once we had refined our techniques at Harvard University we were ready to experiment abroad with Norwegian and French subjects. In which of the two national environments would people go along with the group more and in which would there be greater independence?

Most of the students used in the Norwegian study were students attending the University of Oslo. Because this is the only full-fledged university in Norway, a good geographic representation was obtained. Our test sample included students from beyond the Arctic Circle, from the fiord country of western Norway and from Trondheim, the former Viking capital.

When the study moved to Paris, French students were selected who matched the Norwegians in age, level of education, fields of study, sex, marital status, and—so far as possible—social class. Once again a good geographic distribution was obtained, because students from all parts of France came to study in Paris. A few of the French subjects came from French North African cities. Those used in the experiment were culturally as French as people living on the mainland; they were of French parentage and had been educated in French lycées.

In Norway the entire experiment was conducted by a native Norwegian and all the recorded voices were those of natives. In France the experiments were conducted by native Frenchmen. Much effort was made to match the tone and quality of the Norwegian and French groups. We made many recordings until people who were sensitive to the nuances of both languages were satisfied that equivalent group atmospheres had been achieved.

Twenty Norwegian subjects and the same number of French subjects were studied in the first set of experiments. The Norwegian subjects

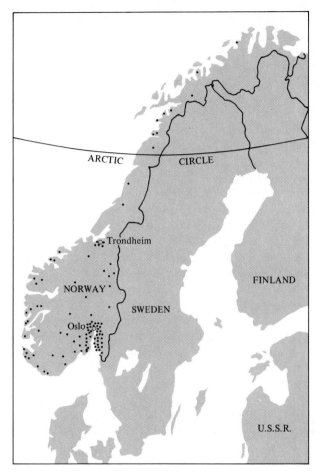

FIGURE 14.2
Norwegian subjects were from the University
of Oslo, which has students from the entire
country. The dots on the map show the home
town or county of the 100 students involved.

conformed to the group on 62 percent of the critical trials (that is, trials in
which the group deliberately voted wrong); the French subjects conformed to the group on 50 percent of the critical trials.

After each subject had taken part in the experiment he was told its
true character and was asked to give his reactions. Almost all participants
in both countries had accepted the experiment at face value and admitted
feeling the strong pressure of the group. A Norwegian student from a
farm in Nordland, above the Arctic Circle, said: "I think the experiment
had a very ingenious arrangement. I had no idea about the setup until it

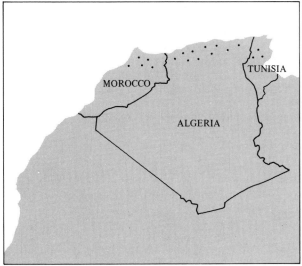

FIGURE 14.3
French subjects were students in Paris chosen
to match the Norwegians as closely as
possible. The dots show the home
department (or area of North Africa) of 95
students.

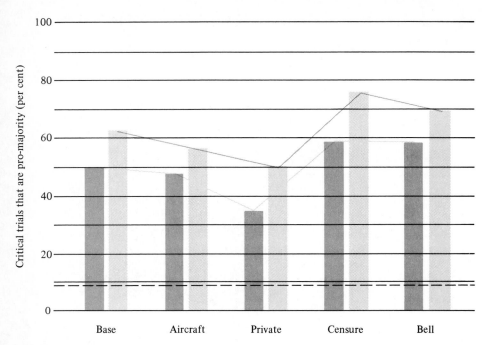

FIGURE 14.4
Level of conformity was higher for Norwegians (light tint) than French subjects (darker tint) in all five test situations, but fluctuated similarly for both. The broken black line indicates the error level of control groups of both nationalities in the absence of pressure. The first set of bars gives results for the basic experiment. In the next situation, significance was increased by an announcement that the test results would affect aircraft safety. This "aircraft" factor was maintained in subsequent tests, in one of which the subjects recorded their answers privately instead of announcing them. In the "censure" situation, critical comments (on tape) stepped up pressure on the subjects. In a final experiment, censure continued and the subjects were allowed to request repetition of the test tones by sounding a bell; fewer Norwegians than Frenchmen proved "bold" enough to do so.

was explained to me. Of course, it was a little embarrassing to be exposed in such a way." A self-critical student from Oslo remarked: "It was a real trick and I was stupid to have fallen into the trap. . . . It must be fun to study psychology." Similar reactions were obtained in France, where students were impressed with the idea of psychological experimentation. (In neither country is psychological research as widespread or as intensive as it is in the U.S., so that subjects are relatively unsophisticated about psychological deceptions.)

It would have been superficial, of course, to conduct just one experiment in Norway, another in France and then draw conclusions. In a second experiment we undertook to change the subject's attitude toward the importance of the experiment itself to see if this might alter the original findings. In this new series of trials (and in all subsequent ones) the subjects were told that the results of the experiments would be applied to the design of aircraft safety signals. In this way their performance was linked to a life-and-death issue. As one might have predicted, the subjects this time showed somewhat greater independence of the group, but once again the level of conformity was higher in Norway (56 percent) than it was in France (48 percent).

One possibility that had to be considered at the outset was that Norwegians and Frenchmen differ in their capacity for discriminating tonal lengths and that this led to the greater number of errors made by Norwegians in the group situation. We were able to show, however, by giving each subject a tone-discrimination test, that there was no difference in the level of discrimination of students in the two countries.

In both of the first two conformity experiments the subjects were required to do more than decide an issue in the face of unanimous opposition: they were also required to announce that decision openly for all to hear (or so the subject thought). Thus the act had the character of a public statement. We all recognize that the most obvious forms of conformity are the public ones. For example, when prevailing standards of dress or conduct are breached, the reaction is usually immediate and critical. So we decided we had better see if the Norwegians conformed more only under public conditions, when they had to declare their answers aloud. Accordingly, we undertook an experiment in both countries in which the subject was allowed to record his answers on paper rather than announce them to the group. The experiments were performed with a new group of 20 Norwegian and 20 French students.

When the requirement of a public response was eliminated, the amount of conformity dropped considerably in both countries. But for the third time the French subjects were more independent than the Norwegians. In Paris students went along with the group on 34 percent of the critical trials. In Oslo the figure was close to 50 percent. Therefore elimination of the requirement of a public response reduced conformity 14 percentage points in France but only 6 percentage points in Norway.

It is very puzzling that the Norwegians so often voted with the group, even when given a secret ballot. One possible interpretation is that the average Norwegian, for whatever reason, believes that his private action will ultimately become known to others. Interviews conducted among the Norwegians offer some indirect evidence for this conjecture. In spite of the assurances that the responses would be privately analyzed, one subject said he feared that because he had disagreed too often the experimenter would assemble the group and discuss the disagreements with them.

Another Norwegian subject, who had agreed with the group 12 out of 16 times, offered this explanation: "In the world now, you have to be not too much in opposition. In high school I was more independent than now.

It's the modern way of life that you have to agree a little more. If you go around opposing, you might be looked upon as bad. Maybe this had an influence." He was then asked, "Even though you were answering in private?" and he replied, "Yes, I tried to put myself in a public situation, even though I was sitting in the booth in private."

A fourth experiment was designed to test the sensitivity of Norwegian and French subjects to a further aspect of group opinion. What would happen if subjects were exposed to overt and audible criticism from the conspiratorial group? It seemed reasonable to expect a higher degree of conformity under these conditions. On the other hand, active criticism might conceivably lead to a greater show of independence. Moreover, the Norwegians might react one way and the French another. Some of my associates speculated that audible criticism would merely serve to annoy the French subjects and make them stubborn and more resistant to the influence of the group.

To test these notions we recorded a number of appropriate reactions that we could switch on whenever the subject gave a response that contradicted the majority. The first sanction, in both Norway and France, was merely a slight snicker by a member of the majority. The other sanctions were more severe. In Norway they were based on the sentence "Skal du stikke deg ut?" which may be translated: "Are you trying to show off?" Roughly equivalent sentences were used with the French group. In Paris, when the subject opposed the group, he might hear through his headphones: "Voulez-vous faire remarquer?" ("Trying to be conspicuous?").

In both Norway and France this overt social criticism significantly increased conformity. In France subjects now went along with the majority on 59 percent of the critical trials. In Norway the percentage rose to 75 percent. But the reactions of subjects in the two countries were even more striking. In Norway subjects accepted the criticism impassively. In France, however, more than half the subjects made some retaliatory response of their own when the group criticized them. Two French students, one from the Vosges mountain district and the other from the Department of Eure-et-Loire, became so enraged they directed a stream of abusive language at their taunters.

Even after we explained in the interview session that the entire experimental procedure had been recorded on tape, many of the subjects did not believe us. They could not understand how we could interject comments with such verisimilitude, particularly since we could not predict how they would respond at any given moment. This was achieved by making use of two tape recorders. One played the standard tape containing tones and the group judgments, with "dead" time for the subject; the other contained only the set of "criticisms" from members of the group. The two instruments could be controlled independently, allowing us to inject a remark whenever the subject's responses made it appropriate. The remarks followed the subject's independent responses immediately, creating a highly spontaneous effect.

Another series of experiments was designed to aid in the interpretation of the earlier findings. For example, many Norwegian subjects rationalized their behavior by stating in the interview that they went along with the others because they doubted their own judgment, and that if they had been given a chance to dispel this doubt they would have been more independent. An experiment was therefore carried out to test this notion. The subject was given a chance to reexamine the stimulus materials before giving his final judgment. He did this by sounding a bell in his booth whenever he wished to hear a pair of tones again. As before, the subject was openly censured by the group if he failed to conform, but he was not censured merely for asking to hear the tones repeated. It turned out that even the relatively simple act of requesting a repetition must be

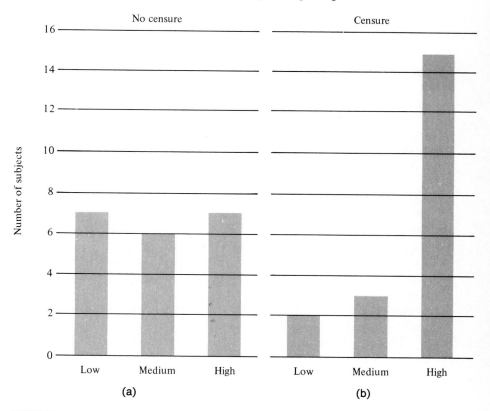

FIGURE 14.5
Effect of censure was to increase conformity. The charts show the degree of conformity among 20 Norwegians in the absence of censure (a) and when censure was introduced in the form of criticism (b). The "low"-conformity category included those who gave 6 or fewer promajority responses out of 16; "medium" is 7 to 11; and "high" is 12 or more.

construed as an act of considerable independence. Only five of the Norwegians asked for a repetition of a tone on any trial, whereas 14 of the French subjects were "bold" enough to do so. And again the French showed more independence over-all, voting with the group on 58 percent of the critical trials, compared with 69 percent for the Norwegians.

The study next moved out of the university and into the factory. When we tested 40 Norwegian industrial workers, we found that their level of conformity was about the same as that of the Norwegian students. There was, however, one important difference. Students were often tense and agitated during the experiment. The industrial workers took it all with good humor and frequently were amused when the true nature of the experiment was explained. We have not yet managed to study a comparable group of industrial workers in France.

No matter how the data are examined they point to greater independence among the French than among the Norwegians. Twelve percent of the Norwegian students conformed to the group on every one of the 16 critical trials, while only 1 percent of the French conformed on every occasion. Forty-one percent of the French students but only 25 percent of the Norwegians displayed strong independence. And in every one of the five experiments performed in both countries the French showed themselves to be the more resistant to group pressure.

These findings are by no means conclusive. Rather they must be regarded as the beginning of an inquiry that one would like to see extended. But incomplete as the findings are, they are likely to be far more reliable than armchair speculation on national character.

It is useful, nevertheless, to see if the experimental results are compatible with a nation's culture as one can observe it in daily life. If there were a conflict between the experimental findings and one's general impressions, further experiments and analysis would be called for until the conflict had been resolved. Conceivably the discrepancy might be due to viewing the culture through a screen of stereotypes and prejudices rather than seeing it with a clear eye. In any case, in our study experiment and observation seem to be in reasonable agreement. For whatever the evidence may be worth, I will offer my own impressions of the two countries under examination.

I found Norwegian society highly cohesive. Norwegians have a deep feeling of group identification, and they are strongly attuned to the needs and interests of those around them. Their sense of social responsibility finds expression in formidable institutions for the care and protection of Norwegian citizens. The heavy taxation required to support broad programs of social welfare is borne willingly. It would not be surprising to find that social cohesiveness of this sort goes hand in hand with a high degree of conformity.

Compared with the Norwegians, the French show far less consensus in both social and political life. The Norwegians have made do with a single constitution, drafted in 1814, while the French have not been able to achieve political stability within the framework of four republics. Though I hardly propose this as a general rule of social psychology, it seems true that the extreme diversity of opinion found in French national life asserts itself also on a more intimate scale. There is a tradition of dissent and critical argument that seeps down to the local *bistro*. The high value placed on critical judgment often seems to go beyond reasonable bounds; this in itself could account for the comparatively low degree of conformity we found in the French experiments. Furthermore, as Stanley Schachter has shown, the chronic existence of a wide range of opinion helps to free the individual from social pressure. Much the same point is made in recent studies of U.S. voting behavior. They reveal that the more a person is exposed to diverse viewpoints, the more likely he is to break away from the voting pattern of his native group. All these factors would help to explain the relatively independent judgments shown by French students.

The experiments demonstrate, in any case, that social conformity is not exclusively a U.S. phenomenon, as some critics would have us believe. Some amount of conformity would seem necessary to the functioning of any social system. The problem is to strike the right balance between individual initiative and social authority.

One may ask whether or not national borders really provide legitimate boundaries for the study of behavioral differences. My feeling is that boundaries are useful only to the extent to which they coincide with cultural, environmental or biological divisions. In many cases boundaries are themselves a historical recognition of common cultural practice. Furthermore, once boundaries are established they tend to set limits of their own on social communication.

For all this, a comparison of national cultures should not obscure the enormous variations in behavior within a single nation. Both the Norwegians and the French displayed a full range of behavior from complete independence to complete conformity. Probably there is no significant national comparison in which the extent of overlap does not approach or match the extent of differences. This should not prevent us, however, from trying to establish norms and statistically valid generalizations on behavior in different nations.

We are now planning further research in national characteristics. In a recent seminar at Yale University students were given the task of trying to identify behavioral characteristics that might help to illuminate the Nazi epoch in German history. The principal suggestions were that Germans might be found to be more aggressive than Americans, to submit more readily to authority and to display greater discipline. Whether these assumptions will hold up under experimental inquiry is an open question.

*N*OTE

1. The research in Norway was carried out at the Institute for Social Research, Oslo, and at the Psychological Institute of the University of Oslo. Special thanks are due to Erik Rinde and Asa Grude Skaard, of these respective institutions, for their generous cooperation. In France, Dr. Robert Pagès, of the University of Paris, was most helpful in securing facilities for the conduct of the research. My research assistants were Guttorm Langaard and Michel Maugis.

*R*EFERENCES

ASCH, S. E., "Effects of group pressure upon the modification and distortion of judgement." In H. Guetzkow (ed.), *Groups, Leadership and Men*. Pittsburgh: The Carnegie Press, 1951.

BLAKE, R. R., and BREHM, J. W., "The use of tape recording to simulate a group atmosphere." *J. Abnorm. and Soc. Psychol.*, 1954, **49**, 311–313.

CASTBERG, F., *The Norwegian Way of Life*. London: W. Heinemann, 1954.

GORER, G., *Exploring English Character*. New York: Criterion Books, 1955.

INKELES, A., and LEVINSON, D. J., "National character: the study of modal personality and sociocultural systems." In G. Lindzey (ed.), *Handbook of Social Psychology* (Vol. II). Cambridge, Mass.: Addison-Wesley, 1954, pp. 977–1020.

McGRANAHAN, D. V., and WAYNE, I., "German and American traits reflected in popular drama." *Human Relations*, 1948, **I**, 429–455.

RODNICK, D., *The Norwegians: A Study in National Culture*. Washington, D.C.: Public Affairs Press, 1955.

SCHACHTER, S., NUTTIN, J., DE MONCHAUX, C., MAUCORPS, P. H., OSMER, D., DUIJKER, H., ROMMETVEIT, R., and ISRAEL, J., "Cross-cultural experiments on threat and rejection." *Human Relations*, 1954, **7**, 403–439.

15

Ethics in the Conformity Experiment: An Empirical Study

———— ❖ ————

A s part of the study of group pressure in Norway, I investigated the subjects' reactions to the ethics of the experiment. In the laboratory, many subjects revealed aspects of their personalities that might be considered unflattering: conformist subjects felt ashamed or even humiliated when, in the interview, they were confronted with the true nature of the experiment. Furthermore, the subject was invited to the laboratory under false pretenses, and was misinformed by the experimenter while he was there. Subjects were deceived into believing (1) that others were present, (2) that the others were answering honestly, and (3) that the experimental findings would have an important humanitarian application. Although subjects were informed of the true character of the experiment immediately after they had performed in it, the ethical issue remains. With a view toward gauging the subjects' reactions to this issue, a questionnaire was distributed to the Norwegian student subjects.

One hundred and twenty questionnaires were distributed approximately two months after the subjects' participation in the experiment. Ninety-six of these were completed and returned. We assume that a few of the twenty-four that were not returned never reached the addressees, because of incorrect addressing, etc.

Excerpted from my doctoral dissertation, *Conformity in Norway and France: An Experimental Study of National Characteristics*, Cambridge, Mass.: Harvard University, 1960, pp. 170–176. Reprinted by permission of the President and Fellows of Harvard University.

However, this is not the only factor. In Table 15.1 we compare performance in the experiment with the number of unreturned questionnaires.

We see that 100 percent of the low conformity subjects, 81 percent of the medium conformity subjects, and only 70 percent of those who had yielded twelve or more times returned the questionnaires.

Thus, in considering the questionnaires, we should keep in mind that there is a systematic bias in favor of the responses of high independence subjects.

In one question we asked the subject how he had felt immediately after performing in the experiment. The open-ended form allowed for maximum freedom of response and, while a variety of moods are expressed, no subject seems to have been shaken too badly. One subject used the word "brutal" but referred only to his experience in the course of the experiment and not to its enduring effects. Most subjects said they were annoyed with themselves for not having penetrated the true character of the experiment.

In another question, we asked whether, from the present perspective, the subject thought the experiment ethical or unethical. In order to stack the cards against the experimenter, we included two negative, one positive, and one neutral response categories. The results are reproduced in Table 15.2.

TABLE 15.1 PERCENTAGE OF PERSONS RETURNING QUESTIONNAIRE AS A FUNCTION OF PERFORMANCE IN THE EXPERIMENT

Degree of conformity	Number of questionnaires returned	Number of questionnaires not returned	Percentage of questionnaires returned
Low	29	0	100
Medium	25	6	80.6
High	42	18	70.0

TABLE 15.2 DO YOU FEEL NOW THAT THE EXPERIMENT WAS ETHICAL OR UNETHICAL?

Very unethical	0
Unethical	8
Ethical	14
Neither ethical nor unethical	69
	91
(No answer)	5
	$N = 96$

Eight persons reported that the experiment was unethical, but some offered qualifying remarks:

> The experiment is unethical because one gets into it on false premises, but I suppose such an experiment can only be set up in such a way.
>   One should perhaps tolerate this much for the benefit of science. All the same, it is not quite right to fool people in this way.

It is clear from the free comments to this question that when subjects judge the experiment to be "ethical" they refer to positive, edifying effects resulting from the experience. Thus one subject in this category wrote:

> I felt as if it was a lesson for me. It's healthy as a prevention against mass mentality.

Others indicated that, despite the discomfort, they had learned much from it.

By far the largest number of subjects declared that the experiment was neither ethical nor unethical. Many indicated that they did not understand how one could use these terms in connection with a scientific experiment. Some responded with the general principle: "Every scientific experiment is beyond ethics." Others pointed out that the ethicality of the experiment would depend on the uses to which its findings were put.

Some students mentioned specific features of the experimental procedure that in their minds kept it aboveboard. One subject wrote:

> When the experiment is kept strongly confidential, and the subjects have volunteered, the experiment in my opinion cannot be either ethical or unethical.

The following themes recur frequently in the students' responses: that subjects had volunteered for the experiment; that the results were kept confidential; and that the purpose of the experiment was explained to them. For most subjects these features counted in favor of the experiment, and compensated for the initial deceptions.

A law student from Oslo expressed the most common reaction when he wrote:

> I must say that the word "ethical"—either with or without the "un"—was never in my thoughts in connection with this experiment. I mean that the test in itself is neither ethical nor unethical, neither moral nor immoral. It might on the other hand serve a moral purpose, namely greater intellectual honesty. If the experiment contributes to this aim, it serves a purpose of immense value.

A less direct approach to the problem was to ask the students how they felt in general about having participated in the experiment. Table 15.3

shows the distribution of answers in terms of the five response categories provided.

It appears that most subjects were glad to have participated, despite the trickery involved. The reasons for this seem to be: First, they understood that any deception used was not primarily for personal gain, but for the advancement of knowledge. They appreciated that they were informed of the true character of the experiment as soon as possible. They understood that whatever their performance may have been, we placed them in a position of trust by revealing the true purpose and methods of the experiment, and they knew that the success of the experimental project depended on their willingness to support this trust. If for twenty minutes we abused their dignity, we reaffirmed it by extending to them our confidence. Third—and this was an unexpected advantage of using tape-recorded stooges—most subjects exhibited relief when they learned that other persons were not really present. The high conformers, especially, were glad that their performances were essentially private, and would be kept confidential.

Again, we remind the reader that twenty-four subjects did not respond to the questionnaire, and they were concentrated among the high conformers. Perhaps, had they responded, we would have had a good many more damaging criticisms on hand. Furthermore, the results are based solely on the sample of Norwegian students. My guess is that responses from the French students would have been more critical. On the basis of the results we have, however, I think it is fair to say that most subjects accept the necessity of deception in this experiment, and do not condemn it morally. That is not to say they should have the last word on the matter. No action is divested of its unethical properties by the expedient of a public-opinion poll; neither is the outcome of such an inquiry irrelevant to the issue.

TABLE 15.3 HOW DO YOU FEEL NOW ABOUT HAVING BEEN IN THE EXPERIMENT?

I'm very glad to have been in the experiment	22
I'm glad to have been in the experiment	48
I am neither sorry nor glad to have been in the experiment	22
I'm sorry to have been in the experiment	1
I'm very sorry to have been in the experiment	0
	93
(No answer)	3
	N = 96

16

Group Pressure and Action against a Person[1]

❖

A great many variations of a paradigm provided by Asch (1951) show that there is an intelligible relationship between several features of the social environment and the degree to which a person will rely on others for his public judgments. Because it possesses merits of simplicity, clarity, and reconstructs in the laboratory powerful and socially relevant psychological processes, this paradigm has gained widespread acceptance as a basic technique of research on influence processes.

One feature that has been kept constant through the variations on Asch's work is that verbal judgment has been retained as the end product and basic index of conformity. More generally, a *signal* offered by the subject as representing his judgment has been the focus of study. Most often the signal has taken the form of a verbal pronouncement (Asch, 1956; Milgram, 1961), though mechanical devices which the subject uses to signal his judgment have also been employed (Crutchfield, 1955; Tuddenham & MacBride, 1959).

A distinction can be made between *signal conformity* and *action conformity* in that the immediate consequence of the former is purely informational; the subject states his opinion or reports on his perception of some feature of the environment. Action conformity, on the other hand, produces an immediate effect or alteration in the milieu that goes beyond a contribution of information. It refers to the elicitation of a *deed* by group forces, the induction of an act that is more than communicative in its effect. The act may be directed toward the well being of

This paper was first published in the *Journal of Abnormal and Social Psychology,* Vol. 69, No. 2 (August 1964), pp. 137–143. Copyright © 1964 by the American Psychological Association. Reprinted by permission.

another person (e.g., a man is induced by group pressure to share bread with a beggar) or it may be oriented toward nonsocial parts of the environment (a delinquent is induced by gang pressure to throw a rock at a shop window).

There is little reason to assume a priori that observations made with regard to verbal conformity are automatically applicable to action. A person may pay lip service to the norms of a group and then be quite unwilling to carry out the kinds of behavior the group norms imply. Furthermore, an individual may accept and even promulgate a group standard at the verbal level, and yet find himself *unable* to translate the belief into deeds. Here we refer not to the distinction between overt compliance and private acceptance, but of the relationship between a genuinely accepted belief and its transformation into behavior.

The main point of the present experiment is to see if a person will perform acts under group pressure that he would not have performed in the absence of social inducement. There are many particular forms of action that can be inserted into a general group-pressure experimental design. One could study sorting IBM cards, or making paper cutouts, or eating crackers. Convenience makes them attractive, and in several valuable experiments investigators have used these tasks to good advantage (Frank, 1944; French, Morrison, & Levinger, 1960; Raven & French, 1958). But eventually social psychology must come to grips with significant behavior contents, contents that are of interest in their own right and are not simply trivial substitutes for psychologically meaningful forms of behavior. Guided by this consideration, a relatively potent form of action was selected for shaping by group pressure. We asked: Can a group induce a person to deliver punishment of increasing severity to a protesting individual? Whereas Asch and others have shown in what manner group pressure can cause a person to pronounce judgments that contradict his thinking, the present study examines whether group pressure causes a person to engage in acts at variance with his uninfluenced behavior.

METHOD

The details of subject recruitment, subject composition, experimenter's introductory pattern, apparatus, and learning task have been described elsewhere (Milgram, 1963) and need only be sketched here.

Subjects consisted of 80 male adults, ranging in age from 20 to 50 years, and distributed in equal numbers, ages, and occupational statuses in the experimental and control conditions.

Procedure for Experimental Condition

General. The basic experimental situation is one in which a team of three persons (including two confederates) tests a fourth person on a paired-associate learning task. Whenever the fourth party makes a mistake the team punishes him with an electric shock. The two confederates suggest increasingly higher shock levels; the experimenter observes in what degree the third member of the team (a naive subject) goes along with or resists the confederates' pressure to increase the voltage levels.

Details. Four adults arrive at a campus laboratory to participate in a study of memory and learning. On arrival each subject is paid $4.50. The experimenter explains that a variety of roles must be performed in the experiment, and that to make role assignments fairly, subjects are to draw printed slips from a hat, each slip designating a particular experimental role. Actually, three of the adults are confederates, and only one naive subject is tested each hour. The drawing is rigged so that the naive subject is always assigned the position, Teacher 3, and Confederate B is always the Learner. The role assignments, which the subjects read from the drawn slips, are as [shown on the next page].

The experimenter explains that the purpose of the experiment is to study the effects of punishment on memory in a context of "collective teaching." Confederate B is taken to an adjoining room and in full view of the others is strapped into an electric-chair apparatus. The experimenter explains the nature of the learning task to the Learner and, passing over a remark made by the Learner concerning a mild heart condition, takes the three teachers to the main experimental room.

They are seated before an imposing shock generator whose essential feature is a horizontal line of 30 lever switches, labeled 15–450 volts, in 15-volt increments. Verbal designations are spread along the line of switches reading: Slight Shock, Moderate Shock, Strong Shock, Very Strong Shock, Intense Shock, Extreme Intensity Shock, and Danger: Severe Shock.

The experimenter restates that the Learner is to be tested on a paired-associate learning task (see Milgram, 1963, for details). Teachers are told that the Learner must be shocked each time he errs in the learning task. The experimenter explains how the level of shock is to be determined:

> Now the amount of punishment given on any trial is decided by the teachers themselves. Each of you will suggest a shock level. And the shock actually administered will be the lowest level suggested by any of the three teachers. In order to keep the experiment running smoothly, give suggested levels in this order: Teacher 1, submit your bid first; Teacher 2, submit your bid second; and Teacher 3, submit your bid third. Remember you can stick to one level or raise or lower your level as you desire, but on any trial, the punishment administered will be the lowest level suggested by any teacher on that trial.

Role title	Participant	Task
Teacher 1	Confederate C	First, you will read word pairs to the Learner. Then you will read a stimulus word along with four possible answers.
Teacher 2	Confederate A	When the Learner gives his answer, you task is to indicate whether he is correct or incorrect. When he has erred you will provide him with the correct answer.
Teacher 3	Naive subject	Whenever the Learner gives an incorrect answer, you will administer punishment by activating a shock generator.
Learner	Confederate B	Your task will be to learn a list of word pairs read to you by Teacher 1.

Thus the naive subject finds himself in a position in which, on any trial, he can effectively control the maximum shock administered to the Learner, e.g., the ground rules of the experiment would permit him to hold the shock level down to 15 volts throughout the laboratory session. On the other hand he may go along with or move in the direction of the group choice. It is the naive subject who actually administers the shock by depressing the appropriate lever on the generator (i.e., he always emerges from the rigged drawing as Teacher 3).

The three teachers each have their roles spelled out for them again, and there remains only the task of giving each a sample shock from the generator before the experiment gets under way.

Behavior of Teachers 1 and 2 (confederates).   According to a prearranged schedule the two confederates at the shock generator call for a one-step increase in the shock level each time the Learner errs. On the first error they both call for Shock Level 1 (15 volts); on the twentieth error they both call for Shock Level 20 (300 volts), and so forth. Their constant unanimity is rendered credible by having Teacher 1 play a somewhat domineering, and Teacher 2 a somewhat submissive type. The confederates, played by adult actors, appear indifferent to the complaints of the Learner.

Behavior of the Learner.   According to a prearranged schedule the Learner responds to the learning task by providing answers in the proportion of three wrong answers to each correct one. There are a total of 40 trials, 30 of them being critical (occasions when the Learner answers incorrectly).

The Learner's responses are not limited to providing answers. As the shocks administered to him become stronger, he grunts, protests, and demands to be let out of the experiment. Each compliment of the Learner is in fact prerecorded on magnetic tape, and is coordinated to a specific shock level. The protests and expressions of discomfort follow spontaneously the administration of an electric shock.

The Learner indicates no discomfort until the 75-volt shock is administered, at which time there is a slight grunt in response to the punishment. Similar reactions follow the 90- and 105-volt shocks, and at 120 volts the Learner shouts to the experimenter that the shocks are becoming painful. Painful groans are heard on the administration of the 135-volt shock, and at 150 volts the Learner cries out that he wants to be released from the experiment, complaining of a heart disturbance. Cries of this type continue with generally rising intensity, so that at 180 volts, the Learner cries out "I can't stand the pain," and by 285 volts his response to the shock is clearly an agonized scream. At 300 volts the victim shouts in desperation that he will no longer provide answers to the memory test, and so forth through 450 volts. In other words, increases in shock level are met by increasingly severe reactions from the person being punished.

It is to be remembered that this is merely a *potential* series of responses. If a shock no higher than the 75-volt level is administered, only a grunt is heard. As a point of procedure, protests were not repeated at the same shock level, e.g., after the first grunt was used in response to Shock Level 75, no further complaints were introduced until and if a higher shock level were used.

Experimental measures.   The principal experimental measure, therefore, is the level of shock administered by the subject on each of the 30 critical trials. The shock levels were automatically recorded by an Esterline-Angus event recorder wired directly into the shock generator, providing us with a permanent record of each subject's performance.

Postexperimental session.   An interview and debriefing session were held immediately after each subject's performance. A variety of background measures was obtained, as well as qualitative reactions to the experimental situation.

Control Condition

The purpose of the control condition is to determine the level of shock the naive subject administers to the Learner in the absence of group influence. One naive subject and one confederate (the Learner) perform in each session. The procedure is identical to that in the experimental condition, except that the tasks of Confederates *A* and *C* are collapsed into one role handled by the naive subject. References to collective teaching are omitted.

The naive subject is instructed to administer a shock each time the Learner errs, and the naive subject is told that as teacher he is free to select any shock level on any of the trials. In all other respects the control and experimental procedures are identical.

RESULTS

Figure 16.1 shows the mean shock levels for each critical trial in the experimental and control conditions. It also shows a diagonal representing the stooge-group's suggested shock level on each critical trial. The degree to which the experimental function moves away from the control level and toward the stooge-group diagonal represents the effects of group influence. Inspection indicates that the confederates substantially influenced the level of shock administered to the Learner. The results will now be considered in detail.

In the experimental condition the standard deviation of shock levels rose regularly from trial to trial, and roughly in proportion to the rising mean shock level. However, in the control condition the standards deviation did not vary systematically with the mean through the 30 trials. Representative mean shock levels and standard deviations for the two conditions are shown in Table 16.1. Hartley's test for homogeneity of variance confirmed that the variances in the two conditions were significantly different. Therefore a reciprocal-of-the-square-root transformation was performed before an analysis of variance was carried out.

As summarized in Table 16.2, the analysis of variance showed that the overall mean shock level in the experimental condition was significantly higher than that in the control condition ($p < 0.001$). This is less interesting, however, than the differing slopes in the two conditions, which show the group effects through the course of the experimental session.[2] The analysis of variance test for trend confirmed that the slopes for the two conditions differed significantly ($p < 0.001$).

Examination of the standard deviations in the experimental condition shows that there are large individual differences in response to group pressure, some subjects following the group closely, others resisting effectively. Subjects were ranked according to their total deviation from

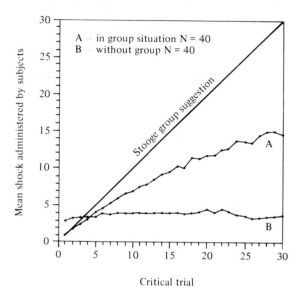

FIGURE 16.1
Mean shock levels in experimental and
control conditions over 30 critical trials.

the confederates' shock choices. On the thirtieth critical trial the most
conforming quartile had a mean shock level of 27.6, while the mean shock
level of the least conforming quartile was 4.8. Background characteristics
of the experimental subjects were noted: age, marital status, occupation,
military experience, political preference, religious affiliation, birth-order
information, and educational history. Less educated subjects (high school

TABLE 16.1 REPRESENTATIVE MEAN SHOCK LEVELS
AND STANDARD DEVIATIONS IN THE EXPERIMENTAL
AND CONTROL CONDITIONS

| Trial | Experimental condition | | Control condition | |
	Mean shock level	SD	Mean shock level	SD
5	4.03	1.19	3.35	2.39
10	6.78	2.63	3.48	3.03
15	9.20	4.28	3.68	3.58
20	11.45	6.32	4.13	4.90
25	13.55	8.40	3.55	3.85
30	14.13	9.59	3.38	1.98

TABLE 16.2 ANALYSIS OF VARIANCE OF SHOCK LEVELS ADMINISTERED IN THE EXPERIMENTAL AND CONTROL CONDITIONS

Source	df	SS	MS	F
Total between individuals	79	966,947.1	12,239.8	
Between experimental conditions	1	237,339.4	237,339.4	25.37*
Between individuals	78	729,607.7	9,353.9	
Within individuals	2,320	391,813.5	168.9	
Between trials	29	157,361.7	5,426.3	96.04*
Trials × experimental conditions (Trend)	29	106,575.4	3,675.0	65.04*
Remainder	2,262	127,876.4	56.5	

*$p < 0.001$.

degree or less) tended to yield more than those who possess a college degree ($\chi^2 = 2.85$, df = 1, $p < 0.10$). Roman Catholic subjects tended to yield more than Protestant subjects ($\chi^2 = 2.96$, df = 1, $p < 0.10$). No other background variable measured in the study was associated with amount of yielding, though the number of subjects employed was too small for definite conclusions.

The shock data may also be examined in terms of the *maximum* shock administered by subjects in the experimental and control conditions, i.e., the highest single shock administered by a subject throughout the 30 critical trials. The information is presented in Table 16.3. Only 2 control subjects administered shocks beyond the tenth voltage level (at this point the Learner makes his first truly vehement protest), while 27 experimental subjects went beyond this point. A median test showed that the maximum shocks administered by experimental subjects were higher than those administered by control subjects ($\chi^2 = 39.2$, df = 1, $p < 0.001$).

The main effect, then, is that in the experimental condition subjects were substantially influenced by group pressure. When viewed in terms of the mean shock level over the 30 critical trials, as in Fig. 16.1, the experimental function appears as a vector more or less bisecting the angle formed by the confederates' diagonal and control slopes. Thus one might be tempted to say that the subject's action in the experimental situation had two major sources: it was partly determined by the level the subject would have chosen in the control condition, and partly by the confederates' choice. Neither one nor the other entirely dominates the average behavior of subjects in the experimental condition. There are very great individual differences in regard to the more dominant force.

TABLE 16.3 MAXIMUM SHOCK LEVELS ADMINISTERED IN EXPERIMENTAL AND CONTROL CONDITIONS

Verbal designation and voltage indication	Number of subjects for whom this was maximum shock	
	Experimental	Control
Slight shock		
15	1	3
30	2	6
45	0	7
60	0	7
Moderate shock		
75	1	5
90	0	4
105	1	1
120	1	1
Strong shock		
135	2	3
150	5	1
165	2	0
180	0	0
Very strong shock		
195	1	0
210	2	0
225	2	0
240	1	0
Intense shock		
255	2	0
270	0	0
285	1	0
300	1	0
Extreme intensity shock		
315	2	0
330	0	0
345	1	0
360	2	0
Danger: severe shock		
375	0	1
395	0	0
405	1	0
420	2	0
XXX		
435	0	0
450	7	1

DISCUSSION

The substantive contribution of the present study lies in the demonstration that group influence can shape behavior in a domain that might have been thought highly resistant to such effects. Subjects are induced by the group to inflict pain on another person at a level that goes well beyond levels chosen in the absence of social pressure. Hurting a man is an action that for most people carries considerable psychological significance; it is closely tied to questions of conscience and ethical judgment. It might have been thought that the protests of the victim and inner prohibitions against hurting others would have operated effectively to curtail the subject's compliance. While the experiment yields wide variation in performance, a substantial number of subjects submitted readily to pressure applied to them by the confederates.

The significance of yielding in Asch's situation is sometimes questioned because the discriminative task is not an issue of self-evident importance for many subjects (Bronowski).[3] The criticism is not easily extended to the present study. Here the subject does not merely feign agreement with a group on a perceptual task of undefined importance; and he is unable to dismiss his action by relegating it to the status of a trivial gesture, for a person's suffering and discomfort are at stake.

The behavior observed here occurred within the framework of a laboratory study presided over by an experimenter. In some degree his authority stands behind the group. In his initial instructions the experimenter clearly legitimized the use of any shock level on the console. Insofar as he does not object to the shocks administered in the course of the experiment, his assent is implied. Thus, even though the effects of group pressure have been clearly established by a comparison of the experimental and control conditions, the effects occurred within the context of authoritative sanction. This point becomes critical in any attempt to assess the relative effectiveness of *conformity* versus *obedience* as means of inducing contravalent behavior (Milgram, 1963). If the experimenter had not approved the use of all shock levels on the generator, and if he had departed from the laboratory at an early stage, thus eliminating any sign of authoritative assent during the course of the experiment, would the group have had as powerful an effect on the naive subject?

There are many points of difference between Asch's investigation and the procedure of the present study that can only be touched upon here.

1. While in Asch's study the *adequate* response is anchored to an external stimulus event, in the present study we are dealing with an internal, unbound standard.

2. A misspoken judgment can, in principle, be withdrawn, but here we are dealing with action that has an immediate and unalterable

consequence. Its irreversibility stems not from constraints extrinsic to the action, but from the content of the action itself: once the Learner is shocked, he cannot be unshocked.

3. In the present experiment, despite the several sources of opinion, there can be but a single shock level on each trial. There is, therefore, a competition for outcome that was not present in the Asch situation.

4. While in the Asch study the focus of pressure is directed toward the subject's judgment, with distortion of public response but an intermediary stage of influence, here the focus of pressure is directed toward performance of action itself. Asch's yielding subject may secretly harbor the true judgment; but when the performance of an action becomes the object of social pressure, there is no comparable recourse to a covert form. The subject who performed the act demanded by the group has yielded exhaustively.

5. In the Asch situation a yielding subject engages in a covert violation of his obligations to the experimenter. He has agreed to report to the experimenter what he sees, and insofar as he goes along with the group, he breaks this agreement. In contrast, in the present experiment the yielding subject acts within the terms of the "subject-experimenter contract." In going along with the two confederates the subject may violate his own inner standards, and the rights of the Learner, but his relationship with the experimenter remains intact at both the manifest and private levels. Subjects in the two experiments are faced with different patterns of social pressure and violate different relationships through social submission.

NOTES

1. This research was supported by Grant NSF G-17916 from the National Science Foundation. My thanks to Taketo Murata of Yale University for computational and statistical assistance.
2. On the first four trials the control group has a higher mean shock than the experimental group; this is an artifact due to the provision that in the experimental condition the shock actually administered and recorded was the lowest suggested by any member of the group; when the subject called for a shock level higher than that suggested by the confederates, it was not reflected in the data. (This situation arose only during the first few critical trials.) By the fifth critical trial the group pressure begins to show its effect in elevating the mean shock level of the naive subjects.
3. J. Bronowski, personal communication, January 10, 1962.

REFERENCES

ASCH, S. E., "Effects of group pressure upon the modification and distortion of judgment." In H. Guetzkow (ed.), *Groups, Leadership, and Men.* Pittsburgh: Carnegie Press, 1951.

——, "Studies of independence and conformity: I. A minority of one against a unanimous majority." *Psychol. Monogr.,* 1956, **70** (9, Whole No. 416).

CRUTCHFIELD, R. S., "Conformity and character." *Amer. Psychologist,* 1955, **10**, 191–198.

FRANK, J. D., "Experimental studies of personal pressure and resistance." *J. Gen. Psychol.,* 1944, **30**, 23–64.

FRENCH, J. R. P., JR., MORRISON, H. W., & LEVINGER, G., "Coercive power and forces affecting conformity." *J. Abnorm. Soc. Psychol.,* 1960, **61**, 93–101.

MILGRAM, S., "Nationality and conformity." *Scient. American,* 1961, **205**, 45–51.

——, "Behavioral study of obedience." *J. Abnorm. Soc. Psychol.,* 1963, **67**, 371–378.

RAVEN, B. H., & FRENCH, J. R. P., "Legitimate power, coercive power, and observability in social influence." *Sociometry,* 1958, **21**, 83–97.

TUDDENHAM, R. D., & MACBRIDE, P., "The yielding experiment from the subject's point of view." *J. Pers.,* 1959, **27**, 259–271.

17

Liberating Effects of Group Pressure[1]

❖

I n laboratory research, the effect of group pressure has most often been studied in its negative aspect; the conspiratorial group is shown to limit, constrain, and distort the individual's responses (Asch, 1951; Blake & Brehm, 1954; Milgram, 1964). Edifying effects of the group, although acknowledged, have rarely been demonstrated with the clarity and force of its destructive potential. Particularly in those areas in which a morally relevant choice is at issue, experimentalists typically examine pressures that diminish the scope of individual action. They have neglected effects that enhance the individual's sense of worth, enlarge the possibilities for action, and help the subject resolve conflicting feelings in a direction congruent with his ideals and values. Although in everyday life occasions arise when conformity to group pressures is constructive, in the laboratory "thinking and investigation have concentrated almost obsessively on conformity in its most sterile forms [Asch, 1959]."[2]

There are technical difficulties to demonstrating the value enhancing potential of group pressure. They concern the nature of the base line from which the group effect is to be measured. The problem is that the experimental subject ordinarily acts in a manner that is socially appropriate. If he has come to the laboratory to participate in a study on the perception of lines, he will generally report what he sees in an honest manner. If one wishes to show the effects of group influence by producing a change in his performance, the only direction open to change is

This paper was first published in the *Journal of Personality and Social Psychology*, Vol. 1, No. 2 (February 1965), pp. 127–134. Copyright © 1965 by the American Psychological Association. Reprinted by permission.

that of creating some deficiency in his performance, which can then be attributed to group influences.

If men tend to act constructively under usual circumstances, the obvious direction of an induced and measurable change is toward inappropriate behavior. It is this technical need rather than the inherently destructive character of group forces that has dictated the lines of a good deal of laboratory research. The experimental problem for any study of *constructive* conformity is to create a situation in which undesirable behavior occurs with regularity and then to see whether group pressure can be applied effectively in the direction of a valued behavior outcome.[3]

EXPERIMENT I: BASE-LINE CONDITION

A technique for the study of destructive obedience (Milgram, 1963) generates the required base line. In this situation a subject is ordered to give increasingly more severe punishment to a person. Despite the apparent discomfort, cries, and vehement protests of the victim, the experimenter instructs the subject to continue stepping up the shock level.

Technique

Two persons arrive at a campus laboratory to take part in a study of memory and learning. (One of them is a confederate of the experimenter.) Each subject is paid $4.50 upon arrival, and is told that payment is not affected in any way by performance. The experimenter provides an introductory talk on memory and learning processes and then informs the subjects that in the experiment one of them will serve as teacher and the other as learner. A rigged drawing is held so that the naive subject is always assigned the role of teacher and the accomplice becomes the learner. The learner is taken to an adjacent room and is strapped into an electric chair.

The naive subject is told that it is his task to teach the learner a list of paired associates, to test him on the list, and to administer punishment whenever the learner errs in the test. Punishment takes the form of electric shock, delivered to the learner by means of a shock generator controlled by the naive subject. The teacher is instructed to increase the intensity of the electric shock one step on the generator on each error. The generator contains 30 voltage levels ranging from 15 to 450 volts, and verbal designations ranging from Slight Shock to Danger: Severe Shock. The learner, according to plan, provides many wrong answers, so that before long the naive subject must give him the strongest shock on the generator. Increases in shock level are met by increasingly insistent demands from the learner that the experiment be stopped because of growing discomfort to him. However, the experimenter instructs the teachers to continue with the procedure in disregard of the learner's protests.[4]

A quantitative value is assigned to the subject's performance based on the maximum intensity shock he administered before breaking off. Thus any subject's score may range from 0 (for a subject unwilling to administer the first shock level) to 30 (for a subject who proceeds to the highest voltage level on the board).

Subjects

The subjects used in the several experimental conditions were male adults residing in the greater New Haven area, aged 20–50 years, and engaged in a wide variety of occupations. Each experimental condition described here employed 40 fresh subjects and was carefully balanced for age and occupational types (see Milgram, 1963, Table 1, for details).

Results and Discussion

In this situation a subject is instructed to perform acts that are in some sense incompatible with his normal standards of behavior. In the face of the vehement protests of an innocent individual, many subjects refuse to carry out the experimenter's orders to continue with the shock procedure. They reject the role assignment of *experimental subject*, assert themselves as persons, and are unwilling to perform actions that violate personal standards of conduct. The distribution of break-off points for this condition is shown in Table 17.1, Column 1. Fourteen of the 40 subjects withdraw from the experiment at some point before the completion of the command series.

The majority of subjects, however, comply fully with the experimenter's commands, despite the acute discomfort they often experience in connection with shocking the victim. Typically these obedient subjects report that they do not wish to hurt the victim, but they feel obligated to follow the orders of the experimenter. On questioning they often state that it would have been "better" not to have shocked the victim at the highest voltage levels. Consider, for example, the remarks of the following obedient subject. He has completed the experiment and is now questioned by an interviewer (who is not the experimenter).

> *I'd like to ask you a few questions. How do you feel?* I feel all right, but I don't like what happened to that fellow in there [the victim]. He's been hollering and we had to keep giving him shocks. I didn't like that one bit. I mean he wanted to get out but he [the experimenter] just kept going, he kept throwing 450 volts. I didn't like that.

TABLE 17.1 DISTRIBUTION OF BREAK-OFF POINTS BY CONDITION

Shock level	Verbal designation and voltage level	Base-line condition (n = 40) (1)	Hypothetical subjects (n = 40) (2)	Disobedient groups (n = 40) (3)	Obedient groups (n = 40) (4)
	Slight shock		3*		
1	15	0	0	0	0
2	30	0	0	0	0
3	45	0	1	0	0
4	60	0	1	0	0
	Moderate shock				
5	75	0	7	0	1
6	90	1	1	0	0
7	105	0	1	1	1
8	120	0	3	0	0
	Strong shock				
9	135	0	2	0	0
10	150	6	9	3←	2
11	165	0	2	4	0
12	180	1	3	1	1
	Very strong shock				
13	195	0	1	4	0
14	210	0	0	12←	0
15	225	0	1	0	0
16	240	0	1	0	0
	Intense shock				
17	255	0	1	0	0
18	270	2	0	4	4
19	285	0	0	0	0
20	300	1	3	2	0
	Extreme intensity shock				
21	315	1	0	3	2
22	330	1	0	0	0
23	345	0	0	0	0
24	360	0	0	1	0
	Danger: severe shock				
25	375	1	0	0	0
26	390	0	0	1	0
27	405	0	0	0	0
28	420	0	0	0	0
	XXX				
29	435	0	0	0	0
30	450	26	0	4	29
	Mean maximum shock	24.55	9.00	16.45	25.70
	Percentage defiant subjects	35.0%	100.0%	90.0%	27.5%

*These three subjects indicated they would refuse to administer even the lowest shock.

Who was actually pushing the switch? I was, but he kept insisting. I told him "No," but he said you got to keep going. I told him it's time we stopped when we get up to 195 or 210 volts.

Why didn't you just stop? He wouldn't let me. I wanted to stop. I kept insisting to stop, but he said, "No.". . . I figured the voltage we were giving him was quite a bit. I wanted to stop but he [the experimenter] kept insisting not to stop. I mean the fellow in there is hollering "I don't want to do it. I want to get out of here. I want to get out of here!"

Why didn't you just disregard what the experimenter said? He says it's got to go on, the experiment.

Do you feel a little upset? Well, I mean I feel concerned about the gentleman in there, I do sir . . . I was getting ready to walk out . . . I couldn't see the point of going on when the guy is suffering in there. I figured he was having a heart attack or something. That's the reason I wanted to stop. . . .

The subject was then dehoaxed carefully and had a friendly reconciliation with the victim.

There is additional evidence that, in shocking the victim to the end of the command series, subjects are engaging in behavior which they disvalue and see as antithetical to personal and social ideas.

Spontaneous shock levels. In an experimental control reported elsewhere (Milgram, 1964), subjects administer any voltage level they wish in the absence of group or authoritarian pressure. Under this condition the mean maximum shock for 40 subjects is 82.5 volts (level = 5.50); in contrast, under command of the experimenter (in the base-line condition described above) the mean maximum shock is 368.25 volts (level = 24.55). When left on their own, subjects administer far lower shock levels than when under command.

Self-image. When persons who have not performed in the experiment are provided with a description of the experimental situation, and are asked to predict their own performance, almost all subjects see themselves as defying the experimenter at some point in the command series. Moreover, they justify their hypothetical behavior in terms of positive qualities of character, employing such statements as "I'm not the kind of person who is willing to hurt others even for the cause of science."

Column 2 of Table 17.1 shows the anticipated break-off points of 40 adult respondents who were asked to predict their own experimental performance. Hypothetical subjects respond in terms of ideals, values, and positive self-conceptions; these values are frequently overridden by the forces engendered in the concrete laboratory situation.

Moral judgment. Twenty undergraduates were asked to render a moral judgment on the issue of obeying or disobeying the experimenter.

After describing the experiment to the respondents in concrete detail, the experimenter asked:

> In terms of the moral and ethical values most important to you, and taking into account the scientific goals served by the research, how *should* you perform in the experimental situation? Should you go through to the end of the experiment or should you break off at some point?

Valued break-off points ranged from 0 to 255 volts with the median at 150 volts. Subjects were also asked to explain at length the values that should guide their behavior in the laboratory situation. A sample statement is given below:

> I would say that one should not even start the shocks, but rather, forcibly withdraw the moment that the outline of the experiment becomes evident. My reasons for saying this are very complex. . . The first is that the society's morals, which I have absorbed, teach that it is wrong to hurt a man. Morals are usually tied in with religion and this is especially true with Christianity. Having been raised, then, in an old fashioned, staunchly Lutheran family I have internalized the view that hurting a man is wrong, and no amount of intellectual reasoning can shake this belief.

Thus, there is a clear consensus that the only behavior consistent with social values and individual conscience is to defy the experimenter at some point before the completion of the command series. Yet there is a marked discrepancy between this value judgment and the actual performance of subjects in the laboratory. Despite their protests and obvious conflict in shocking the victim, a substantial number of subjects are unable to defy the experimenter's authority, and proceed to administer the highest shock levels commanded by him.

EXPERIMENT II: GROUPS FOR DISOBEDIENCE

We may now examine in what degree group influence can release the subject from authoritarian control, and allow him to act in a direction congruent with his values and personal standards.

The strategy is to replicate Experiment I, but with this difference: the subject is placed in the midst of two peers who defy the experimenter and refuse to punish the victim against his will. In what degree will the pressure created by their action affect the naive subject's behavior?

Technique

Forty fresh subjects were studied in this condition. The procedure is identical to Experiment I with these exceptions: Four persons appear at the laboratory to take part in an experiment on "the effects of collective teaching and punishment on memory and learning." Three subjects are confederates of the experimenter and one is a naive subject. The experimenter explains that three teachers and one learner are to be used in the study, and by means of a rigged drawing, the naive subject is assigned the position of Teacher 3. The roles of Teacher 1, Teacher 2, and learner are filled by the confederates. The learner is strapped into the electric chair and the three teachers are seated before the shock generator. Teacher 1 is told to read the list of work pairs. Teacher 2 informs the subject if he is correct or incorrect in his answers, and Teacher 3 (the naive subject) administers punishment. As in Experiment I, the subjects are instructed to raise the shock level one step each time the learner makes an error. (More detailed descriptions of the group technique can be found in Milgram, 1964.)

Behavior of confederates.   The confederates comply with the experimenter through the 150-volt shock. After the 150-volt level is administered Teacher 1 informs the experimenter that he does not wish to participate further, because of the learner's complaints. (It is at the 150-volt shock level that the learner makes his first vehement protest.) The experimenter insists that the subject continue. However, Teacher 1 is not swayed by the experimenter's commands, gets up from his chair in front of the shock generator, and takes a seat in another part of the room. Since the experimenter's efforts to get the subject to return to the generator are futile, the experimenter instructs the remaining two subjects to continue with the experiment. Teacher 3 (the naive subject) is to handle the reading of word pairs, in addition to his regular job of administering electric shock to the learner.

After Shock Level 14 (210 volts) is administered, Teacher 2, expressing concern for the learner, refuses to participate further. The experimenter makes strong efforts to have him continue, but he too leaves his chair in front of the generator and seats himself at an opposite corner of the room, saying "I'm willing to answer any of your questions, but I'm not willing to shock that man against his will: I'll have no part of it."

At this point the naive subject is seated alone in front of the shock generator. He has witnessed the defiant actions of two peers. The experimenter orders the naive subject to continue with the experimental procedure by himself, indicating that it is essential that the experiment be completed.

Results and Discussion

The break-off points of the naive subjects in Experiment II are shown in Table 17.1, Column 3. The arrows at Shock Levels 10 and 14 indicate the points at which each of the confederates defied the experimenter.

Comparing the proportion of obedient to defiant subjects in Experiments I and II, we see that the effect of the confederates' pressure was substantial. In Experiment I, 26 subjects proceeded to the end of the command series; less than one-sixth of this number obeyed fully in the group setting (obedient versus defiant subjects $\chi^2 = 25.81$, df = 1, $p < 0.001$). These results are presented graphically in Fig. 17.1. The mean maximum shock in Experiment II (16.45) was also significantly lower than in Experiment I (24.55, $p < 0.001$).[5]

After Shock Level 14 the second confederate defies the experimenter. Before Level 15 is administered, 25 naive subjects have followed the defiant group, while at the corresponding point in Experiment I only 8 subjects have refused to follow the experimenter's orders. The confederates appear to exert some influence, however, even on those subjects who do not follow them immediately. Between Voltage Levels 17 and 29, 11 subjects in Experiment II break off, while only 6 subjects do so in Experiment I.

In sum, in the group setting 36 of the 40 subjects defy the experimenter while the corresponding number in the absence of group pressure is 14. The effects of peer rebellion are most impressive in undercutting the experimenter's authority. Indeed, of the scores of experimental variations completed in the Yale study on obedience none was so effective in undermining the experimenter's authority as the manipulation reported here.[6]

How should we account for the powerful effect of the experimental

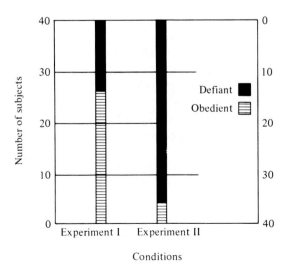

FIGURE 17.1
Proportion of obedient and defiant subjects in
Experiments I and II.

manipulation? It is probable that in Experiment I many subjects come near to performing the defiant action but cannot quite bring themselves to the point of disobedience. The additional pressure of the group members leads to an increment in the forces oriented toward defiance; the increment is of sufficient strength so that, in combination with pressures for defiance already present, many subjects are carried over the threshold of disobedience.

The strong liberating effect of the peers brings to mind the powerful effect of a partner in Asch's (1951) study. In that experiment negative pressures originated within the group itself so that the conflicting agents (partner versus majority) were internal to the group boundary; in the present study the peers free the subject from an influence that is *external* to the group. Additionally, the partner's support in Asch's study leads to a response that is fundamentally similar in form but different in value from that of the erring majority. In the present study the peers initiate a radically different order of response, one which has no antecedent in the course of the laboratory hour, and which destroys the very framework of the experiment.

Reactions to the confederates. The reactions of naive subjects to the defiant confederates varied considerably and were in part dependent on the exact point where the subject himself defied the experimenter. A subject who quit simultaneously with the first confederate stated, "Well, I was already thinking about quitting when the guy broke off." Most defiant subjects praised the confederates with such statements as, "I thought they were men of good character, yes I do. When the victim said 'Stop' they stopped [Shock Level II]."[7] "I think they were very sympathetic people . . . and they were totally unaware of what was in store for them [Shock Level 14]."

A subject who defied the experimenter at Level 21 qualified his approval: "Well I think they should continue a little further, but I don't blame them for backing out when they did."

A few subjects acknowledged the importance of the confederates in leading to their own defiance: "The thought of stopping didn't enter my mind until it was put there by the other two [Shock Level 14]." "The reason I quit was that I did not wish to seem callous and cruel in the eyes of the other two men who had already refused to go on with the experiment [Shock Level 14]." The majority of subjects, however, denied that the confederates' action was the critical factor in their own defiance.[8]

The fact that obedient subjects failed to follow the defiant group should not suggest that they did not feel the pressure of the confederates' action. One obedient subject stated:

I felt that I would just look like a real Simon Legree to these guys if I just went on coolly and just kept administering lashes. I thought they reacted normally, and the first thing that came to my mind was to react as they did. But I didn't, because if they reacted normally, and stopped the experiment, and I did the same, I don't know how many months and days you'd have to continue before you got done.

Thus this subject felt the burden of the group judgment, but sensed that in the light of two defections he had a special obligation to help the experimenter complete his work. Another obedient subject, when asked about the nervousness he displayed in the experiment, replied:

I think it was primarily because of their actions. Momentarily I was ready to go along with them. Then suddenly I felt that they were just being ridiculous. What was I doing following the crowd? . . . They certainly had a right to stop, but I felt they lost all control of themselves.

And a third obedient subject criticized the confederates more directly, stating:

I don't think they should have quit. They came here for an experiment, and I think they should have stuck with it.

A closer analysis of the experimental situation points to a number of specific factors that may contribute to the group's effectiveness:

1. The peers instill in the subject the *idea* of defying the experimenter. It may not have occurred to some subjects as a response possibility.
2. The lone subject has no way of knowing whether, in defying the experimenter, he is performing in a bizarre manner or whether this action is a common occurrence in the laboratory. The two examples of disobedience he sees suggest that defiance is a natural reaction to the situation.
3. The reactions of the defiant confederates define the act of shocking the victim as improper. They provide social confirmation to the naive subject's suspicion that it is wrong to punish a man against his will, even in the context of a psychological experiment.
4. The defiant confederates remain in the laboratory even after withdrawing from the experiment (they have agreed to answer post-experimental questions). Each additional shock administered by the naive subject now carries with it a measure of social disapproval from the two confederates.
5. As long as the two confederates participate in the experimental procedure there is a dispersion of responsibility among the group members for shocking the victim. As the confederates withdraw, responsibility becomes focused onto the naive subject.[9]

6. The naive subject is a witness to two instances of disobedience and observes the *consequences* of defying the experimenter to be minimal.

7. There is identification with the disobedient confederates and the possibility of falling back on them for social support when defying the experimenter.

8. Additionally, the experimenter's power may be diminished by the very fact of failing to keep the two confederates in line, following the general rule that every failure of authority to exact compliance to its commands weakens the perceived power of the authority (Homans, 1961).

Hypothesis of Arbitrary Direction of Group Effects

The results examined thus far show that group influence serves to liberate individuals effectively from submission to destructive commands. There are some who will take this to mean that the direction of group influence is arbitrary, that it can be oriented toward destructive or constructive ends with equal impact, and that group pressure need merely be inserted into a social situation on one side of a standard or the other in order to induce movement in the desired direction.

This view ought to be questioned. Does the fact that a disobedient group alters the behavior of subjects in Experiment II necessarily imply that group pressure can be applied in the other direction with similar effectiveness? A competing view would be that the direction of possible influence of a group is not arbitrary, but is highly dependent on the general structure of the situation in which influence is attempted.

To examine this issue we need to undertake a further experimental variation, one in which the group forces are thrown on the side of the experimenter, rather than directed against him. The idea is simply to have the members of the group reinforce the experimenter's commands by following them unfailingly, thus adding peer pressures to those originating in the experimenter's commands.

EXPERIMENT III: OBEDIENT GROUPS

Forty fresh subjects, matched to the subjects in Experiments I and II for sex, age, and occupational status, were employed in this condition. The procedure was identical to that followed in Experiment II with this exception: at all times the two confederates followed the commands of the experimenter; at no point did they object to carrying out the experimental instructions. Nor did they show sympathy for or comment on the discomfort of the victim. If a subject attempted to break off they allowed the experimenter primary responsibility for keeping him in line, but contributed background support for the experimenter; they indicated their disapproval of the naive subject's attempts to leave the experiment with such remarks as: "You can't quit *now*; this experiment has got to get done." As in Experiment II the naive subject was seated between the two confederates, and in his role of Teacher 3, administered the shocks to the victim.

Results and Discussion

The results, presented in Table 17.1, Column 4, show that the obedient group had very little effect on the overall performance of subjects. In Experiment I, 26 of the 40 subjects complied fully with the experimenter's commands; in the present condition this figure is increased by 3, yielding a total of 29 obedient subjects. This increase falls far short of statistical significance ($\chi^2 = 0.52$, df = 1, $p > 0.50$). Nor is the difference in mean maximum shocks statistically reliable. The failure of the manipulation to produce a significant change cannot be attributed to a ceiling artifact since an obedient shift of even 8 of the 14 defiant subjects would yield the 0.05 significance level by chi square.

Why the lack of change when we know that group pressure often exerts powerful effects? One interpretation is that the authoritarian pressure already present in Experiment I has preempted subjects who would have submitted to group pressures. Conceivably, the subjects who are fully obedient in Experiment I are precisely those who would be susceptible to group forces, while those who resisted authoritarian pressure were also immune to the pressure of the obedient confederates. The pressures applied in Experiment III do not show an effect because they overlap with other pressures having the same direction and present in Experiment I; all persons responsive to the initial pressure have already been moved to the obedient criterion in Experiment I. This possibility seems obvious enough in the present study. Yet every other situation in which group pressure is exerted also possesses a field structure (a particular arrangement of stimulus, motive, and social factors) that limits and controls potential influence within that field.[10] Some structures allow group influence to be exerted in one direction but not another. Seen in this light, the hypothesis of the arbitrary direction of group effects is inadequate.

In the present study Experiment I defines the initial field: the insertion of group pressure in a direction opposite to that of the experimenter's commands (Experiment II) produces a powerful shift toward the group. Changing the direction of group movement (Experiment III) does not yield a comparable shift in the subject's performance. The group success in one case and failure in another can be traced directly to the configuration of motive and social forces operative in the starting situation (Experiment I).

Given any social situation, the strength and direction of potential group influence is predetermined by existing conditions. We need to examine the variety of field structures that typify social situations and the manner in which each controls the pattern of potential influence.

NOTES

1. This research was supported by two grants from the National Science Foundation, G-17916 and G-24152. The experiments were conducted while the author was at Yale University. Pilot studies completed in 1960 were financed by a grant from the Higgins Fund of Yale University. My thanks to Rhea Mendoza Diamond for her help in revising the original manuscript.
2. Exceptions become more numerous in moving from the experimental domain to the practice of group therapy and training groups. And surely the *philosophy* of group dynamics stresses the productive possibilities inherent in groups (Cartwright & Zander, 1960).
3. Another solution would be to wait until people who perform in a naturally destructive way come to the laboratory and to use them as subjects. One might deliberately seek out a group of recidivist delinquents who would ordinarily behave in a disvalued manner, and then study group effects on their performance. This would, of course, limit the study to an atypical population.
4. Descriptions of the shock generator, schedule of protests from the learner, and other details of procedure have been described elsewhere and will not be restated here (Milgram, 1963, 1964).
5. Of course the mean maximum shock in the experimental conditions is tied to the precise point in the voltage series where the confederates' break-off is staged. In this experiment it is not until Level 14 that both confederates have defied the experimenter.
6. See Milgram, 1965/1974, for additional experiments.
7. Numerals in brackets indicate the break-off point of the subject quoted.
8. Twenty-seven of the defiant subjects stated that they would have broken off without the benefit of the confederates' example; four subjects definitely acknowledged the confederates' rebellion as the critical factor in their own defiance. The remaining defiant subjects were undecided on this issue. In general, then, subjects underestimate the degree to which their defiant actions are dependent on group support.
9. See Wallach, Kogan, and Bem (1962) for a treatment of this concept dealing with risk taking.
10. See, for example, the study of Jones, Wells, and Torrey (1958). Starting with the Asch situation they show that through feedback, the experimenter can foster greater independence in the subject, but not significantly greater yielding to the erring majority. Here, too, an initial field structure limits the direction of influence attempts.

REFERENCES

ASCH, S. E., "Effects of group pressure upon the modification and distortion of judgment." In H. Guetzkow (ed.), *Groups, Leadership, and Men.* Pittsburgh: Carnegie Press, 1951.

———, "A perspective on social psychology." In S. Koch (ed.), *Psychology: A Study of a Science.* Vol. 3. *Formulations of the Person and the Social Context.* New York: McGraw-Hill, 1959. Pp. 363–383.

BLAKE, R. R., & BREHM, J. W., "The use of tape recording to simulate a group atmosphere." *Journal of Abnormal and Social Psychology,* 1954, **49,** 311–313.

CARTWRIGHT, D., & ZANDER, A., *Group Dynamics.* Evanston, Ill.: Row, Peterson, 1960.

HOMANS, G. C., *Social Behavior: Its Elementary Forms.* New York: Harcourt, Brace, 1961.

JONES, E. E., WELLS, H. H., & TORREY, R., "Some effects of feedback from the experimenter on conformity behavior." *Journal of Abnormal and Social Psychology,* 1958, **57,** 207–213.

MILGRAM, S., "Behavioral study of obedience." *Journal of Abnormal and Social Psychology,* 1963, **67,** 371–378.

———, "Group pressure and action against a person." *Journal of Abnormal and Social Psychology,* 1964, **69,** 137–143.

———, "Some conditions of obedience and disobedience to authority." *Human Relations,* 1965, **18,** 57–76.

———, *Obedience to Authority: An Experimental View.* New York: Harper & Row, 1974.

WALLACH, M. A., KOGAN, N., & BEM, D. J., "Group influence on individual risk taking." *Journal of Abnormal and Social Psychology,* 1962, **65,** 75–86.

18

The Drawing Power of Crowds of Different Size[1]

❖

I n a typical urban setting, when a group of people engage in an action simultaneously, they have the capacity to draw others into the crowd. The actions of the initial group may serve as a stimulus for others to imitate this action. A careful analysis of the details of crowd formation is of obvious interest to a society in which collective action plays an increasingly important part in social life. One theoretical formulation that bears on this problem is that of Coleman and James (1961).

Coleman and James assumed that there is a "natural process" by which free-forming groups acquire and lose members and thus reach specific maximum sizes. They have developed a model that generates a size distribution that closely approximates the actually observed size distribution of many thousands of groups. The central assumption of their model of acquisition and loss are "a constant tendency of a group member to break away, independent of the group, thus producing a loss rate for the group proportional to size; and an acquisition rate for each group proportional to the number of single individuals available to be 'picked up [p. 44].'" Thus the growth of a group is independent of the size of the group and dependent only upon the number of persons who are available to join the group. However, Coleman and James pointed out that "a contagion assumption—that is, an assumption that a person is more likely to join a large group than a small one [p. 44]," might be needed in their model. (Their use of the

This paper was written in collaboration with Leonard Bickman and Lawrence Berkowitz, and was first published under the title "Note on the Drawing Power of Crowds of Different Size," in the *Journal of Personality and Social Psychology*, Vol. 13, No. 2 (1969), pp. 79–82. Copyright © 1969 by the American Psychological Association. Reprinted by permission.

term "contagion" is not entirely accurate, since this term does not signify in any direct way that a large group is more effective in attracting new persons than a small one. It is preferable, in this connection, to use the phrase "assumption of initial group size.")

This paper reports on the effects which crowds of different sizes had on passersby, following the quantitative approach to the study of crowd behavior outlined by Milgram and Toch (1969).

A few of the basic concepts used in this study need to be clarified. First there is the *stimulus crowd*. This was provided by the investigators and varied in number from 1 to 15. If the crowd is to draw onlookers, then it must be exposed to an *available population*. The population may be finite, and thus exhaustable, or it may be continually replenished as in the present study. The population may also be in various *states of activity*, that is, sitting around (as at a beach) or moving along paths. The available population in the case of the present study consisted of the stream of

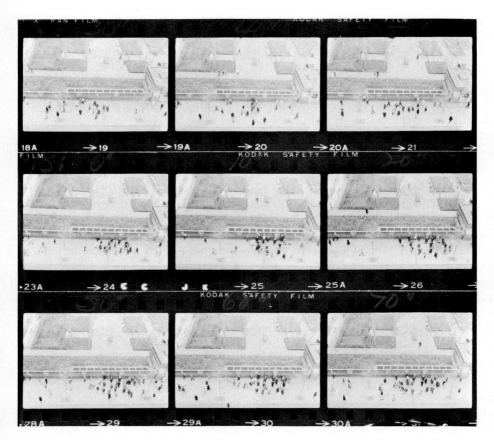

FIGURE 18.1
Photographs used in the analysis of crowd growth.

pedestrians moving along a major city thoroughfare. Finally, the crowd must exhibit some sort of *observable action* that the population can imitate or in some manner respond to. In the present study the stimulus crowd stood on the pavement and looked up at the window of a nearby building. This action, or parts of it, could be adopted by the passersby. The passerby could simply look up at the building where the crowd was staring without breaking stride, or he could make a more complete imitative action by stopping and standing alongside the crowd. Analyses were undertaken for both types of responses.

In sum, the investigators wanted to see in what degree crowds, varying in size from 1 to 15 persons, and all performing the same observable action, would draw persons into their activities.

METHOD

Subjects

The subjects were 1,424 pedestrians on a busy New York City street who passed along a 50-foot length of sidewalk during thirty one-minute trials. The study was conducted on two winter afternoons in 1968.

Procedure

A 50-foot length of sidewalk was designated as the area of observation. At a signal, flashed from the sixth-floor window of an office building across the street from this area of sidewalk, a group of confederates (stimulus crowd) entered the middle of the observation area, stopped, and looked up at the sixth-floor window. This gaze was maintained for 60 seconds. At the end of this period the group was signaled to disperse. After the area was cleared of the gathered crowd the procedure was repeated using a different size stimulus crowd. Five randomly ordered trials were conducted for each of the six different size stimulus crowds. The stimulus crowds were composed of 1, 2, 3, 5, 10, and 15 persons. Motion pictures were taken of the observation area for the 60 seconds during which the stimulus crowd maintained its gaze at the window.

Data Analysis

The motion pictures were analyzed to determine the total number of persons who passed through the observation area and their behavior. Pairs of judges counted the number of persons entering the field; within this group, the number of persons who looked up; and finally the number of persons who stopped.

RESULTS

The first question is whether the number of persons who stop alongside the crowd increases as the size of the stimulus crowd increases. The data are provided in Fig. 18.2 (broken line). While 4 percent of the passersby stopped alongside a single individual looking up, 40 percent of the passersby stopped alongside a stimulus crowd of 15. An analysis of variance was performed on the mean percentage of persons who stopped alongside the crowd (Table 18.1). This analysis indicates that the size of the stimulus crowd significantly affects the proportion of passersby who stand alongside it.

But the influence of the stimulus crowd is not limited to those who stop and stand alongside it. For a larger number of passersby partially adopt the behavior of the crowd by looking up in the direction of the crowd's gaze, while not, however, breaking stride and standing alongside it. Here again the influence of the stimulus crowd increases along with its size. While one person induced 42 percent of the passersby to look up (whether or not they also stopped), the stimulus crowd of 15, all looking in the same direction, caused 86 percent of the passersby to orient them-

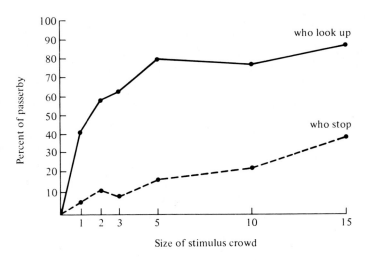

FIGURE 18.2
Mean percentage of passersby who look up and who stop, as a function of the size of the stimulus crowd.

TABLE 18.1 ANALYSIS OF VARIANCE
OF THE PROPORTION OF PASSERSBY
WHO STOP AS A FUNCTION OF THE
SIZE OF THE STIMULUS CROWD

Source	SS	df	MS	F
Between	0.423	5	0.085	20.63*
Within	0.099	24	0.004	
Total	0.522	29		

*$p < 0.001$.

selves in the same direction (Fig. 18.2, solid line). An analysis of variance again confirms the difference in means (Table 18.2).

A trend analysis for unequal intervals was performed on the data (Gaito, 1965). There is a significant linear trend ($F = 101.7$, $p < 0.01$) and a nonsignificant quadratic trend ($F = 0.42$) for the passersby who stopped. However, for the passersby who looked up, there are both significant linear ($F = 57.2$, $p < 0.01$) and quadratic ($F = 11.6$, $p < 0.01$) components. This bears on a recent discussion of Gerard, Wilhelmy, and Conolly (1969). In their study, conformity increased in linear fashion as a function of group size, in contrast to Asch (1951), who found a curvilinear relationship. The present study shows that a single set of group-size manipulations can generate both types of functions, depending on the specific dependent variable selected for analysis.

A comparison of those who stop and those who look up shows that while both behaviors increase with the size of the stimulus crowd, the percentage of those who only look up is always higher than those who stop, regardless of the size of the stimulus crowd. It appears that the more demanding, in time or effort, the behavior, the less likely it is that the passerby will join it.

Two additional points need to be made. First, it is clear that while the effects of a precipitating group of a given size for the subsequent growth of the crowd were studied, the size of the stimulus crowd increased as

TABLE 18.2 ANALYSIS OF VARIANCE
OF THE PROPORTION OF PASSERSBY
WHO LOOK UP AS A FUNCTION OF
THE SIZE OF THE STIMULUS CROWD

Source	SS	df	MS	F
Between	0.628	5	0.125	16.28*
Within	0.187	24	0.008	
Total	0.815	29		

*$p < 0.001$.

soon as persons joined it. Thus, the effect of a stimulus crowd of *constant* size was not studied. In order to do this it would be necessary to withdraw a member of the stimulus crowd as soon as a passerby joined it.

Second, the maximum size which the crowd attains is dependent not only on the initial size of the crowd, but also on the nature of the stimulus to which the passerby is directed. In the present study, passersby were oriented by the gaze of the crowd to a scene that had no special holding power. (Pedestrians looked up to the sixth floor of an office building where some dimly perceived figures were peering back from inside. It was not a scene of compelling interest.) If, instead, an acrobat were performing on the building ledge, the interest of the scene would likely hold crowd members for a longer period of time, and the crowd would grow to a larger maximum size within a one-minute interval (the size of the crowd at any given moment being equal to the initial stimulus crowd plus additions minus withdrawals). There is some logical basis for joining larger crowds: all other things being equal, the larger the crowd, the more likely its members are attending to a matter of interest.

The results of this study show that the number of persons who will react to, and join in, the observable behavior of a stimulus crowd is related to the size of the stimulus crowd. These findings contradict the acquisition assumption of the Coleman and James model. The acquisition rate is not, as they assume, dependent only upon the number of persons available to join the group. (For the present study, the mean number of such individuals was not significantly different for the different size stimulus crowds.) An assumption of initial group size is indeed necessary.

NOTE

1. This study arose out of a graduate seminar in social psychology conducted by the first author at The City University of New York. Among those who took part in the present study were Stuart Baum, Sheryl Bruder, Fay Crayne, Victor Ernoult, Susan Flinn, Bert Flugman, Henry Glickman, Michael Hoffman, Marcia Kay, Jo Lang, Elaine Lieberman, Nicholas Papouchis, Arthur Shulman, Henry Solomon, Sheila Sperber, and Mark Silverman. The study was supported by The City University of New York and by a small grant from the National Institute of Mental Health, Number 16284-01.

REFERENCES

Asch, S. E., "Effects of group pressure upon the modification and distortion of judgment." In H. Guetzkow (ed.), *Groups, Leadership, and Men*. Pittsburgh: Carnegie Press, 1951.

Coleman, J. S., & James, J., "The equilibrium size distribution of freely-forming groups." *Sociometry*, 1961, **24**, 36–45.

GAITO, J., "Unequal intervals and unequal N in trend analysis." *Psychological Bulletin*, 1965, **63**, 125–127.

GERARD, H. B., WILHELMY, R. A., & CONOLLY, E. S., "Conformity and group size." *Journal of Personality and Social Psychology*, 1968, **8**, 79–82.

MILGRAM, S., & TOCH, H., "Collective behavior: crowds and social movements." In G. Lindzey & E. Aronson (eds.), *The Handbook of Social Psychology*. Vol. IV (2nd ed.). Reading, Mass.: Addison-Wesley, 1969.

PART 4

——— ❖ ———

The Individual in a Communicative Web

INTRODUCTION

I f the world were drained of every individual and we were left only with the messages that passed between them, we would still be in possession of the information needed to construct our discipline. For every truly socio-psychological phenomenon is rooted in *communication*. If influence is to be exerted by one person on another, some message must pass from the influencing source to its target, whether it be an eloquently persuasive argument, a fleeting scowl, or the distal messages that modern technology allows. By this fact, social psychology acquires scientific potential, for what passes from one person to the next necessarily enters the public and thus measurable domain.

Several articles in this section began as personal experiences that were eventually transformed into an experimental inquiry. Perhaps an account of the diffusion traceback study, which has not been previously published, best illustrates this interplay.

In 1954, I lived in a graduate dormitory at Harvard University. The dormitory rooms did not have private telephones, but there was a pay telephone in the hallway about 100 feet from my room. Students both made and received calls at the pay phone. The telephone often rang many times before a student bestirred himself to walk from his room to answer it, then summoned the person requested by the caller. The problem was that there was no norm or custom prescribing how often to perform this civic chore. When the telephone rang, no one in the dorm knew who it was for. Who then should answer it? As a possible solution I devised a formula, inscribed it on an index card, and posted it near the telephone. It stated: "To share equitably the burden of answering this phone, students should answer the phone two times for each call they receive. (This is to take account of those occasions when a call is received for you, and you are not in.)" The message served as a guideline in a previously normless situation.

Five years passed. I left the dormitory, spent a year in Norway and one in France, then in 1959 I returned to Harvard. While making use of a pay phone in a neighboring dormitory, I noticed near the telephone a card that stated: "To share in the burden of answering this telephone, it is traditional for students to answer the phone two times for each call he receives . . . etc." The notices were spread far and wide. This cultural item had become diffused. It was now a tradition, yet it had started as the act of a single person. That is how many items must work their way into the general culture. A person inscribes a bit of graffiti: "Kilroy was here," or, "Taki 183." It catches on, diffuses widely, and seems to be everywhere. But is it possible to trace the item back to its original source?

The problem of tracing cultural items to their origin was again revived in 1966 in a conversation with my colleague, Dr. Lane Conn. We had begun our discussion with the premise that many items of information, fads, and styles are spread in a community by person to person, word-of-mouth communication. Verbal crazes, such as the now defunct "swifties" or "Polish jokes," are one form which such communication can take, whereas rumors and the widespread diffusion of antiscientific attitudes represent another more significant level. We wondered whether we could start with some item of information then circulating in society and trace it backward to its point of origin by asking each individual to tell us where he or she had learned of the item of information, and to continuously move the inquiry one step backward until we found the true origin of such a fad. To avoid the contaminating problem of the mass media, we would work with items that were not likely to be communicated over the radio or through newspapers. Our underlying model was that information, jokes, or fads ultimately had a beginning in some human source, and we could trace it back to that source. We speculated, for example, that perhaps all "Polish jokes" which were then sweeping the country may have started with a single beer-drinking piano player somewhere in a Chicago bar. And through our systematic network search we would find him, much as the small world method zeros in on the target person.

As it turned out, we did not launch this society-wide study, but the following year my experimental social psychology class managed to examine the diffusion-traceback phenomenon on a more modest experimental scale.

The class initiated a message we hoped would diffuse throughout the community. Once the message had been circulated we would apply our trace-to-origin procedure. Since we knew the actual origin of the message, we would be able to assess the accuracy of the procedure, i.e., whether the procedure correctly brought us back to the known point of origin. First, we needed to create a message that could be passed along on a person-to-person basis. We did this by creating a little story, a joke, that anyone could hear by calling our telephone number. An automatic answering unit repeated the joke each time the number was called. (After some trial and error, we decided to use a moderately sexy joke for this purpose, one that seemed to appeal to Harvard freshmen! A sultry young voice at the other end of the line reminisced about a romantic evening, followed by the revelation that the caller was a father!)

To get the communication process going, we sent a postcard to each of five freshmen living in the Harvard Yard. The card stated: "Call this number, just for fun, 887-5532." Our assumption was that the joke was so funny, the freshmen would pass the number on to their roommates, and so on. And this indeed proved to be the case.

A few hours after the postcards arrived, the calls started to come in. And they increased in frequency until our telephone line was jammed with calls. After 320 calls had been received, our machinery was so overloaded it broke down. Still, the 320 calls gave us enough diffusion data to initiate the second part of the study: to trace the entire pattern of diffusion and see if we could trace it back to the five Harvard freshmen who had received the original postcards.

We located people who had heard the joke by interviewing students in the undergraduate dining rooms and by placing an ad in a local newspaper. We asked each person where he had learned of the telephone number, then followed up on this information much as an epidemiologist would follow up on people known to have been infected with a contagious disease. Through careful and systematic work, the class was able to trace the diffusion network back to the original five freshmen. Thus, on a small scale, the diffusion traceback procedure worked well.

Mr. John Fryer, one of the students in the course, gave a precise account of the diffusion patterns:

> . . . the information (about the phone number) stayed largely within the Harvard freshman class. Of the 123 persons who learned about the telephone number, 103 were Harvard freshmen. The other 20 persons included 7 residents of the towns of Arlington, Brighton, and Lincoln, 2 Radcliffe freshmen, 5 Wellesley students, 3 Harvard upperclassmen, 1 freshman proctor, 1 Boston College student, and 1 student from Hiram College, Ohio . . . Within the freshman class, the channels of diffusion were largely determined by proximity. Beginning with about 0.5 percent of the freshman class in the first wave, the information spread to about 8 percent of the freshman class.

The appeal of the method used above is that it does not assume *a priori* categories of social structure, but allows such structures as are actually operative to be revealed through communicative processes. We have not applied this procedure to a society-wide process, but this remains an interesting prospect.

In the articles reprinted in this section, I have used communicative acts both as tools and as objects of sociopsychological inquiry.

Almost all of us have had the experience of encountering someone far from home who, to our surprise, turns out to share a mutual acquaintance with us. This kind of experience occurs with sufficient frequency so that our language even provides a cliché to be uttered at the appropriate moment of recognizing mutual acquaintances: We say, "My, it's a small world." "The Small World Problem" aims to elucidate this latent communication system, whose properties turn out to be interesting and more readily discerned through mathematical analysis than casual intuition.

What is the use of such a study? The criticism implied in this question has never bothered me, for any activity seems to me of value if it satisfies curiosity, stimulates ideas, and gives a new slant to our understanding of the social world. Nonetheless, I confess to being pleased when a medical investigator informed me that he found the small world method uniquely suited to his study of viral diffusion.

The use of a communication system as a tool is best illustrated in "The Lost Letter Technique." One attractive feature of the technique is that it uses a very ordinary event—coming across a lost letter—as the basis of measurement. And it moves away from an exclusively verbal study of attitudes, which, because of its convenience, comes so easily to social psychologists and other survey scientists. Indeed, what it seemed to do was allow us to survey deeds and use this as a sociological datum. True, how a person disposes of a letter addressed to "Friends of the Nazi Party" is not a very large deed (perhaps we should call it a "microdeed"), but when aggregated with the responses of many other people and compared with an experimental control, it does tell us something about how people act toward such an organization, and even whether they are willing to help or hinder it by their acts.

Society has never worried more about the effects of messages than it has about the messages transmitted on television. The concern arises because of the sustained exposure to television by the country's youth, and the high incidence of violent behavior depicted in this medium. Does viewing such violent behavior stimulate violence in the community? Social science could hardly formulate a question of greater significance for public policy. But the empirical question is not easily answered, as the excerpt from "Television and Antisocial Behavior" demonstrates.

Despite the negative character of the research findings, I am not yet willing to accept them as conclusive answers to the question of violence on television. Indeed, other investigators studying this issue have reported effects of television on the commission of antisocial acts. But in truth, the quality of the investigations is not compelling. In principle, it seems that repeated and sustained exposure to violence ought to have an effect on individuals, but experimentation has thus far failed to demonstrate it.

The essay on photography attempts to explore the sociopsychological meaning of this "image freezing" medium. Since the analysis of photography is my current burning interest, let me say a little more about it. There is a special reason why photography deserves more attention by the psychologist than, say, the act of tying our shoelaces. Photography is a technology used to extend specifically psychological functions: perception and memory. It can thus teach us a good deal about how we see and how we remember. The challenge is to identify psychologically interesting components of photography and to deepen our understanding through analysis and experimentation.

Photography is not necessarily a social act. We may take pictures of inanimate objects and not even show the photographs to others. But most generally, the social context powerfully conditions our photographic behavior. This seems a useful working assumption. Photographic behavior, therefore, ought to be subject to sociopsychological analysis.

One may inquire, for example, into the effects of a camera's presence on social behavior. One reasonable hypothesis is that prosocial behavior is encouraged and antisocial behavior is inhibited when people are aware that they are being photographed. To study this, one of my students, Maya Heczey, recently compared the size of contributions to a medical charity by individuals who are photographed and those who are not as they make their donations. She found that in the presence of the camera, people give substantially larger donations to a medical charity. She also found that antisocial behavior is inhibited: Substantially more automobiles stop at an intersection (bearing a stop sign) when a person is present at the intersection taking pictures than when the person is present without the camera.

The experiment touches on the deeper issue of the degree to which people feel accountable for their actions, and how this affects their behavior. At one extreme, a person may perform an act unobserved by others. But even behavior performed in the presence of others has a transitory quality. It is enacted, then disappears. The camera carries the documentation of the act beyond the situation in which it was carried out. It thus alters levels of anonymity, responsibility, and deindividuation. The camera is the "individuating" device par excellence, always recording a *particular* person or thing. The photograph, by permanently documenting the action, implies the polar opposite of anonymity and accordingly enhances social control.

A host of interesting questions may be raised about photography as a human activity: How can we describe the social relationship between the photographer and the person photographed? What is the nature of the pose assumed by the person photographed? To what extent is the pose influenced by cultural factors? How does the nature of the photograph a person takes change from childhood to maturity? Who within the family takes photographs and who is photographed most often? What does this tell us about the inner emotional life of the family? To what extent does taking a photograph prevent a person from fully savoring the special qualities of the moment in exchange for a future record of it? When we photograph an event, do we necessarily become an impersonal spectator of it; does this diminish our ability to respond to the event in other ways? These questions chart experimental paths that remain to be explored.

19

The Small World Problem

--- ❖ ---

The problem concerns the manner in which individuals are linked, through bonds of kinship and acquaintance, into complex networks, and the means of devising efficient paths connecting any two points within the network. For the sake of simplicity, let us call this "the small world problem," a phrase long current in our language, but first employed in the social sciences by Ithiel Pool (cited in Rand, 1964).

The simplest way of formulating the small world problem is: "Starting with any two people in the world, what is the probability that they will know one another?" A somewhat more complex formulation, however, takes account of the fact that while persons X and Z may not know each other directly, they may share a mutual acquaintance—that is, a person who knows both of them. One can then think of an acquaintance chain with X knowing Y and Y knowing Z. Moreover, one can imagine circumstances in which X is linked to Z not by a single link, but by a series of links, that is, *X-a-b-c-d—y-Z*. That is to say, person X knows person *a* who in turn knows person *b*, who knows *c*, . . . who knows *y*, who knows Z.

Therefore, another question one may ask is: given any two people in the world, person X and person Z, how many intermediate acquaintance links are needed before X and Z are connected? There are two general philosophical views on the small world problem. Some people feel that any two people in the world, no

This paper was first published in *Psychology Today* magazine, Vol. 1, No. 1 (May 1967), pp. 60–67. Copyright © 1967 Ziff-Davis Publishing Company. All rights reserved. This paper later appeared in somewhat modified form in *Interdisciplinary Relationships in the Social Sciences*, M. Sherif and C. W. Sherif (eds.), Chicago: Aldine, 1969, pp. 103–120. Illustrations are from the Sherif volume. Reprinted by permission of Alexandra Milgram.

matter how remote from each other, can be linked in terms of intermediate acquaintances, and that the number of such intermediate links is relatively small.

There is, however, a contrasting view that sees unbridgeable gaps between various groups. Given any two people in the world, they will never link up, because people have circles of acquaintances which will not necessarily intersect. A message will circulate in a particular cluster of acquaintances, but may never be able to make the jump to another cluster. This view sees the world in terms of isolated clusters of acquaintances. The earlier view sees acquaintances in terms of an infinitely intersecting arrangement that permits movement from any social grouping to another through a series of connecting links.

Concern with the small world problem is not new, nor is it limited to social psychologists like myself. Historians, political scientists, and even city planners have spoken of the matter in quite unambiguous terms. Jane Jacobs (1961), who has written on city planning, expressed it in terms that many of us have entertained as children.

> When my sister and I first came to New York from a small city, we used to amuse ourselves with a game we called Messages. The idea was to pick two wildly dissimilar individuals—say a head hunter in the Solomon Islands and a cobbler in Rock Island, Illinois—and assume that one had to get a message to the other by word of mouth; then we would each silently figure out a plausible, or at least possible, chain of persons through which the message could go. The one who could make the shortest plausible chain of messengers won. The head hunter would speak to the head man of his village, who would speak to the trader who came to buy copra, who would speak to the Australian patrol officer when he came through, who would tell the man who was next slated to go to Melbourne on leave, etc. Down at the other end, the cobbler would hear from his priest, who got it from the mayor, who got it from a state senator, who got it from the governor, etc. We soon had these close-to-home messengers down to a routine for almost everybody we could conjure up (pp. 134–135).

The importance of the problem does not lie in these entertaining aspects, but in the fact that it brings under discussion a certain mathematical structure in society, a structure that often plays a part, whether recognized or not, in many discussions of history, sociology, and other disciplines. For example, Henri Pirenne (1925) and George Duby (1958) make the point that in the dark ages communication broke down between cities of western Europe. They became isolated and simply did not have contact with each other. The network of acquaintances of individuals became constricted. The disintegration of society was expressed in the growing isolation of communities, and the infrequent contact with those living outside a person's immediate place of residence.

THE UNDERLYING STRUCTURE

Sometimes it is useful to visualize the abstract properties of a scientific problem before studying it in detail; that is, we construct a model of the main features of the phenomenon as we understand them. Graph theory, which is concerned with the mathematical treatment of networks, provides a convenient way of representing the structure of acquaintanceships. (Harary, Norman, and Cartwright, 1965)

Let us represent all the people in the United States by a number of points. Each point represents a person, while lines connecting two points show that the two persons are acquainted. Each person has a certain number of firsthand acquaintances, which we shall represent by the letters $a, b, c, \ldots n$. Each acquaintance in turn has his own acquaintances, connected to still other points (see Figs. 19.1 and 19.2).

The exact number of lines radiating from any point depends on the size of a person's circle of acquaintances. The entire structure takes on the form of a complex network of 200,000,000 points, with complicated connections between them. One way of restating the small world problem in these terms is this: given any two of these points chosen at random from this universe, through how many intermediate points would we pass before they could be connected by the shortest possible path?

There are many ways to go about the study of the small world

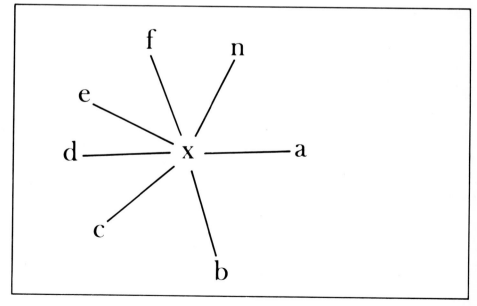

FIGURE 19.1
Acquaintances of X, $a, \ldots, n$.

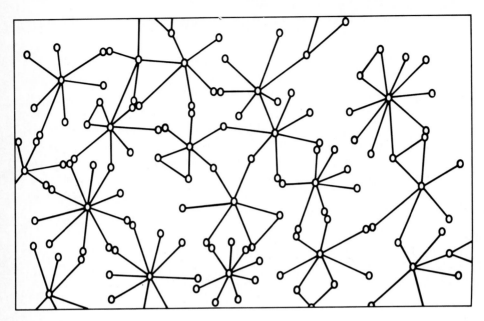

FIGURE 19.2
Network of acquaintances.

problem, and I shall soon present my own approach to it. But first, let us consider the contributions of a group of workers at MIT under the leadership of Ithiel de Sola Pool. Pool, working closely with Manfred Kochen of IBM, decided to build a theoretical model of the small world, and the model parallels closely the idea of points and lines shown in Figs. 19.1 and 19.2. To build such a model certain information needs to be known. First, you have to know how many acquaintances the average man has. Surprisingly, though this is a basic question, no reliable answers could be found in the social science literature. So the information had to be obtained, and Dr. Michael Gurevitch, then a graduate student at MIT, set about this task. Gurevitch (1961) asked a variety of men and women to keep a record of all the persons they came in contact with in the course of 100 days. It turned out that on the average, these people recorded names of roughly 500 persons, so that this figure could be used as the basis of the theoretical model. If every person knows 500 other people, what are the chances that any two people will know each other? Making a set of rather simple assumptions, it turns out that there is only about one chance in 200,000 that any two Americans chosen at random will know each other. However, the odds drop precipitously when you ask the chances of their having a mutual acquaintance. And there is better than a 50–50 chance that any two people can be linked up with two intermediate acquaint-ances.

Of course, the investigators were aware of the fact that even if a man has 500 acquaintances, there may be a lot of inbreeding. That is, many of the 500 friends of my friend may be actually among the people I know anyway, so that they do not really contribute to a widening net of acquaintances. Figure 19.3 illustrates the phenomenon of inbreeding by showing how the acquaintances of X feed back into his circle of acquaintances and do not bring any new contacts into the structure.

It is a fairly straightforward job to check up on the amount of inbreeding using one or two circles of acquaintances, but it becomes almost impossible when the acquaintance chain stretches far and wide. There are just too many people involved to make a count practical.

So the main obstacle in applying a model of this sort is the problem of social structure. Although poor people always have acquaintances, it probably turns out that they tend to be among other poor people, while the rich speak mostly to the rich. It is exceedingly difficult to assess the impact of social structure on a model of this sort. If you could think of the American population as only 200,000,000 points, each with 500 *random* connections, the model would work. But the contours of social structure make this a perilous assumption, for society is not built on random

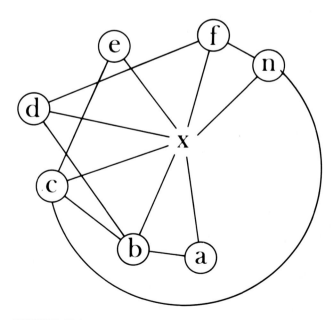

FIGURE 19.3
Inbreeding.

connections among persons, but tends toward fragmentation into social classes and cliques.

But could the problem admit of a more direct experimental solution? The Laboratory of Social Relations at Harvard gave me $680 to prove this was the case. My approach was to try to find an experimental method whereby if two persons were chosen at random, it would be possible to trace a line of acquaintances that linked the two.

Let us assume for the moment that the actual process of establishing the linkages between two persons runs only one way: from person A to person Z. Let us call person A the *starting* person, since he will initiate the process, and person B the *target* person. Then we would ask the starting person to try to establish contact with the target person using only a chain of friends and acquaintances. We could then see how long the chain was, and study many of its other properties. Of course, the starting person cannot, at the outset, know what the complete chain looks like: he cannot see beyond the circle of his immediate acquaintances, and the chance that anyone of his immediate acquaintances would know the target person is small. The starting person cannot see beyond the first link, he can only start the process on its way, by moving it one step toward the target.

The general procedure was to obtain a sample of men and women from varied walks of life. Each of these persons was given the name and address of "Target Person" (that is, an individual chosen at random living somewhere in the United States). Each of the participants was asked to move a message towards the target person using only a chain of friends and acquaintances. Each person could transmit the message to one friend or acquaintance who would be more likely to know the target person than he was. The friend would repeat the process until the message reached the target person. Messages may only move to persons who know each other on a first-name basis.

As a crude beginning, we thought it best to draw our starting people from some distant city such as Wichita, Kansas, or Omaha, Nebraska (from Cambridge, these cities seem vaguely "out there," on the Great Plains or somewhere). So letters of solicitation were sent to residents in these cities asking them to participate in a study of social contact in American society. (For certain purposes, residents of the Boston area were also used.) It was necessary to select a target person and the first individual to serve in this capacity was the wife of a Divinity School student living in Cambridge. In a second study, carried out in collaboration with Jeffrey Travers, the target person was a stock broker who worked in Boston and lived in Sharon, Massachusetts. To keep matters straight, I will refer to the first study as the Kansas study and the second study as the Nebraska study. These terms indicate merely where the starting persons were drawn from. Each person who volunteered to serve as a starting person was sent a document, which is the main tool of the investigation (see Fig. 19.4). I suggest that it be scrutinized to learn the flavor and details of the procedure, but let us quickly review its main contents. The document contains:

1. The name of the target person as well as certain information about him. This orients the participant toward a specific individual.

2. A set of rules for reaching the target person. Perhaps, the most important rule is stated in box 4; *"if you do not know the target person on a personal basis, do not try to contact him directly. Instead, mail this folder . . . to a personal acquaintance who is more likely than you to know the target person . . . it must be someone you know on a first-name basis."* This rule sets the document into motion, moving it from one participant to the next, until it is sent to someone who knows the target person. Then, rule 3 takes over and the chain is completed.

3. A roster on which the subject affixes his name. This tells the person who receives the letter exactly who sent it to him. The roster also has another practical effect; it prevents endless looping of the document through a participant who has already been an earlier link in the chain. For each participant can see exactly what sequence of persons has led up to his own participation.

4. A stack of fifteen business reply cards.

Several other features of the procedure need to be emphasized. First, the subject operates under the restriction that he can send the folder on only to one other person. Thus, the efficiency with which the chain is completed depends in part on the wisdom of his choice in this matter. Second, by means of the business reply card, we have continuous feedback on the progress of each chain. The cards are coded so we know which chain it comes from and which link in the chain has been completed. The card also provides us with relevant sociological characteristics of the sender and receiver of the card. Thus, we know the characteristics of completed, as well as incompleted, chains. Third, the procedure permits experimental variation at many points.

In short, the device possesses some of the features of a chain letter, though it does not pyramid in any way; moreover it is oriented toward a specific target, zeros in on the target through the cooperation of a sequence of participants, and contains a tracer that allows us to keep track of its progress at all times.

The question that plagued us most in undertaking this study was simply: Would the procedure work? Would any chains started in Kansas actually reach our target person in Massachusetts? The answer came fairly quickly. Within a few days after initiating chains in Kansas, one of the documents was returned to the target person, the wife of a Divinity School student. The document had started with a wheat farmer in Kansas. He

COMMUNICATIONS PROJECT

322 EMERSON HALL HARVARD UNIVERSITY CAMBRIDGE, MASSACHUSETTS 02138

We need your help in an unusual scientific study carried out at Harvard University. We are studying the nature of social contact in American society. Could you, as an active American, contact another American citizen regardless of his walk of life? If the name of an American citizen were picked out of a hat, could you get to know that person using only your network of friends and acquaintances? Just how open is our "open society"? To answer these questions, which are very important to our research, we ask for your help.

You will notice that this letter has come to you from a friend. He has aided this study by sending this folder on to you. He hopes that you will aid the study by forwarding this folder to someone else. The name of the person who sent you this folder is listed on the Roster at the bottom of this sheet.

In the box to the right you will find the name and address of an American citizen who has agreed to serve as the "target person" in this study. The idea of the study is to transmit this folder to the target person using only a chain of friends and acquaintances.

> **TARGET PERSON**
>
> Information about
> the target person
> is placed here.

HOW TO TAKE PART IN THIS STUDY

1 ADD YOUR NAME TO THE ROSTER AT THE BOTTOM OF THIS SHEET, so that the next person who receives this letter will know who it came from.

2 DETACH ONE POSTCARD. FILL IT OUT AND RETURN IT TO HARVARD UNIVERSITY. No stamp is needed. The postcard is very important. It allows us to keep track of the progress of the folder as it moves toward the target person.

3 IF YOU KNOW THE TARGET PERSON ON A PERSONAL BASIS, MAIL THIS FOLDER DIRECTLY TO HIM (HER). Do this only if you have previously met the target person and know each other on a first name basis.

4 IF YOU DO NOT KNOW THE TARGET PERSON ON A PERSONAL BASIS, DO NOT TRY TO CONTACT HIM DIRECTLY. INSTEAD, MAIL THIS FOLDER (POST CARDS AND ALL) TO A PERSONAL ACQUAINTANCE WHO IS MORE LIKELY THAN YOU TO KNOW THE TARGET PERSON. You may send the folder on to a friend, relative, or acquaintance, but it must be someone you know on a first name basis.

Remember, the aim is to move this folder toward the target person using only a chain of friends and acquaintances. On first thought you may feel you do not know anyone who is acquainted with the target person. This is natural, but at least you can start it moving in the right direction! Who among your acquaintances might conceivably move in the same social circles as the target person? The real challenge is to identify among your friends and acquaintances a person who can advance the folder toward the target person. It may take several steps beyond your friend to get to the target person, but what counts most is to start the folder on its way! The person who receives this folder will then repeat the process until the folder is received by the target person. May we ask you to begin!

Every person who participates in this study and returns the post card to us will receive a certificate of appreciation from the Communications Project. All participants are entitled to a report describing the results of the study.

Please transmit this folder within 24 hours. Your help is greatly appreciated.

Yours sincerely,

Stanley Milgram, Ph. D.
Director, Communications Project

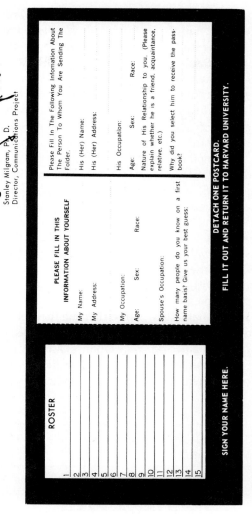

ROSTER

1
2
3
4
5
6
7
8
9
10
11
12
13
14
15

SIGN YOUR NAME HERE.

**PLEASE FILL IN THIS
INFORMATION ABOUT YOURSELF**

My Name:

My Address:

My Occupation:

Age: Sex: Race:

Spouse's Occupation:

How many people do you know on a first
name basis? Give us your best guess:

**DETACH ONE POSTCARD.
FILL IT OUT AND RETURN IT TO HARVARD UNIVERSITY.**

Please Fill In The Following Infomation About
The Person To Whom You Are Sending The
Folder.

His (Her) Name:

His (Her) Address:

His Occupation:

Age: Sex: Race:

Nature of His Relationship to you. (Please
explain whether he is a friend, acquaintance,
relative, etc.)

Why did you select him to receive the pass-
book?

FIGURE 19.4
Document used in the small world problem.

passed it on to an Episcopal minister in his home town, who sent it to a minister who taught in Cambridge, who gave it to the target person. Altogether the number of intermediate links between starting person and target person amounted to *two!*

As it turned out this was one of the shortest chains we were ever to receive, for as more tracers and documents came in, we learned that chains varied from 3–10 intermediate acquaintances, with the median at 5.5. Figure 19.5 shows what may be regarded as the main finding of the study; the distribution of 42 chain lengths from our Nebraska study, in which 160 persons started in an attempt to reach a stock broker who resided in Sharon, Massachusetts. The median number of intermediate persons is 5.5, which is, in certain ways, impressive, considering the distances traversed. Recently, I asked a person of intelligence how many steps he thought it would take, and he said it would require 100 intermediate persons, or more, to move from Nebraska to Sharon. Many people make somewhat similar approximations, and are surprised to learn that only 5.5 intermediaries will—on the average—suffice. Somehow it does not accord with intuition. Later, I shall try to explain the basis of the discrepancy between intuition and fact.

It is reasonable to assume that the theoretically pure number of links needed to complete the chains is even less than that shown by our findings. First, since our participants can only send the folder on to one of their 500 possible contacts, it is unlikely that even through careful selection they will necessarily, and at all times, select a contact best able to

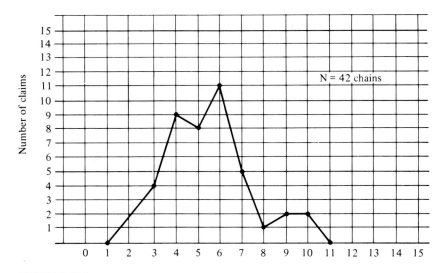

FIGURE 19.5
Number of intermediaries needed to reach target person. Each chain started in Nebraska and reached a target person in Massachusetts.

advance the chain to the target. On the whole they probably make pretty good guesses, but surely, from time to time, they overlook certain possibilities for shortcuts. The chains obtained in our empirical study are less efficient than those generated theoretically.

Secondly, the only basis for moving the folder to the target person is to work along certain highly rational lines. That is, a certain amount of information about the target person concerning his place of employment, place of residence, schooling, etc., is given to the starting subject, and it is on the basis of this information alone that he selects the next recipient of the folder. Yet, in real life, we sometimes know a person because we chance to meet him on an ocean liner, or we spend a summer in camp together as teenagers, yet these haphazard bases of acquaintanceship cannot be fully exploited by the participants.

There is one factor that could, conceivably, work in the opposite direction, that is, give us the illusion that the chains are shorter than they really are. There is a certain decay in the number of active chains over each remove even when they do not drop out because of reaching the target person. Of 160 chains that started in Nebraska, 42 were completed and 128 dropped out. These chains die before completion because a certain proportion of participants simply do not cooperate and fail to send on the folder on each remove. Thus, the results we obtained on the distribution of chain lengths occurred within the general drift of a decay curve. It is possible that some of the uncompleted chains would have been longer than those that did get completed. To account for this possibility, Professor Harrison White of Harvard has constructed a mathematical model to show what the distribution of chain lengths would look like if all chains went through to completion. In terms of this model there is a transformation of the data, yielding longer chains.

EXAMINING THE CHAINS

There are several features of the chain worth examining, for they tell us something about the pattern of contact in American society. Consider, for example, the very pronounced tendency in our Kansas study for female participants to send the folder on to females, while males tended to send the folder on to other males. For a total of 145 subjects involved in the study, we find:

Female	→	Female	56
Male	→	Male	58
Female	→	Male	18
Male	→	Female	13

that is, subjects were three times as likely to send the folder on to someone of the same sex as someone of the opposite sex. This is true when the target person is female, less true when the target person is a male. Exactly why this is so is not easy to determine, but it suggests that certain kinds of communication are conditioned strongly by sex roles.

Subjects also indicated on the tracer cards whether they were sending the folder on to friends, relatives, or acquaintances. In this same series, 123 cards were sent to friends and acquaintances, while only 22 were sent to relatives. Cross-cultural comparison would seem useful here. It is quite likely that in societies which possess extended kinship systems, relatives will be more heavily represented in the communication network than is true in the United States. In American society, where extended kinship links are not maintained, acquaintance and friendship links provide the preponderant basis for reaching the target person. I would guess, further, within certain ethnic groups in the United States, a higher proportion of familial links would be found in the data. Probably, if the study were limited to persons of Italian extraction, one would get a higher proportion of relatives in the chain. This illustrates, I hope, how the small world technique may usefully illuminate varied aspects of social structure, as well as cultural topics.

In Fig. 19.6 we show what kind of people were involved in some typical chains that stretched from Nebraska to Massachusetts.

Each of us is embedded in a potential small world structure. It is not enough to say, however, that each acquaintance constitutes an equally important basis of contact with the larger social world. For it is obvious that some acquaintances are more important in establishing contacts with broader social realms: some friends are relatively isolated; others possess a wide circle of acquaintances, and contact with them brings the individual into a far-ranging network of additional persons.

Let us consider in detail the pattern of convergence crystallizing around the target person of our second target person, a stock broker living in Sharon, Massachusetts, and working in Boston. A total of 62 chains reached him,[1] 24 of these at his place of residence in a small town outside of Boston. Within Sharon, fully sixteen were given to the target person by Mr. Jacobs, a clothing merchant in town. He served as the principal point of mediation between the target person and the larger world, a fact that came as a considerable surprise, and even something of a shock for the target person. At his place of work in a Boston brokerage house, ten of the chains passed through Mr. Jones, and five through Mr. Brown, business colleagues of the target person. Indeed, 48 percent of the chains to reach the target person were moved on to him by three persons: Jacobs, Jones, and Brown. Between Jacobs and Jones there is an interesting division of labor. Jacobs mediates the chains advancing to the target person by virtue of his residence. Jones performs a similar function in the occupational domain, and moves 10 chains enmeshed in the investment-brokerage network to the target person (Fig. 19.7).

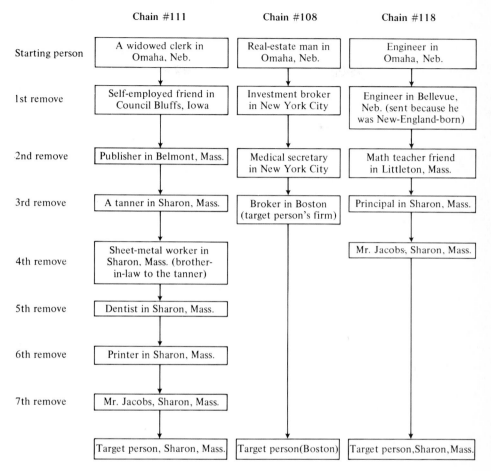

	Chain #111	Chain #108	Chain #118
Starting person	A widowed clerk in Omaha, Neb.	Real-estate man in Omaha, Neb.	Engineer in Omaha, Neb.
1st remove	Self-employed friend in Council Bluffs, Iowa	Investment broker in New York City	Engineer in Bellevue, Neb. (sent because he was New-England-born)
2nd remove	Publisher in Belmont, Mass.	Medical secretary in New York City	Math teacher friend in Littleton, Mass.
3rd remove	A tanner in Sharon, Mass.	Broker in Boston (target person's firm)	Principal in Sharon, Mass.
4th remove	Sheet-metal worker in Sharon, Mass. (brother-in-law to the tanner)		Mr. Jacobs, Sharon, Mass.
5th remove	Dentist in Sharon, Mass.		
6th remove	Printer in Sharon, Mass.		
7th remove	Mr. Jacobs, Sharon, Mass.		
	Target person, Sharon, Mass.	Target person (Boston)	Target person, Sharon, Mass.

FIGURE 19.6
Typical chains in the Nebraska study.

More detail thus comes to fill out the picture of the small world. First, we learn that the target is not surrounded by acquaintance points each equally likely to feed into an outside contact; rather, there appear to be highly popular channels for the transmission of the chain. Second, there is differentiation among these commonly used channels, so that certain of them provide the chief points of transmission in regard to residential contact, while others have specialized contact possibilities in the occupational domain. For each possible realm of activity in which the target is active, there is likely to emerge a sociometric star with specialized contact possibilities.

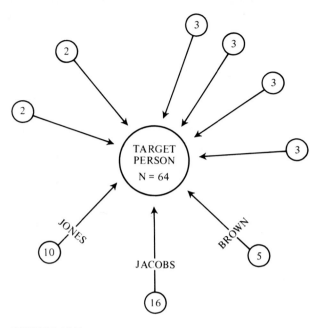

FIGURE 19.7
Convergence through common channels (includes 42 chains that started in Nebraska and 22 that started in the Boston area).

GEOGRAPHIC MOVEMENT

Geographic movement from the state of Nebraska to Massachusetts is striking over the several links. Figure 19.8 shows the progressive closing in on the target area with each new person added to the chain. There are some cases, however, in which a chain moves all the way from Nebraska to the very neighborhood in which the target person resides, but never quite makes the necessary contact to complete the chain. Some chains have died only a few hundred feet from the target person's house, after a successful transmission of 1000 miles. Social communication is sometimes restricted less by physical distance than by social distance.

The major research focus for future inquiry calls for changing the relationship between the starting person and the target person. If the two are drawn from different class backgrounds, does this decrease the probability of completing the chain? Does it increase the number of links?

In collaboration with Charles Korte, I am now applying the small world method to the study of communications in subgroups in American society; namely, Negro and white persons. We will have Negro starting

1305 miles	(starting position)
710 miles	first remove
356 miles	second remove
210 miles	third remove
79 miles	fourth remove
44 miles	fifth remove
20 miles	sixth remove
Target area	seventh remove

FIGURE 19.8

Geographic movement from Nebraska to Massachusetts. The chains progress toward the target area with each remove. The figure shows the number of miles from the target area with each remove averaged over all chains, completed as well as incomplete. For example, by the sixth remove, the average chain (assuming it is still active) is 20 miles from the target area. The target area is defined as any location less than 20 miles from Boston.

persons and target persons, and white starting persons, and try to trace the lines of communication between them. We would first like to ask: In what degree are the racial lines surmounted? Can any sizable fraction of the communications get through the racial barrier? If the answer is affirmative, what is the typical locus of transition? Does it occur at the neighborhood level? At the place of work? We are particularly interested in the persons who serve as links between Negro and white groups. In what way do they differ from others in the chain? Do they tend to occupy particular professional categories, such as minister, teacher, etc.? Is there any easier flow between Negroes and whites in Northern or Southern locales? Perhaps some new light can be cast on the structural relationships, between Negro and white communities by probing with the small world method.

As stated previously, many people were surprised to learn that only 5.5 intermediaries will, on the average, suffice to link randomly chosen individuals, no matter where each lives in the United States. We ought to try to explain the discrepancy between intuition and fact.

The first point to remember is that although we deal directly with only 5.5 intermediaries, behind each of them stands a much larger group of from 500 to 2500 persons. That is, each participant selects from an acquaintance pool of 500 to 2500 persons the individual he thinks is in the best position to advance the chain, and we deal only with the end product of a radical screening procedure. Second, there is an element of geometric progression implicit in the search procedure, and there is nothing more alien to mathematically untutored intuition than this form of thinking. As youngsters, any of us were asked the question: If you earned a penny a day and the sum were doubled each day, how much would you have earned by the end of a 30-day working period. Most frequently people give answers on the order of $1.87 or $6.45, when in fact the sum is more than \$10,000,000 for one 30-day working period, the last day alone yielding \$5,368.709.12 in wages. Elements of geometric progression with an increase rate far more powerful than mere doubling underlies the small world search procedure, and thus, with only a few removes, the search extends to an enormous number of persons.

Finally, when we state there are only 5.5 intermediate acquaintances, this connotes a closeness between the position of the starting person and the target persons, but this is in large measure misleading, a confusion of two entirely different frames of reference. If two persons are 5.5 removes apart, they are far apart indeed. Almost anyone in the United States is but a few removes from the President, or from Nelson Rockefeller, but this is only as seen from a particular mathematical slant and does not, in any practical sense, integrate our lives with that of Nelson Rockefeller. Thus, when we speak of five intermediaries we are talking about an enormous psychological distance between the starting and target points, a distance which only seems small because we customarily regard "5" as a small, manageable quantity. We should think of the two points as being not five persons apart, but five "circles of acquaintances" apart—five "structures" apart. This helps to set it in its proper perspective.

There is an interesting theorem based on the model of the small world. It states that if persons from two different populations cannot make contact, that no one within the entire population in which each is embedded can make contact with any person in the other population. Said differently, given person a embedded in population A (which consists of his circle of acquaintances), and person b embedded in population B, if a cannot make contact with b, then:

1. No other individual in A can make contact with b.
2. No other individual in A can make contact with any other individual in B.
3. In other words, the two subpopulations are completely isolated from each other.

Conceivably, this could happen if one of the populations were on an island never visited by the outside world. In principle, any person in the United States can be contacted by any other in relatively few steps, unless one of them is a complete and total hermit and then he could not be contacted at all.

In sum, perhaps the most important accomplishment of the research described here is that—although people have talked about small world connections, and have even theorized about it—these are, to my knowledge, the first empirically created connections between persons chosen at random from a major national population.

Although the study started with a specific set of questions arising from the small world problem, the procedure illuminates a far wider set of topics. It reveals a potential communication structure whose characteristics have yet to be exposed. When we understand the structure of this potential communication net, we shall understand a good deal more about the integration of society in general. While many studies in social science show how the individual is alienated and cut off from the rest of society, from the perspective of this study a different view emerges: in some sense, at least, we are all bound together in a tightly knit social fabric.

NOTE

1. This includes the 42 originating in Nebraska and 20 additional chains originating in the Boston area.

REFERENCES

DUBY, G., AND MANDROU, R., *Histoire de la Civilisation Française.* Paris: Colin, 1958.

GUREVITCH, M., "The social structure of acquaintanceship networks." Unpublished doctoral dissertation, Massachusetts Institute of Technology, 1961.

HARARY, F., NORMAN, R. Z., AND CARTWRIGHT, D., *Structural Models: An Introduction to the Theory of Directed Graphs.* New York: Wiley, 1965.

JACOBS, J., *The Death and Life of Great American Cities.* New York: Random House, 1961.

KORTE, C., AND MILGRAM, S., "Acquaintance networks between racial groups: Application of the small world method." *Journal of Personality and Social Psychology,* 15(2), 1970, 101–108.

PIRENNE, H., *Medieval Cities: Their Origins and the Revival of Trade.* Princeton, N.J.: Princeton University Press, 1925.

POOL, I. DES., Unpublished memorandum, Massachusetts Institute of Technology.

RAND, C., *Cambridge, U.S.A.: Hub of a New World.* New York: Oxford University Press.

TRAVERS, J., AND MILGRAM, S., "An experimental study of the small world problem." *Sociometry,* 32(4), 1969, 425–443.

20

The Lost–Letter Technique

———— ❖ ————

hroughout the summer and fall of 1967, the Communists staged a series of strikes, terrorist attacks and civil disorders in the British Crown Colony of Hong Kong. The aim was to apply pressure to the British and, some experts said, to dislodge them. The political sympathies of the 4,000,000 people in Hong Kong, an active, vibrant city precariously perched on Red China's doorstep, were largely unknown. Harrison Salisbury of the *New York Times* noted that pictures of Chiang Kai-shek were displayed in shop windows of the overseas Chinese merchants, but wondered whether portraits of Mao Tse-tung hung in the back rooms. What exactly were the political loyalties of the overseas Chinese?

In 1967, the populace of Hong Kong stood firm. Despite the disorder, they did not join the Communist cause. The outcome was an unexpected relief to many Westerners, but it came as no surprise to our small research team. A few months earlier, we had obtained evidence that the majority of Chinese in Hong Kong favored Taiwan over Peking, and that they would act on their political loyalties.

The evidence consisted of several hundred letters, identical in content but differently addressed. They constituted the most recent application of an experimental method for assessing community orientations toward political institutions: the Lost-Letter Technique.

We shall return to the study in Hong Kong, but first, let me tell you how a lost-letter study is conducted—and why.

This paper was first published in *Psychology Today* magazine, Vol. 3, No. 3 (June 1969), pp. 30–33, 66, 68. The technique was first described in the article "The Lost-Letter Technique: A Tool of Social Research," by S. Milgram, L. Mann, and S. Harter, *Public Opinion Quarterly*, Vol. 29 (Fall 1965), 437–438. Copyright © 1969 Ziff-Davis Publishing Company. All rights reserved.

At the root, the technique is a simple one. An investigator distributes—drops—throughout a city a large number of letters, addressed and stamped but unposted. A person who comes across one of these "lost" letters on the street must decide what to do: mail it? disregard it? destroy it?

There is a widespread feeling among people that one *ought* to mail such a letter. This behavior is so widely acknowledged as proper that an item on the Weschsler Adult Intelligence Scale is based on it. This feeling also prevails in Chinese-speaking communities. In some circumstances, however—when the letter is addressed to an organization the finder thinks highly objectionable—he may *not* mail it. Thus, by varying the addresses on the letters and calculating the proportion returned for each address, one can measure sentiment toward an organization.

The technique gets around certain problems inherent in the survey interview—the usual method of assessing attitudes. When a research team wants to test public sentiment on a social issue, it ordinarily chooses a representative group of persons from the community, and questions them. The methods for selecting a representative sample have been worked out in very careful fashion, and are so effective that a sample of only 1200 persons can be used to predict national trends with great accuracy. But it remains true that once the person is selected for questioning, the information must come through a structured conversation. The resulting measurements measure only what the person *says*. This exclusive focus on verbal accounts, though of great utility, seems an unwise fixation in any scientific social psychology. It ought to be possible to measure *deeds* on a large scale and in a way that permits experimental variation.

In the lost-letter method, the respondent is not asked to speak; instead he is presented with a chance to act in regard to an object with political and social attributes. The basic premise of the technique is that his action will tell us something of how he relates to that object. By mailing the lost letter, he aids the organization in question; by disregarding or destroying the letter he hinders it. And he has defined his relationship toward the organization by the quality of his actions.

People confronted with interviews and questionnaires know they are in a special situation. They know that they have been chosen for study and that their behavior will be scrutinized. As Milton Rosenberg of the University of Chicago has shown, their concern with the way their responses will be evaluated can have a strong effect on what they say.

This problem is particularly acute in research concerning politically sensitive issues. A Chinese merchant in Kowloon is unlikely to tell an interviewer that he is willing to take actions to advance the fortunes of Peking.

Several years ago, in my graduate research seminar at Yale, I, along with Leon Mann and Susan Harter, developed a technique that avoided these problems—one that would measure attitudes without people's knowledge, through their actions instead of their words. The lost-letter technique was one solution. Lost letters have been used to inflame a populace and to study personal honesty, but we were interested in using the returns as a clue to how people felt and—more important—how they would act toward different political organizations. The information we gained would be sociological, not psychological. We would not know about the individuals who returned the letters, but we would have a return rate specific to each organization, and thus useful for certain purposes. The nature of the procedure guaranteed the anonymity of those who took part.

NAZIS AND COMMUNISTS

The first study, carried out in New Haven, was intended not to tell us something new about the world, but to show whether the technique would work at all. Members of the seminar addressed 100 envelopes each to two organizations that would doubtless prove unpopular with New Havenites, *Friends of the Nazi Party* and *Friends of the Communist Party*. As a control, we addressed 100 more to an organization about which we expected people to feel positively, *Medical Research Associates*, and 100 to a private person, *Mr. Walter Carnap* (see Fig. 20.1).

The envelopes, all addressed to the same post office box in New Haven, contained identical letters. The letter was straightforward but, we felt, could interact suggestively with each address (see Fig. 20.2).

We distributed the letters in 10 preselected districts in New Haven— on sidewalks, in outdoor phone booths, in shops, and under automobile windshield wipers (with a penciled note saying "found near car"). Each letter had been unobtrusively coded for placement and section of city and, in a final bit of cloak-and-daggermanship, each envelope was sealed in a way that would show us later whether or not it had been opened. Then we waited. In a few days the letters came in, and as we had predicted—in unequal numbers. Whereas 72 percent of the Medical Research letters and 71 percent of the personal letters came back, just one-quarter of the Nazi and Communist letters were returned (see Table 20.1).

A considerable number of the envelopes had been opened: 40 percent of the Communist letters, 32 percent of the Nazi ones, and 25 percent of the Medical Research letters. Apparently people were more reluctant to tamper with a personal letter, for Mr. Carnap's mail came through 90 percent intact. The least returned letters were also the most opened. The trend held not only from letter to letter, but from location to location.

The initial results and the discrepant return rates showed that the basic premise of the technique held up: the probability of lost letters being returned depends on the political and social attributes of the organization

M. Thuringer

Medical Research Associates
P.O. Box 7147
304 Columbus Avenue
New Haven 11, Connecticut

Attention: Mr. Walter Carnap

M. Thuringer

Friends of the Communist Party
P.O. Box 7147
304 Columbus Avenue
New Haven 11, Connecticut

Attention: Mr. Walter Carnap

FIGURE 20.1
Sample envelopes in the lost-letter study.

to which they are addressed. Having established this, we could then apply the lost-letter technique to other circumstances where the answers were hard to obtain by conventional means.

In the realm of imagination the lost-letter technique seemed like a lazy man's social psychology, consisting of nothing more than dropping envelopes here and there, and waiting for the returns. But in actual practice, the physical distribution of letters to predesignated locations is a difficult and exhausting chore. Aching feet were common. We tried distributing the letters from a moving car, but this had to be done in darkness. The envelopes tended not to fall where we meant them to; also, as often as not, they landed wrong-side up.

Later, we tried an air drop over Worcester, Massachusetts (after requesting and receiving an official exemption from the city's littering ordinances). This did not work well either. Many letters, of course, came to rest on rooftops, in trees and in ponds. Worse still, many were swept directly into the aileron structure of the Piper Colt, endangering not only

```
                                                    4/3/63


  Dear Walter,

        Just a note to tell you that the plans have been changed.

  The speaker can't be in New Haven in time for next week's

  meeting, so bring the two reels of film instead.  My guess is

  the film will have a very good effect on the group, particu-

  larly the new members.  I'll try to get a few recent

  acquaintances to show up.

        Grace and I are flying to Chicago as usual, but we'll

  be back in time for the meeting.  Regards from my brother, and

  keep up the good work.


                                      Best,
                                         Max
```

FIGURE 20.2
Letter for all seasons. The wording of lost letter in New Haven test
is ambiguous enough to be "sent" to a variety of addresses.

TABLE 20.1

| | Placement | | | |
Address	Shops	Cars	Streets	Phone booths	Percent return
Medical Research Associates	23	19	18	12	72
Personal letter	21	21	16	13	71
Friends of the Communist Party	6	9	6	4	25
Friends of the Nazi Party	7	6	6	6	25
Total	57	55	46	35	48

the results but the safety of the plane, pilot and distributor. In the end, we never did find a substitute for legwork.

To facilitate the research, some legal spadework seemed useful. We obtained permission of the Post Office Department to use the names of fictitious organizations. And a week before the New Haven study began, I told the FBI of our work, hoping to save our Government the expense of pursuing an illusory conspiracy. The agent I spoke with seemed appreciative and even offered to let me know how many reports his office received from the citizenry. As things turned out, however, when I phoned again, the agent said he had forgotten my earlier call. Half the force, he hinted, was out on the case. The number of reports that had come in was now classified and unavailable to me.

ON RACE

The New Haven study showed that the technique could work. We next wanted to see if it could be applied to a current social issue. In 1963, tensions over racial integration in the Southern states were at a peak. Newspaper headlines reported dramatic confrontations at motels and restaurants. A Yale graduate student, Mr. Taketo Murata, drove south from New Haven with a batch of letters addressed to pro-civil rights groups and anti-civil rights groups. He dispersed them in black and in white neighborhoods in North Carolina tobacco towns. Inside, as before, was the same letter. The returns showed a neat reversal across neighborhoods. In black neighborhoods, the pro-civil rights letters were returned in greater numbers, while from Caucasian residential areas the "Council for White Neighborhoods" came in more strongly. Thus the techniques seemed applicable to a real social issue and was also responsive to a demographic variable. Mann and Murata repeated the study in a Connecticut industrial town, where the results, though tending in the same direction, were less clear, reflecting the more moderate sentiments on racial integration in the North at that time. The growth of militant Northern civil rights activity in the past six years could conceivably lead to stronger differentials in response. In general the more divisive a society, the more likely the differences in return rates of letters relevant to social issues. In an extreme case, when a country has polarized into hostile camps, neither side will mail any letters for the other.

AN ELECTION

The technique had one serious shortcoming: we had no objective evidence of its validity. True, the Medical-Research letters had come in more strongly than the political-extremist letters, and the civil-rights letters reflected the neighborhoods in which they were dropped in a way that made sense, but we needed an exact criterion against which the results could be assessed. The 1964 Presidential election provided the opportunity. Working closely with Dr. Rhea Diamond, I distributed the following letters in several election wards of Boston: Committee to Elect Goldwater, Committee to Defeat Goldwater, Committee to Elect Johnson, and Committee to Defeat Johnson.

The results were summarized by the *Harvard Crimson* a few days before the election: "SOC REL FINDS PRO-LBJ BOSTONIANS WON'T MAIL LETTERS TO ELECT BARRY." And the historical record shows that the lost-letter technique correctly predicted the outcome of the election in each of the wards. But, although the technique identified the trend, it badly underestimated the strength of Johnson support. Overall, it gave Johnson a scant 10 percent lead over Goldwater when the actual lead in these wards was closer to 60 percent. This suggests that *the difference in return rates of letters will always be weaker than the extent of actual difference of community opinion.* Even if a person plans to vote for Johnson he may still be a good enough fellow to mail a pro-Goldwater letter. And some letters are always picked up and mailed by children, illiterates, and street-cleaners. There is a good deal of unwanted variance in the returns.

In this election study the letters placed on car windshields provided the best results (see Table 20.2).

Thirty-seven letters for each one of the four committees were dropped. There seemed to be two reasons for the superior predictive power of windshield letters. First, it is more likely that adults, and therefore voters, will encounter them. Second, a letter found on a car windshield, as opposed to one found on the street, seems more in one's personal possession and is more likely to be disposed of according to personal whim.

*M*AO VERSUS CHIANG

The lost-letter technique really showed us things we already knew, or soon would know. It was not so much that the technique confirmed the *events* as the fact that *events* confirmed the technique. Could the lost-letter technique be applied to a situation where the answers were not clearly known and would be difficult to get? The situation of the 17 million

TABLE 20.2

	Johnson	Goldwater
Committee to elect	25	9
Committee to defeat	13	27

overseas Chinese provided an interesting case in point. How would they respond to an extension of Red Chinese power? Were they pro-Mao or pro-Nationalists? These are questions difficult to investigate with ordinary survey methods, but perhaps they would yield to the lost-letter technique. I wanted to disperse throughout Hong Kong, Singapore, and Bangkok letters addressed as follows: Committee for the Taiwan Government, Committee for the Peking Government, Committee to Overthrow Mao Tse-Tung, Committee to Overthrow Chiang Kai-shek and (replacing Medical Research Associates) Committee to Encourage Education.

Almost at once problems arose. Riots between the Malays and the Chinese began in Singapore just before our experimenter arrived. And in spite of written consent from the Malaysian Government, he was put back onto the plane almost as soon as he arrived at the airport. We postponed the Singapore study. The following year our experimenter in Hong Kong, a journalist from that city who had offered to distribute the letters and had been paid in advance, disappeared. After many months a Chinese colleague of mine reached him by telephone. The would-be-experimenter said that in China research takes a *very long time.* In truth, he had absconded with the research funds. I decided to go to Hong Kong myself, stopping only in Tokyo to confer with Robert Frager, who was to assist me in this study. Informants warned us that distributing "overthrow" letters in the Crown Colony would be unwise.

In the end we used all five addresses in Bangkok and Singapore but only the pro-Mao pro-Chiang, and Education letters in Hong Kong. The letters themselves were a Chinese equivalent of the straightforward earlier letter (see Fig. 20.3). All were addressed to a post office box in Tokyo, where many political organizations are located. One serious problem was the possibility of post office interference in the mailing of the letters. Even if the letters were returned to our Tokyo headquarters in unequal numbers, how could we be certain that post office policy was not producing the result? Perhaps postal officials systematically removed pro-Communist letters while sorting mail. We therefore introduced an experimental control by personally dropping several coded letters of each type directly into mailboxes served by various post offices in each city. The controls arrived in Tokyo intact, assuring us that differences in response rates were not due to postal policies but to the different response of the man in the street to the political attributes of the letters.

We employed groups of Chinese students as distributors. The students prepared written reports, some of which captured the ambiance of the Chinese study. Typical is this one:

"This is the first job which I think most embarrassing for I have to drop 100 letters on streets and roads as I walk along in Kowloon side. The Colony is always crowded and the pedestrians seem to stare at me when I have the intention of dropping a letter which has been addressed and stamped. In order to carry out my job efficiently I went to several bus

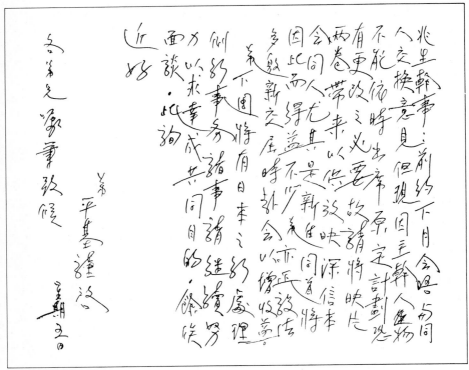

(a)

Executive Secretary Shiu Sang:
     We have previously arranged for a gathering of our
friends sometime next month for the exchange of views.
But I'm afraid that the plan has to be revised, since the
central figure will not be able to be present in time. Will
you please, therefore, bring with you the two reels of film
to the meeting for the purpose of showing. I'm confident that
these will be highly useful to our members, particularly
those new members. I am also trying to get as many new
acquantances as possible to come.
     I shall be going to Japan next week for the purpose of
handling some routine official business, and shall be back
as soon as it is through in order to be present at the
meeting.
     May I remind you to continue with your greatest effort
for our common cause so as to ensure its accomplishment.
     Best regards. All the brothers ask me to say "Hello"
to you.
                              Your younger brother,

                              Ping Kai

(b)

FIGURE 20.3
(a) Chinese letter used in the Hong Kong study. (b) Translation from the Chinese.

stops and knelt down, pretending to deal with my shoes. By doing so I left the letter on the road as I stood up and proceeded on my way.

"The dropping of letters became difficult as I came to Kowloon Isai Village, the re-settlement. Here the dwellers are very mixed. There are people even on the staircase which is dirty and moisty. However the letters must be dropped and so I just dropped the letters on the sidewalk casually and carefully. If some people stare at me, I just gave them a smile. . . . It is a delight for me to observe in some areas where I have dropped the letters, the letters disappeared (as I came back the second time). Obviously they have been picked up by somebody else."

We found that substantially more pro-Chiang than pro-Mao letters were picked up and mailed. The returns were consistent, and taken together, the findings from the three cities showed a statistically pro-Taiwan feeling on the part of the overseas Chinese.

While I would hardly offer the superior return rate of pro-Chiang letters as definitive proof of the sentiment of overseas Chinese toward Peking and Taiwan, it is certainly evidence worth feeding into the total equation of political assessment. And it makes sense too. In Hong Kong, thousands of residents are political escapees from mainland China; and in Bangkok and Singapore many are engaged in small family business and would be hurt seriously by an extension of Communist power and influence.

Other investigators now have used the lost-letter technique to study attitudes toward Vietnam, and the McCarthy-Johnson primary in Wisconsin, with varying results. While the technique seems to reflect gross differences of opinion, it fails to reflect the subtle differences that are more typical of social disagreement. Yet when the study starts with an interesting idea, interesting results sometimes follow. For example, William and Melissa Bowerman, graduate students at Harvard, distributed anti-Nazi letters in Munich, and found a depression in the return of anti-Nazi letters in specific neighborhoods of that city. Thus, they pinpointed the areas of strongest neo-Nazi sentiment.

Some advice to persons who wish to employ the lost-letter technique:

1. In order to get significant differences between control and experimental letters, they must be distributed in sufficiently large numbers. No fewer than 100 and preferably as many as 200 letters should be assigned to each cell of the experimental design. There is much uncontrolled variance and it can only be transcended by using large numbers.

2. The lost-letter technique is not very good for subtle issues, or in connection with issues that do not arouse very strong feelings. It only works for issues in which there is clear-cut polarization, and which arouse a high level of emotional involvement.

3. There is no simple way to estimate population parameters from the differential response rates. On the whole, the procedure should not be used where sample survey technique is equally convenient or applicable, but primarily when the respondent's knowledge that he is involved in a study seriously distorts his response.

REFERENCES

MERRIT, C., AND FOWLER, R., "The pecuniary honesty of the public at large." *Journal of Abnormal and Social Psychology, 43*, 1948, 90–93.

MILGRAM, S., Comment on "A failure to validate the lost-letter technique." *Public Opinion Quarterly, 33* (2), 1969, 263–264.

MILGRAM, S., MANN, L., AND HARTER, S., "The lost-letter technique: a tool of social research." *Public Opinion Quarterly, 29*, 1965, 437–438.

WEBB, E., CAMPBELL, D., SCHWARTZ, R., AND SECHREST, L., *Unobtrusive Measures: Nonreactive Research in the Social Sciences.* New York: Rand McNally, 1966.

WILLIAMS, L. E., *The Future of the Overseas Chinese in Southeast Asia.* New York: McGraw-Hill, 1966.

21

Television and Antisocial Behavior: Field Experiments

❖

INTRODUCTION

This is a report of research designed to test whether the content of television programs has a measurable effect on behavior. It aims more specifically at discovering the extent to which an antisocial act depicted on television stimulates imitation among its viewers. We hope that in addition to its substantive findings the report will contribute to the methods by which such studies are pursued.

The Present Inquiry

Two main principles shape the present inquiry. The first is that we study the effects of television under natural circumstances. This applies both to the viewing situation and to the setting in which the potential influence of the program is

Excerpted from the book *Television and Antisocial Behavior: Field Experiments,* written in collaboration with Lance Shotland, New York: Academic Press, 1973. Copyright © 1973 by Academic Press, Inc. The research was supported by a grant from the Office of Social Research, CBS, Inc. Reprinted by permission of Academic Press.

assessed. Laboratory studies typically create an aura in which the act of "aggression" loses all socially significant meaning.

The second principle is that logically compelling results can be obtained only by using an experimental design, one in which the investigator varies the value of the suspected cause and notes whether that leads to corresponding variations in the suspected effect. In this investigation, the content of a television program is subjected to controlled variation.

We expose the viewer, under a naturalistic set of circumstances, to a television program depicting antisocial behavior. The viewer is then presented with temptations in real life similar to those faced by the television character. The question is whether the television character's depicted actions influence the real life behavior of the viewers. And, of course, we run a control, a parallel condition featuring a television drama in which antisocial behavior was not an element.

What antisocial act should be used? It must be nontrivial, and hence constitute a meaningful antisocial act by the subject; it must be specific, so that the subject's commission of it can be clearly linked to its television enactment; but it must not be so grave an act that, should it be imitated outside the laboratory, the community would actually suffer serious consequences. And finally, it had to be embedded in a proper dramatic context.

The interplay of these requirements led us to settle upon an act in which the protagonist of a drama destroys a medical-charity collection-box and steals its contents. The act was well suited to our purposes: devoid of personal violence, it yet had real antisocial significance—destruction, theft, and moreover, theft from a beneficent social institution.

The next step was to embed the act in a proper dramatic context. We considered creating a special television program, with new characters, and presenting it as a television "special."[1] But this entailed two major problems: First, it is very hard to generate large audiences for special dramatic programs, and the larger the audience we could obtain for the purpose of our study, the better. Second, we did not wish to alert the audience to the fact that something was afoot; we wanted the antisocial act to appear in as natural a context as possible. These factors convinced us that it would be better to embed the act in an existing television series, which for practical reasons had to be a CBS program.

We rejected such programs as *Mission Impossible* and *Mannix* because they regularly depict such a degree of violence that our experimental act would appear trivial by comparison. We also rejected such a situation comedy as *My Three Sons*, which lacks the serious tone needed for the study.

In the end, we selected *Medical Center*, a typical hospital drama whose many episodes were entirely independent of one another, connected only by Dr. Gannon and a few other abiding characters. It would be feasible to write an episode around our planned incident without affecting the overall series, and the show, rated among the top 15, could deliver the sizable audience our experiment demanded. *Medical Center* seemed optimal for our purposes.

The Scenario

The scenario, created for the purposes of this experiment, was to have at its core the smashing of medical charity boxes.

The program centers around Tom Desmond, a young, white attendant at the Center, a recent father and owner of a small boat, with which he earns some extra money. At the beginning of the program, Tom quits his job, then changes his mind and asks Dr. Gannon to rehire him, but the job is no longer available. Tom's need for money grows desperate; his wife has fallen ill and he has defaulted in payments on the boat.

Meanwhile, Dr. Gannon, participating in a drive to raise funds for a community clinic, appears on a telethon and informs viewers that collection boxes for the charity have been distributed throughout the city. (The boxes, in fact, have been in evidence at the hospital during the opening sequences of the episode.)

As the critical sequence approaches, we find the dispirited Tom in a bar; one of the collection boxes appears unobtrusively in a corner. The television set is tuned to Gannon, who is asking viewers to call in pledges. Frustrated and angry, Tom dials the telethon but instead of making a pledge he pours abuse into the telephone. He calls in again, and is again abusive. Finally, he picks up a bludgeon, smashes the collection box, pockets the contents, and runs into the street.

An exciting sequence ensues: to a pulsating jazz accompaniment and with quick camera work, Tom roams the streets searching out more collection boxes. He finds one and smashes into it, pockets the money, and runs on to another and another. He finds five in all, and he smashes and pilfers all of them.

There is little question that this antisocial sequence, which occurs in the last quarter of the program, constitutes the dramatic highpoint of the episode.

Four Stimulus Programs

In order to provide stimulus material for experimental comparisons, the story was written and filmed in three separate versions. Two of the versions use the outline above and differ only in the consequences to Tom. The third version omits the antisocial sequence.

Version 1: antisocial behavior with resulting punishment (WP). After Tom smashes the last charity box, he is apprehended by the police and jailed. He learns that it was unnecessary for him to break into the charity banks, for Dr. Gannon was willing to lend him the money needed to retrieve his boat. His marriage also appears to have broken up. This is a conventional ending, in that broadcast code requirements state that crime must not go unpunished.

Version 2: antisocial behavior, no punishment (NP).   After the crime is committed. Tom is chased by the police. But he eventually escapes to Mexico, where his wife will join him. Since the culprit gets away with the crime, this program would not ordinarily be shown on television.

Version 3: prosocial behavior (PRO).   In the prosocial version, Tom never breaks into the charity displays, although he seriously considers it, nor does he make any abusive telephone calls. He gets to the point of raising a bludgeon to break the boxes, then he thinks of his wife and child, and refrains from doing so. Finally, he drops a coin into one of the charity displays.

Neutral story.   It is possible, of course, that the mere suggestion of an antisocial act on television is sufficient to provoke its imitation, whether or not the act is actually carried out. For example, a group of TV conspirators might talk about blowing up the Empire State Building without actually doing so, and this could conceivably be sufficient to instill this idea in someone. Therefore, we thought it best to use an unrelated episode of *Medical Center* as part of the experiment. For this purpose, we employed a sequence centering on a love affair between a foreign service officer and his long-suffering lady friend. This episode is romantic, sentimental, and entirely devoid of any violence or antisocial behavior.

Thus, four stimulus programs were used through the course of the experiment. Version 1 would test whether the depiction of an antisocial act engenders imitation. But because viewers of that version might be inhibited from imitation because the protagonist was punished, we would test another group with Version 2, in which he is not punished. Version 3 would indicate whether the mere contemplation of an antisocial act might motivate one in the same situation to commit the act, or whether Desmond's restraint and charitable contribution would induce prosocial imitation. And finally, the neutral program would provide a base line: the incidence of antisocial behavior among subjects who had not seen any of the experimental programs.

Assessing the Effects of the Program: General Idea

The next step in the logic of the design is to assess the effects on viewers of the several versions of the stimulus program. Toward this end, groups which have seen different versions of the program need to be exposed to an authentic charity display, and a comparison of the destruction rates of the several groups would constitute the principal experimental datum.

We recruited our subjects and exposed them to our stimulus program in a preview theater, over the air, or via simulated broadcasts on closed circuit television. And we promised all subjects a prize for their participation—a General Electric transistor radio.

The gift-distribution center was on the 23rd floor of 130 West 42nd Street, an office building of somewhat faded distinction surrounded by a motley assortment of shops and banks, and pornographic bookstores, and movie houses. It is a busy and informal thoroughfare, where our subjects feel no necessity to dress up to make an appearance, which meant one less impediment to their participation.

Upon arriving on the 23rd floor, our subject could consult a directory, which directed him to the office of *Bartel World Wide* or one of the five other dummy gift-distribution firms we had set up for the study. The furnishings of all were virtually identical and entirely conventional. No office personnel were to be seen.

Two other elements, critical to our experiment, were in each office: a handwritten note taped to the counter that, in the first experiment, said:

NOTICE

We have no more transistor radios to
distribute. This distribution center
is closed until further notice.

wording designed to dash the subject's hope that he would get the prize he was promised. We intended, too, that the brusque notice would suggest that no one was present; that the subject was alone in an office where he had anticipated a pleasant experience rather than the frustrating one he was now undergoing.

It was upon the other critical element of furnishings that the subject could, if he were inclined, imitate Tom Desmond's antisocial behavior: a display mounted on one of the walls bearing a poster that showed a surgeon treating a little girl, a picture of a hospital ship, and the words, "Where There Is Hope There Is Life. Project Hope. A people-to-people program of medical education and treatment for developing nations." And mounted on the display, a clear plastic container with some change, a ten-dollar bill and four singles, one of which (dubbed The Dangling Dollar) stuck slightly out of the container.

This was the focus of our experiment: would the subject emulate the antisocial behavior he had seen in the television drama? Had that experience increased the likelihood of his behaving in a similar way? Concealed television cameras enabled us to watch.

In a few minutes the subject would leave the office and retrace his steps to the door that had admitted him to the corridor, only to find it locked. Arrows direct him to the exit; following them, he finds himself not at the elevators, but in a small room. A clerk appears at a teller's window and politely asks, "Are you here for your radio, sir? Sorry about the inconvenience, but we're distributing the radios here, since the *Bartel* people are ill. Do you have a gift certificate?"

Upon countersigning the certificate (so that we could later check whether the recipient of the radio had indeed seen the stimulus program), he received his prize neatly boxed, was thanked for coming, and left, his contribution to socio-psychological research at an end.

EXPERIMENT 1: THE FIRST PREVIEW SCREENING

At the outset, we did not wish to broadcast the stimulus material on regular television channels; we needed to develop and refine our assessment techniques without "wasting" the program on several million viewers. The problem was to expose a sufficient, but not excessive, audience to the program. Our approach was to bring several hundred participants together in a midtown auditorium and show them a version of the stimulus program on film. Then we assessed the effect of the film on their behavior.

Recruiting the Audience

We wanted a large but not unwieldy audience, a cross section of the population with a good proportion of young men and disadvantaged minorities, federal statistics (Uniform Crime Reports, 1970) having shown that most thefts other than shoplifting are committed by those segments of the population.

We used two recruitment methods. In the first, we advertised in the *New York Daily News, The Amsterdam News,* and *El Diario,* the New York Spanish-language daily, asking readers to send in a coupon if they cared to receive a transistor radio in return for giving us their reaction to a TV program they would see.

We also recruited participants from the streets, distributing business reply cards at subway stations in both black and white neighborhoods during rush hours, and at high schools at the end of the school day. The postcard bore the same copy as the newspaper ad except for the addition of a line restricting the participants' age to 16 to 40.

We received 1018 responses, which we divided into four groups (one for each of our experimental programs and the fourth, neutral one), balancing the groups for age and, through random assignment, for other characteristics.

In a few days we sent our respondents invitations on a *Television Previews* letterhead, informing them that they could bring a friend if they wished but that the friend would not be eligible for a prize. And we instructed the four groups to appear at one of four specified screenings (on consecutive Thursdays, at 6 and 8 P.M.) at the Network Television Preview Theater. (This theater had, in fact, been used to gauge audience reaction to TV programs and commercials for marketing and advertising concerns for several years; we could capitalize on the theater's authenticity to enhance our credibility.)

Of the 1018 persons who were sent invitations, a total of 607, constituting groups of between 137 and 162, actually reported to the theater.

Presentation of Stimulus Programs

At the Network Television Preview Theater, participants found a comfortable auditorium, manned by a staff of professional ushers, who collected their letters of invitation, led them to their seats, and distributed questionnaires and writing instruments. Five minutes after the scheduled hour, a master of ceremonies welcomed the participants, and discussed the need that people in television have for the opinions of viewers. He informed the subjects they would see a preview of *Medical Center,* and that we would be interested in their opinions of the program. Participants filled out some preliminary questions on age, sex, and television viewing habits. Then, the lights dimmed, and subjects were exposed to a one-hour episode of the stimulus program, projected in color on the theater's professional-size movie screen. No commercials were shown.

After the screening, the emcee led the audience through the rest of the questionnaire, reading the questions and pausing while they wrote their answers, turning at last to the gift certificate, which they were to sign. He then instructed the audience to take their certificates to *Bartel World Wide* or one of the other companies specified on the certificate, at the time also specified there (M, Tu, W, F 11–7; Sat 9–5), where, he said, they would countersign and surrender the certificates in exchange for their radios. Subjects were then thanked for coming and dismissed.

The gift certificate procedure enabled us to solve a major technical problem: we had to assess the behavior of several hundred subjects at the gift-distribution center, but we could not have them all arrive simultaneously, for we wanted them exposed individually to the charity display. It would not be realistic to schedule each subject for a specific hour and minute to pick up the transistor radio. The solution was to stagger the pick-up dates over a one-week period, and also over six gift companies. In this way we hoped to keep subject collisions to an acceptable level. To minimize effects idiosyncratic to any of the six laboratory testing rooms, half of each audience was directed to a different testing room on different days.

Subjects

Three-hundred and forty-two, or 70 percent of those who received gift certificates came to the laboratory for their radios. Fifty-three of these subjects were eliminated from our analysis because they were interrupted just before or during the test by other arrivals, encounters which we felt might have affected the spontaneity of their behavior.[2] Of the remaining 289 subjects, 89 percent were male, 12 percent had not completed high school, 14 percent had completed graduate or professional schools, 17 percent were between 15 and 19, 14 percent were over 50, 25 percent were nonwhite.

Assessment Procedure

From the time the subject reached the 23rd floor and stepped off the elevator to the time he left, he was observed via concealed television cameras. Working at monitors in the control room, we coded descriptions of the subject and his behavior. We noted whether the premium office was empty when he entered it and whether he entered alone; whether he stole from the collection box or donated to it; whether he took other items from the office, or whether his behavior was entirely neutral.

Additionally, fractional behavior that could lead to antisocial or prosocial behavior was noted. Thus, we noted whether the subject attempted to pry open the donation box, and whether or not he was successful in doing so. These fractional behaviors were coded because the stimulus material may lead to the initiation of an antisocial act that is not consummated. Moreover, we considered this detail pertinent to our study because an unfilled antisocial action is, before the law, nonetheless culpable; witness such legally defined crimes as *attempted* murder, *attempted* robbery, and so on.

Upon entering any of the unoccupied offices, our subjects looked about and discovered the notice taped to the counter. Their reaction was typically one of annoyance: they would pace the room, walk behind the counter, sometimes scrawl obscenities on the notice. Subjects invariably focused their attention on the charity display, with its pictures of the surgeon and child, the medical ship, and the attached collection box. This was the critical juncture. In nearly all cases, the subject left the room within a minute or two of his arrival.

Results

Before examining the effects of specific viewing conditions, we need to ask whether any antisocial behavior occurred at all, irrespective of viewing condition. For the total absence of such behavior in any subjects would indicate that there was really no temptation present, or that there were features of the testing situation that completely inhibited antisocial action. Table 21.1 shows that this is not the case.

The fact that subjects engage in some antisocial action establishes the technical adequacy of the assessment situation, but it does not yet address the main experimental question: what is the effect of different viewing conditions on the rate of antisocial behavior? The results are shown in Table 21.1.

The three experimental programs (prosocial, antisocial with punishment, antisocial without punishment) do not differ among themselves by any statistical test in the breakage or theft rates they produced. However, the breakage rate in the neutral program (2.8 percent) appears lower than that produced in the antisocial WP condition (8.5 percent) though this trend does not reach statistical significance ($p = 0.14$, one-tailed). Yet, it is the lowest breakage rate of any of the four programs, so perhaps the depiction of Tom Desmond's antisocial act did influence behavior. But the numbers are small, and the finding inconclusive; we need replication to strengthen the case.

EXPERIMENT 2: THE FRUSTRATION STUDY (WITH HERMAN STAUDENMAYER)

Our first experiment yielded some slight evidence that an antisocial drama might engender imitation. We wanted now to strengthen the case and, at least as important, to study the conditions under which imitation obtains. More specifically, we wanted to see if frustration was a necessary condition for imitation of the antisocial act seen in the stimulus program. Or would a program lead to imitation, even without frustrating circumstances?

Second, we were aware of the fact that the reaction to the frustrating note was quite strong, and came to dominate the mood of the participant. Perhaps differences due to the stimulus programs would be brought more sharply into relief without frustration; perhaps, the reaction to frustration was so strong that it masked the effects of some of the treatment conditions.

Third, there is a well-known theory in social psychology that frustration leads to aggression (Dollard, Doob, Miller, Mowrer & Sears, 1939), yet

TABLE 21.1 PROPORTION OF SUBJECTS PERFORMING ANTISOCIAL ACTS ACCORDING TO STIMULUS PROGRAM IN EXPERIMENT 1*

	Stimulus programs					
	Neutral (n = 72)	Prosocial (n = 67)	Antisocial WP (n = 71)	Antisocial WP (n = 79)	All versions (N = 289)	Significance of difference† (df = 3)
Broke into bank and stole money	2.8% (2)	4.5% (3)	8.5% (6)	5.1% (4)	5.2% (15)	$\chi^2 = 2.49$, n.s.
Removed Dangling Dollar only	4.2% (3)	6.0% (4)	4.2% (3)	0.0% (0)	3.5% (10)	$\chi^2 = 4.33$, n.s.
Unsuccessfully attempted to break into bank	4.2% (3)	11.9% (8)	8.5% (6)	3.8% (3)	6.9% (20)	$\chi^2 = 4.92$, n.s.
Stole other items from room	13.9% (10)	13.4% (9)	8.5% (6)	7.6% (6)	10.7% (31)	$\chi^2 = 2.46$, n.s.

*The first four categories of antisocial behavior are not mutually exclusive. A single individual would have been scored for three acts if (a) he unsuccessfully attempts to break into bank, (b) removes the Dangling Dollar, and (c) steals items from the room. A final convention: If a subject breaks into the charity bank and steals the money, he was scored for the first category (broke into bank and stole money), but was not scored for the second category (removed Dangling Dollar only), since in breaking into the bank, the Dangling Dollar becomes part of the general loot. The percentages reported in the tables are the percentages of subjects performing each specific antisocial act. This system is employed throughout, unless otherwise specified.

†Two tests of significance were used throughout, chi square and the Fischer exact test. Chi square was used when the expected frequencies per cell were six or greater, with one degree of freedom. All chi square values are corrected for continuity when df is equal to 1.

The Fischer exact test was used when expected frequencies per cell were less than six. The Fischer exact test yields probabilities directly (i.e., significance levels), and the absence of a χ^2 value in our reporting of significance indicates the Fischer exact test was employed. Significance levels are reported up to $p = 0.30$. Beyond 0.30, we simply designate n.s. (nonsignificant). All reported significance levels are two tailed, unless otherwise specified.

there have been few tests of this notion in naturalistic circumstances. The experiment would give us insight into the general proposition.

Fourth, we wanted some assurance that our dependent variable— breaking into the collection box—was a responsive variable, one that really moved if acted on by appropriate forces. Perhaps the breakage rate was so inherently stable that no experimental manipulation could alter it. If this were true, we could never show the effect of different stimulus programs. The present experiment, therefore, constitutes a test of the sensitivity of our dependent measure. (For details of recruitment procedure and subjects, see pp. 23–29, Milgram, S. and Shotland, R.L., 1973.)

How Frustration Was Reduced

The point at which frustration was strongly aroused occurred when the participant came to pick up the transistor radio and encountered the terse message in the empty distribution office. And this was the point where frustration could be markedly reduced. The technical problem was to expose the participant to the empty office, while at the same time reducing his disappointment. This was done, quite simply, by substituting a new message for the old, one that was considerably more polite, and which informed him that he was about to receive his transistor radio. The new notice read:

NOTICE
Sorry to inconvenience you, but this office
is temporarily closed because of illness.
Kindly pick up your radio in Room 1800 of
this building, where an office will be
kept open until 7 p.m.
Thank you for your cooperation.
—The Management

Results

The data presented in Table 21.2 show that neither antisocial version of our program elicited significantly greater rates of antisocial behavior than did the neutral program; no significantly greater incidence of breakage and theft is associated with the WP version (3.0 percent) than with the neutral program (8.2 percent); nor did the NP version (7.6 percent) fare better. Our other indices yield similar results; theft of the Dangling Dollar did not occur significantly more often with either the WP or NP group (4.0 percent and 7.6 percent) than with the neutral program group (5.9 percent).

TABLE 21.2 PROPORTION OF SUBJECTS PERFORMING ANTISOCIAL ACTS ACCORDING TO LEVEL OF FRUSTRATION AND STIMULUS PROGRAM

	Stimulus program						Significance of differences (df = 2)	
	Neutral		Antisocial WP		Antisocial NP		Among high frus. conditions	Among low frus. conditions
	High frus. (n = 85)	Low frus. (n = 85)	High frus. (n = 101)	Low frus. (n = 89)	High frus. (n = 92)	Low frus. (n = 36)	(n = 278)	(n = 210)
Broke into bank and stole money	8.2% (7)	2.4% (2)	3.0% (3)	0 (0)	7.6% (7)	0 (0)	χ^2 = 2.76, n.s.	χ^2 = 2.97, n.s.
Removed Dangling Dollar only	5.9% (5)	2.4% (2)	4.0% (4)	0 (0)	7.6% (7)	0 (0)	χ^2 = 1.19, n.s.	χ^2 = 2.97, n.s.
Unsuccessfully attempted to break into bank	3.5% (3)	1.2% (1)	1.0% (1)	1.1% (1)	4.4% (4)	0 (0)	χ^2 = 2.13, n.s.	χ^2 = .42, n.s.
Stole other items from room	8.2% (7)	1.2% (1)	6.9% (7)	0 (0)	9.8% (9)	0 (0)	χ^2 = .52, n.s.	χ^2 = 1.48, n.s.

Similarly, thefts of other items by the WP and NP audiences (6.9 percent and 9.8 percent) were no greater than by viewers of the neutral program (8.2 percent). Nor did the WP or NP audiences make significantly more attempts at prying into the collection box than did the neutral program audience (1.0 percent and 4.4 percent versus 3.5 percent).

Thus, we did not replicate the trend of the first experiment and that finding is now in grave doubt. The data also show that the high frustration level we induced does not, in fact, mask other behavioral effects, for when we reduced frustration, we still failed to get effects attributable to differences in the stimulus programs.

But quite aside from the effects of the stimulus programs, the presence of frustration proved to be an extremely powerful determinant of antisocial behavior. We can see this most clearly by comparing the percentage of subjects who committed any antisocial acts in the frustration (18.7 percent) and no frustration (2.9 percent) conditions, as shown in Table 21.3.

Six times as many subjects commit antisocial behavior when frustrated. Moreover the greater frequency of antisocial behavior holds over all categories, and in each of the three stimulus groups. For example, theft from the bank (breakage plus Dangling Dollar) is 11.9 percent when subjects are frustrated and 1.9 percent when subjects are not frustrated ($\chi^2 = 15.56$, $df = 1$, $p < 0.001$).

Our results show, therefore, that the theft rate is, in principle, a responsive dependent variable. Manipulations of level of frustration substantially boost the theft rate; but our manipulation of stimulus programs in contrast did not affect the theft rate in any clear-cut way.[3]

TABLE 21.3 EFFECTS OF FRUSTRATION ON COMMISSION OF ANTISOCIAL ACTS*

Stimulus program	High frus- tration	n	Low frus- tration	n	Significance of difference between high and low frustration conditions (df = 1)
Neutral	21.2%	85	5.9%	85	$\chi^2 = 7.24$, $p < 0.008$
Antisocial WP	13.9%	101	1.1%	89	$\chi^2 = 8.88$, $p < 0.003$
Antisocial NP	21.7%	92	0	36	$\chi^2 = 7.70$, $p < 0.006$
All versions	18.7%	278	2.9%	210	$\chi^2 = 27.20$, $p < 0.001$

$N = 488$

*Includes any antisocial act: 21.2 percent indicates that this percentage of the 85 subjects in the High frustration Neutral condition performed an antisocial act.

EXPERIMENTS 3–6: GENERAL DISCUSSION

An additional series of four experiments (reported fully in "Television and Antisocial Behavior: Field Experiments") pursued the matter further.

Experiment 3 dealt with the effects of a model. We embedded a reminder of the antisocial behavior in the testing situation (a smashed bank) that we thought might interact with the stimulus program and add impetus to the antisocial response.

Experiment 4 dealt with eliminating the time gap between seeing the antisocial programing, and having the opportunity to imitate it. We arranged that our subjects could imitate the antisocial act even as they watched the program.

In Experiments 5 and 6, the stimulus programs were broadcast on network television, and home viewers tested for an imitative response.

While the antisocial behavior of breaking into the charity bank was manifested in all of the above experiments, it occurred with the same frequency for those who saw the antisocial version of the program and those who saw a neutral control.

We return to a detailed account of further experiments.

EXPERIMENT 7: THE TELEPHONE STUDY

There is a serious limitation in the experimental model we have worked with thus far. To understand it, we must consider the nature of the mass media. Stimulus content is transmitted to a very large number of people from an emitting source. Several million people across the country watched the *Medical Center* episode used in this study. Influence on only a very small fraction of the viewers could constitute an important *social* fact, but it would not emerge as a statistical fact in the experiment just outlined. For the assessment procedure by its very nature could test only a relatively small sample of those millions.

Let us say, for example, that the antisocial program influenced only one-tenth of 1 percent of the viewers—one person in a thousand; then fully a thousand of each million who saw it would be affected—a number of obvious social significance. Yet, our methods would not detect this fact because each of our experiments, necessarily limited in the numbers it can deal with, is based upon at most 500 subjects. And although that number is unusually large in terms of social-psychological experimentation, it would not tell the story, for one-tenth of 1 percent of 500 is *less than a single subject.*

It appears, then, that our method can disclose only much larger effects, those on the order of, say, 10 percent of the entire viewing audience. On that scale, if a million New Yorkers saw our WP-version, and 100,000 of them imitated the antisocial act, we could with our present methods detect the program's influence. But what if we are dealing with a phenomenon involving only one-hundredth of that number?

To overcome this limitation (1) we could employ extremely large numbers of subjects in the assessment situation, or (2) attempt to locate and use a subject population that was considerably more prone to influence by the media than the general population. A possible third course is to have very good information on *all* the antisocial imitation that occurs after our broadcast, not only in the laboratory but in the community at large. We did, in fact, seek precisely that data from several charity drives that were using collection boxes at the time of our broadcast; but all of them, reluctant to disclose the extent to which their efforts were vitiated by theft, declined to cooperate.

We can summarize the problem by stating that while the stimulus is transmitted to millions, the assessment procedures are geared to several hundred. We need to devise an assessment procedure that is sensitive to the fact that only a small fraction of those exposed to the program may be influenced by it. We need to show on television an antisocial act that anyone viewing in his own home could imitate with impunity, and which, if imitated, would be signaled to us. Toward this end, a second antisocial act was designed into the *Medical Center* episode. Namely, Tom Desmond makes two abusive telephone calls to a medical charity.

Desmond's antisocial use of the phone occurs when he responds to Dr. Gannon's telethon plea for pledges. In the first call, Tom says:

Hello, Telethon. I wanna talk to Gannon, Dr. Joseph Gannon . . . I got a message for him. Tell him I think his clinic stinks. Tell him it's nothing but a crummy monument to his crummy ego. It . . .
(*Click at the other end of the line.*)

In Tom's second call:

TOM: Hello, is Gannon still busy? I wanna talk to him.
OPERATOR: He's busy sir: do you wish to make a contribution?
TOM: No, I'm not making any contribution to your stinkin' clinic! How much money you got so far?
OPERATOR: I don't have that figure, but if you wish to add to . . .
TOM: Well, instead of ADDING money, you can start subtracting. You're gonna start LOSING money any minute now!
(*Tom hangs up.*)

The next task, from a technical standpoint, was to provide the viewer with a convenient opportunity to imitate the abusive calls. This was done in the following way: immediately following the *Medical Center* episode, a public service commercial appeared, in which viewers were asked to call in pledges to an authentic medical charity, Project Hope.

The 30-second public service spot, which was sandwiched between commercial messages, featured an attractive Eurasian girl, seated alongside a model of the hospital ship HOPE, and requesting viewers to call in telephone pledges for this charity. Meanwhile, a local telephone number was overlayed on the screen, so that viewers would know what number to call.

A bank of telephone operators was trained to receive pledges and to write down all comments made by the callers. The calls were also recorded, a fact that the operators acknowledged by saying:

> Thank you for your call, which we will record to insure accuracy. Do you wish to make a pledge to Project Hope?

With the stimulus and appeal broadcast, the opportunity and means for imitation were at hand. If only one-tenth of 1% of the estimated 1,235,000 homes in New York tuned in to *Medical Center* imitated Tom, more than a thousand abusive calls would be forthcoming. We could compare that figure to the response of a control group—a similar audience that saw the public-service message immediately following a neutral *Medical Center* episode the week before. Would the proportion of abusive calls be greater following Tom's example?

(We were aware, of course, that there would be a limitation in our data: the basic unit would be the received telephone call, but we could not know whether a single individual would call a number of times, or whether every call would come from a different person. But since the same possibilities would inhere in the calls following both the stimulus and neutral programs, we would assume that the number of repeat calls is the same in both cases and so cancel each other.)

(For details of the first tests of the telephone study in Chicago and Detroit, see pp. 45–46, Milgram, S., and Shotland, R.L., 1973.)

There remains the question, of course, of how many persons who saw the original *Medical Center* episode were also likely to see the spots. According to the A. C. Nielson Company, 21.7 percent of the 5,200,000 television homes in the New York area were tuned in to *Medical Center* (at least during its last quarter-hour) on April 21, when the antisocial WP-version and the first set of Project Hope appeals appeared. And between 70 and 90 percent of those who saw the subsequent spots had also seen the program: e.g., 85 percent of those who saw the spot during the 11 o'clock news had also seen the critical *Medical Center* segment.[4]

Results

A total of 193 telephone calls were received in response to the Project Hope spots in New York, 124 in the week in which the neutral version of the program was presented, and 69 in the week in which the antisocial version was presented. The data are shown in Table 21.4.

TABLE 21.4 TELEPHONE RESPONSES TO PROJECT HOPE APPEALS FOLLOWING NEUTRAL AND ANTISOCIAL WP PROGRAMS IN NEW YORK

| | Stimulus program | | Significance of df = 1 |
	Neutral (n = 124)	Antisocial WP (n = 69)	
Clearly antisocial	6 (4.8%)	4 (5.8%)	χ^2 = 0.00 n.s.
Possibly antisocial	14 (11.3%)	4 (5.8%)	χ^2 = 1.00 n.s.
Pledge of funds	15 (12.1%)	14 (20.3%)	χ^2 = 1.73 n.s.
Wants further information	14 (11.3%)	10 (14.5%)	χ^2 = 0.18 n.s.
Hang up without response	60 (48.4%)	34 (49.3%)	χ^2 = 0.00 n.s.
Miscellaneous (includes children, but not antisocial)	15 (12.1%)	3 (4.4%)	χ^2 = 2.30 p < 0.13
Totals	124	69	

We did not find an increase in percentage of abusive calls resulting from the program. Indeed, as we analyze the language of those calls that did come in, we see that not one of them actually imitates Tom Desmond's language. There is no use of the words "stinkin' crummy ego," nor does any caller threaten to diminish the money of Project Hope. Rather, we find a small array of sexually abusive comments that in no way seems to have been increased by the program.[5]

It is possible, of course, that a more interesting or stimulating antisocial action by Desmond would have inspired more imitation. If, for example—and this is purely speculative—we had shown him dialing a number that released the money in a pay phone, thousands of viewers might have dialed that number. It is also possible that the call he did make did not integrate into the motives of potentially antisocial viewers. The motives for breaking into a charity box seem clear enough if one is poor and needs money; the motives for making an abusive call are less so.

Of course, telephone calls reported in the mass media sometimes do appear to inspire imitation. The announcement on a television newscast of a few bomb threats seems to be dismayingly fruitful: as many as 4000 calls have clogged the New York City Police Department's switchboard on such occasions.

The differences between such perversely inspiring stimuli and those of our experiment are not entirely clear, though two points are worth noting. First, newscasts of bomb threats refer to real events, not to theatrical fictions, and may for that reason be more potent; and second, the gratification for calling in a bomb threat may not reside in the verbal delivery of the message, but in viewing its consequences, that is, the arrival of the police, clearing of the building, etc.

It is possible, also, that the abusive calls stimulated by the program were deflected to some other organization, and that somewhere in the city, a charity drive was receiving many antisocial comments stimulated by the program. But this is speculation, and in any case, we ought to have received at least a portion of those calls. We certainly made it easy enough for the stimulated subject to direct his abusive comments at Project Hope.

So far as the method used here is concerned, we believe that it is a promising one. It is potentially a very sensitive procedure and, possibly with some change in the stimulus material, could demonstrate imitative effects. In any case, it is clear from the experiment that not just any antisocial action shown on a single television program is likely to produce imitation. If this were so, we would have received hundreds of abusive calls in imitation of Tom Desmond's action on television. More than a million people saw the program in the New York City area, but our data show that the program had no effect in stimulating imitation of his action.

(The last experiment in this series was on the effect of seeing the antisocial stimulus as "news" rather than fiction. Those interested should refer to pp. 51–55 of Milgram, S., and Shotland, R.L., 1973.)

CONCLUSIONS

This research started with the idea that viewers imitate some of the antisocial action they see on television. We set out to measure actual imitation of a television depicted act. We created a program in which the act—breaking into a charity bank—is shown repeatedly, and with considerable dramatic impact. We created an assessment situation in which antisocial acts and imitation could easily occur.

In a first experiment, subjects saw one of four stimulus programs in a preview theater, and were then tested at a gift-distribution center. Result: a trend, though not statistically significant, that one of the antisocial programs engendered imitation. We wondered whether the high level of frustration experienced by the subjects obscured the effects of the stimulus program; we eliminated frustration in Experiment 2. Result: no evidence of imitation. We thought a model or booster placed in the assessment situation might interact with the stimulus program and produce an effect. Result: negative. We reduced the time delay between seeing the television act and the occasion for imitating it, by embedding both in the same situation. Result: negative. We broadcast the stimulus material in New York and St. Louis and again sought to measure imitation, but there was none. We changed the material from dramatized fiction to real life incidents presented on the news. Result: no imitation. We adopted a new paradigm of investigation in the telephone study, by giving an opportunity to any viewer to immediately imitate the act by calling in an abusive message. We hoped this would be a very sensitive measure that could pick up even slight effects. But again, we found no evidence that the antisocial program engendered imitation. We looked for efforts in subpopulations, and here the results were equivocal. We did our best to find imitative effects, but all told, our search yielded negative results.

Two quite different interpretations of the results are possible: First, the programs did, in reality, stimulate a tendency in our subjects to perform antisocial acts, but our measurement procedures were deficient. Second, there was no imitative tendency induced by the program.

Let us consider the first possibility: The program had a potential for inducing imitation. Why might we have missed it?

First, the imitative response may occur in the subject at another point in time or space, and not within the assessment situation we had set up. Perhaps, a year from now, a subject on the threshold of breaking into a charity bank will be influenced by the program.

Second, perhaps we did not test the right subject population. Conceivably, people below the minimum age for this study would have been measurably influenced by the program. We chose to limit our subject population out of practical considerations and because we did not want to provoke mere children into imitating antisocial behavior. (Of course, we did study teenagers, but conceivably, television affects even younger children.)

Or, perhaps in the very process of recruiting subjects for our study, we eliminated those most likely to have been influenced by the program. It requires a certain discipline to come to a preview theater, fill out a certificate, and then show up at the gift-distribution center. Perhaps some delinquents in the population were excluded by this procedure. However, the fact that we did get considerable antisocial behavior in the laboratory does, somewhat, weaken this argument.

Fourth, it is possible that the program stimulates imitation in only a very small fraction of the viewing audience, and we could not pick this up with the numbers used in our assessment procedures. However, we did introduce the telephone procedure to get around this, though using a quite different antisocial act. Perhaps if we could combine the sensitivity of the telephone measure with the motivational properties of the theft measure, an effect might have been discovered.

And, of course, we can go on endlessly. For when an experiment yields no differences between the experimental and control conditions, there is an infinitude of factors that may account for this. However, these are merely speculations, and do not have the status of evidence until they are themselves converted to tested operations. Often we ourselves thought we had figured out why we were not getting imitative effects, converted this notion into an experiment, only to fail again in our search for an effect.

Let us assume now that our measuring procedure is completely adequate and that, in fact, the stimulus material does not induce imitation. This would still not mean, however, that television does not stimulate antisocial behavior. Let us consider the factors not treated by the experiments described here.

1. It is possible that the television depiction of a different antisocial action would have engendered imitation. Perhaps, an antisocial act that contains the germ of a new criminal technique is more likely to be imitated. Note the series of parachute hijacks that appears to have been, in part, due to the dissemination of this technique by the mass media.
2. Perhaps it is not so much the depiction of one antisocial act, as the cumulative impact of numerous violent actions shown on television, from childhood onward, that predisposes a person to commit antisocial behavior. Conceivably, our subjects have been so sated with the depiction of crime on television that they are already maximally stimulated, and our program can add no further to it.
3. Or a more indirect mechanism may be at work, namely, that the norms and attitudes of society are changed by the frequent depiction of violence, so that even a person who has not viewed television will be influenced by it through his absorption of general social attitudes.
4. Perhaps the manner in which Desmond breaks into the charity banks did not stimulate imitation, because his actions were depicted dramatically rather than casually.

All of these possibilities exist, but are outside the scope of the present investigation. We can only urge that other investigators apply themselves to the study of these variables.

What then is the contribution of the present study? First, the evidence it has generated must be taken seriously, and serve as a constraint on discussion of television's effects. For the results of the present experiment are not that we obtained *no findings*, but rather that we obtained *no differences* in those exposed to our different stimulus programs. The research thus consistently supports the null hypothesis.

It is possible that people have been entirely too glib in discussing the negative social consequences of the depiction of television violence. Personally, the investigators find the constant depiction of violence on television repugnant. But that is quite different from saying it leads to antisocial behavior among its viewers. We have not been able to find evidence for this; for if television is on trial, the judgment of this investigation must be the Scottish verdict: Not proven.

Second, we hope the study has cleared the way methodologically for much new research. We believe that the general experimental paradigms presented here are by no means exhausted in the present investigation. The use of new stimulus material, younger populations, and modified assessment procedures can only further our knowledge of television's effects. The telephone study, though yielding no evidence of imitation in the present investigation, does point to the kind of experimental paradigm needed for further inquiry.

Not that the present paradigm is the only useful approach. Far from it. We carried it out because it seemed to us logical to start with a single program; if we could have demonstrated imitative effects in this single program, we could without equivocation have concluded that television stimulates antisocial behavior. That we did not find an effect does not exclude this possibility. We believe that future inquiry should direct itself to the long range effects of television, of many programs, over time.

Finally, in this research, a major television network extended its resources to social scientists wishing to study the possible effects of television depicted antisocial behavior. We regard this, not as the fulfillment of television obligations to society, but as a firm precedent, on which future investigation shall move ahead.

*N*OTES

1. Actually, a special program was written, incorporating the antisocial act. But it was a poor program dramatically, and we deemed it unacceptable for the purposes of the experiment.
2. Inclusion of these "excluded" subjects in the analysis of results does not alter the outcome of any experiment reported in this book.
3. In interpreting the meaning of the findings, two factors should be noted. First, the specific type of frustration is one in which the subject feels cheated, in that he does not get the reward he expected and feels he deserves. It is frustration centering on a breach of contract. One may therefore find his stealing items from the store to be somewhat "justified," in that in removing ashtrays, artificial flowers, and pictures from the company office he is "getting his due from them." However, the theft from a national charity can in no way be justified, since the money does not belong to the gift company in question. It has nothing to do with the fact that the company did not come forth with the promised radio. Thus, it is a case of the displaced effect of frustration.
4. Data based on the Nielson Station Index New York Instantaneous Audimeter, April 21, 1971. Data subject to qualifications.
5. The identical analysis was performed on the calls that came in response to the Project Hope spot immediately following the neutral and experimental programs. Since these were closest in time to the program, we thought they might be more likely to show imitation. But this was not the case. Twenty-four calls came in immediately after the neutral episode, with one clearly antisocial and two possibly antisocial messages. Thirty-six calls immediately followed the antisocial *Medical Center* broadcast, with one antisocial message.

*R*EFERENCES

ASCH, S. E., "Studies of independence and conformity: A minority of one against a unanimous majority." *Psychological Monographs,* **70** (9), 1956.

BAKER, R. K., AND BALL, S. J., *Violence and the Media.* Washington, D.C.: National Commission on the Causes and Prevention of Violence, 1969.

DOLLARD, J., DOOB, I. W., MILLER, N. E., MOWRER, O. H., AND SEARS, R. R., *Frustration and Aggression.* New Haven: Yale Univ. Press, 1939.

FESHBACH, S., AND SINGER, R. D., *Television and Aggression.* San Francisco: Josey-Bass, 1971.

LATANÉ, B., AND DARLEY, J. M., *The Unresponsive Bystander: Why Doesn't He Help?* New York: Appleton, 1970.

MILGRAM, S., "Some conditions of obedience and disobedience to authority." *Human Relations.* **18** (1), 1965, 57–176.

MILGRAM, S. AND SHOTLAND, R. L., *Television and Antisocial Behavior: Field Experiments.* New York: Academic Press, 1973.

SINGER, J. I. (ed.), *The Control of Aggression and Violence: Cognitive and Physiological Factors.* New York: Academic Press, 1971.

UNIFORM CRIME REPORTS 1970., *Federal Bureau of Investigation, United States Department of Justice,* Washington, D.C. (Superintendent of Documents, U.S. Government Printing Office.)

UNITED STATES PUBLIC HEALTH SERVICE., *Television and Social Behavior: An Annotated Bibliography of Research Focusing on Television's Impact on Children.* National Institute of Mental Health, 1971.

22

The Image
Freezing Machine

--- ❖ ---

I

The habit of taking pictures is now so widespread, we forget how recent it is. At the beginning of the nineteenth century only a talent for drawing or painting would allow a person to visually record what he saw. At the end of the century anyone could do it with the aid of a simple rectangular box. He looked into a small ground glass window, framed the picture he wanted, then pushed the shutter. Kodak did the rest.

The best way to grasp the human significance of photography is not to think of camera, film, and tripod as something external to human nature, but as evolutionary developments as much a part of human nature as his opposable thumb. A deficiency existed, of sorts, in the way our sensory and information storing capacities functioned. They had limits, and photography was one way to overcome those limits. The limit in human functioning is simply this: Although we can see things very well, we cannot store what we see so that we can reliably bring up the image for repeated viewing. Instead, visual images are incompletely stored in memory, often in a highly schematized form, and subject to decay and distortion.

Moreover, memory is private. It resides in the neural structure of the individual, and does not directly take the form of an external object that others can see.

This paper originally appeared as a series of three articles for the *ASMP Journal of Photography in Communications, Bulletin 75* (a magazine for professional photographers) in April, June, and August 1975. Reprinted by permission of Alexandra Milgram.

And when the person dies, all of the images stored in his brain vanish, along with all the other information he possesses.

It is the perishability of our visual experience that led men to seek to fix it by externalizing it: by placing it on something more permanent, and more available to public scrutiny than the brain. A first solution to this problem came about through the development of skills in painting and drawing. Man had the capacity to depict what he saw by representing those forms and colors on an external surface, such as the wall of a cave, or papyrus, silk, or canvas. But it required a special talent to do this, which only a fraction of men possessed.

An optochemical means for recording of visual images was achieved in the nineteenth century: Photography allowed anyone to freeze a moment of visual experience, and thus to augment his memory, to preserve it beyond his own lifetime, and to show others what he saw. To a psychologist this new capacity to fix and externalize visual experience is intriguing, for it immediately raises the question: what did people choose to render into permanent photographic images?

In principle, the camera could be used to record any visual event: stars, lakes, garbage, loaves of bread, anything. But the fact is that, overwhelmingly, what people wanted to record was images of themselves. The growth of portrait photography in the nineteenth century is astonishing, even by today's standards of rapid technological exploitation. The nineteenth century absorbed photography with a voracious thirst that revealed the extraordinary need for an image freezing machine. The process was scarcely known before 1839; within twenty years commercial studios had sprung up in New York, London, Paris, and Basel. A hundred thousand daguerreotype portraits were made in Paris in 1849. By 1860 New York City claimed more than fifty photo-portrait studios. It is true that some photographers could make a living taking pictures of far-away places and selling them. But overwhelmingly the business end of the enterprise rested on photo-portraiture. That is what people wanted most of all.

To understand how special this fact is, consider that when later in the century, the technical means for recording not visual but auditory events became possible, there was no such rush to get oneself recorded. Indeed, while people wanted pictures of themselves, they wanted sound recordings not of their own voices, but of impersonal cultural objects—above all, music.

So the recording of the visual aspect of experience, and the auditory aspect, are skewed in enormously different ways. Even today, there are hundreds of record stores in which we shop for sound recordings of musical groups. But picture stores, in which we shop for recorded images, are not to be found on anything like this scale.

We need to go a little deeper into the contrasts between visual and auditory recording. There is a scene in the film *Edison: The Man* that is revealing. Spencer Tracy, having just invented the phonograph, tries to persuade his infant son to say something into it, so that he can have a recording. But the infant refuses to say anything; and this vignette serves as a running gag through the film. The scene reminds us that the recording of sound depends on a performance, while visual recording does not. The photographed person may remain passive, and still be recorded. This contrast between the passivity of photography and activity of sound recording reaches down to the very origin of the physical energies underlying the two processes: the energy for a voice recording originates in the activity of the speaker, but the energy for a photograph of him is external in origin, merely light that has bounced off him. You can photograph a corpse but not record him on a cassette. The potentially passive nature of the object photographed colors the entire process. It means the camera captures what one is, a state of being. One doesn't have to do anything for it. It merely soaks you in. Perhaps that is why voice recording studios, which require performance, have never developed on anything like the scale of photographic studios.

The phenomenon of photographic portraiture is even more revealing when we consider the stereotyped nature of portraiture. After all, even if a man wants a visual record of himself, he may want a record of himself doing something worthwhile, such as giving money to a poor beggar, helping a lame animal, or lending a tool to a neighbor. Instead, we find men and women seated before cameras, in general not doing anything, just looking, at most aided by a prop of a book or surrounded by other family members. People did not want so much a photographic rendering of themselves performing a specific action, as they wanted a general statement of their character. The sources of this attitude are not hard to find. To some extent they derive from traditional oil portraiture, and the camera was merely a cheap way to get the equivalent of an oil painting. Then, too, the early technology of photography did not permit action shots, and it was to the photographic entrepreneur's advantage to do all his work in the studio. But most of all, it was a desire to have not specific actions, but one's general likeness recorded for posterity. Although the subject knew that he had nothing to do but sit and be photographed, he realized that the full burden of a multitude of moods and moments would come to be represented by that single exposure of the camera. The burden placed on that moment was very substantial, and motivated the subject to work for an optimal image: he posed.

We all make some adjustment as we take account of the person we are dealing with. Our facial muscles, poses, and posture are subtly altered as we speak to a child, a lover, or a judge. Even half-consciously we are able to adjust ourselves to act in a manner appropriate to the specific situation. But the problem of a photograph is that, although it is taken in one situation, it may be seen by many people and in many situations. How then are we to adjust to the camera? How can we create a facial expression that is of generic usefulness, and not useful merely for a narrowly defined occasion?

The most typical strategy, particularly when photography was first coming into general use, was to use a socially conventional face, and express as much civic virtue as possible in the exposed moment, an attitude that, together with the technical necessity of holding a stationary position for a matter of minutes, led to the bland, stilted photographs which was the typical product of the nineteenth century Daguerrian studios.

There was one human experience which all human beings had known in the nineteenth century, which led them to underestimate the truthfulness of the camera. I am not speaking of portraits by artists, which were limited to the well-to-do, but a more mundane experience: the mirror. If you had never had a photograph taken of yourself, the best clue to what it would look like was based on what you had seen in the mirror. And that is where the surprise came in. For individuals almost never reject what they see in the mirror, but hundreds of Daguerretypes were angrily denounced by men and women who knew they were more comely than the photograph showed. What they should have learned is that the psychological preparations made before looking into a mirror are such that we do not affront our own self-image. Even today, individuals are constantly rejecting unflattering snapshots, firmly believing that they could never look as bad as the photograph showed. But such reactions rarely come upon looking into a mirror. Perhaps the old, "a mirror offers us a thousand faces; we only accept one," contains the relevant wisdom. The camera, by freezing our faces at a particular moment, from a particular viewpoint, often gives us one of those faces which we would prefer not to accept. But, unlike the mirror, we cannot make those instantaneous adjustments, turns of the head, lowering of the eyelids, search for the exact angle, that defuses the offending image. Rather we count on the photographer to function as a kind of ego supporter and photograph us as we would like to be presented to that generic constituency which is the audience of all photographs.

II

Photography is a way of recording, for further scrutiny, the visual aspect of things. Only one other sensory modality, hearing, has been similarly susceptible of recording. We do not as yet have adequate technologies for recording experiences of smell, touch, or taste. And we do not seem to feel much need for developing them. But of the need to have a visual record, there can be no doubt, as the growth of a vast photographic industry attests.

But it is not just the fact of capturing a likeness that is the essence of photography. We know that life masks can be made which depict the person's physiognomy in three dimensions, or at least in bas-relief. Yet such techniques never acquired the popularity of photography. Of course, there is the matter of the greater convenience of photography. But beyond that, the reduction of the image to the two dimensional plane is the crucial element.

Consider that stereoscopic photographs were available as early as the mid-nineteenth century, yet only play a minor part in photography. Color film, though of high technical excellence, has found a secure place in photography, but it has not supplanted black and white, which continues to exert an attraction to millions of photographers, particularly those of artistic bent. It is the abstracting quality of the black and white two-dimensional photograph that appeals to many over the greater verisimilitude of stereoscopy and color. It remains to be seen whether the recently discovered hologram, with its uncanny shifting parallax, will force a fundamental change in emphasis. History suggests that though holograms may develop a significant niche of their own, they will not supplant the ordinary black and white print.

The viewer is part of the process of photography. As we look at photographs, Rudolph Arnheim has pointed out, we see them through a special attitude which conditions our response to them. Unlike painting, in which we know that every detail is created by the effort of the painter, the photograph is interpreted as the product of a mechanical process. As soon as the camera is clicked, images within its view are encoded without further human effort onto the film. Details may be recorded without any necessary intention on the part of the photographer. Indeed, he may discover things in his picture he was not aware of at the time he took it. For the camera provides a mechanical and exhaustive rendering of visual surfaces, within the range of its technical capacities. This directness and infinite inclusiveness confer on photographs a high degree of credibility. We are more likely to believe that an object depicted in a photograph really existed than, say, an object depicted in a painting. The truthfulness of the camera is not, of course, guaranteed by this fact. Photographs may be faked, or they may be unrepresentative of what they purport to depict. But even here, if we examine the photographs carefully enough, some detail in the photograph itself may belie the photographer's claim.

People possess a photographic urge, an enormous desire to fix the image of things in a form they can later consult. And it is, for many people, an urge to fix the image through their own efforts. The pictures one can buy outside a famous landmark are no substitute for the pictures one has taken, even if the quality of the commercial product is superior to one's own. It is seizing the image through one's own act that seems uniquely satisfying.

The act of taking a picture, like the act of seeing itself, takes place in a broad range of human situations. When we are alone or with others, whether we are taking a picture of a rock or a lover, it always involves some sort of exchange, whose terms we may now explore.

First, there is the trade-off between the passive enjoyment of a unique moment, and the active process of photographing it. The man who sees a beautiful scene, and has his camera, stops to take a picture; but the photographic act may interfere with his fully savoring the experience. There is not only the minor inconvenience of carrying a few pounds of camera equipment, but the interruption of a fully spontaneous set of activities by the need to stop to take pictures, and divide one's attention between enjoyment of the scene and the mental set needed to photograph it. The photographic act devalues the moment, as one trades the full value of the present instant for a future record of it.

The very meaning of human activities, such as travel, comes to be transformed by photographic possibilities. We seek out places not only for their beauty, but because they are suitable backgrounds for our pictures. A group of tourists, Nikons hanging about their necks, sees its arrival at the Eiffel Tower as the consummation of a photographic quest. The place comes to be subordinate to its photographic potential. The value of our vacation will depend not only on what we experience at the moment, but on how it all comes out in the pictures. It is the contamination of the pleasurable present, by the photographic urge, that prompts growing numbers of vacationers to leave the camera home.

But if the photographing act is best seen as an exchange, this is most clearly present when we photograph other people. What kind of exchange is it? The English language is quite blunt about it. A photographer takes a picture. He does not create a picture or borrow one, he takes it. A camera bug travels to a foreign country, sees a peasant in the field, and takes a picture of him. Now why does the photographer think he has the right to snatch the image of the peasant? It is true the photographer invests time, film, and effort into taking the picture, but I find it hard to understand wherein he derives the right to keep for his own purposes the image of the peasant's face. "Give it back, give it back," the peasant might cry, "It's my face, not yours."

Photography is an exchange, obviously unfair, and the native who once allowed himself to be photographed, just to be pleasant, in time may realize he is giving away something for nothing: his image. There is, of course, the pride he may feel of having been deemed worthy as a subject of photography, but in the long run this type of glory wears thin, and the native may decide to charge the photographer, as boys in the Caribbean do with increasing frequency. The relationship becomes a professional one.

Naturally, it is convenient for photographers to carry on their activities with the assumption that individuals, tacitly at least, give their assent to being photographed. (I am referring now not to the use of the photograph, which is bound by legal constraints, but to the act of photographing others, which is considerably less controlled by law.) But just how do people feel about giving away their image? How many people would actually agree to have their picture taken by a stranger for some unspecified purpose?

To study this, my students and I recently went into the streets of midtown Manhattan and, camera in hand, each of us asked a stranger: "May I take your picture?" If asked to explain his motives, the student answered simply, "I'm interested in photography." We posed the question to more than one hundred people in Bryant Park and on 40th and 42nd Streets.

In the street 35 percent allowed us to take their picture, while 65 percent refused. Hands went up over the face, people scowled, or walked hurriedly—reminding us that the act of photographing has given rise to a whole set of gestures which never existed before the camera. Gestures of the photographer, gestures of the subject allowing or refusing to be photographed. (Presumably, before the press photographer came on the scene, criminals rarely held their hands over their faces or dug their faces into contortional positions when arraigned.) Photography has created an entirely new choreography of human body movement.

In Bryant Park itself, the population divided evenly into those who assented and those who refused. Females were less willing than males to have their picture taken (but we need more data to confirm this). The willingness of people to have their picture taken interacts subtly with mood temperament and the exact pose and circumstance of the potential subject. Of the six people lounging on the grass whom we approached, five agreed to have their picture taken, an astonishingly high proportion. We have just begun this socio-psychological inquiry into the act of photographing, but one thing is already clear. The culture of photography is so widespread, and the normality of taking pictures so deeply rooted, that everyone understood what it meant to be photographed, and took the request in stride.

The importance of this fact can only be understood in comparison with other requests one might make. For example, a few years ago our class went into the New York subway. Each student stood in front of a seated passenger, and asked: "May I have your seat?" However trivial the request may seem, it is extremely difficult to utter, and for some impossible. (My own experience was one in which I was paralyzed, virtually unable to carry out the subway assignment; and after having carried it out I felt an enormous need to justify my request by appearing sick or faint.) But the act of asking if one might take someone's picture had none of these qualities—it flows naturally and is self-justifying. It is part of a shared culture. Perhaps in our culture we are profligate with our image because we feel the photographer does not really take it from us, but simply reproduces it, a form of visual cloning in which the original is not diminished, even while multiples of itself are created.

Every culture varies in the degree to which it is camera shy. The photographer can feel it in the reluctance he may have of taking pictures of the natives in any particular locale. Sometimes it seems an intrusion, an aggressive act. One solution, a friend once suggested, would be to have a camera deliver up to two pictures each time the shutter was snapped, one for the photographer and one for the subject. I suppose an SX-70 could be rigged up easily enough to do just that.

As I say, it is a cultural matter, and who knows where wisdom resides? In Peru, the Indian women run away when you aim the camera at them, and they look at you suspiciously even if you finger the camera. Maybe they are right, and the custom of letting strangers take our pictures bespeaks an inexcusable indifference to our own image. Who knows what the tourist with the Nikon will do with our image. Maybe he will laugh at it when he gets back home, use it for darts, or as a stimulus for bizarre sexual experiments.

But now we are slipping into insubstantial fantasies when a far more significant question remains in the relationship between the photographer and his subject. The question concerns the capacity of some photographers to render portraits of greater artistic depth than others. Some attribute this to the superior selectivity of the master photographer: he seeks out faces of potential interest, then selects the right moment to snap the shutter. No doubt this is part of the process. But when we examine photographs of, let us say Diane Arbus, we begin to understand that the psychological consistency in the faces of many diverse individuals must in part be due to the photographer's capacity to induce a certain attitude or expression in the subject, that a subtle psychological relationship exists between photographer and subject, in which the photographer—or at least some photographers—play a part in creating the faces they photograph.

But even the most mundane occasion for taking a snapshot involves us in a relationship, and moreover it is a relationship that others perceive and in some degree respect. For the photographic act occurs within a normative field, i.e., we don't just take photographs. The activity is circumscribed by certain social rules that are widely shared, even if they are implicit. People will exert some effort, for example, to avoid interference with the relationship. But how can this be measured?

We start with the idea of a "privileged space" between the photographer and his subject. There is a line of sight and it possesses a certain degree of inviolability. But just how much inviolability? The reluctance of bystanders to violate the line of sight is a measure of the strength and legitimation which they ascribe to the photographic act.

Our initial experiments on this topic were carried out on a major New York City thoroughfare (42nd Street between 5th and 6th Avenues). The street is characterized by heavy pedestrian flow, and the pavement is conveniently divided into four lanes by pavement scratch lines (see Fig. 22.1).

The subject to be photographed posed along the inner wall of the street, the Bryant Park gate. Another student stepped back to the half width of the sidewalk, and held a camera to her eye as if to take a picture. The photographer held the camera for a five-minute period; observers counted how many people interrupted the line of sight between camera and subject, and how many people deviated to walk around it. In the first condition, the photographer stood at the point midway between the wall and the gutter. In the second condition, the photographer moved back to the 3/4 position (so that pedestrians only could squeeze through by using the remaining quarter of the sidewalk) and again held the camera to her eye for a five minute period. And finally, the photographer moved all the way back to the curb so that there was no way a pedestrian could pass without breaking the line of sight, except by ducking, waiting, or walking into the street.

The results speak well for the respect shown the photographic relationship: 90 percent respected the line of sight in the first condition, 69 percent in the second, and 37 percent even when the entire sidewalk was blocked. It should give photographers heart to note that to avoid breaking

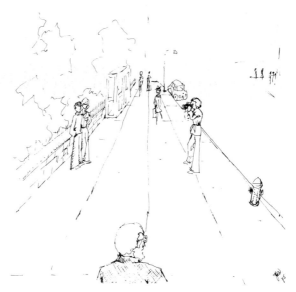

FIGURE 22.1
Illustration of the arrangement for the line-of-sight study. The photographer is shown taking a picture at the 3/4 mark.

the line of sight, a third of the New Yorkers detoured into the street, waited, or ducked very low.

To what extent is the special subject-photographer relationship being respected and to what extent is it the act of taking a picture being respected? A further experiment allowed us to check this. We substituted an inanimate object for the human subject, and performed the same line of sight variations. There are a far greater number of penetrations of the line of sight when the photographer is taking a picture of an object, rather than of another person. So the social relationship definitely plays a part in strengthening the inviolability of the line of sight.

We might ask whether any activity involving two people, and not only photography, would generate a similar deference. In another experimental condition our two experimenters abandoned the camera, and started playing ball from the 1/2, 3/4, and 4/4 positions on the 42nd street sidewalk, lobbing and rolling the ball to each other. Here there was far less respect for the relationship, and 91 percent of the pedestrians walked through (in the 3/4 position) compared to 31 percent when a photograph was being taken.

And people muttered that the pair had no right to play ball on the midtown sidewalks. But this remark was never made for the act of photographing. This suggests an important point: many activities, such as playing ball, are confined to a definable locus: in a school yard, in a park, etc. But there is no such definition for the act of taking a picture. Indeed, we work the other way: any place is considered appropriate for taking a picture, unless it is specifically excluded by violating sanctity or privacy, as in funeral parlors and brothels.

III

The job of the photographer and that of the psychologist interested in photography are very different. The photographer seeks to capture a particular moment on film; the psychologist tries to explain why the photographer is taking the picture, and how motives, perceptual processes, and emotional factors come into play. He tries to do this through research, conducting experiments, and formulating questions open to inquiry. It is odd that Eastman Kodak spends vast sums on research in film chemistry, but so little research has been carried out on the larger social and psychological processes of photography.

Consider, for a moment, not the history of psychology, but its history within a single individual. An important set of psychological questions concerns the way in which a person learns to take photographs. Although children, for example, are reported to have a clear, naive vision of things—imbued with wonder and freshness—the fact is that there are no great child photographers. Perhaps we have simply not placed the camera in the child's hands at the sufficiently early age, but I am skeptical of this argument, having seen large numbers of photographs taken by my own children. On the whole, the freshness, and even artistry we often find in children's drawings do not translate into their photographic view. Psychologists have studied children's drawings for many years now, and find that the drawings change systematically with age, and can often tell us a good deal about the mental processes of the child. But can photography be used in this way? What if we gave every two-year-old a camera, and studied the pictures he took over the span of a lifetime. What would we learn about the child, and about the growth of photographic skill as he matures? Perhaps there are Piagetian stages of development that will be revealed through a study of children's photographs. Is there a systematic shift in what he photographs, and how he photographs it, comparable to systematic stages in the use of language and thought? The matter is worth looking into.

There is another side of the relationship of photography and human development. The individual learns not only how to take pictures, but also how to appear in them, that is, to pose. Infants, we know, are not self-conscious about cameras. They do not know what the camera is for, and this innocence allows us to capture their naive actions. But the child learns very quickly, and by five or six may not be able to stand in front of a camera without grimacing, and feeling ill at ease. In most individuals, this awkward feeling is gradually brought under control of an adjustive response: a pose. Studying how poses change over time, in different social classes, in different cultures, and through the growth and maturation of the individual, is a first-class problem for research.

The photographic process itself may help in the analysis of this aspect of photography. Eadweard Muybridge used the camera to obtain a sequence of pictures of humans and animals in action, so that he could better analyze the components of locomotion. We could do well to apply Muybridge's technique to the act of photography itself, as a way of better understanding it. How might it be used to study, for example, the pose?

Here is one possible scenario: A person comes to a portrait studio to have his picture taken. From the moment he enters the studio, a camera covertly takes a series of pictures of the person, perhaps one every ten seconds or so. The photographer performs his normal functions, poses the subject as he usually does, and snaps a series of portraits. By examining the portraits in the longer sequence taken by the hidden camera, it becomes easy to see how the official pose differs from the unposed pictures. It will help us to understand the adjustments the individual makes to the camera. The method would be particularly instructive when a master portrait photographer is at work, for we would then be able to trace photographically the means by which he brings his subject to the desired appearance for the portrait.

This technique is easy, but some questions are hard to answer even through ingenious experiments. Why, for example, are some people photogenic and others are not? Is it a matter of the perceptual effects in that certain three dimensional forms translate more flatteringly into flat photographs than others; or do some people come alive before a camera, and relate to it with a radiance and warmth elicited by no other stimulus, while others twist their faces into anxious masks? Probably both factors are at work, but a little research into the matter wouldn't hurt.

One of the most challenging areas for research deals with the psychological characteristics of the professional photographer. Certainly, some kind of visual intelligence is needed for this type of work. But beyond that, the forms of activity are so varied that different constellations of motives and abilities are probably at work in different domains of the photographic profession.

As to why people become photographers, the answers are probably as dependent on chance and circumstance as in any other occupation. But are there any "hidden" motives underlying the practice of the photographer's craft?

Freudian psychology might say that the profession of photography is a subliminated form of voyeurism, and underlying every lifelong commitment to photography is some remnant of the desire to catch a glimpse of the primal scene, i.e., sexual intercourse between parents. Like the little boy peeking at that special scene, the photographer positions himself to view an event, not to intervene in it, but to passively register it.

We need not take this interpretation seriously in order to acknowledge that a good photographer does require an extraordinary balance of passive and aggressive tendencies. He needs the aggressiveness to intrude himself into situations where he is often irrelevant, and sometimes unwanted. Photographs of funerals, accidents, and grief-stricken moments are not generally offered up to the photographer; they are taken by him, as a thief snatches diamonds. At the same time, there is a passive component to photography, for the photographer must keep himself receptive to the images presented by the environment, and let them enter his camera.

Without overstating the case, we note how easily photography was presented as a highly sexualized activity in Antonioni's *Blow-Up*. Generally, to the working photographer, none of these factors will seem particularly important, since he is preoccupied with making a living, trying to please the client and turn a profit, worrying about competition and his integrity, wondering whether to fake a news photo, or whether to lend a hand to a suffering accident victim rather than simply photograph him. These conscious conflicts are no less important than so-called subconscious ones.

Photographs can constitute an important psychological document about an individual. Robert Akaret's sensitive book, *Photoanalysis*, shows how far one can go in interpreting the psychological meaning of individual snapshots. But one can also use the aggregate of photographs in an individual's possession as an index of his psychic life. First, people ordinarily photograph only what interests them. If we examine the photographs a person has taken during his lifetime, we will be able to discern the things that were important to him, and those that were not. It is probably as good a measure as we have of his enduring lifetime cathexes. One friend I know concentrated on hundreds of nature scenes, and very few of his wife, an indication of where his true passions resided—a fact also confirmed by his recent divorce.

My colleague, Dr. Stuart Albert, has suggested that we examine the entire content of family photo albums to see which events are recorded, and which are not. He believes that we photograph mostly during periods of rapid change and growth, thus explaining the preponderance of photographs of children in their period of rapid maturation.

Through the family photo album, the family constructs a type of fairy tale. Only the happy moments tend to be shown: birthdays, bar mitzvahs, weddings and vacations. Families construct a pseudo-narrative which highlights all that was life-affirming and pleasurable, with a systematic suppresion of life's pains. (At least, I have not yet seen a family album in which funerals and suicides are depicted). However imperfect, the album is for most contemporary families the only narrative available of its history, having supplanted the family Bible, where, in earlier times, a record of births, deaths, and marriages was maintained.

Photography, I am convinced, is ready for an invasion of psychologists, experimentalists, who will not be satisfied to hear there is something called the "decisive movement"; they'll want to show just how long it is, and find out what would happen if Cartier-Bresson were saddled with a camera whose shutter snapped unpredictably from five to thirty seconds after depressing the release button. Would he miss all the good shots? The psychologists will want to know whether the immediate feed-back of a Polaroid system facilitates the learning of photographic skills, and whether certain personality types among photographers prefer color or black and white. The psychologist will want to probe into the enormous credibility of photographs (viewers tend to believe the things they show really happened). They will want to know who in the family takes the photographs, and examine the patterns of photographs a person takes over a lifetime.

But perhaps the most interesting set of questions concerns the photographs themselves, and the socio-imagistic reality they create. Let me explain. We start with the fact that photographs are often treated as compelling and incontrovertible evidence that the events depicted in them actually happened. This is overlaid by the fact that the photograph constitutes a reality, valued in and of itself. We all know the joke about the grandmother traveling with her grandchildren. A fellow passenger remarks on how attractive the children are. The grandmother rejoins: "That's nothing, let me show you their pictures." The pictures constitute a reality of their own, and evoke emotions, attitudes, and convictions. Photographs, therefore, not only depict realities, they create a new plane of reality to which people respond.

There is a universe of events that we smell, a universe that we hear, and there is also a universe of events whose existence is embodied in photographs. Thus, each year we eagerly await the official Chinese Communist May Day photograph to see who is photographed alongside the Chairman, and who has been displaced. The official photograph is not only a reflection of the political reality, but itself solidifies that reality, becomes an element in it.

The question that arises for purposes of research, therefore, is: to what degree will events that exist in photographs exert an effect outside the photograph? For example, if we stop two strangers on the street, ask them to pose momentarily, and take a picture, have we thereby created through the photograph a bond that previously did not exist? If the photograph is circulated to others, will the two individuals, fortuitously brought together in the photograph, tend to be treated as a pair? Does the photograph act back on the real world, and begin to shape that world?

Events happen, not only in the real world, but in photographs as well, and this new focus of action may exert a devastating power. House detectives have known this for years. A photograph showing a political candidate shaking hands with a Communist Party official can kill his chances for re-election, even when the photograph is faked.

Or, consider a more typical case. An aspiring young lawyer gets to see President Carter for five minutes. A photograph is taken of the two men chatting. The lawyer proudly hangs it behind his desk. The image freezing machine has done its work. Clients see the photograph, are impressed, draw inferences. The lawyer need never mention the photograph. It resoundingly speaks for itself, a powerful new element in the lawyer's career. The lawyer has learned through personal experience what prophets of photography have long suspected: a photograph does not only record events. It creates them.

NOTE

1. The sketch on page 317 is by Judith Waters.

REFERENCES

AKERET, R. U., *Photoanalysis: How to Interpret the Hidden Psychological Meaning of Personal and Public Photographs.* New York: Wyden, 1973.

ARNHEIM, R., "On the nature of photography." *Critical Inquiry,* Sept. 1974, **I,** 149–161.

BECKER, H., "Photography and sociology." *Studies in the Anthropology of Visual Communication,* 1974, **5,** 3–26.

NEWHALL, B., *The History of Photography.* New York: Museum of Modern Art, 1964.

SONTAG, S., "Photography." *New York Review of Books,* Oct. 18, 1973; Nov. 13, 1973; and Apr. 18, 1974.

23

Candid Camera

———— ❖ ————

Since 1947 millions of television viewers have watched the program *Candid Camera,* created by Allen Funt. The program consists of filmed records of people spontaneously responding to unusual and sometimes bizarre situations set up by the producer. In a representative episode, a naive person approaches a mailbox in order to deposit a letter, and is startled to find a voice from within the mailbox addressing him. The camera focuses on the responses of the person to this anomaly, and typically the reactions of a sequence of individuals confronting this situation are shown. Each episode ends by informing the person that the experience he has undergone is part of a *Candid Camera* episode. In the course of a single program, four or five different situations are shown.

The *Candid Camera* program merits examination for several reasons. First, the very fact of a program built on the exposure of spontaneous human behavior is itself symptomatic of broader cultural currents which we need to examine. Second, the *Candid Camera* episodes constitute a repository of documented behavior of potential interest to social scientists. We are not the first to recognize this value. James Maas and his associates at Cornell University have classified and annotated more than 1,500 such episodes. But we need to assess both the utility and the limits of such an archive. The value of such material will depend in part on their methods of collection. Here we note an interesting feature of the *Candid Camera* program: it participates, at least fractionally, in the methodology of the social sciences.

For social science, *Candid Camera* possesses a number of attractive features. First, each episode begins with a question about human behavior, for which we do not fully know the answer. The question is examined in concrete circumstances somewhat the way an experimental social psychologist might proceed in his

Written in collaboration with John Sabini, this article first appeared in *Society*, vol. 16, pp. 72–75. Reprinted by permission.

laboratory. An illustrative question might be: "How would a customer in a clothing store react if the salesman took out a tongue depressor and started to examine the customer with it?" One senses that a question such as this touches on a larger sociological issue centering on role theory. We might tend to think that in the case of the above episode, because the clothing salesman's act is so bizarre, none of the clients will go along with it. The filmed records show, however, that at least some clients do cooperate with the salesman; thus, the procedures seem capable of yielding surprises, perhaps even making discoveries.

At least one group of social scientists, experimental social psychologists, shares with *Candid Camera* the idea that one ought to create synthetic situations as a means of revealing human behavior. For social psychologists, the synthesized situation is called the experiment. For *Candid Camera*, it is a typical program episode. Both experimentalists and Funt construct situations into which the participants are brought, but which are unfinished, the completion of the scene being accomplished by the performance of the person. The exact character of the performance is seldom entirely known by those who set up the situation. Indeed, behavior which deviates from what is expected, that is, surprises, are particularly valued by those who organize such occasions.

An obvious merit of *Candid Camera* is that it presents us with behavior, not just hearsay. Through the visual and auditory document, we are able to see how certain situations are set up and exactly how people respond to them. It is not merely a statement of how people think they *would* act or feel they *ought* to act in a given situation; it is a record of how they do in fact act. We are presented with a richly textured, though unanalyzed, record which is precise at the level of the individual case. Such firsthand data would seem to be of considerable value in any science of human behavior.

Because the behavior has been recorded on film, it can continually be reexamined by social scientists, a task now facilitated by the availability of an annotated archives of *Candid Camera* episodes. Generally, in social science, we must be content with an account of an event provided by the investigator. But this account, whether in quantitative or verbal descriptive form, is an abstraction taken from a more complex behavioral situation which is no longer accessible to us. While experiments, and often sociological observations, are in principle replicable, there are many practical limitations to such replication. How much more satisfactory it is to have access to the actual behavior, or at least filmed records of such behavior. We may find in such iconic material features which would never be mentioned in a skeletal verbal account, and we are better informed of the exact tone or expressive character of the event.

Moreover, the events depicted in *Candid Camera* are embedded in the stream of everyday life. Funt creates his episodes in a variety of familiar environments: hotel rooms, banks, on the street, in parks, in bars and canteens, in zoos, elevators, bowling alleys, and numerous other settings that individuals encounter in their daily rounds. Those who serve as confederates play a variety of real life roles: bartenders, salesmen, bank clerks, etc. Insofar as sociological theory has as its goal the explanation of real life behavior, Funt's ecological imagination would seem to be a considerable advance over the more sterile methods which remove subjects from the natural contexts of life.

Candid Camera shares another feature with certain social science strategies. It gives us a new vision through the disruption of the habitual. It frequently makes evident what we take for granted by altering some of the normal assumptions of daily life. Thus, when a client enters a clothing store, and the salesmen begins to examine the client with a tongue depressor, the audience laughs because of the discrepancy between normal expectancies as to the appropriate behavior of the salesman, and the behavior actually engaged in. It has often been observed that harmoniously functioning systems may be more difficult to analyze than those that show some degree of dysfunction. Freud believed that by using neurosis as a point of departure, he could better understand how the normal processes of personality work. Ethnomethodologists such as Harold Garfinkel attain an understanding of the normal rules of everyday life by deliberately violating them. Funt frequently relies on a similar disruption of the usual in order to generate insights.

A further merit of *Candid Camera*'s materials is embodied in the very name of the enterprise: the behavior is observed without the awareness of the participant. Ethically, this aspect of *Candid Camera* is problematical; scientifically it is indispensable to a full understanding of human behavior. The essence of a social situation is not merely that there are two people present, but that each of the parties has a representation of the other in his field of awareness. When a person is aware that he is being photographed or filmed or merely observed, he reflexively calls into play a range of self-presentational mechanisms. These include both censorship mechanisms (he suppresses certain behaviors, such as picking his nose) and positive acts (he smiles, straightens his shoulders). When a person is not aware that he is being photographed or observed, he has no chance to make the adjustments needed for a social encounter. Thus *Candid Camera* presents us with behavior uncontaminated with the reactivity of an observer. (Sometimes, however, Funt will use a confederate to create a needed social scene, or to provoke the behavior of the target.)

Funt states that *Candid Camera* catches the person "in the act of being himself." More precisely, the camera catches the person acting under the belief that he is unobserved, or at least that his behavior is not being recorded for the later scrutiny of others.

A final point which social scientists may admire in *Candid Camera* is the sheer creativity evidenced over the years in the construction of *Candid Camera* episodes: taxis that split in half; drivers that land their automobiles in trees; waitresses in an ordinary diner who break into a Broadway chorus as they serve apple pie; bystanders who suddenly find themselves on a stage in the midst of a theatrical performance; walls that vanish, mailboxes that talk, etc. The sheer variety and inventiveness of the incidents is undeniable. Funt is not interested in sociological theory per se, but his incidents are informed by a keen, though unarticulated, intuition about the forces that shape behavior in a social context.

But *Candid Camera* is not social science, nor are its materials free of problems for use by scientists. Before examining such deficiencies, let us start by pointing to the most obvious difference between *Candid Camera* and scientific research. This concerns the institutional framework within which each is conducted. Above all, *Candid Camera* is a commercial activity. The overriding goal of the producer is to create materials that can be sold to a network or a sponsor. Such materials are saleable insofar as they are able to attract and hold a large television audience. Thus, within this framework the entertainment value of an episode is the ultimate test of its worth. Funt treats his incursions into the study of human behavior as a marketable commodity, and each episode has a dollar and cents value. The scientific deficiencies of the *Candid Camera* material stem from its origin as commercial entertainment.

The most obvious scientific deficiency of *Candid Camera* is the lack of adequate sampling. There is no guarantee that the behavior depicted is typical behavior. Indeed, we have every reason to feel that the selections actually used in *Candid Camera* are chosen for their maximum value as entertainment. Funt indicates that he often shoots at a film ratio of 100/1; thus, even when a sequence of respondents is shown, we cannot assume the persons depicted represent anything other than a highly uncharacteristic sets of responses.

Consider the situation in which a delivery boy finds Funt bound and gagged, asks whether the victim ordered a hamburger, then leaves nonchalantly when Funt indicates no. Clearly, the laughter promoted by this response indicates that it is entertaining. But is the behavior typical? We are not told how many delivery boys needed to be filmed before this particular boy left the incident. It seems that the more appropriate response of untying the victim, and offering him assistance, would be less amusing to an audience and thus likely to appear in the *Candid Camera* archives. We have no systematic record of the range and centrality of responses to any given situation. We are thus presented with behavior which is shown to be possible (and of no small value for this reason) but with no idea of its probability.

Moreover, we are only shown those segments of the subject's behavior which produce a maximally humorous impact. We are not shown sequelae which may be critical to establishing the meaning of the behavior as experienced by the subject. In the episode cited above, we are not informed whether this particular delivery boy left the scene of his victim permanently, or whether, upon leaving what he perceived to be a dangerous situation, he immediately called the police. This latter possibility would give an entirely different interpretation to the delivery boy's behavior.

Candid Camera differs from scientific experiments in another important way. Experiments take account of and proceed beyond work that has already been done. Thus an experiment can be evaluated by the degree to which it contributes to the cumulative growth of a discipline. Funt does not evaluate his episodes by this criterion. All that is required is that each episode differs in some way from what has gone before, and that it be entertaining. Thus, while the *Candid Camera* episodes grow in number, they do not accumulate in any specifiable direction. *Candid Camera* is thus an enterprise that offers novelty, but not progress.

Candid Camera shares with experimental social psychology the observation of behavior within constructed situations, but social psychologists make use of experimental variation, in which one systematically alters the situation to find the causes of behavior. Moreover, an experiment must have a certain degree of precision and control. Each subject must confront the same stimulus; there must be a specifiable and metrical aspect to both the stimulus and the response. Some would argue that the quantification of experimental social psychology has led to an impoverished picture of human behavior. But merely to record behavior, for all its surface vitality, gives us no clue as to its significance in some larger framework of understanding. We are left with raw material which may amuse us, but which in itself explains nothing.

In sum, the *Candid Camera* record is probably more important in raising than answering questions, since it is a haphazard rather than a disciplined approach to the study of human behavior. The questions the *Candid Camera* sequences ask are often of the "What would happen if . . ." variety, selected to produce interesting and amusing effects rather than to elaborate a system of causal explanations. This lack of conceptual discipline at the outset of its inquiries finds its parallel in a lack of rigor in the documentation of results; the responses to the situations one sees may not be representative, since entertainment value rather than adequate sampling is the criterion for selection. Further, the film record falls short as a report of empirical results since it does not select, from all that a subject does, the scientifically interesting component. Since the sequences do not flow from some larger body of conceptual issues, there are no criteria for selecting important questions from less-significant possibilities or from abstracting the most important response dimensions. These scientific criticisms are quite irrelevant, of course, to the producer of *Candid Camera*, since his aim is to entertain rather than to inform.

Let us consider further how *Candid Camera* entertains. One important determinant of the viewer's response is his relative superiority to the subject on the screen. The audience is in on the joke; acting from this privileged perspective of full information, viewers laugh at the target's confusion or dilemma rather than share in it.

Instructions in how to respond begin with the show's opening moments, which create an unserious tone. As the show progresses, the viewer is instructed by the narrator about exactly what to look for; his comments reinforce the notion that what we are about to see will be funny. Studio laughter accompanies each episode as a way of continually defining the actions as funny, prompting the home viewer to experience the scene as amusing, rather than feeling sympathy or compassion for the victim's plight, or searching to understand it.

The audience is also offered an opportunity to see things to which it usually has little access. The situations involve circumstances which might not occur without intervention in a lifetime of observation. Although these situations may be somewhat bizarre, they are not beyond the audience's understanding. In order to understand the subject's response, the audience must be given some inkling of the perception of the situation from the subject's point of view. The *Candid Camera* technique invites the viewers to put themselves in place of the subject; they know what he is thinking; they laugh because they can see that his mode of thought will lead to ineffectual or inappropriate behavior. The behavior is funny rather than inexplicable or weird, precisely because the viewer can enter the phenomenology of the subject and understand that it is the unreasonableness of the circumstances rather than irrationality on the part of the subject which produces the maladaptive behavior.

The ability of *Candid Camera*-like techniques to expose the usually covert processes of an actor's phenomenology has made them an attractive tool for theorists of a phenomenological bent. It is apparent that the Garfinkel-type demonstrations, so intimately linked to ethnomethodology, are precisely in the mold of *Candid Camera* episodes. Like *Candid Camera* writers, ethnomethodologists deal with human action from the standpoint of the actor's perception of the situation, the likelihood of his constructing meaning out of novel and even bizarre circumstances, and the belief that he will respond to situations in terms of the meanings he can impute to them. Indeed, we may speculate that *Candid Camera,* a cultural phenomenon of 30 years standing, has exerted an intellectual influence in stimulating ethnomethodological thought. In *Candid Camera,* we see repeated demonstrations of the ethnomethodological arguments that people continuously construct meanings out of the flux of daily life, even out of incongruity. We laugh at the person's struggle to extract meaning out of a situation so constructed as to frustrate this effort.

Much of the impact of *Candid Camera* results from the impression that people have been trapped into showing themselves as they "really are." The target's self-presentational mechanisms are thwarted by his incomplete understanding of the real situation. The audience sees him vainly attempting to maintain his proper self in the absence of proper understanding. The attempt to maintain an adequate self fails for a variety of reasons. One aspect of an adequate self-presentation is giving an appropriate response to one's environment, but what is an adequate response to a talking mailbox? In other cases, the subject attempts to conceal a deficiency he believes is personal, while the audience knows that it is the environment which is impossible. (In one sequence, subjects conceal the fact that they cannot open a packet of sugar, while the audience knows that the packet cannot be opened.)

People may appear foolish if they unnecessarily lose their cool when the situation is quite normal, but they can be made to appear just as foolish when they attempt to maintain their cool in an abnormal situation. In stable, everyday experience, self-presentation can be maintained by enacting habituated patterns of behavior; in the extraordinary circumstances of the *Candid Camera* films, the audience sees people actively structuring a self out of the stacked opportunities the situation provides. *Candid Camera* repeatedly shows us that people operate with a certain amount of good faith and trust and that they have certain habitualized or routine ways of dealing with situations that may sometimes be misplaced in the face of bizarre circumstances.

There are several senses in which we may examine *Candid Camera* as a cultural phenomenon. First, we may ask in what way *Candid Camera* is an expression of the larger culture. What continuities does it have with other cultural forms? Is it a completely new form of activity or does it emerge from precedents?

The spirit of *Candid Camera* is largely the spirit of the prank or the practical joke. Consider the archetypic prank. A person walks along the street, sees a wallet lying on the pavement and attempts to pick it up. The wallet is attached to a string which is then pulled out of the reach of the person just as he stoops to pick it up. The person is initially startled, then realizes he has been the butt of a joke. If the prank is performed on April 1, its perpetrators will normally jog the person into a realization of its significance by announcing, "April Fool!" thus giving a cultural legitimacy to their activity and undercutting hostile reaction from the victim by admonishing him to be a "good sport."

Funt has extended April Fool's Day to a year-round activity. Moreover, the program has achieved a certain cultural penetration. Instead of announcing "April Fool," each episode typically ends when Funt says, "Smile, you're on *Candid Camera*." Upon hearing these words, subjects are almost always taken aback. Before responding to this interpretation, they search out the camera to confirm the interpretation. Indeed, pointing to the presence of a concealed camera to support the assertion that the person has been filmed has become part of the ritual of *Candid Camera*. Suddenly, all of the confusing and even bizarre events that preceded these words fall into place. The subject is thus grateful that the strain placed on his coping with the environment was nothing but an extended practical joke. Confusion suddenly crystallizes into a meaningful interpretation. *Candid Camera* has acquired a genuine cultural standing insofar as the words, "Smile, you're on *Candid Camera*" give meaning and legitimacy to the events that preceded them.

At an aesthetic level, the *Candid Camera* program elevates the practical joke to the limits that a large budget, technological sophistication, and admirable ingenuity allow. Whatever else one may say about it, asking a cab driver to follow a car which splits in half is a masterful practical joke. *Candid Camera* is funny in part because it is an extension of a preexisting form of humor.

The practical joke is not the only cultural precedent for *Candid Camera*. Western society offers many other instances of creating an entertainment out of the manner in which people spontaneously respond to unusual and unforeseen circumstances. Pitting people against others in gladiatorial combat, or more perversely, placing people in combat with carnivorous animals, drew a substantial audience to the Roman arena. Like the early Christians entering the arena, the participants in *Candid Camera* do not choose to be in the situation. Unlike the Roman arena, *Candid Camera* must create its entertainments within a fairly tightly circumscribed boundary of individual and legal rights. A *Candid Camera* participant may be confused, embarrassed, or made anxious by the situation in which he is placed, but these are transient emotions which are presumably limited to the situation in which they are generated, and the consequences are certainly less serious than, say, being devoured.

Unlike Funt, the Roman impresario was given free rein to create bold and gory entertainments. The critical difference was this: in Rome, audiences and actors were of juridically different statuses. Christians, captured warriors, etc., were presumed to be devoid of those rights which ordinary Romans enjoyed. But in both cases an audience is entertained by the sight of people forced to cope with circumstances that are out of the ordinary and not entirely predictable. *Candid Camera* perpetuates the spirit of the Roman arena, but as vitiated by the limits imposed by an egalitarian political culture, and without the punitive intent of the Colosseum. In *Candid Camera*, the presumed equality between spectator and participant serves an important dramaturgical effect, facilitating identification between the two.

There is another sense in which *Candid Camera* is closely tied to culture. Many episodes rely on a precise knowledge of the prevailing cultural practice, and derive their humor from a violation of cultural expectancies. Much *Candid Camera* humor, therefore, is effective only within the particular culture in which it was constructed. For example, in one episode, male workers enter a physician's office for a physical examination. The physician turns out to be an attractive woman. The workers feel awkward when they're asked to undress before her. The audience titters at this embarrassing situation. It is clear that such a response can occur only in a society in which women physicians do not typically examine men. Even within other parts of modern society, say in Scandinavia or the Soviet Union, the embarrassed and awkward response of the workers would be less likely. Some *Candid Camera* episodes which prove successful in America do not travel well.

In their willingness to tinker with social reality for the purpose of observing behavior, both social science and *Candid Camera* display a fundamental irreverence toward the existing social order, and thus—some would say—participate in the analytic, disintegrative tendencies of modern life. But for *Candid Camera*, at least, there are clear boundaries to irreverence. Funt carefully avoids incidents or the use of persons that would be regarded as offensive by segments of the population. ". . . we lean over backward not to use a weak or poor sample of a black person . . . if a guy looked as if he was too rough or too ignorant, or too Uncle Tom, I left him out of the picture." Moreover, while Funt does not regard the everyday operation of the social order as sacred, he treats certain social activities as immune from *Candid Camera*'s intrusions. For example, *Candid Camera* does not create episodes intruding upon real funerals; nor does it carry out a prank on a person's wedding night, however rich the possibilities for humor. This would be considered too deep a violation of the couple's privileged moments. *Candid Camera* maps for us the domain of the sacred by leaving such activities alone. Like the prankster, it tweaks at the culture, without doing serious violence to it.

Finally, as its very name implies, *Candid Camera* is utterly dependent upon the technical culture of western society, and specifically on the availability of instruments for audiovisual recording. Thus, it was not possible to undertake an enterprise such as *Candid Camera* until the present century. At best, it was possible, through the use of actors, to recreate a scene that the participants thought was covert (as in Hamlet's recreation of the poisoning of his father). But this is a far cry from the detailed filmic documentation of behavior enacted under the illusion of being ephemeral and unobserved.

READINGS SUGGESTED BY THE AUTHORS

CORNELL CANDID CAMERA COLLECTION/CATALOG. Department of Psychology, Cornell University, Ithaca, New York.

FUNT, ALLEN. "What Do You Say to a Naked Lady." In Alan Rosenthal, ed., *The New Documentary in Action: A Casebook in Film Making*. Berkeley: University of California Press, 1971: 251–53.

GARFINKEL, HAROLD. "Studies of the Routine Grounds of Everyday Activities." *Social Problems* 11 (Winter 1964): 225–50.

MAAS, JAMES, AND TOIVANEN, KENNETH. "Candid Camera and the Behavioral Sciences." *Teaching of Psychology* 5 (No. 5, 1978): 226–28.

24

Reflections on News

❖

Let me begin with a confession. I am a news addict. Upon awakening I flip on the *Today* show to learn what events transpired during the night. On the commuter train which takes me to work, I scour the *New York Times,* and find myself absorbed in tales of earthquakes, diplomacy, and economics. I read the newspaper as religiously as my grandparents read their prayerbooks. The sacramental character of the news extends into the evening. The length of my workday is determined precisely by my need to get home in time for Walter Cronkite. My children understand that my communion with Cronkite is something serious and cannot be interrupted for light and transient causes.

But what is it, precisely, that is happening when I and millions of others scour our newspapers, stare at the tube, and pour over the news magazines that surround us? Does it make sense? What is news, and why does it occupy a place of special significance for so many people?

Let us proceed from a simple definition: news is information about events that are going on outside immediate experience. In this sense, news has always been a part of the human situation. In its earliest form, it took the shape of an account brought by a traveler, or a member of the group who wandered further than the rest and found water, game, or signs of a nearby enemy. The utility of such information is self-evident. News is a social mechanism that extends our own eyes and ears to embrace an ever wider domain of events. A knowledge of remote events allows us to prepare for them and take whatever steps are needed to deal with them. This is the classic function of news.

News is the consciousness of society. It is the means whereby events in the body politic are brought into awareness. And it is curious that regimes which we call *repressive* tend to exhibit the same characteristic of repressed personalities;

Reprinted from the *Antioch Review,* vol. 35, no. 2–3 (Spring–Summer 1977), pp. 167–170. Copyright © 1977 by the Antioch Review, Inc. Reprinted by permission of the Editors.

they are unable, or unwilling, to allow conflictive material into awareness. The disability stems from deep insecurities. The censoring of the repressed material does not eliminate it, but forces it to fester without anyone's rationally coming to grips with it.

Inevitably news comes to be controlled by the dominant political forces of a society. In a totalitarian regime the government attempts to create the image of a world, and of events, that reflects most favorably on those in power. The democratization of news, which goes hand in hand with the diffusion of political power among those governed, is a relatively recent development whose permanence cannot be assured. Democracies are far better able to cope with the reality of events than are totalitarian regimes. Such regimes promulgate a myth of their omnipotence, and are threatened even by events outside the control of the political process. Thus, typically, the Soviet press does not report air crashes, and even natural disasters such as earthquakes are suppressed, out of the notion—rooted in political insecurity—that the event in some manner reflects badly on the regime.

The question for any society is not whether there shall be news, but rather who shall have access to it. Every political system may be characterized by the proportion of information it has which is shared with the people and the proportion withheld. That is why the growth of secret news-gathering agencies, such as the C.I.A., is a troubling one for a democracy. It appears our government wants to keep some news to itself.

At a deeper historical level we can see that news in its present form is closely tied to the rise of economy, and specifically to the exploitative and risk elements of capitalism. For the nineteenth-century merchant, news meant reports of his ship, of resources to exploit, and the means of minimizing the risk element inherent in entrepreneurship by gaining as much information as possible before his competitors. News services, such as Reuters, developed to serve business and investment interests, who discovered that getting the news quickly was the first step to financial gain.

In a civilization in which all activities tend toward commercial expression—for example, our own—news becomes a product to manufacture and dispense to the consumer. Thus a large-scale industry for the production and consumption of news has evolved. We ingest it with the same insatiable appetite that moves us to purchase the manifold products of our commercial civilization.

News under such circumstances tends toward decadent use. It no longer serves first the classic function of giving us information on which to act, or even to help us construct a mental model of the larger world. It serves mainly as entertainment. The tales of earthquakes, political assassinations, and bitterly fought elections are the heady stuff of which drama or melodrama is made. Happily, we are able to indulge our taste for thriller, romance, or murder mystery under the guise of a patently respectable pursuit. All enlightened people are supposed to know what is going on in the world. If what is going on also happens to be thrilling and exciting, so much the better.

Another feature of the decadent use of news is its increasing ritualization. The information becomes subservient to the form in which it is delivered. News is broadcast every evening, whether or not there is vital information to be conveyed. Indeed, the problem for the news networks is to generate sufficient news to fill a given time period. The time period becomes the fundamental fact, the framework into which events must be fitted. As in any ritual, the form persists even when a meaningful content is missing.

Those groups whose survival and well-being are most affected by remote events will be most persistently attuned to them. For example, Israelis, who view the survival of their state as a day-to-day contingency, are among the most news-oriented people in the world. During periods of crisis, portable radios blare in buses and in the market place. Jews, in general, have felt the need to develop antennae for remote events because of a communal insecurity. Any event, no matter how remote—even a farcical *putsch* in Munich led by a paper hanger—may grow into a formidable threat. Thus, constant monitoring of events is strongly reinforced.

Although I am a news addict, my addiction is strongest for news that in many respects seems most remote from my own life and experience. International news receives top priority, followed by national domestic news, and finally—and of least interest—local news. I feel more concerned reading about a student strike in Paris than a murder in my own neighborhood. I am especially uninterested in those news programs that provide a constant litany of fires and local crimes as their standard fare. Yet there is a paradox in this. Surely a criminal loose in my city is of greater personal consequence than an election outcome in Uruguay. Indeed, I sometimes ask what difference it makes to the actual conduct of my life to know about a fracas in Zaire, or a train wreck in Sweden. The total inconsequence of the news for my life is most strikingly brought home when we return from a vacation of several weeks where we have been without any news. I normally scan the accumulated pile of newspapers, but cannot help noticing how little difference it all made to me. And least consequential of all were those remote international events that so rivet my attention in the normal course of the week.

Why this interest in things far away, with a lesser interest in events close at home? Perhaps it is essentially a romantic impulse in the projection of meaning into remote countries, places, and people. Such a romantic impulse stems from a dissatisfaction with the mundane reality of everyday life. The events and places described in the news are remote, and thus we can more readily fix our imaginative sentiments to them. Moreover, an interest in news reinforces the "cosmopolitan" attitude which characterizes modern life, a desire to focus not only on the immediate community, but on the larger world. It is thus the opposite of the "provincialism" which characterized an earlier rural existence.

Living in the modern world, I cannot help but be shaped by it, suckered by the influence and impact of our great institutions. The *New York Times*, *CBS*, and *Newsweek* have made me into a news addict. In daily life I have come to accept the supposition that if the *New York Times* places a story on the front page, it deserves my attention. I feel obligated to know what is going on. But sometimes, in quieter moments, another voice asks: If the news went away, would the world be any worse for it?

25

Cyranoids

————— ❖ —————

Since 1977 I have been conducting research on cyranoids. *Cyranoids* are people who do not speak thoughts originating in their own central nervous system: Rather, the words that they speak originate in the mind of another person who transmits these words to the cyranoid by means of a radio transmitter. The cyranoid receives these words by means of a tiny FM receiver with connecting earphone fitted inconspicuously in his or her ear.

Although cyranoids appear to be engaged in normal conversation, they are actually doing something quite different: They are only relaying speech word-for-word that is beamed to them from a distal source. Every word spoken by the cyranoid is unoriginal. Cyranoids shadow the speech of their "sources," who, like Frank Morgan in "The Wizard of Oz," remain poised in another room eagerly spewing their words into a microphone and listening attentively to the proceedings so that they can feed their lines to the cyranoid on cue.

Before proceeding, it is useful to define our terms. First, let us call the person who is originating the speech the *source*. The person who transmits the talk to a third person will be called the *cyranoid*. And the third person, to whom the speech is directed, can be termed the *listener* or *interactant*.

Why study cyranoids? The original idea arose while analyzing a hypothetical world in which the thoughts of one person would come out of another person's mouth. What would be the main sociopsychological consequences of such a world? Would there be a weakening of verbal constraints on the sources, since they no longer suffered the immediate consequences of their talk? What insights

Talk delivered at the 1984 Convention of the American Psychological Association in Toronto, Canada, August 16, 1984. Reprinted by permission of Alexandra Milgram.

would technique give into issues of individual accountability and person perception? Is such a procedure technically feasible? And how could we explore this experimentally?

In our studies we found that, while there is considerable variation in the ability to shadow speech, many subjects could track exceedingly well, introducing a delay of a half second or less between the source's utterance and the cyranoid's echoing and often creating an impression of astonishing naturalness in their speech. The interactant, normally a naive subject, engages in conversation with the cyranoid and cannot hear the source directly but only as mediated by the person with whom she or he is face-to-face.

Of course, only a component of the source's communicative output is transferred to the cyranoid, the specifically verbal component. The appearance of the cyranoid, and his or her social features, such as age, sex, and race, are not altered. Our studies show that although cyranoids may track word-for-word the utterances of the source, the cyranoids contribute emotional and affective properties to their speech that tend to be distinctively their own. Moreover, the social characteristics of the cyranoid, for example, age, may govern the kinds of conversation that interactants are disposed to engage in. But more of that later.

Several streams of research are relevant to the cyranic technique. Gordon (1973) devised a wireless "bug in the ear" communication for training and therapy, and a considerable number of studies have used this technique. The bug-in-the-ear research differs in an essential respect from the studies I have been carrying out: It neither aims at, nor achieves, cyranic functioning. The messages transmitted by the clinical supervisor are quite fragmentary, designed to guide or influence the trainees, rather than provide the full linguistic template of their speech. The clinical supervisor addresses comments *to* the trainee, while in cyranic functioning, the source speaks *through* the cyranoid. The latter features gives cyranic functioning its special character.

A second related line of research has been carried out in experimental linguistics. The exact latencies required for repeating speech originating in others was measured by Marslen-Wilson (1973). To move from the temporal analysis of speech shadowing to the cyranic mode requires a shift of conceptual focus and the additional step of inserting the "shadower" into a social situation so that the shadowed speech is responded to by another individual.

Finally, a few years after my investigation had gotten underway, research using a similar technique was reported by Schwitzgebel and Taylor (1980). These investigators and I had proceeded in total independence of each other until 1980, when Schwitzgebel wrote to me about an article he had seen about my work.

SOME FINDINGS

What is it like to see a cyranoid in action? To the naive subject conversing with the cyranoid, there is nothing special about the person functioning in the cyranic mode. Indeed, he or she seems quite normal. This is perhaps one of the most remarkable findings of our studies, that people can interact with a cyranoid over a period of 20 minutes or more, engage in give-and-take conversation, probe, ask questions and leave the situation feeling that one has engaged in a perfectly normal interaction with a perfectly normal, spontaneously functioning individual. The fact that everything the other person said originated in the mind of a distal source, that the cyranoid was simply echoing speech received by radio, simply doesn't enter into the picture. We call this the "cyranic illusion." Specifically, it is the illusion that one has been dealing with an autonomously functioning person.

The illusion is determined by three facts: First, on the part of the naive interactant, there is the deeply rooted expectation that in speaking to someone, the words uttered are generated out of the other person's own central nervous system. The second fact which allows for this illusion is that the speech-tracking capacities of individuals are such that it is technically possible to create an appearance of spontaneity. Prior to undertaking this research, we did not know that this would be so. The third fact is that the discrepancy between the verbal and nonverbal behavior of the cyranoid is not so contradictory as to render the illusion unsustainable.

In one experiment we tried to obtain systematic measures of the strength of the cyranic illusion. Twenty naive subjects were used in this experiment; they were recruited through a newspaper advertisement to take part in a study of person perception. Subjects were asked to interview a person, who unknown to them, was a cyranoid, and they were given a set of guideline questions, dealing both with personal and political issues, mainly nuclear disarmament. Subjects were free to ask additional questions if they wished. In each case, the source was the same 50-year-old professor transmitting to the cyranoid from an adjacent room. Four different cyranoids were employed in the study: Ken, a 16-year-old black male high school student; Jay, a 16-year-old high school student of Korean origin; Christine, a 22-year-old female graduate student; and Stuart, a 32-year-old white male graduate student. Each subject interviewed one cyranoid. After the interview subjects were asked, "Please indicate your general impression of the person you just interviewed with regard to such features as maturity, poise, intelligence, likability and sincerity." Here are some of the written characterizations provided by the subjects.

A 33-year-old man described Christine:

I think that a great amount of honesty and sincerity characterized all her answers. Her initial nervousness notwithstanding, I think that she exhibited a fine amount of poise throughout the questioning. She seemed to me to be quite intelligent and was always, as I said earlier, honest to a fault and sincere in everything she said.

A 33-year-old female subject described the same cyranoid:

Christine is a lovely woman. She is poised, intelligent, likable and sincere. She has a pulse on our time, is informed and a great help to mankind.

A 43-year-old female administrator took quite a shine to Jay, a 16-year-old Korean cyranoid. The interview broadened to the point where the subject began to discuss some of her marital problems with him. She characterized Jay this way:

He was very likable, open, interested in the subject and in the interviewer and had firm opinions and knowledge of the subject. He showed a great deal of maturity and poise—in that he had risked the experience and made eye contact throughout. I think he was very sincere.

In addition, subjects were asked to rate the cyranoid on a number of personality scales and to indicate their agreement or disagreement with statements that started with "The person I interviewed . . ."

. . . was quite normal

. . . was under the influence of alcohol or other drugs

. . . made odd grimaces and gestures during the interview

. . . spoke by receiving radio messages and repeating them to me

Not a single subject accepted this last interpretation.

At the end of the session subjects were informed by the experimenter of the true situation, which explanation was often buttressed by showing the earplug in the cyranoid's ear, the radio receiver and transmitter, and demonstrating the technique. Some who had engaged the cyranoid in interesting, and sometimes personal, discussion felt the loss of a person. The cyranoid they had encountered was composed of a mixture of the source's words and the medium's own affective and personal qualities. This personality they had encountered was a synthetic creation of the experimental procedure and had no existence apart from the hybridization which the experiment created.

ANOMALIES

The power of the cyranic paradigm lies in the independent variability of the source and the medium. Thus a source of any given characteristic can be linked to a medium of any characteristic. This allows us to create extreme disparities between the two. For example, an 11-year-old medium may be prompted by a 50-year-old source, or vice versa. What is it like to deal with such a person? How will a child be perceived if animated by a mature adult? What degree of latitude do people allow before they judge the person bizarre, deviant, or simply not credible? The questions posed here are of substantial role-theoretic interest, for they allow us to examine the degree of interchangeability of behaviors, attitudes, and language between people who occupy substantially different social statuses.

In the time allotted, let me describe one experiment we carried out that highlights these issues. Our cyranoids in this study were an 11-year-old boy, Jason, and a 12-year-old boy, Omri. They were chosen for their mimetic skills. Both attended elementary schools and were, respectively, in the sixth and seventh grades. They were each interested in theatrical careers and attended an acting school on weekends. Both boys were intelligent and personable. As cyranoids, they performed brilliantly, echoing their source with uncanny quickness and skill, yet contributing a youthful charm of their own. It is unfortunate that we cannot show here videotapes of their performances as cyranoids. They are so convincing as authentic, coherent personalities it is hard to believe that their words were animated by a source, transmitting his words by radio.

We recruited high school teachers to form an interview panel and interrogate each boy "so as to get a good picture of what he is like and what he knows." The panel was further instructed to "Ask whatever questions you feel will best reveal the child's intellectual potential. Your questions should touch on several areas: science, literature and current events, for example. And try to probe the limits of the child's knowledge in each area so that you would be able to recommend a grade level for each subject." Each panel of teachers was to interview two children in turn. For each session one of the children was a cyranoid and the other functioned autonomously. (The roles would be reversed for the next panel so that for each of the two boys we obtained judgments made of him while a cyranoid and while functioning on his own.)

The teachers were seated around a small conference table. Each boy was in turn brought in for the interview by a group of as many as six teachers. After each interview session, the teachers individually responded to open-ended questions and gave scaled judgments of the person they had just interviewed.

The results are too detailed to report fully here, but in general we can say that both boys were well regarded by the teachers. When teachers were asked to assign each boy to an appropriate grade level in the fields of English, science, math, art, and social studies, Jason as a cyranoid was elevated at least 2 years in each subject over his autonomous performance and 4 years over his actual grade level, i.e., the sixth grade. In the field of art, Jason received a mean score of twelfth grade, compared to an eighth-grade level when he was on his own. In social studies he was elevated from ninth to tenth grade, a gratifying improvement to the source, who, as I have indicated, was a professor of psychology.

In the case of Omri, the pattern is somewhat different. Omri proved so impressive in control conditions, when he functioned on his own, that in general, the source, though he huffed and puffed, was unable to elevate Omri's performance as a cyranoid. That is not to say Omri didn't get high marks. Consider these characterizations of him as a cyranoid: A 53-year-old mathematics teacher wrote:

> Omri is a very bright, articulate, highly intelligent and likable young man. He seems mature beyond his years. Given more time and permission to give tests we could conceivably come to the conclusion that he is a prodigy. He is very much interested in all the topics we touched upon, more so in philosophy, arts and science than in math. . . . It was a pleasure to talk to the young man, to listen to him. His vocabulary is stunning, so good for a person so young. Very pleasant personality.

A 56-year-old library teacher wrote:

> I felt embarrassed after a while doing this interview. This young person had as much or more information about the world in all its aspects—artistic, scientific, intellectual, than I can ever hope to have. He challenged the quality of questions we asked. He was poised and expressive (hands, face). He was fascinating and again for me a little frightening. I feel his self-confidence is almost overwhelming. He also jogs!!

A 65-year-old art teacher wrote:

> The boy showed great maturity and self-confidence. He was at ease, very intelligent—warm and honest; a very likable boy with great potential.

Thus, however disparate the nature of a 12-year-old boy and a 50-year-old professor may be, the teachers were able to integrate these aspects into a coherent impression of the cyranoid.

Finally, a teacher of secretarial studies wrote that there was an aspect of his behavior that disturbed her: "He exhibited poise to a degree but he seems to be the type of individual who likes to have things on his own terms. In this aspect there is a mixed degree of maturity. From the intellectual point of view he is mature, but emotionally I feel he is still to achieve maturity. He is sincere in his beliefs but I feel he cannot be opposed graciously. . . ." But then she added, "Omri is very possibly on a near genius level."

We see from all these remarks that a certain personality may be transmitted through the cyranoid, as well as purely intellectual content.

At the end of each questionnaire the statement appears: "I can now tell you that there was a very unusual feature in the interview situations you participated in today. Could you indicate what it was?"

The mathematics teacher, noticing the earplug in Omri's ear, wrote: "Maybe the boys had a physical disability? Were the boys hearing impaired? One of them appeared to be wearing a hearing aid."

But that is about as far as the teachers got. None suspected that they were not speaking to an authentic, autonomous person.

Let me now make several general observations about the study I have just described. The technique is an extraordinary prism through which to understand how people form judgments of others. For in a significant degree, the opinions teachers formed of our child cyranoids depended as much on the teacher as on the child, and the questions asked and avoided. Teachers varied in how they approached their questions, the best of them allowing the cyranoids' responses to guide their interview, the worst never seeing beyond the possibilities of an average 11-year-old.

Moreover, we see how general preconceptions did not allow the teachers to get anywhere near the appropriate grade level of the cyranoid in some subjects. After all, to assign a Ph.D. to a tenth-grade class of social studies does no great honor to his Harvard degree. Often, teachers themselves simply did not have the knowledge, information, or inclination to ask adequate questions or to make adequate judgments. As the source, I was hoping they would ask the cyranoid about Freud, Jung, Adler, or at least Darwin and Wittgenstein, but some teachers stuck to fractions and parts of speech.

We thus see very clearly how the impressions people form are to some extent generated by their own interaction with the stimulus person, the things they bring out and suppress. It is not enough, as some studies in our field do, to present a subject with a prepackaged description of a stimulus person, for in the real world the subject significantly shapes those aspects of the person to which he is exposed.

CONCLUSION

The paradigm described here has many interesting research possibilities. For example, one can rotate several sources behind a single cyranoid. The question is whether subjects will have any sense that they are not dealing with a unitary individual. When we have done this, that is, when several experimenters alternated in prompting the same cyranoid, sometimes on a minute-by-minute basis, we found no perception of a fragmented personality. What is the implication of this finding for the notion that personality in some sense is a unified phenomenon?

Another line of research concerns not the cyranoid, but the source. The "disinhibition hypothesis" argues that sources may express attitudes and viewpoints through the cyranoid they might not otherwise externalize, because the sources no longer have to directly confront the consequences of their speech. Such consequences are, instead, displaced onto the cyranoid. After all, this is why Cyrano de Bergerac was able to profess his love for Roxanne, using the handsome Christian as his mouthpiece.

Defining the limits of the cyranic technique is no less important than examining its potential. We found, for example, that unlike Omri and Jason, some cyranoids cannot project warmth and have a telltale, distant glaze in their eyes. Other people are simply not very good at speech echoing, and even those who can echo speech may garble it if they don't grasp its meaning. Thus, one of our cyranoids, who was in real life a shoeshine boy, transmuted the sentence "Plato was a great philosopher" into "Plato was a great falafaler"—that is, one who makes falafel, which, for all I know, he might have been.

Although the exact scientific significance of the cyranoid remains difficult to pinpoint, it nonetheless is a highly evocative phenomenon. The phenomenon evokes a range of instances in which the self is intruded upon or taken over by an external source. Paranoids claim they hear voices beamed to them by radio. So do our cyranoids, and they are right. Every culture deals at some level with the substitution of one's authentic self by an external presence. Psychoanalytic culture refers to such a process in the formation of narcissistic character; primitive cultures speak of demonic possession. The theoretical root of cyranic studies, therefore, centers on the concept of self and the conditions under which such selves are perceived by others even under the radical deformations induced by the cyranic technique.

REFERENCES

COLLIGAN, D. Report of Milgram cyranoid research. *Omni,* vol. 2, March 1980, pp. 108–115.

GORDON, D. A. A mobile, wireless "bug-in-the-ear" communication system for training and therapy. *Behavior Therapy,* vol. 6, 1975, pp. 130–132.

MARSLEN-WILSON, W. Linguistic structure and speech shadowing at very short latencies. *Nature,* vol. 224, 1973, pp. 522–523.

MILGRAM, S. Technique of mediated speech as a tool in social psychology. Grant proposal submitted to the National Science Foundation. 26 February 1979.

ROSTAND, E. *Cyrano de Bergerac.* 1897. English translation by Brian Hooker, 1923. New York: The Modern Library, Random House, 1936.

SCHWITZGEBEL, R., & TAYLOR, R. Impression formation under conditions of spontaneous and shadowed speech. *Journal of Social Psychology,* vol. 110, 1980, pp. 253–263.

Name Index

Subject Index

acceleration, vehicular, 15
acquaintance, 259–263, 264, 273–274
  chain, 61, 263, 264, 265, 268–269, 270–271
  circles, 261, 263
  links, 259–260, 268, 273–274
  see also familiar stranger
acquiescence, 32
  to group, 127–128
  see also authority
acquisition of crowd members, 245, 250
act, antisocial, 256–257, 287–308
  communicative, 256
  induction of, 219–220
  morally significant, 125
  photographic, 315–322
action:
  against person, 219–229
  against queue jumper, 51 *ff.*
  conformity, 196, 219–229
  of a crowd, 245–250
  measure of, 278–286
activity, city and town, 17
  human, photography, 257–258
  states of, 246
adaptations to city life, 17, 20, 23, 26
adolescent perceptions of city, 28
aggregation, in mental maps, 73–74
aggression, 144, 154, 158, 159
alienated, influencing the, 196
alienation, 17, 118
altruism, 125, 133
  in cities, 12–13
ambience, measurement, xxi, 1, 2
  in New York, 21–23
  in Paris, 21–23, 26–28
  sources of, 26–28, 114–124
American, experimenters in Paris, Athens, Boston, 24
  internment camp, xxxii
  preconceptions, 24
  reaction to Genovese case, 32
  society, 158, 201, 264, 269, 270, 272

  see also Boston; Chicago; New York; United States
anecdote, 3, 168–169, 170, 174–175
anonymity, benefits of, 18
  consequences of, 17–18, 154
  level of, 257
  in lost letter procedure, 278
  urban, 17–18, 68–71
  see also familiar stranger
anonymous strangers, 18–19
anxiety, inhibitory, xxiv
  obedience experiment, xxiv
  in subway experiment, xxiv
archives of Candid Camera, 324
arrondissements, 89–90, 104–108
associations of Paris:
  mental, 98
  verbal, 99
Athens, helpfulness in, 24
atmosphere, urban, 21–23
atriums, and perceptions of skyscrapers, 123
attitude, assessing, 277–278
  toward experiment, 208–209
  toward McCarthy-Johnson, 285
  measurement, through actions, 278–286
  toward Vietnam, 285
  urbanite, 20
auditory variation of Asch experiment, 197
  see also noise
authority, 125–126
  background, 151–153
  closeness of, 145, 147
  diminished, 241
  disobedience to, 127, 136–160
  experimenter as, 128, 138, 159, 169–171, 183, 241
  and the group, 198
  legitimate, 191
  medical, 130
  obedience to, 127, 136–160, 183
  pressure of, 130, 183
  rejection of, xx
  structure of, xxxii

DISCARD

Crosscurrents / Modern Critiques
Third Series

Edited by Jerome Klinkowitz

In Form: Digressions on the Act of Fiction
  Ronald Sukenick

*Literary Subversions: New American Fiction and the Practice of
Criticism*
  Jerome Klinkowitz

The Fiction of William Gass: The Consolation of Language
  Arthur M. Saltzman

Critical Angles: European Views of Contemporary American Literature
  Marc Chénetier

Zoltán Szilassy

American Theater
of the 1960s

Southern Illinois University Press
CARBONDALE AND EDWARDSVILLE

Printed in the United States of America

Edited by Susan H. Wilson
Designed by Design for Publishing, Inc.
Production supervised by Kathleen Giencke

89 88 87 86   4 3 2 1

Library of Congress Cataloging in Publication Data
Szilassy, Zoltán, 1947–
    American theater of the 1960s
    (Crosscurrents/modern critiques. Third series)
    Includes index.
    1. Theater—United States—History—20th century.
2. Experimental theater—United States.   3. American
drama—20th century—History and criticism.   I. Title.
II. Series.
PN2266.5.S95   1986   792'.0973   85-8405
ISBN 0-8093-1227-1

Contents

Crosscurrents/
Modern Critiques/
Third Series

I N THE EARLY 1960s, when the Crosscurrents/Modern Critiques series was developed by Harry T. Moore, the contemporary period was still a controversial one for scholarship. Even today the elusive sense of the present dares critics to rise above mere impressionism and to approach their subject with the same rigors of discipline expected in more traditional areas of study. As the first two series of Crosscurrents books demonstrated, critiquing contemporary culture often means that the writer must be historian, philosopher, sociologist, and bibliographer as well as literary critic, for in many cases these essential preliminary tasks are yet undone.

To the challenges that faced the initial Crosscurrents project have been added those unique to the past two decades: the disruption of conventional techniques by the great surge in innovative writing in the American 1960s just when social and political conditions were being radically transformed, the new worldwide interest in the Magic Realism of South American novelists, the startling experiments of textual and aural poetry from Europe, the emergence of Third World authors, the rising cause of feminism in life and literature, and, most dramatically, the introduction of Continental theory into the previously staid world of Anglo-American literary scholarship. These transformations demand that many traditional treatments be rethought, and part of the new responsibility for Crosscurrents will be to provide such studies.

Contributions to Crosscurrents/Modern Critiques/ Third Series will be distinguished by their fresh approaches to established topics and by their opening up of new territories for discourse. When a single author is studied, we hope to present the first book on his or her work, or to explore a previously untreated aspect based on new research. Writers who have been critiqued well elsewhere will be studied in comparison with lesser-known figures, sometimes from other cultures, in an effort to broaden our base of understanding. Critical and theoretical works by leading novelists, poets, and dramatists will have a home in Crosscurrents/Modern Critiques/Third Series, as will sampler-introductions to the best in new Americanist criticism written abroad.

The excitement of contemporary studies is that all of its critical practitioners and most of their subjects are alive and working at the same time. One work influences another, bringing to the field a spirit of competition and cooperation that reaches an intensity rarely found in other disciplines. Above all, this third series of Crosscurrents/Modern Critiques will be collegial—a mutual interest in the present moment that can be shared by writer, subject, and reader alike.

Jerome Klinkowitz

Preface

How Dare I . . . ?

INDEED, HOW DARE I—a middle-aged, Eastern European comparativist at a small university in a tiny country with my amateur singer-performer past, with my ESL and International Anguish—write a book concerning American theater in the 1960s? I shall tell you.

Even the most scantily informed average American citizen realizes that the widespread discontent and revolt that led to the Hungarian turmoil of 1956 and to its subsequent failure was a turning point, no matter how it is interpreted this or that side of paradise. As a teenager, unable to understand what was happening to us, I grew up with the sixties and only later came to understand the catalyst role of the late fifties. More and more information found its way to and from us. The Iron Curtain had been perforated!

My high-school years coincided with the early sixties, when we were taken aback by the messages of John Lennon, Bob Dylan, Pete Seeger, Joan Baez, and the like; and my undergraduate years (after I made the unhappy choice of becoming a lay preacher rather than a folk singer) were full of literary and theatrical sensations coming from the West. We were happy to swallow Kafka and Proust, Camus and Sartre, and Kierkegaard and Heidegger in one big gulp; but, in my case, O'Neill, Wilder, Miller, and Williams opened my eyes to the "otherness of the other." Semiclassics though they were, I needed a fresher view—in about 1970 I landed with Edward Albee. Strangely enough, this choice followed the logic of my sixties. Along with knowing about "John, Paul, George, and Ringo," we *did* know of Bessie Smith and Elvis Presley, of George Gershwin, Charlie Parker, and Louis Armstrong. An early play like *The American Dream* challenged not only those in the title, but us, as Europeans. And *Who's Afraid of Virginia Woolf?* was a mock-rhetorical question whose relevance could not be denied by any adherers to the Spenglerian heritage.

Horizons widen all the time. While doing my doctorate in 1974, I had to acquaint myself with Albee's contemporaries and their possible position in long-term development. In the sixties, Martin Esslin was the kind of European soothsayer who placed all these writers into the relevant, but mostly convenient, scheme of "absurdists" (1960 to 1968). For me, Esslin, Jan Kott, Peter Brook, and so on, are part of the same innovative theatrical generation: a generation that knew almost too much of its predetermined heritage—a generation that would soon be radically changed. The case was different when Europeans tried to absorb the American phenomena. A European-American cultural commuter like Charles Marowitz certainly did a good job of introducing *New American Drama* (1966) and *Off-Broadway Plays* (1970) in the Penguin paperback series. The publication of these two works was a promising sign for those who wanted to know that the Little Theater movement in the United States had not been stopped by either the First or Second World Wars. Thus, "Off Broadway" really came to mean a continuity represented by the Provincetown Players premiering O'Neill before World War II and Albee after it. For better or for worse, I became familiar with Richardson, Schisgal, Horovitz, Guare, and their colleagues. Then came my long visit to the United States in 1978. It was at this time that I realized that Off-Off-Broadway was no younger than Off Broadway, and that regional theater activity was no poorer, in comparison to New York City, than that produced by any other alternative field. I also found out that theater revolutionaries had not necessarily come from behind the coulisses but that often they had arrived at dramatic solutions while trying to sell—aesthetically and ethically, rather than financially speaking—their action painting, mobile sculpture, atonal music, and the like. My knowledge continued to broaden as I became acquainted with the activity of the Living Theater and Open Theater on the one hand and with newcomers like Van Itallie and Shepard on the other.

My choice of the material discussed in this book, by definition and by necessity, is restricted to the representative samples that have come within my reach. This, of course, is not to say that the neglected areas are less substantial. Although I share both the hopes and doubts of performance reconstruction theorists (*TDR*, 103, fall 1984), my efforts in selectively reconstructing the theatrical atmosphere of an entire decade, might, perhaps, help those who would want to evaluate the seemingly random mainstream of side- and crosscurrents.

In offering these observations, I would like to extend my warmest thanks and acknowledgments to the follow-

ing persons. First and foremost to Dr. Jerome Klinkowitz, most helpful friend and scholar. No less affection
is due to Barrie Stavis, friend and playwright, a portion
of whose life's work I have been lucky to introduce in
Hungary. Horizons widen, as they say, until views of so
different generations and nations can amalgamate. I owe
special thanks to professors of the English and Theater
departments at the University of Minnesota, especially
to Dr. Kent Bales, my academic adviser. I have enjoyed
an intellectually and emotionally stimulating friendship
with Paul Walsh, who was a graduate student and teaching assistant at the University of Minnesota during my
stay there. If we meet again for a longer period of time,
we must write up our notes for our coauthored book,
The Room-Sized Metaphysics of Twentieth-Century Drama.
The ensemble whose continuous efforts, from the sixties
to the time I met them, have deeply impressed me, was
the Provisional Theater of Los Angeles. Trying to avoid
sentimentalism, from my personal helpers who helped
me to understand theater and to survive life. I list only
a few, namely: Dr. Clara Györgyey, Dr. Enikö Molnár-
Basa, Dr. Annette T. Rubinstein, Laurel Hollowaty,
Irene Palamar, Martha Lampland, Kate Karakassis, Julius Novick, Ronald Tavel, Richard Kostelanetz, and Jan
Wheelock. And, of course, my numerous Hungarian
friends and colleagues who have given me constant help,
most specifically to earlier reader of this research project
and book: Dr. Charlotte Kretzoi, Dr. György Székely, Dr.
Tamás Bécsy, and Dr. Gábor Mihályi. For linguistic and
stylistic advice I owe special thanks to Helen Thomas,
Christine Lilley, (Great Britain), and Jeff Harlig and
John Murtha (United States). Dr. István Pálffy, chairman
of the Debrecen University English department, Dr.

Myron Simon, Fulbright Professor in 1983–1985, and the Debrecen group of Americanists—led by Dr. Zoltán Abádi-Nagy—offered valuable criticism and good advice. And for revising my manuscript into a readable style, many thanks to Julie Huffman-Klinkowitz.

Zoltán Szilassy

1985

Introduction

THE SEMILEGENDARY and somewhat nostalgically viewed decade of the 1960s, with its "imaginative acts in a decade of change,"[1] has already provoked handfuls of general monographs[2] that recount the politico-social, intellectual, aesthetic, and popular background of the period. The field of dramatic theory and criticism in the United States, however, has been treated quite differently. Studious literary historians, comparativists, and compilers of literary bibliography—C. W. E. Bigsby of England and Walter J. Meserve of the United States, for example—complain about the chaotic and not entirely up-to-date-condition of American dramatic theory and criticism. Examining Meserve's research, Bigsby comments that "in compiling bibliographical essays for the annual *American Literary Scholarship* Meserve found himself repeatedly lamenting the standard of material he was reviewing. In 1966 he observed that few of the books or essays which he had read would have any lasting value because few American people take American drama seriously. The following year he found critical material on American drama to be extremely slight, poorly written, ineffectively substantiated . . . and mak-

1

ing confused and commonplace remarks."[3] Meserve repeats this view elsewhere,[4] and Bigsby goes on to allude to the simple fact that the first substantial monograph on Arthur Miller was written in England while the first on Edward Albee came from Belgium.[5]

There is an apparent contradiction between these opinions and the intimidating multitude of commentaries and critical reviews published first in important dailies, weeklies, and theater journals and then later collected in volumes of criticism. American dramatic and theater criticism in the late 1960s made as ample use of the well-established clichés as the criticism of fiction, poetry, or any of the beaux-arts—all these fields suffering from the same social frustration and the need to become multimedial, modern, or postmodern. These new coinages had been predetermined in part by the vogue of the day, and those vogues were often European imports. The Theater of Cruelty (Artaud), the Theater of Commitment (Brecht, Piscator), and the Poor Theater (Grotowski) had all appeared in the American "empty space" (Brook), in the last case as part of the sixties. But long before that, Esslin's early classification of the so-called Albee generation as "parallels and proselytes of the 'Theatre of the Absurd' "[6] in Paris had for a long time haunted the critical evaluation of the same generation both at home and abroad.

It took at least a *Who's Afraid of Virginia Woolf?* before speculation about indigenous American theatrical heritage could once again take shape. Besides these haunters from Europe, later to include also Jan Kott and Charles Marowitz, the haunted themselves contributed to the fruitful chaos in terminology. Somewhat similar to the way Esslin treated the Theater of the Absurd,

Michael Kirby spared no universally cultural or genetic expense in creating the category, "Theater of Happenings." Kirby did for happenings what Esslin did for the dramas loosely linked by the category of the "Theater of the Absurd": he gave them a coherent and profound analysis that resulted in a too-rigid set of categories and theories. Yet, terms are less important than what they describe, and the fact that the happeners came to protest against some of Kirby's misinterpretations does not reduce his importance. The category "Happening," owing its origin to Allan Kaprow and its first conclusive theory to Kirby, must necessarily have been replaced by a more collective rendering of all the possible liminalities (events, activities, intermedia, and so on), both aesthetic and social. Each subgenre did have its respective father-progenitors (Beckett, Cage), artists and occasional theorists (Ionesco, Kaprow), and apologist-theoreticians (Esslin, Kirby). Nor did Esslin, in the long run, stick to his own categorization, choosing to refer to the same dramas as "metaphors for states of mind."[7] Kaprow and Kirby seem to have arrived at the same autic category of auto-performance in the unheroic seventies.[8]

On yet another level, the clear-sighted and sharp-tongued Robert Brustein had first tried to sum up his views in *The Theatre of Revolt* (1965) but then very aptly reversed his hypothesis in *Revolution as Theatre* (1970). Other fervently circulating coinages are also attributed to him, such as *Seasons of Discontent* (1967) and the not-too-convincing category of the *Third Theatre* (1969). George Wellwarth has extended the history of *The Theatre of Protest and Paradox* (1964) from Ibsen to Albee, just as Lionel Abel did with his *Metatheatre* (1963) from the Greek classics to Genet. Walter Kerr burst onto the scene with *Theatre in Spite of Itself* (1963). One might endlessly enumerate thought-provoking and fancy titles of volumes of collected theater criticism, which, in spite of having momentarily hit the mark from this perspective, seem to have brought about an equally endless beating around the bush. The situation was no less chaotic during the second half of the sixties, when the enigma of Alternative Theater seems to have incorporated all these attempts at definition. The numerous ways of "offending the audience" which existed at that time were analyzed and received no less generalized tags, such as Radical (protest, guerilla, yippie, street) Theater (Arthur Sainer, 1975) and Environmental and/or Ritual Theater (Richard Schechner, 1973).

One cannot, however, blame the theater critics, literary historians, or aesthetes. The necessity of fastening on labels comes from the wishful thinking of those in charge who try to see order in disorder and vice versa. Literary or art history is likely to take over the same ready clichés, providing they are general enough to be cyclized in order to point out the seemingly or really necessary genesis of the point made. In this way, American drama history had to speak about the psychologizing twenties and the political thirties, just as recent attempts at differentiation had to juxtapose the fifties and the sixties. Not even inaccurate but rather lacking in unaccounted for details, these labels and studies can be questioned only from the standpoint of a relatively larger horizon.

It is not only the European and American history of art which offers ready clichés to summarize all these, but my field also. Critics, whether to slight, to generalize, or to use as a catch-all, often speak of a neo-advantgarde atmosphere. The original category of the avant-garde—put by some people as derriére-garde—must undergo a reevaluation. The more so with this rejuvenated category, which is good enough to show similar backgrounds of various crisis periods in American (or any other) society but which is bad enough to neglect the specific differences between the same periods by way of analogizing too readily. Thus, "neo-avant-garde" is as good a descriptor as any to account for the relative continuity of the Little Theater movement in the United States; on the other hand, it fails to illustrate the differences between particular little theaters, differences necessitated by input from various microperiods.

Instead of blindly accepting once-accurate clichés, why not reconsult Aristotle and Hegel in defining what is and what is no longer drama? Georg Lukács did this as early as 1909 in *History of the Development of Modern Drama*[9] during a no less complicated period. There and then he prophesized the development of a nondramatic character. Antidrama of any kind still preserves the medium and heritage of the literary theater. This neo-Hegelian approach has helped Hungarian critics to swallow Albee in almost the same gulp as Miller and Williams. Some readily acknowledge him as a rebellious part of the post–Ibsen / Chekhov / Strindberg heritage (something Albee himself admits) and joyfully announce that naturalism is not dead. Others would interpret Albee's dramas as rites of passage in the theatrical sense.

Experts in theater criticism should switch over to the innate, sociologically documented definitions of Greek, medieval, and Elizabethan theater practice, to the double dramaturgy and modelization of all communal play-like events, since we are getting steadily closer to scenarios (playscripts) and their medium-determined and audience-profligated realizations than to dramas, predescribed by the classicist use of the category. Talk of revolutionary theater should be withheld until revolution consists only of socio-historico-critical implications or protest communicated via a traditional medium like drama-as-playscript.

The seemingly or deliberately nonliterary-minded intermedia, in spite of all their attempted spontaneity and access to an unbiased audience, still worked with preconceived parameters, willingly or unwillingly in the spirit of Cage's idea of aleatory composition. Just as in the case of more traditional media (film, television), with intermedia one can presuppose the existence of some kind of scenario, however vague it may be. In contrast with the rebellious drama that still is a literary product as well as a playscript for a would-be production, to read scenarios (for example, Kaprow's, Dine's and Oldenburg's happenings) in book form would never give the same kind of experience as "being there." A similar pseudo-experience would be to read *Hair* without the benefit of listening to the recording at the same time. I must stress that the partial role of literary criticism should not, even in this case, be underestimated. It cannot be mere chance that retrospective description of some happenings resembles free verse or a surrealist dream in wild prose. This fact takes us back to the idea of preconceived parameters verbalized in at least two different ways: either in a vague scenario or else during series of repeated rehearsals or talks, or both.

My approach would be that of an interdisciplinary nature, by which the delicate balance of a binary system of paradoxes made the theatrical equilibrium work during the American 1960s. The rebellious drama, still somewhat attached to the literary heritage and to the Establishment, was a revolutionary tradition offering analyses of the false illusion of the American Dream. In spite of the fact that this model owed much of its revolt to coexisting, established theater activities, I should be inclined to include here most of Albee's early dramas, Kopit's early bravado (*Oh Dad, Poor Dad*), the French tradition-oriented early plays of Richardson,[10] and even *succès de scandale* plays like *The Brig* and *The Connection*. Comparatists and literary historians are especially likely to follow the thread of development from *Waiting for Lefty* through *Waiting for Godot* and up to *The Connection*. Here again is an example of analogizing too readily. I would, however, classify these three as dramas, *Waiting for Godot* becoming a kind of happening only when performed in a prison or in a lunatic asylum, as actually happened in the United States, and *The Connection* as still preserving the post-Pirandello spirit despite its local color given by jazz, junk, and Off Broadway.

The politico-socially, ethnically, or ritually inclined and the only too numerous intermedia provided a traditionally revolutionary (neo-avant-garde) and topically revolutionary (sub-or counterculturally provoked) atmosphere for the Off-Off-Broadway. The genesis of Off-Off-Broadway obviously goes back to at least as far as that of Off Broadway, but the mode became dominant, and sometimes chic, only in the second half of the sixties. The case is complicated further by the fact that, more or less during the same period, another strong decentralizing tendency came to be felt: that of Beyond Broadway—national theater centers outside New York City—[11] with the vogues of regionalism and community theater.

As far as survival and output in the seventies are concerned, some kind of conclusion might be drawn from the fact that the neopicaresque ensembles of seemingly less anarchist type (Schechner's Performance Group, Schumann's Bread and Puppet Theatre, Bruler's Mabou Mines, the San Francisco Mime Troupe) have managed to survive, whereas those no less picaresque but more prone to assimilating nihilist and alienating effects of the rotting European culture—ensembles like the Firehouse in Minneapolis, Le Living, and Open Theatre—have ceased to exist. This, however, does not deny the influence, perhaps more revolutionary, of the latter groups. The proof of the pudding may indeed be in the eating, but an international set of La Mama theaters is not definitive proof that they are more profound than the Becks' or Chaikin's.

Thus, the outside observer from Europe may still have hope that the Americans will keep or rather develop the kind of theatrical equilibrium that made the sixties unforgettable both at home and abroad.

Part 1

The Rebellious Drama

1

Edward Albee: First among Equals

I WISH TO AVOID RESPONDING to the critics' and the critics' critics' opinions here in this chapter.[1] As I read plays by Edward Albee or saw them performed on stage, they always had such a strong impact on me that I felt like an East European McMurphy under the treatment of a severe yet humanistic American nurse. Otherwise, I could dedicate a chapter to Albee in my literary autobiography the way Richard Kostelanetz does in his *Recyclings:* "edward clearly most substantial several american who come in last years . . . expect albee 36 continue time write of excellence . . . it hard first define ultimate in single themes diverse subjects [but!] trace lines style sensibility.[2] *And so on,* just as I firmly share Albee's "ceterum censeo" in the case of New Carthago; with due alteration in details, I envisage him not sitting, but dancing macabre—a new Marius—on the ruins of the American Dream.

Albee's private life has never interested me, especially in the sense that omniscient critics are likely to view his output. I see eye to eye with Pierre Brodin who, after raising the fundamental question, does away with the rumors in the elegant way a scholar truly should:

Premiére bagarre: ces piéces ne sent-elles pas essentiellement des histoires a peine deguisées d'homosexuels? . . . Disent ces critiques Albee déteste irremédiablement les femmes. Son oeuvre entiére n'est elle pas colorée par cette phobie? Ou bien, estiment les tenants d'une autre école, s'agit il–simplement de la guerre entre les sexes et de la dénonciation des vertus étouffantes de la femme américaine? Le symbole de *Mom* ne représentet-il pas un aspect authentique, fondamental, de la civilization d'aujourd'hui?[3]

Having already partially broken my promise, I must state my point clearly. Without deeply immersing myself in musicology, I shall treat Albee's lifework like toccatas and fugues composed upon a relatively stable vision of Life. I know that I am not alone in searching for the main line and the deviations in an important writer's works. Perhaps the most telling and the most easily decodable title that Albee has ever produced is *A Delicate Balance*.[4] I consider it not only the name of any frustrated family's desired equilibrium but also that of Albee's personal technique of fusing tradition and innovation. In contrast with the main trends of criticism, I shall also pay attention to the relative "flops," such as *The Death of Bessie Smith, FAM and YAM, The Sandbox, Tiny Alice, Box–Mao–Box,* and *Everything in the Garden*— fugues or, rather, experiments as laboratory accessories to the worldwide hits (toccatas) like *Who's Afraid of Virginia Woolf?, A Delicate Balance,* and in my opinion *Seascape* and *The Lady from Dubuque*. In addition, I shall point to similarities between Albee and his peers rather than dwell on his too–often mentioned heritage of O'Neill, Williams, Strindberg, Ibsen, and Chekhov.

Although *The Zoo Story* (1959–1960) can be interpreted as a clarion for the sixties, most literary and theater historians exaggerate its importance. Many view this work as representative of all the problems that Albee would deal with later: the hopelessness of the American Dream, noncommunication, cliché-talking, illusion versus reality, sexual misery, the psychopathology of nonconformism, the near musical arrangement, and so forth. I am inclined to think that the non-conformism of Jerry and George (*The Zoo Story* and *Who's Afraid of Virginia Woolf?*) and the conformism of Peter and Nick, respectively, differ quite a bit.

Another possible misinterpretation is that of placing Albee's early works exclusively in the so-called Theater of the Absurd.[5] Disregarding *The Sandbox* and *The American Dream, The Zoo Story* is no more than "absurdist." The simple stage props of two benches could be connected to Beckett's single tree in *Waiting for Godot*, and one could speculate on the two characters' colloquial usage of the category of absurd. But the author's instructions for placement of the two benches, in "Manhattan, Central Park," should not be forgotten. This is not an "empty space," as Peter Brook would put it, but a place where all ends meet. To imagine a neutral area between East and West Berlin is something like trying to imagine a similar space between the upper East and West Sides of New York City—so vast are the differences between the two. Therefore, the two benches are not the same as those in Eugène Ionesco's multiplying *Chairs* and neither is the attitude of their owners. Albee means to say exactly what he says.

The DOG monologue is continuely commented upon. Playing with anagrams and words tempts anyone who knows that there is wordplay in Beckett's milestone work, *Waiting for GOD-ot* (Godet? Godin?). I would offer yet another analogy, via anagrams and analogous situations. Bertolt Brecht, in his early period, wrote a short story very much in the Kafkaian way entitled *Brief Über eine Dogge* (1925), which described much the same situation.

Above and beyond all these considerations, I think that I find the main virtue of Albee's clarion play to be that of its having found the actual local color of that American day, whether or not it is related to O'Neill's *The Hairy Ape*. The relevant point here is that a reinterpretation has been achieved. Both Yank and Jerry are hopeless outsiders; their reintegrating efforts meet with different results, no matter how suicidal they both may be.

The Death of Bessie Smith (1959–1960) is not, in my opinion, a deviation from the absurdist techniques that Albee experimented with as a young playwright. One must not forget that it was not only the Theater of the Absurd (Beckett, Ionesco, Adamov, Genet) that influenced Albee and the whole of American drama but that *the* absurd, as viewed by Camus and other French philosophers and playwrights, also played a large part. A list of Albee's favorite playwrights is almost confusing in its diversity: O'Neill and Williams, Aeschylus and Sardou, Brecht and Beckett, Pinter and Behan, and generation-mates Richardson and Gelber. An Albee workshop has always been a furor-dominated one.

The lonesome and lovesick Jerry in *The Zoo Story* (somewhat like Jimmy Porter in John Osborne's *Look Back in Anger*, 1956) is an unsuccessful "trumpeter" complaining with his verbal solos to the empty heavens as well as to his one and only listener, Peter. *The Sandbox* is a clarinet-like improvisation on the same problem, with the difference that the shrill whinings of Grandma are even less likely to meet any sympathetic reaction—with the exception of the solaces from the Young Man. Finally, the trombone-like chiding of the Family by the grandmother in *The American Dream* intensifies the same problem. One is always alone, mind kids, especially when the Van Man is coming for any of you.

In contrast to what most critics think, I find *The Death of Bessie Smith* to be highly relevant to the period in question. It seems to be the first "combo" that Albee managed to get together. In the Doctor and Nurse's heavily charged conflict, like that of a tenor and alto saxophone, the cruel improvizations of George and Martha (*Who's Afraid of Virginia Woolf?*) are in the making. The importance of *Bessie Smith* does not lie solely with the well-known name, the well-known racial problem, and all that jazz. Well-known blues are in the background; more obscure, thought-provoking blues are in the forefront. This is what one sees and hears. When the Doctor calls the Spanish Civil War "the last great cause," he is echoing somewhat Jimmy Porter's complaint: "There are no good brave causes left" (John Osborne, *Look Back in Anger*, 1956). The Doctor can no longer use the knife the way Jerry does; the development points toward the status-quo of New Carthago.

The Sandbox was an occasional play, a cynical, grotesque one, requested by the organizers of the Experimental Theater Festival in Spoleto (1959–1960).[6] At times, Albee has commented that this play forms the apex of his work, almost faultless in its entirety of only fourteen minutes. Grandma's dying, as a rite of passage, calls forth numerous associations from world literature. Shakespeare's seventh period person gets into the sand(box), one might associate Evelyn Waugh's darkest humor in *The Loved One*, and the cruelty displayed is somewhat similar to what is being presented in Fukazava Hichiro's *The Song of the Pilgrim*. The subtext of this play can be found more readily in Ionesco's *The Bald Soprano* than in the seemingly parallel play by Samuel Beckett, *Happy Days* (1961). Mom and Dad's pleasantries remind us more of the Smiths in Ionesco's play than of any Estragon or Vladimir exchanges, although these were probably influential for the young Albee also. This motif of "organized dying" will return in *All Over* as the pseudonaturalism of the *intérieur*.

Albee himself speaks clearly on *The American Dream* (1960–1961): "The play is an examination of the American Scene, an attack on the substitution of artificial for real values in our society, a condemnation of complacency, cruelty, emasculation and vacuity: it is a stand against the fiction that everything in this slipping land of ours is peachy-keen."[7] Contrast this with Charles Marowitz's comment expecting some sort of "objective correlative," with which I disagree: "In merely stating his main character and not developing him, Albee loses a marvellous opportunity for satire. The strikingly handsome, appallingly vapid All-American Boy is a peculiarly American Tragedy. . . . When we see him admired by his elders—what a clean-cut fella!—, courted by women—what a dreamboat!—, idealized by his pals (a great guy!) and wooed by the big industry boys (he'll go far, that one!), we tend to forget that he is a fatuous, hollow, football-toting, orgiastic primitive.[8] Daddy and Mommy have gotten a richer characterization in this play than in *The Sandbox*, not to mention the appearance of the Ionescoean character, Mrs. Barker, who will reappear as a "Long-Winded Lady" in *Box-Mao-Box*. Then, of course, there is the Kafkaistic-Pinterian "Van Man" soon to come.

The Sandbox and *The American Dream* are important not only for their usefulness in pointing out correlations but as micromodels that help us to reestablish the ancient European philosophical drama. *The Sandbox* makes the universe seem a priori absurd, whereas *The American Dream* offers an a posteriori analysis of how absurd existence may become if real values are exchanged for pseudo ones. Both plays can be appreciated within the framework of the rite of passage, but individual approaches must be worked out. The message is motivated by anxiety-ridden humanism; any theatrical production is, by way of necessity, motivated by the then-existing or accepted tragicomic-theatrical rituals.

The October 14,1962, premiere of *Who's Afraid of Virginia Woolf?* in the Billy Rose Theater has been registered in theater history as much of a landmark as Osborne's *Look Back in Anger*. Both playwrights made the "error" of creating post–World War II classics that haunted them throughout the rest of their lives and to which all other work was automatically compared. Praise came from such diverse sources as Thornton Wilder, Marcel Achard, and John Gielgud. Even formidable critics like John Simon, Walter Kerr, and Robert Brustein had to give a complimentary nod. When coming to my interpretation of the play, I must, once again, disagree with Marowitz whose picaresque theatrical adventures I highly admire. He speaks, I think, too *ex cathedra*: "*Who Is Afraid of Virginia Woolf?* is a generalized social indictment, and it is this generality that so weakens its case. Its psychological tensions are real enough; its political attitudes assumed and unconvincing. First class updated Strindberg perhaps, but very bogus Ibsen."⁹

Statements instead of arguments—these are what Marowitz makes in his writing. The English critic is still misled by the *empassibilite* power of Freud, nee Strasberg, or vice versa, on Broadway. The problems may be the same as those in *The American Dream*, but in this play they have to do with the intelligentsia who are not in the mainstream of the river. The intellectuals are especially likely to show the symptoms of "other-directedness," as pointed out by Riesman.¹⁰

Following W. G. Knight's interpretation of Hamlet, one ought to reverse the cast. The Ambassador of Death is Nick and the Hamletian figure is George. Martha serves as Gertrude, and Honey as Ophelia. Nick controls Honey's flirtations much as Laertes controls Ophelia. The actor (Ben Piazza) chosen for the roles of the Young Man in *The Sandbox, The American Dream*, and in *Who's Afraid of Virginia Woolf?* demonstrates this continuity. Albee only slightly takes sides in this eternal quarrel. His primary aim is to show *confrontation*. The responses and sympathies of any given audience may change in accordance with generational inclination, but one thing is certain: oscillation is provided, give or take whatever one likes. These aging Hamlets and Claudiuses are acting younger and younger.

Personally, I do not consider Albee's "second" classic, *A Delicate Balance* (1966), a lesser product than *Who's Afraid of Virginia Woolf*. Comparatists usually try to point out Strindbergian influences in the first and Chekhovian reminiscences in the second. The period between 1962 and 1966 clearly illustrates Albee's workshop continuity, with the advent of many adaptations such as *The Ballad of the Sad Café* from Carson McCullers' novel (1963), *Malcolm* from James Purdy's novel (1965), and, although slightly out of process relatively speaking, the adaptation of Giles Cooper's *Everything in the Garden* (1969).

Both *Who's Afraid of Virginia Woolf?* and *A Delicate Balance* are akin in the sense that both present more or less stabilized infernoes of stability. Agnes has inherited Martha's "keeping together," just as she has her long-windedness. It is Claire, however, who retains the al-cohol-stinking, truthsaying attitude, confessing too much of what should be hidden. Tobia's monologue (or "aria" as Albee puts it), delivered when he tries to deal with unexpected visitors, is a display of full emotional anxi-ety—an aria oscillating between fear and courage and necessity and retrievement. The musical sphere moves between tears and laughter, shouts and silence, and all the tones in between, providing fugues on the ever-existing and ever-changing life situations.

Before further analysis of the group of adaptations, it would be advisable to concentrate on the ambiguous mid-product of the sixties, that is, *Tiny Alice* (1964–1965). I share Albee's opinion that the critics made too much fuss about the interpretation of the play; it can either be taken as a modern "mystery play," or, as Albee puts it, a "devant-garde" experiment on what theater was like forty years ago. This was a time when Albee heartily agreed with one of his idols, Eugene O'Neill, in main-taining that while most contemporary plays deal with man's relationship to other men, he was concerned only with the relationship between man and God. Playwrights must present the "sickness" of today's existence and then offer new cures.

Tiny Alice, then, may be interpreted as a modern mystery or morality play verging on the two zones of Existence: from Here to Eternity. If interpreted as a morality play, there are simple enough possibilities for decoding: the Lawyer would represent the openly sinful World, the Cardinal would represent the hypocritically sinful Church, and the Butler would represent temptations of a mixed kind. Alice herself could be anything from an earth mother symbol to a sex ad; her castles, both the real and the miniature, simply offer a space where the Everymen of our day can have their fun and games. "New senecanism" is one of the too-readily available critical approaches,[11] but when concentrating on the main antihero, Julian, the Lay Brother's dilemmas or polylemmas, I would hint at a readier parallel provided by T. S. Eliot in his *Murder in the Cathedral.* For me, relative innocence and firm readiness for martyrdom connect Julian and Thomas Becket. But all the dramatis personae forcing him into martyrdom are "realistic" enough characters—more fitting in a play by Shaw than by Eliot.

As stated previously, I should like to group Albee's adaptations on the basis of a forgettable divertimento: *FAM and YAM.*[12] A routine European comparatist would now bring in Pim and Bom from Beckett's *Comment c'est,* but my approach is different. I consider this particular improvisation of Albee's rather a short essay, in dramatic form, on the possibilities of a YAM (Young American Playwright) contrasted with those of a FAM (Famous American Playwright).

It would be beside the point to give a detailed analysis of *Malcolm* (1965) and *The Ballad of the Sad Café* (1963), and even less so of the unpublished *Bartleby* (1961), although the choices of Albee as "YAM" are more than typical in opposition to a "FAM" like Inge. But this YAM had to make his home-based or European-based choice when selecting his sources for dramatic adaptation, and depending on his genetically or ethnically minded preferences, he could choose anything from Whitman to Faulkner or from Gide to Witkiewicz. For example, *Everything in the Garden* (1969) was an adaptation of the Englishman Giles Cooper's play. There are not too many differences between the plays, but even the minor changes Albee has made deserve attention. The housewife in the English version collects the silver paper of cigarette packs for donation, whereas the American housewife hunts for gift coupons. There is a vast difference (one that critics usually dislike) in that Jack, the cynical millionaire in both plays, makes a comeback in Albee's play even after his death and, in fact, is given the role of an absurdist narrator. It is worth emphasizing that both authors retain the desire to frighten their good neighborhood with the danger of the still prevalent attitude of "keeping up with the Joneses."

The twin or triple play *Box and Quotations from Chairman Mao Tse Tung* (1968) is, in fact, a return to the experimental technique of the " Paris School," a fugue system in my analogy. Theater critic Martin Duberman is astonishingly mild in reacting to these strange plays: "The first play: *Box,* despite some nice incidental seagull and ocean effects was otherwise pretentious gibberish. But some of the intricate monologues in *Quotations . . .* had considerable power, effectively suggesting that nothing belongs, that personal memory, and public utterances alike numb us by their meaningless repeti-

tion.[13] I believe that here Albee is getting closest to the
kind of musical arrangement that Cage, née Stravinsky
and Bartók, is about to create and in which some Europeans (Beckett, *Words and Music,* 1962; Harold Pinter,
The Lover, 1963) had been experimenting. A single
quote—"all that falling!"—brings to mind the Bible,
Beckett's biblical title *(All that Fall,* 1957), the Miltonian
ambivalence of the "Fall," and Eliot's "London Bridge is
falling down."

A commentary on Albee's sixties work cannot disregard *All Over,* in spite of the fact it was produced in 1971
(I will come back to *Seascape* [1975] and *The Lady from
Dubuque* [1980] in chapter 6). *All Over* seems to be a
return to the results already produced by *Who's Afraid
of Virginia Woolf?* and *A Delicate Balance.* However, there
are strikingly different evaluations of this play. On one
hand it earned the title of "club bore" for Albee,[14] but
on the other hand Kerr was somewhat sympathetic toward the playwright for having discovered a sort of "artistic detachment" in treating his toccata line.[15]

I still owe the reader a personal view of Albee as "first
among equals." The European comparatist cannot help
but have a feeling of déjàvu in Albee's case. That is why
I quote Alan S. Downer: "Beckett's black allegories of
emptiness and despair have played in every city and
college theater in the country, but American playwrights
have responded by creating grotesque allegories whose
comic vitality mocks the emptiness of their characters'
attitudes."[16] Albee himself said:

The avant-garde theater is fun: it is free-swinging, bold, iconoclastic and often wildly funny. If you will approach it with a
child-like innocence—putting your standard responses aside—

for they do not apply—if you will approach it on its own terms, I think you will be in for a liberating surprise. I think you may no longer be content with plays that you cannot remember halfway down the block. You will not only be doing yourself some good, but you will be having a great time, to boot. And even though it occurs to me that such a fine combination is sinful, I still recommend it.[17]

Why should Albee have to choose a single model of writing plays? Why should we exclude Friedrich Dürrenmatt *contra* Beckett, Peter Weiss *contra* Sartre, Ionesco *contra* Arthur Miller from among our favorites? Each is pertinent. The enemy is a common one—not the "box-office draw" but the "titillating dangerousness" rather than shock or catharsis.

Albee has been attacked by some critics for courting the Broadway audience while posing as an avant-garde dramatist at the same time. One could witness his growing interest in verbal and thematic spareness (no less rich in fun and games) as the sixties passed and seventies went by. But Foster Hirsch's ironic question "who's afraid of Edward Albee?"[18] becomes increasingly relevant over the years when we see him survive all of his crossroads with newer and newer creative turns.

2

Varieties of the Albee Generation

EVEN A RELATIVELY RECENT study complains that American drama has been a neglected part of the survey of American literature.[1] Some say that there had never been an American drama of any literary distinction, and therefore it was unable to undergo a rebirth in the twentieth century.[2] Still, at its best, it is twentieth-century American drama that deserves something better than Ambrose Bierce's definition of contemporary drama as "the art of adapting from French."[3] Although the mainstream has never lost its indebtedness to the Chekhov-Ibsen-Strindberg tradition and, lately, to the European Theaters of Revolt, the Americanization of the European heritage is a process specially worth studying.

Like European theater, American theater is in close touch with new movements in art and literature, searching beyond realism and naturalism to show more than reality and penetrating into human existence to reveal man in his essence. The works of progressive American drama disclose the corruption of the American Dream and offer reactions against the American Condition, the false alternative of which is violence and / or conformism. There have been changes in playwrights' attitudes, too. The conflicts that made O'Neill or Clifford Odets choose the form of tragedy now provide gallows humor and the form of tragicomedy of Albee and his peers. American drama, which was sociologically or pathologically oriented, under the European influence of the sixties seems to have turned toward room-sized metaphysics. To find a terminology to account for all the changes of theatrical atmosphere, both in Europe and America, is, however, difficult.

In 1969, during a symposium devoted to the Theater of the Absurd, a strong discussion centered around the appropriateness of that term. Even Martin Esslin, who had fastened the label onto various dramatists, created another, less satisfying label that seems to reflect the never-ending storm of controversy surrounding the actual existence of this movement.[4] The theatrical revolution, arriving on the stage in two waves—that of the fifties, manifested by the Angry Young Men, and that of the sixties, revealed in the Theater of the Absurd—brought about various speculations about a neo-avant-garde atmosphere. Now that these periods no longer exist, one can evaluate them more objectively and, in some cases, with a greater degree of accuracy.

The first wave in the fifties was simply a revival of a particular strain of the Theater of Emotional Intensity as represented by John M. Synge, Sean O'Casey, Maksim Gorki, and O'Neill, which started with an angry revolt and ended with the Idea of Involvement and the rediscovery of Bertolt Brecht. The second wave fulfilled its avant-garde task more successfully by producing a renaissance of the grotesque in dramatic art and by discovering the new possibilities of the genre of tragicomedy. From among many related tendencies, the Theater of the Absurd became the slogan of the day. It was a medium that could express its neo-existentialist message with the simplicity and clarity of an ancient formula—clownery—relying on verbal nonsense as well as on abstract scenic effects in the continuous tradition of mime and black humor. It was often enriched by a poetic or even surrealistic treatment of the dramatic material.

This, however, made it all the more difficult to pinpoint and separate the Theater of the Absurd from other neo-avant-garde theatrical strivings like the Theater of Cruelty. The possibility for differentiation was, even so, given within the limits of the Theater of the Absurd by the very technique of clowning. There was a more or less common approach coming from the common metaphysical roots of existential message: absurdity, nonsense-talking, and clichés were heaped on the stage, first to disguise and then to reveal despair and anguish. But the authors also wanted to find the "national colors" in which this basic message would be best represented. This meant a perhaps unwanted but natural shift from the individual to the social Inferno of Man. No mentors, not even Beckett, could provide their followers with an overall technique for Absurd Drama; all had to invent their own clowning, paraphrasing their very own national and spiritual-cultural heritage. Thus, soon after the appearance of the prototypes for Absurd Drama (for example, Beckett's *Waiting for Godot* [1953] and Ionesco's *The Bald Soprano* [1950]), various "parallels and proselytes" emerged who can more rightfully be called "absurdists" rather than writers of Absurd Drama. Having achieved a pyrrhic victory in the Anti-Theater versus

Conservative Theater battle, the Theater of the Absurd soon found its national expression in various parts of the world, including America.

In America, the new dramatists who emerged in the sixties and who had their works premiered Off Broadway were ostensibly influenced by Beckett, Ionesco, Jean Genet, and so on; but in reality they adopted only the stylistic traits of these writers.[5] The metaphysical inclination was paraphrased in accordance with the traditions of Off Broadway traceable as far back to 1915 (The Provincetown Players and the early O'Neill), the Idea of Protest being the focus of "new idealism." Esslin, even in the revised edition of *The Theatre of the Absurd* (1968), speaks of "the relative absence of dramatists of the Absurd in the United States."[6] For Esslin, Arthur Kopit's play, *Oh Dad, Poor Dad, Mamma's Hung You in the Closet and I'm Feeling So Sad* (1960), illustrates how difficult it is in America to use the convention of the Theater of the Absurd.[7] Difficult it may be, but Kopit's "art of adapting from French" really hits the mark.

Described as "a pseudo-classical tragifarce in a bastard French tradition," the play portrays a fragile young man's collision with the outside world that his dominating mother has deprived him. The mother-son relationship very much resembles the one in Tennessee William's *Suddenly, Last Summer* (1958). Madame Rosepettle, in many respects a parallel figure to Dürrenmatt's Old Lady, and Jonathan, her son, arrive at a lavish hotel in Havana with heaps of luggage, including the corpse of Madame Rosepettle's late husband in a coffin. The pets of the wandering household include Rosalinda the talking fish and two Venus's-flytraps, which also appear in *Suddenly, Last Summer*. The lady soon drives the entire staff of the hotel mad with her eccentric demands. Meanwhile, Rosalie, a naughty babysitter living in the neighborhood, watches Jonathan with growing interest. She tries unsuccessfully to involve Jonathan in a love affair.

Madame Rosepettle herself has an affair with Commodore Roseabove, the aging but amorous bachelor-millionaire. The setting for their "love-story" might have been designed by Blanche Du Bois, with its "two flickering candles, a bottle of champagne, a flower vase with one wilting rose protruding, a Viennese waltz playing softly in the background." The actual designer, Madame Rosepettle, intends however to remain faithful to the memory of her late husband and the frustrated commodore is unable to see through the tricks of the mysterious woman. In the growing frenzy of a real Cuban carnival, Jonathan kills the Venus's-flytraps, the talking fish, and finally Rosalie, who has decided to have a final go at seducing him. Madame Rosepettle, returning from the seaside where she has indulged in her usual sport of disturbing lovers with her electric lamp, finds the girl on her bed buried under the "fabulous stamp-book-and-coin-collection" of her son. As a mother to her son she asks him: "What is the meaning of this?"

Obviously, the question applies not only to the final situation but to the entire play. This question challenges Jonathan, the audience, and the drama critics. It would be too simple to assume that the play is a mere parodistic joke and the meaning, therefore, of no importance (if there is a meaning at all). To risk a "serious interpretation" would, perhaps, be in utter contradiction with the spirit of the play. The question is whether the fun is convincing in itself or whether one must read between the lines to find out who is being parodied and why.

Kopit wrote this play while an undergraduate at Harvard. (Remember Professor Baker's earlier seminar!) It shared the usual fate of American avant-garde plays. First it was performed abroad. It had a less than moderate *succès de scandale* in London during 1961. After the premiere, a critic writing for *Variety* asserted that it was only "too evident" that the play was intended to be against Ionesco and the absurdists.[8] The *Plays and Players* article tried to be offhand, saying that this high-school burlesque was likely to be remembered only because of its extraordinarily long title.[9] In West Germany and Poland, Kopit's play found a much warmer reception.[10] A Parisian critic seems to have found different, if not too flattering reminiscences in the play. "A bogus Williams parody," he writes, "Yankee burlesque for boulevard audiences."[11] The Off-Broadway production in 1962 was directed by Jerome Robbins, the famous choreographer-director. The orgiastic lights, Debussy's music, and, above all, the play, won at once the hit-or-flop battle. Since then there have been several hundreds of performances in the United States and even the cold-blooded audiences of London changed their minds, applauding the 1965 revival of the play at the Piccadilly Theatre.[12]

How can one account for the worldwide success of this "Yankee burlesque for boulevard audiences?" Who is being parodied, Williams or Ionesco? Ibsen or Beckett? O'Neill or Dürrenmatt? To illustrate the viewpoint that all are being parodied and not one in particular, and obvious parallel offers itself, a play and a playwright of very similar reputation: Alfred Jarry and his *Ubu Roi* (1896). The partly intentional, partly sincere childish naiveté, the grandiosely absurd, puppetlike characters of both plays serve the same simple slogan, "Èpater les bourgeois," and are aimed against different types of the common practice of melodrama. Jarry's drama is a cosmic farce ridiculing the historical melodrama, whereas Kopit's aims at the sociopathological melodrama. The Grand Guignol in each case is to confront the member of the audience with the horror of their own complacency and ugliness.

The first sentence in Kopit's play—"Put it in the bedroom!"—is less sensational than the by now classic "Merde" on Jarry's stage. Later on, however, when we learn that *it* refers to the corpse of Madame Rosepettle's late husband, we begin to suspect that the young member of the Harvard drama seminar is challenging a whole succession of dramatists, flirting with the absurdity of transcendentalism on the stage. The bedroom also brings forth a number of associations which verify that it must be the chosen center of the homemade universe. The bedroom is the latent center of the horizon where the sunset is "full of magenta and wistaria blue, to say nothing of cadmium orange and cerise," in Madame Rosepettle's words. O'Neill's heroes are sometimes likely to give similarly exalted descriptions: "I could feel the night wrapped around me like a gray velvet gown lined with warm sky and trimmed with silver leaves!"[13]

It is not only Madame Rosepettle who resembles many pathologically great American dramatic heroines; her son, Jonathan, is also the ad absurdum variety of classically weak figures (Sebastian in *Suddenly, Last Summer*, Laura in *The Glass Menagerie*). Esslin's main objection to Kopit's play is that "the author underlines the painfully Freudian aspects of his fantasy."[14] For me, Kopit offers a satire of the painfully Freudian aspects of the fantasy of American dramatic tradition; the corpse hung in the closet is also the corpse of Freudian determinism long since worn out. The clichés uttered by the poor, book-wormish, stuttering Jonathan reveal the same chaos that is characteristic of the representatives of the old generation. The possibilities for communication are as depressing as in Ionesco's *The Bald Soprano*, or, going even further back, in Anton Chekhov's *Three Sisters* (1901),[15] referred to many times.

The significance of this play, therefore, apart from any parodistic effects, lies first of all in its offering a grand, metaphysical farce, in its giving a clownish interpretation of human life as mirrored by theatrical conventions and innovations. The conventions falsely stress the heroism; the innovations do the same with the antiheroism of the individual, both in history and in private. This kind of apocalyptic clowning, including elements of philosophical tragicomedy, makes the plays of Jarry, Frank Wedekind, and Stanislaw Witkiewicz filter into Kopit's misfits and transforms the great characters of the American theatrical tradition into Madame Tussaud's blood relations. Besides provoking laughter, Kopit's "distorting mirrors" intensify the reverse of social violence—individual helplessness.

As previously stated, in the early sixties, these four playwrights, Albee, Jack Richardson, Kopit, and Jack Gelber, distinguished themselves as the best prospects for the future of the American theater since the postwar emergence of Williams and Miller. The four became acquainted and, especially in the season of 1962 to 1963, were simultaneously active in the Playwright's Unit of the Actor's Studio in New York.[16]

The young generation of playwrights shared a general dissatisfaction with the Theater of Sentiments and the Theater of Verisimilitude, which had dominated the American stage in the previous decades. Psychological realism as a dramatic style, still very much dependent on Freud's and Jung's postulates and faithfully observed behaviorism as an acting style, relied on the methodization of Konstantin Stanislavsky's system—resulting in maintaining a room-sized destiny for small pimples. The young ones were once more ready for iconoclasm and wild fun. Just as Harold Pinter's and David Storey's characters talk in recognizably British dialogues, so the young American playwrights have definitely Americanized the Absurdist message. Even Kopit, who had entered the stage with his Jarrylike bravura (*Oh Dad, Poor Dad,* 1961) switched over to the reconsideration of the American Past with *Indians* in 1968.

From Richardson's four important plays, *The Prodigal* (1960), *Gallows Humour* (1961), *Lorenzo* (1963), and *Xmas in Las Vegas* (1965), it is *Gallows Humour* that attracted the most attention and received surprisingly good, worldwide critical reviews.[17] The following detailed investigation of the play will take into account both its positive and more doubtful connotations that have contributed to its general success. For just as the effect of Albee's *The Zoo Story* is somewhat marred by its melodramatic climax, Richardson's *Gallows Humour,* consisting of two closely related one-acters, in many respects fails to illustrate its title and consequently goes back to the very traditions it tries to sweep off the stage.

Even Off Broadway, the seemingly simple term, *comedy,* was in need of expurgation. Richardson says in the preface to the play:[18]

Any specific references to *Gallows Humour* with such absolutes as Cervantes, Molière, and Shakespeare still in the reader's mind would be an impertinence which no amount of Shavian bluster could make palatable. I've mentioned them not for the sake of any comparison, but to purge, if only for a moment, the term comedy of all its Broadway connotations and to hint that, at its best level, the word is far more applicable to *Oedipus Rex* than to *Under the Yum Yum Tree*. . . . I insist only that the very best and oldest clowns be chosen as examples.

He also suggests that *tragicomedy* should be written as one word, without a hyphen, aligning himself thus with those who would wish to break down the distinction between the tragic and the comic. But tragicomedy is a *sui generis* genre; rhetoric does not go well with it. Shavian bluster is, indeed, not characteristic of Richardson, but Shavian exuberance seems to be an integral part of *Gallows Humour*.

The play is preceded by a prologue, related by an actor dressed as Death. Having first apologized for his appearance, he readily admits that his theatrical fame ended with morality plays. Still, he dwells upon the subject for quite a while, nostalgically recalling the good old days. Then comes a similarly elaborated complaint about the present, culminating in a premature disclosure of the techniques and moral of the play: what the audience is going to see is not the same as actually seeing it. John Tanner will be justified by Don Juan Tenorio, but Troilus and Hamlet would still pass for beatniks and Joan of Arc is daily prevented from coming back. Only they are tragicomic heroes.

Lucy, the state prostitute in a bright yellow blouse and tight black skirt, is anxious to do her job properly. The criminal, Walter, a former lawyer, is one of the better sort, a nontattooed type of murderer who beat his wife to death with forty-one blows with a golf club. Lucy gets to wheel in the last dinner, served on silver dishes. The

Warden serves Lucy with the compliments of the state, an innovation in the penal program. He, also, wants to have his share of the "happening" and celebrates the innovation as something "touchingly human," taking some of the sting out of the anticapital punishment arguments. Walter is at first too shy, then reticent, and does not even touch the batter-fried chicken he ordered for dinner. Lucy has a go at one leg, which immediately makes the Warden come out with some of his "official" humor: "Look at her go after that chicken, Walter. How many men would love to be in that piece of meat's place. And you are going to get the chance."[19] And off he dashes with, "I want to see a contented face, Walter, when I return."

Lucy gives an account of her profession and informs Walter that at present her reputation is at stake. If she fails, she will have to take to deeper layers of rouge, longer eyelashes, and darker stockings. Now and again she moves closer, attempts to caress him, and smooths her blouse. Walter does not give in. During the days that he has spent here, he worked out a second-by-second plan for his last hour. He wants to sew on his loosened number patch, the only sign of his identity. Walter relates the story of his life:

I knew exactly what to pray for, how often a month I should have sex (four times, only with my wife) . . . how stern I should be when my children spilled their soup . . . everything from constellation to subways seemed to be moving at my rhythm. . . . And then came the Gogarty trial . . . Mrs. Ellen Gogarty versus The Municipal Bus Company. The woman's son, age thirty-five, had been run over and completely mashed by one of their vehicles. The light had been with him, and the bus driver, by eyewitness account, had been drunk and singing "Little Alice Bottom" when the accident took place. . . . Just before the jury was about to file out, Mrs. Gogarty began to hiccup. . . . With the occasional change in pitch there was almost a little tune coming out of her . . . and then comes the laughter . . . the wait is a very short one . . . and they announce a verdict against her. . . . I knew then that it was all over, and that a sneeze, hiccup, or crooked nose could twist those impressive sentences into gibberish. . . . Oh, I'd been cheated, Lucy, and gradually I began to grow angry—mad in fact— until one morning, with everything spinning about me in complete disorder, I struck back. My poor wife happened to be closest at hand, and for all I know I might have thought I was on the golf course until I felt the club make contact with her skull.[20]

Arguments and counterarguments. After experiencing disorder, Walter falls back into line again. "I have my number, a room that never changes, meals that arrive punctually to the moment. . . . The world has boundaries again and I know my place in it."[21] Nobody has the right to upset this order, especially in this crucial hour. Lucy, drawing on her official terminology, compares Walter to a happy, still-life whore and makes him admit that he was only frightened that he might begin to enjoy that dizzy world too much. The murder was only an escape from temptation. And now, having admitted it, what is there to lose? Lucy triumphs.

Again, the curtain rises on the early morning confusion of Phillip the executioner's suburban kitchen-dining room. Phillip demands a black hood from the Warden. Martha, the executioner's wife, wants Phillip to finish his oatmeal. She agrees with the Warden that if Phillip needs a change, he should get in some fishing instead of wearing a morbid black hood. Something must indeed be wrong with Phillip. There are a number of symptoms: he used one of his slippers for an ashtray and then tucked it beneath his pillow, a banjo and a Swedish book are discovered, a pair of red socks found. He has refused to renew their country club membership or make a donation to the Red Cross.

Martha and the Warden begin to resurrect old grievances and past memories and this culminates in a passionate kiss. They even try to fix an assignation but cannot arrange it because of their busy schedule. The Warden asks for another kiss and Martha refuses. He kisses her anyway and Phillip comes in, his black hood over his head. "Now that you two have kicked up your heels a little bit, I see no reason why I shouldn't follow suit."[22] But who is responsible for that?—you put her in my arms—the Warden says. Then, in a stylish speech (the vocabulary is nautical this time), he ends by saying: "Remember, Phillip, no matter how attractive you find the mermaids on the rock they wrap their appealing green tails around, the important thing is to keep sailing on course."[23]

The couple now face each other. Martha inquires whether he is planning to go out and make love to the Warden's wife. Phillip says no, he simply wants to get away and become something like those fellows he has been hanging in the last few months. Martha asks him to help with the dishes first. Phillip, towel and plate in his hand, goes back to his visions about having a new suit made, going to a tropical land, and seeing mirages. Meanwhile, he puts on an apron and winds the dishtowel into a strangling cord. He says that he would like to return to his original job but on a freelance basis, finding all the dead branches that need pruning. Martha tries to talk him out of this by mentioning all the urgent appointments they have made. Phillip is ready to leave, but the door will not open. Martha makes him even more frantic. She insists that the door will not open because he does not want it to open. "You are an official executioner a little paunchy through the middle, with thinning hair and obedient attitude. That's as close as you'll ever be to a murderer."[24] In his despair, Phillip tries to strangle his wife with the help of the black hood, but the only result is Martha's sardonic outcry: "This is the closest we've come to sex in years!" There is nothing left for Phillip but to get rid of the hood, tightly button up his uniform, take his handkerchief, and kiss his wife goodbye. A broken man, he starts for the door. It springs open. Curtain.

The symbols of the executioner's private life are somehow more convincing than the requisites of Walter's everyday life. Clichés are used here, too (slippers used as an ashtray to show rebellion), but the things that mark Phillip's desperate attempt to escape (a pair of red socks, a banjo, a Swedish book) are chosen illogically enough to suggest the general idea of nondefinable frustration. The hood is an excellent device. Parallel with the attempt to use it, it also hints at the problem of identity.

It is extremely natural that the couples should be played by the same actor and actress. This theatrical effect, however, is again one that does not really contribute to the tragicomical character of the play. It is indeed difficult to tell the hangman from the hanged, the wife from the prostitute, the warden from the prisoner, if they are shown to us as seemingly or necessarily different aspects of the same existence, that of Everyman. Rather than a tragicomedy, *Gallows Humour* appears to be a kind of modern *Lehrstück*, a parable-play.

Not just *Gallows Humour* but all of Richardson's plays are unified by his persistent and strongly held view of the human predicament as man's forced participation in a destructive conflict between fundamental opposites: life, individuality, imaginative illusion accompanied by chaos on the one hand; death, conformity, reality, and order on the other. As a parable-play, *Gallows Humour* is nearer to works by Dürrenmatt and Jean Anouilh than to Brecht; it is richer in paradoxes than in tragicomic effects.

I think that one can forgive Walter for being as cool in his last hour as any Richard Dudgeon could be. The female characters of the play are also too sure of themselves, as if they were led, too, by the Shavian "will to live." Just as with Shaw, it is difficult to distinguish between the rhetoric used and the rhetoric that is being mocked. The title and the general idea of the play must have presented too much of a temptation for the playwright. This is perhaps why he tries to think in terms of tragicomedy, but, at the same time, cannot prevent the weeping of the willow tree from developing into gallows humor. If interpreted as a tragicomedy, *Gallows Humour* provokes no repercussions. If, however, it is taken for what it is, a peculiarly American form of the parable-play, it deserves a better judgment. "What is so effective in *Gallows Humour* is that the play does not tackle conformity merely as a concept, a large, generalized evil, but as a particularly nauseating form of human repression."[25]

One has to admit that *Gallows Humour* and similar Off-Broadway experiments are fighting a sincere battle against plays like *Under the Yum Yum Tree*. That battle, however, began long ago with the advent of the Little

Theater movement. It is far more difficult to fight against the clichés of the Theater of Sentiments, against things that had once been innovation but by now were simply platitudes. In particular, the complaints of the antiheroes about their humdrum lives cannot yet do without the "oh, my"-stuffed lyricism of insect-sized nightmares and realities. Clownery, if taken seriously, could do with lots of laconic statements like: "Nothing happens, nothing goes, it's awful." Sticking a needle into somebody's back, struggling with doors that will not open, trying to strangle a pepper mill, and throwing chicken bones about are also clownery, but the face of Buster Keaton or Charlie Chaplin go better with them than that of Willy Loman or a mask of Dionysus. Off Broadway will probably retain its position as Broadway's loyal opposition, until we no longer visit theaters of Sun City or Utopia.

Earlier in this chapter, I tried to describe the two plays I consider models for the sixties. I also tried to illustrate two, somewhat different approaches taken by the Americanist in Hungary. As I dealt with Kopit's play I relied on its being relatively well known in Hungary and was therefore more scholarly and concise. As Richardson is virtually unknown, I retold the plot. The latter approach, though "schoolmarmish," does have its advantages. I share the Belgian comparativist Gilbert Debusscher's view[26] that Richardson is important because he firmly belongs to the French reinterpretation of the classical Greek heritage. Some aspects of "gallows humor," however, escape his attention; an American or a Hungarian would see the same things in a somewhat different light. So much for Richardson; I will now return to Kopit, my number two favorite of the decade.

For if Richardson signifies the survival of the classical French heritage, Kopit marks the survival of the "bastard French" tradition that includes Beckett, Arthur Adamov, Genet, and Ionesco.

Kopit's last important work I know of is his radio-play *Wings* (1977–1978), which became a successful theater production at Yale Drama School.[27] I mention it only to point out Kopit's "survival"; the play itself is beyond my chronological interest. The previously mentioned *Indians* (1968–1969) is a different cause not only because it belongs to the decade in question but because of its place in an interesting side stream that I will refer to in chapter 3. Just like Robert Lowell's *The Old Glory*, the play's title in itself is an ironic provocation. The "Indians" that appear in the sky are, in spite of their ethnic tragedy, necessary to illustrate the pseudoglorious myth of Buffalo Bill as the representative of white superiority. It is little wonder that the play's European and American popularity was attributable to the cavalcade-like production of the Royal Shakespeare Company; this production was directed by Peter Brook in somewhat the same vein as their *Marat/Sade* production, although very different in itself. Kopit shows himself to be a member of the Albee (loner that he was) generation with this play, which is a revision of the *American Dream*, just as *Wings* shows similar orientation to Albee's *Listening* (1975), also intended as a radio-play. Revisiting the past or reacting to the present is also typical of Albee, as his *The Death of Bessie Smith* and *Box-Mao-Box* bear witness.

In contrast to what others think, I consider Kopit's experimentational technique between *Oh, Dad, Poor Dad* and *Indians* worth more consideration than it receives. When those one-acters, improvisations, and trifles were

collected to give Mermaid Publishers a volume,[28] Kopit
chose the most challenging title for it: *The Day the Whores
Came Out to Play Tennis* (not the best play of the volume—
a Chekhovian *trouvaille* lacking the original genius). *The
Questioning of Nick* and *The Conquest of Everest* are really
no more than divertimentos. *Sing to Me through Open
Windows* does have a Williamsian furor and a Beckettian
discipline. The play I should most like to call attention
to is the Joycean-sounding *Chamber Music* (1965), with
echoes from *One Flew over the Cuckoo's Nest, The Brig* and,
specifically, from Pinter's *The Birthday Party* and Dürrenmatt's *The Physicists*. I do not think that Kopit studied
all these works in a scholarly manner in order to write
his play, but they may have been lurking in the back of
his mind, just as others were when he wrote *Oh, Dad,
Poor Dad*. In *Chamber Music,* the latent sadism and ma-
sochism and the manifest paranoia and schizophrenia
of the inhabitants of the lunatic asylum, chosen to represent the world in miniature, like the hotel in *Oh, Dad,
Poor Dad,* culminate in murder. The severe choreography of their lives reminds me of Kenneth L. Brown's
The Brig and of Kesey's *Cuckoo's Nest.*

The male and female patients of the asylum are sep-
arated from one another, and it is not surprising that
the women, who wear culturally parodistic nicknames
like Gertrude Stein, think that the men are planning to
attack them. The women, in defense, want to kill one
of their own in order to show that they are capable of
violence and murder. They try to find a "candidate" by
way of a democratic vote, but their efforts turn into
hysterical havoc that displays the inner love and hate
relationships of the smaller groups within the whole. In
the end, they choose as a victim the one who thought

she was perfectly safe, having chaired the discussion and the vote. She had provoked mass hysteria without thinking that she, too, could become its victim—a special case of Catch-22. This kind of cruel truth, however, can only be achieved within the confines of the lunatic asylum because even though the Outer World may, in fact, be as crazy, it is not considered as such. The solution is as if Dürrenmatt's physicists were able to kill their manipulator, the Owner, or as if Stanley could strike back at Goldberg and McCann in Pinter's *Birthday Party*.

The Hero (1964) should receive attention in part 2 because it was written as a pantomime-script. But it does not because this fugue of Kopit's is an excellent example of what I mean by *inter*mediality as opposed to the ever-existing multimediality of the stage and the uses and misuses of the latter as practiced by the mass media. A Man (Adam?) paints an oasis for the Woman (Eve?), illustrating that even in a sunbleached desert the drip-drop illusion can help the sufferers.

The rather lonely and iconoclastic Kopit is seldom satisfied with his own works. "My usual reaction when re-reading things I have written is sadness at not having thrown them out," he says. My usual reaction is just the opposite. The images from Kopit's dramatic distorting mirrors—even if some think they are "classy"—are as typical as those non-theater-goers may get from Woody Allen's movies or, *mutatis mutandis,* from Disneyland spectacles. His output may be smaller than that of Albee, but one can trace the main line *(Oh, Dad, Poor Dad, Chamber Music, Indians,* and *Wings)* as toccatas of the period in question and be happy with his experimental fugues, described above.

The second half of the sixties, apart from the new performances to be dealt with in part 2 brought with it dozens of successful playwrights. I have chosen Jean-Claude Van Itallie for a special, short discussion because I firmly believe that he continues, in a sense, the tradition of O'Neill, Miller, Williams, and Albee in newly disclosing the once pertinent corruption of the American Dream. (Later on, Sam Shepard will partly join this line, but he must wait for discussion in the last chapter. Shepard's real career, I believe, belongs to the seventies, although he started well back in the sixties. The seventies is a decade "in search of an author," just as are Pirandello's six characters.)

Apart from Van Itallie's commitment to the Open Theater, I consider his *America, Hurrah!* (1966) to have been as much of an explosion as Albee's *The Zoo Story* had been—a mid-sixties clarion. Unlike Albee's *The American Dream* and like his *The Zoo Story, America, Hurrah!* is exteriorized the way Miller had taken his salesman out of the family house and into the wilderness of motels and the like. The play, consisting of three, closely related one-acters, first takes us through the routine questioning of any Nick (cf. Kopit) who is about to undertake a new job. Then we are introduced to the work of television pollers, and we learn that they are no less miserable than any typists (cf. Schisgal's work). Finally, we come to the archetypal scene of Americans, "on the road" as Kerouac would have put it, but with a new attitude toward the institution of the motel. This is the only playlet where puppetry is used and the only one to reach its climax and ritual in murder. But it seems as if all the characters were "supermarionettes," in the Craig or Bread and

Puppet fashion. It also seems that the strings are being manipulated by a perverse system of pseudovalues of a complete Establishment. Added to this impression are other "magical mystery tours" in the land of "air-conditioned nightmare" (Miller) or "neon-smiles," as documented by Wolfe. Isn't this once again a "danse macabre,"as envisaged by Bosch?

The Little Men as seen by Ionesco and Albee might at least be blamed for preparing the concrete for their crypts to come. But Van Itallie's little men make us search for the Grand Marionetteers behind the coulisses. After one step backward, this is one step forward, as we had already seen "ominiscient writers" with too much hidden sympathy for the Becky Sharps and the Becky Thatchers, respectively.

There are many of the Albee generation, called such for simplicity's sake, who deserve attention here. However, I will deal with them in my next chapter to illustrate the richness of the dramaturgical kaleidoscope of the American sixties.

3

The Dramaturgical Kaleidoscope
of the Sixties

DRAMA, even in the so-called revolutionary periods, always finds itself thrown back on worthy and durable traditions by a cultural expectation reinforced by the practical ties of theater. Just as Albee is ready to admit that recent American drama still owes much to the post–Ibsen/Chekhov tradition,[1] the grand old dads of American theater (most notably Lee Strasberg, Harold Clurman, Robert Lewis, and Elia Kazan) have always stressed their indebtedness to Stanislavsky's teachings.[2] It is not only the one-time glory of Group Theater one must consider in this respect, but the activity of the Actors' Studio that produced the most lasting Kazan, Miller, and Williams hits.

The Actors' Studio, founded in 1947 by Kazan, Cheryl Crawford, and Lewis, all former members of the Group Theater, inherited a version of the Method enriched by other components. Within the scope of this work, I shall concentrate on the common aspects of Stanislavsky's system and its adapted version: the Method. The leaders of the Actors' Studio (Kazan and Strasberg) especially emphasize two items of Stanislavsky's theories and practice: the important role of improvisation and situative exercises during the preparation for the play and the "effective memory," necessary for the actor in deriving his characterization from his personal experience. He must "re-act" rather than "act," "be" and not "do."[3] Stanislavsky's books helped a great deal in establishing the theoretical basis of the Method (*My Life in Art,* 1924; *An Actor Prepares,* 1926; two posthumous books: *Stanislavsky Rehearses Othello,* 1948; *Building a Character,* 1950). Even in the shattering fifties and sixties when the Theater of Sentiments was cruelly attacked and when the usual charge against a member of the Actors' Studio was that "he overacts his underacting," Clurman was able, most astutely, to defend the Method.

Ever since the end of the Second World War, the young American has more than ever begun to seek himself as a person. . . . The young folk of the Fifties felt the need to throw off the constrictions of conformism—the affliction of a too highly organized industrial society devoted to mass production. . . . The Method has a particular appeal to the young American actor who, like every other member of the community, is subject to its moral climate, because while not the whole of the Stanislavsky System, it emphasizes the inner nature of the actor's self, the truth of his private emotion as the prime source of artistic creativity. . . . Too frequently he tends to make a cult of it—when this occurs: it becomes a distortion of art in general and of Stanislavsky's teaching in particular.[4]

Stanislavsky's system as a working method can still rival carefully elaborated practical theory, including Brecht's with which it is most frequently juxtaposed. Although there are some very significant differences,

the common end of both is to shake both the performers
and the audience out of their complacency and expectation of the status quo. The general slogan of the century seems to be "creative participation." This way or
another, it can be achieved only if we all exercise our
minds and bodies. The following quatrain, satirizing the
situative exercises compulsory for the members of the
Actor's Studio, might have been a comment on the activity of any Grotowski-oriented group:

> Be a tree, be a sled,
> Be a purple spool of thread,
> Be a storm, a piece of lace,
> A subway train, an empty space.[5]

Brook has remarked that the way for the American
success of the Royal Shakespeare Company was prepared by the successes of Kazan, Miller, and Williams.[6]
Referring back to Clurman's opinion, one finds the explanation for this in the well-adapted formula of Stanislavsky's theory of identification with one's role. In an
age when it is becoming clear that the false alternative
of choice is violence and/or conformism, the performers
and the audience are once again to share the basic premises of a morally critical attitude, just as in Shakespeare's time. This way, even the extremes of a pessimistic
vision are acceptable: the requisites of absurd drama can
equally be found in Shakespeare's *Troilus and Cressida*
and in Las Vegas. Recent interpretations of the catharsis-
problem also reinforce the importance of methexis beside mimesis.

As mirrored in the never-too-distorting images of theatrical success, the ability of American audiences to iden-

tify with very different heroes (Yanks and Joneses, Dion Anthonies and Browns, Mr. Zeroes and Macbeths, Georges and Marthas, Willy Lomans and Blanches, beat and soul children from *Hair* and *Jesus Christ Superstar*) seems to be inexhaustible. This, however, is not a peculiarly American phenomenon. Provided we are still ready to accept the theatrical happening as a (perhaps modernized) magical mystery tour, it "for a certain space of time allows us not to be ourselves but our reflections, impersonations, doubles and dreamchildren, our possibilities and theoretical incarnations."[7]

It is illogical, therefore, to prefer either tradition or revolution, as if they were offered as choices. What is offered for analysis is their interdependence and interaction. A worthy tradition prepares the way for a revolution to come—telling the truth leads to a rebellion and producing tension leads to a blow-up.

The theatrical innovations, brought about by the fifties and sixties, ostensibly clashed with the remnants of the scattered tradition of the Theater of Sentiments. The common enemy, however, seems to have been the unmasked melodrama or the titillating happy ending, leaving the audience and the performers wallowing in the pseudoharmony of conformist values.

Albee's *The Sandbox* or *Box-Mao-Box* seemed only for a while to be more revolutionary than, for instance, Elmer Rice's *The Adding Machine* (1923). It was soon discovered that those trying to evaluate the recent relationship between tradition and revolution were also searching for an applicable terminology that would help to shake off the unnecessary remnants of Panglossian theatrical complacency. Without finding the necessary terminology, the excesses of the Theater of Sentiments were counterposed and corrected by the severe visions of the Theater of the Absurd and by the collective power of happenings. Possibly incurring the risk of attaching temporary labels, one may safely refer to either as the far end of the development. Even when I casually point to the middle, I find a statement by Sartre worth quoting here: "As a successor to the theater of characters we want to have a theater of situation. The people in our plays will be distinct from one another not as a coward is from a miser or a miser from a brave man, but rather as actions are divergent or clashing, as right may conflict with right or wrong with wrong."[8]

If one wants to witness the new search for terminology, there is another opinion, which, if it were voiced at an imaginary conference where the participants included all those mentioned here, should provoke no serious objection:

We use comedy, as we use tragedy, to give form to social dilemmas, for until we have such forms we cannot communicate with ourselves or with others as actors in a drama of social order. The Theater of the Absurd is therefore a cautionary drama which, as it confronts us with its multiple levels of dehumanization, warns of the catastrophe lurking at the end of our present course. The whole thrust of this theater is to make us see ourselves as we are by exposing the comfortable lies with which we insulate ourselves from the real world.[9]

Without Stanislavsky's efforts to transfer the accent from the well-established patterns of the external to experimental internal effects, from the traditional solid truth of history, manners, and customs to the truth of feelings, moods, and expression, our theatrical prophets, whether or not conscious of Stanislavsky's contribution, could not have been as iconoclastic as they believe themselves to be. There is a laconic statement from Gordon Craig, commenting on Stanislavsky's direction of *An Enemy of People:* "The audience smile all the time that they are not being moved to tears."[10]

Many sophisticated European and American regular drama readers and theatergoers have probably heard less of Barrie Stavis than of, for example, Williams or Miller. Their peer, Stavis is one of America's major playwrights acknowledged at home who is also highly respected abroad. The core of his life's work, up to now, his historical drama-tetralogy about heroes who need "neither gods, not tyrants" and who are punished for threatening the social order by speaking the truth, is a convincingly unique body of work offering historical insight as well as paradigm of the "humanist alternative."[11] *Lamp at Midnight,* on Galileo Galilei, inaugurated the second round of the Off-Broadway movement (*New Stages,* 1947), preceding The Circle in the Square production of Williams's *Summer and Smoke* by five years or so. *The Man Who Never Died,* about labor leader and songwriter Joe Hill, has been translated into about two dozen languages, and more than twenty theatrical productions were planned worldwide to celebrate the one-hundredth anniversary of Hill's birth in 1979. *Harpers Ferry,* about John Brown's raid, was the first American play ever done by the Guthrie Theater in Minneapolis, one of the major regional centers of theatrical innovations. I choose *Coat of Many Colors* for particular comment because I think the choice and elaboration of this subject is specifically typical of the 1960s atmosphere, for the period of violence, disruption, and upheaval. All plays written by Stavis are concerned with the use and misuse of political power, but Joseph's example, both as a skillful politician and economist and as a banished revolutionary brings Stavis nearer to the black humor dominating the sixties' stage. This seems to have happened "automatically," since Stavis did not originally have a very high esteem for contemporary writing. When he talks of the mainstream he would like to fit into, he means the classical Greek and Roman theater, the Elizabethan theater, Ibsen, O'Casey, George Bernard Shaw, and "one and one-half plays" of Miller *(The Crucible* and *Death of a Salesman)*. In his opinion, "the theater of cruelty, the theater of the ridiculous are interesting side-streams . . . the theater of the absurd is a dead end, excepting the great Godot . . . and a couple of similar plays."[12]

Joseph's well-known story in Stavis's version is radically changed "only" in its denouement—Joseph the revolutionary is ultimately sent to die in the wilderness by his former "collaborators": Potiphar's wife, Vashnee, the "high priestess" of Joseph's time of turmoil, and Pharaoh. The constant mordant humor of the play comes from the way in which the insiders react to the rebellious activities of the outsider. The analogy between prehistoric times and modern times is clear. "Joseph lives in an age dominated by terror, in which the world of nature seems all powerful, and mankind accepts the need for magic. Into this world Joseph brings the need for human reason and the application of human wisdom."[13] In a chaotic age, (one might ask oneself which age is not) both the revolution and the recovery of human values is inevitable.

Joseph is a traditionally tragic hero not only because he threatens the powers and privileges of state and priestly authority but also because he commits the "fatal mistake" of adopting the methods of the cynical Establishment: "manipulating men for his own ends, though these ends will be good for the very people he drives. The workers whom he has put to forced labor on his nature-taming project will not allow themselves to be enslaved even for their own good."[14] In spite of the tragic ending, the audience is more likely to remember the wry humor manifested in Joseph's career and numerous escapes.

When I was about to translate *Coat of Many Colors* into Hungarian,[15] I asked the author about his diverse sources for the work in question. He responded:

The artistic seed for a play about Joseph was formed when I was 5–8. Remember my being raised in a highly orthodox Hebrew family where going to the synagogue—prayers, benedictions, and Biblical commentaries—was a ritual. . . . Much later I began to see how to develop the theme of power in mordant and ironic terms, and yet, at the same time, with humanist perception. My thinking of power (how it is obtained and then maintained and the uses to which it is put and for whose benefit it is used) has been determined by my own twentieth-century understanding and experience. In this sense the play is a parable of the twentieth century politics. And the fact that the material is handled in ironic, sardonic, often bitter terms, and yet there are long passages which are terribly funny on the stage is, as I see, a major indication of my maturity in handling this complex structure of power.[16]

This would seem to be an obsession with the politics of the contemporary scene, but another laconic ars poetica helps to illuminate all these statements: "My two major literary inspirations are Shakespeare and the Bible."[17]

In recent years, Stavis has been occupied with forming the network for his ongoing tetralogy and with visiting and supervising the worldwide theatrical productions of his first tetralogy (ranging from Russia to socialist to noncommitted Third World countries). The planned second tetralogy shows Stavis as a true preserver of the wider implications of the Monroe Doctrine. He has completed his play on George Washington (*The Raw Edge of Victory*) and is about to write his next plays on Miguel Hidalgo and Simón Bolívar, two liberators of Central and South America. His life's work, up to now, seems to offer a didactically humanistic alternative to the "other mainstream" that shows the sometimes rapid, sometimes slow collapse of the civilization in the shadow of Spengler's dark prophecy, *Untergang des Abendlandes*.

One might wonder why I have attributed this much space to Stavis, whereas I shall refer to Williams and Miller only briefly. On the one hand, I believe that the latters' semiclassics should be dealt with in separate monographs or articles, and, indeed, many scholars have already offered their opinions in this manner. On the other hand, when I talk about the dramaturgical kaleidoscope of the sixties, I have to emphasize that Stavis has provided Europeans with yet another bit of the local color present in America. Williams and Miller have also given us insights into basic American problems without their denying their regionality (Williams) or ethnicity (Miller), but they somehow seem to fit into the European tradition more so than Stavis. Stavis takes historical problems as seriously as, for example, a classic like Friedrich

Schiller and several forgettables belonging to the Theater of Commitment did at one time.

The richness of the kaleidoscope is amazing, and I should pay more attention to the O'Neillian heritage and to other important figures like Lillian Hellman and, especially, Thornton Wilder. But the comparison of O'-Neill and Albee[18] is a comparativist article or a university seminar topic that can not be undertaken here. Of Wilder, suffice it to say that may think *Our Town* (1938) and his early short experiments should be taken as predecessors to the attitude discussed here. His *Skin of Our Teeth* (1942) and Archibald MacLeish's *J. B.*, much later, still come out rather bad when compared to Shaw's "gradiose failure," *Back to Methuselah.* I believe Williams's *The Night of the Iguana* (1961) deserves a much more "stroboscopic" production than the ones I have seen, giving more pictorial stress to the storm shaking Monte Verde Hotel (as in Kopit's *Oh Dad, Poor Dad*), to the German "invaders" parade and songs, and to many other details in order to illustrate Shannon's ancient dilemma, "hell is myself" or "hell is other people." Williams's interesting one-acters collected, in print, under the title *Dragon Country*,[19] again deserve the attention of a Williams fan.

Somewhat similar is the case of Miller's *After the Fall* (1964). It would be interesting to point out the "hit or flop or both" problem of its having been produced at Lincoln Center (New York City) but that has been done brilliantly by Julius Novick, *Village Voice* critic and writer.[20] I should, however, call the American readers' attention to the fact that this was the very play that confused those European critics who had been only too ready to read a difference into Williams's "psychopathologizing" and

Miller's "being committed." Few know about Marilyn Monroe, and they know even less about the first working title (*Inside His Mind*); and *An Incident at Vichy* (1969), as good a play as it is, reassured them in their being right. The Vichy play is frightening enough, but I, before a decisive World War III, am likely to think about it as a remainder and reminder of previous shocks, and my feelings are mixed.

Poets and novelists occasionally visiting the stage as authors make the kaleidoscope no less complicated. I found the novelists' contribution (for example, Joseph Heller's *We Bombed in New Haven*, 1968; Saul Bellow's *The Last Analysis*, 1964; Kurt Vonnegut's *Happy Birthday, Wanda June*, 1970) interesting, but singular enough, as if they were one-time excursions into the theater. The case with Lowell's *The Old Glory* (1964) is different. Fitting excellently into his work as a poet, it is, in my opinion, a semiclassic work somewhat out of the sixties mainstream but joining the line of American tragedy. There was a possibility in the sixties, too, for dissent from the dissenters; this is represented by Stavis, Lowell, and even Kopit's *Indians* (1969). Peculiar "visions and revisions" of the American past always seem to interest Europeans in the long run, whereas Andy Warhol-like sensations, though wildly funny and even "pertinent," do not last very long. I think this explains the relatively recent European popularity of plays like Paul Foster's *Tom Paine*. Albee and some of his generation were first more warmly accepted in Europe than in America (compare, for example, the case of Albee's *The Zoo Story* or Schisgal's *The Typists*); Foster's play spread together with the La Mama Troupes and without them, too.

Before switching over to the second part of my book, I must explain what I mean by two interrelated models, rebellious drama as heritage and intermedia as innovation (and vice versa), by describing their common and uncommon characteristics.

Rebellious drama:

1. Space and time relationships: close, even frightening space; environmentalia not yet in the forefront as main (anti) heroes but as signifiers of the human condition. "Hell is myself" or "hell is other people" can still correlate this type of drama to the classic three unities. Time is the present, much relying on Ibsen's analytical technique, Chekhov's stalemate positions, and Strindberg's pseudorevolutions. Interior set first, unit set second; even the mixtures show the claustrophobia of dramatic characters (family home, farm, office, regular bar, etc.). Example: New Carthage Campus is as suffocating to George as Martha's flat in *Who's Afraid of Virginia Woolf.*

2. Plot and characters: still family drama or nonfamily characters in everyday (office) contact and, perhaps at random, in neutral places (Central Park, Burger King.) The rites of passage do not occur before the audience—they are monologized upon.

3. Denouement and catharsis: the death of tragedy, excepting a few cases, is inevitable as George Steiner has prophesied it. The cyclical "when and where" questions stand for the "then and there" missing links. Earlier, the chorus asked the questions and commented upon the happenings. Now, the main characters ask the questions and there is no one to answer or even comment.

Intermedia (to be dealt with in detail in part 2):

1. Space and time relationships: frighteningly "empty" space, peopled by objects instead of characters. Hell is fetish and/or technology. Time is "apocalypse now." The randomly selected place is any place. Exterior is a park, subway, street corner, deserted house, steps of a temple; interior is a disrupted flat, empty garage, or anything "underground."

2. Plot and characters: the intermedia like to work with much more "plot" and many more "characters," involving the spectator-participants. Preconceived parameters, improvised plot, spontaneous activity; an "event," if possible.

3. Denouement and catharsis: shock-catharsis technique for and against the "audience." Any climax is desirable, liminalities are no longer frontiers, and vice versa. Example: "Paradise Now!" which goes well together with "Apocalypse Now." As visions the productions are pessimistic, as prophecies the productions are optimistic, eschatologically speaking.

And now a final glance at the list of the peculiar multitude of playwrights the sixties has offered Off, Off-Off, and Beyond Broadway. For want of illustration, I will disregard the entire sphere of musicals, no matter how influential they might have been. Ethnically oriented theater, because of its multidimensions, and rebellious or even anarchist as it is, finds its place briefly in part 2. Black playwrights the stature of James Baldwin and LeRoi Jones (Imamu Amiri Baraka) deserve individual monographs. Nor will I analyse Michael Smith and Arthur Sainer, whom I consider energetic theater-experimenters and critics rather than playwrights. I consider John Guare's seventies comeback (*The House of the Blue Leaves*) more important than his sixties one-acters (*Cop Out; Muzeeka*). Guare's favorites are no less surprising than Albee's. "Why should not Feydau and Strindberg be married?" he asks.

Like Guare or Lanford Wilson, Murray Schisgal is also a phoenix nowadays, but during my research I found his highly esteemed one-acters (*The Typists; The Tiger,* 1961–1963) to be a sum of his influences. Unlike Marowitz, I do not think Ionesco is the most pronounced,[21] I am more inclined to discover Pinterian echoes. *Luv!* (1964) was dissatisfying for all of us, but that may have been attributable to poor European productions.

I can attribute only a respectful nod of recognition to Charles Horowitz (remembered because of his film-script of *The Strawberry Statement* rather than for his much anthologized *The Indian Wants the Bronx*), María Irene Fornés, Ronald Tavel (his collaboration with the Theater of the Ridiculous needs a different apparatus), Terence McNally, and Megan Terry (now with the Omaha Magic Theater).

The facts to be discussed in part 2 indicate that it is impossible to find one single dramaturgical rival to the methodization of Stanislavsky's system as embodied by the activity of the Actors' Studio inheriting the Group Theater techniques. It took Richard Burton and Elizabeth Taylor to make a worldwide success out of the film version of *Who's Afraid of Virginia Woolf.* In the more apathetic seventies, it was Burton again who took the role of the psychiatrist-narrator in Peter Shaffer's *Equus*—as psychopathologically oriented as any play by Williams, or for that matter, as Paul Zindel's *The Effect of Gamma-*

Rays on Man-in-the Moon Marigolds, another seventies' hit. Nevertheless, there was something different in the air during the sixties, but rebellious drama was unsatisfactory in itself to express this new tension. Bob Dylan was booming, Elvis Presley still lived, and Beatlemania was in full swing; new prophets (Carlos Castaneda, R. D. Laing, Claude Lévi-Strauss) were chosen while the Ginsbergs of the fifties were still active. Norman O. Brown, Timothy O. Leary, Abbie Hoffman, Jerry Rubin, Eldridge Cleaver, and others testify about the theatrical nature of protests and revolts. Consequently, theater is going to borrow more and more from the multi- and intermedia of the streets, from life itself.

Part 2

The Intermedia

4

Happenings and New Performance Theories

IT IS DIFFICULT to discuss happenings and new
performance theories since at least to my knowledge,
there exists no comprehensive history of the happenings, nor is there any all-embracing definition that could
account for the diversity of the environmentalia, *mise en
scène,* and message of these "events." The new performance theories are even vaguer, since their recent critical interpretations speak of no less than a role in our
so-called postmodern culture.[1] Another obvious difficulty is that it is impossible to accurately reconstruct the
authentic atmosphere of these intermedia (as they later
came to be called) from the sketchy scenarios, photographs, and impressionistic criticism available. The happenings as products of immediate impulses must have
relied intensely upon an interaction with the particular
historical, social, political, and artistic background from
which they had grown.

Thus, instead of analyzing individual artists' *oeuvres,*
I limited this section to a quick summary of some relevant critical responses to the happenings. There seem

to be three crucial *K's* in attaining an essential understanding: the texts of Kaprow, Kirby, and Kostelanetz.[2] Despite their basic introductory essays, all three works are anthologies of scenarios and opinions rather than direct summaries concerning the movement in a wider range of social or artistic references. Each has, however, unique value owing in part to the different nature of their compilers' activity in the neo-avant-garde of the sixties. Although the official name-giver of the strange genre of happenings was Allan Kaprow, father-creator (*18 Happenings in 6 Parts,* 1959), it was in fact Michael Kirby, then a theorist and one of the editors of *TDR,* who seems to have done for the happening what Esslin had done for the Theater of the Absurd—give it a coherent and genetically deducted theory. Parallel to this, Kaprow's and John Cage's roles somewhat resemble those of Ionesco and Beckett, respectively—Kaprow as the everchanging artist and occasional theorist of the movement and Cage as the father-generator and archetypal creator of the same, acknowledged as such by most happeners.

Kirby introduced his book with a pointed essay in which he outlined the way happenings are related to the European, classic, avant-garde movements: futurism, constuctivism, dadaism, and surrealism. Thus, he focused on the significance of happenings for the neo-avant-garde theater. While pointing out the origins of this particular and complex form of American culture, he did not forget to claim that it too was "original," by relating it to action painting and abstract expressionism and casting a glance at the proto- and pre- stimuli of films (Chaplin, the Marx Brothers) and dance (Martha Graham, Merce Cunningham).

Chronologically and logically speaking, Kaprow's book seems in many ways to have been a direct response to Kirby's. As an artist-participator, Kaprow is absolutely correct in tracing the genesis of happenings from the New York art scene of the fifties. This even enables the collector of those fifties items to consider the existence of proto- and pre- happenings. Kostelanetz, art critic and writer,[3] was therefore able to make implicit references to the differences between Kirby's and Kaprow's accounts in his own book.[4] His characterization of happenings as "still theatrically-minded intermedia" allows us to connect his conceptions with what Richard Schechner, director and critic, much more a Greenwich Village type than a real happener, calls "new performance theory."[5] Many interpreters vaguely call it the "new" (rebellious, protesting, and soon) American theater of the sixties.

It should be clear by now that my intention here is to more or less agree with the genetically inclined theoreticians (Kirby, Kostelanetz) and, paradoxically enough, not to disagree with the artists involved (Kaprow, Schechner). I would rather view their productions and utterances in "radical juxtaposition" to all other possible interpretations, as is methodically suggested by Susan Sontag.[6]

The unpleasant task of trying to define what happenings are (or rather what they were) is unavoidable. Some general maxims, risking the summary of a century-long, general background are no less indispensable. As Jerome Klinkowitz has put it:

The major topic of art in this century, most critics agree, has been its own art history. . . . Music, fiction, poetry, cinema, theatre, dance and even the popularly expressive forms of anthropology showed evidence of such fruitful self-attention, making the Sixties an intellectually active period to match the historical and social turmoil encountered nearly every day. . . . Each form of art, then, became a radically full experience as a result of its respective aesthetic challenge. What first had threatened to be a loss or even extinction, became the way to great enrichment. Less is definitely more.[7]

Since there is no denying the fact that the happenings came from nontheatrical origins and since their outcome was, by all means, "theatrical," inasmuch as they presupposed the presence of a sympathetic and/or hostile "audience" (those who would formerly go to openings, readings, exhibitions, and concerts), later and similar events and activities (Street and Guerilla Theater) could bring about a perhaps vaguer but more applicable definition: artistic "liminalities, places of fruitful chaos."[8]

Kirby, as a theorist, arrived at a too precise and somewhat biased definition, according to which happenings might be described as a form of theater (this is what many of the happeners protested against) "in which diverse and *alogical* elements, including nonmatrixed performing, are organized in a compartmented structure."[9]

On the other hand, the eclectic Schechner, later also confronted with the growing influence of Grotowski's theory and practice and with the renaissance impact of Antonin Artaud's teachings (also present in some happeners' works), chose to retrospectively illuminate the difference between what he called "traditional" and "new" performance in a very tactful way, with strong Brechtian reminiscences.[10] In spite of his numerous allusions to proto-cultures, he, however, fails to establish the same valid contacts between European and American culture that Kirby is so eager to point out—very possibly because of the different type of intellectual horizon Schechner has in mind. For him, the conclusions of the sixties, "teatrum mundi" seem to have a Marshall McLuhanized interpretation of Lévi-Strauss's ideas on the tribality of all human culture. Kirby, however, is ready to admit all the connotations that may come from his deriving the word *merz* from *kommerz*, just as *pop* may be derived from *popular*. His genetic approach to happenings may, however, be summarized as a theoretical glance at the only-too-numerous possibilities of the various modes of perception in the ever-changing time-space relationships. In this respect, the relative kinship of the happenings to the Theater, working with traditional concepts of the same, is fully justified.

Kaprow, as an artist, probably first saw the happenings as a more or less logical extension of the assemblages he had been making in the preceding years. Cage's Zen-inspired theories of aleatory composition offered a base and methodology for incorporating controlled and uncontrolled materials in a single work. In later years, however, Kaprow, too, would join the practitioners and theorists of American neo-avant-garde theater in calling attention to the ritual aspects of performance. As early as 1961, happenings were catching the suspicious attention of the art world establishment. Again, Kaprow was one of the first to notice the dangers that the "new type of artist" had to face; because of the entire "corrosive system," the artist, whose *sui generis* task was to create "moral rights," might have become "repetitive at best, and at worst, chic."[11] At the same time, when he tried to theoretically point out what he meant by "theater with a difference," he still had to fight with "arch-traditional"

ideas, saying that the happenings had no structured beginning, middle, or end. He could not, however, account
for the programmed, scripted, and (often, if not always)
rehearsed nature of the happenings. As Paul Walsh has
put it: "Whether chance elements were used in composition or performance . . . the artist was always in control of certain predetermined parameters which might,
in turn, be termed as 'preconceived scripts or scenarios'
within which the activities took place."[12] The authenticity
of these "chance elements" was, therefore, of crucial
importance, since it directed the selecting artist towards
a minimum application of tarty art, replacing it with,
for example, conceptual art and art-as-arena in the spirit
of Jackson Pollock. Some particular results of all these
were not unlike a Wagnerian bad dream of the "synthesis
of the arts" upon which the "junk-culture had been superimposed."[13]

Here I should mention another figure, Ken Dewey,
who was, perhaps, the first happener to publicly recognize the political implications and anarchist strain of
the new art form. He saw the happenings as a possible
means for reanimating theater by renewing ancient links
with primitive and medieval theater through the kin-
esthetic contact between the purpose of primitive ritual
and the people who practice it.[14] In later years, some
representatives of the New York neo-avant-garde theatre, especially the Becks' Living Theatre and Schechner's
The Performance Group, would, like Dewey, attempt to
reestablish links with the primitive and ritualistic theater.
Theorists like Kirby and Kostelanetz would, however,
always clearly distinguish betwen the "play-like" early
production of Le Living (for example, Gelber's *The Connection,* 1959) and their later, more communal and more

happening-like pieces (*Paradise Now!* 1968). They also admit, however, the seminal importance of the early neo-avant-garde drama, for example, Albee's *The Zoo Story* (1960).

In the mid-sixties, most of the happeners went on with their individual explorations of spatialization, duration, and performance. Kirby, as a theorist, was still in the forefront, as one can see from the winter 1965 issue of *TDR*. The dimension of nonmatrixed performances was often pushed to the extreme in that human figures were sometimes treated as other "objects," parts of the environment. This, in turn, resulted in bulks of hostile theater criticism defining the happenings as violent, anti-human abstractions. But, since the sixties' atmosphere seems to have been preoccupied with real and stylized violence, even this conservatist challenge helped the renaissance of the Theater of Cruelty as manifested by Artaud and Grotowski.

Kaprow gradually moved away from the idea of happenings as communal performances and , by now, seems to have arrived at the conception of auto-performance.[15] He felt the Kirby's emphasis on the history of avant-garde performance theories falsified the aesthetic experience that the happenings were striving for. In response, Kirby used his newly created vocabulary of performance theory to distinguish happenings from what he called "Activities and Events." [16] The numerous and multicolored Activities and Events (Fluxus, Yip, Guerilla, and so on) also offered the possibility of different, more politically minded interpretations for other critics. Franck Jotterand, for example, stresses the interrelatedness of all these events.[17] Lee Baxandall suggests that happenings went out into the street to become part of the mock social revolution waged by the counterculture in the latter part of the sixties.[18]

Mixing the vocabularies of Freud, Herbert Marcuse, Lévi-Strauss, and Marshall McLuhan, Kostelanetz has called happenings the "art for the age of informational overload as well as the era of polymorphously libidinal leisure that is superceding the era of phallic concentration, whether at orgasmic pleasure or productive work."[19]

The spontaneous approach to the necessity for a non-representational, total theater was another method to summarize the importance of the happenings for drama critics like E. T. Kirby. He seriously spoke of happenings as another step toward the synthesis of the arts which had been preached by Wagner, Appia, Craig, and the Symbolists.[20] Very similar roots, however, could lead to a very different outcome. The new performance theory Schechner advocated was to "distinguish performance as a social science rather than a branch of aesthetics."[21]

As one can see, the few relevant "insiders" mentioned here approached the happenings with the unavoidable bias of their personal preoccupations. This suggests, as Walsh wisely put it, that "this movement originating from the visual arts may perhaps have been side-tracked by the practitioners of the neo-avantgarde theater."[22] But because of the three K's, the sidetrack itself is significant, and, apart from its justified claims to "originality," it also bears the heavy imprints of European "origins."

Three thought-provoking elements seem to have pre-determined the formation of the category in the title: the dramatization of life by the media, deliberate blurring of the boundaries between genre and genre, Art and Life, and the emphasis on functioning and surviving in a highly technological environment.[23] The appearance of new performance theories is closely related to the century-long loosening of the structure of traditional drama as a literary genre and, in theater, as a playscript. Other obvious stimuli have come not only from other theatrical activities, pantomime, dance, musical comedy and tragedy, happenings, and so on, but also from sister arts like atonal music, action painting, and mobile sculpture.

Alternative theater is trying to compensate for the lack of traditional dramatic heroes by giving an overwhelming emphasis to the intense presence of the performer. The earlier, psychologizing-sociologizing theater characterized the dramatic situation and the charge of the conflict with the help of an analytical method enriched by the innovations of the "isms" (outback, flashback, dream and surrealist logics, fantasies, visions, remembrances of the subconscious, and so on). The performer of the alternative theater torments both himself and the audience (compare Artaud, Grotowski, Weiss, Peter Handke) when he confesses the paralyzing effects of environmentalia fetishism, allegorizing about the remaining rags of illusion or by seriously and parodistically presenting the nearly catatonic state of Things versus Characters. Thus, a vicious paradox develops the haphazard indeterminism of pseudoactions (or those of the few remaining "real" actions, like violence within and without; drug addiction as biochemical violence, suicide, and so on; and ritual murder; ritual rape and manifestations of subculture). They function partly because of environmental determinism, to which the human reaction is estrangement and alienation; the resulting visions are highly pessimistic, post-Spenglerian, post-Nietzschean, yet, nevertheless, metaphysically oriented.

At the beginning of the decade, the radically experimental American little theater activity was not yet free
from Brechtian influences. All the more so because any
protesting social and/or artistic movement seems always
to have been slightly "leftist": red with anger and pink
in considerations. While actually performing, the performer was watching the performance, himself turning
into something like a third factor: a bridge between the
performance and audience. In fact, this beginning was
a preparation for later developments when the rage of
protest and creation made the ensemble expect active
participation from the audience; this time not only in
the Brechtian but in many other (Artaud-, Grotowski-,
and Brook-like) ways, too. Parallel to this, another type
of V-effect had a strong influence on experimental theater life: the cosmic absurd of the Paris "school"—Beckett,
Ionesco, Genet, Arthur Adamov, and so on. (The French
existentialists—Camus, Sartre, Jean Giradoux, Anouilh—had not been without their influence, either.)
Whichever clarions one thinks of, all presented a basic
challenge to the well-established and still influential hereditary dramaturgical standards embodied by O'Neill
and his disciples like Miller and Williams. This appears
to be even more the case if one considers the theatrical
realizations on Broadway and its beneficial satellite-system Off Broadway.

The young artists of the period (such as playwrights,
directors, performers, and happeners) were more sure
about what they did not want to do than about what
they did. The protest against commercialized theater
swept them, for a longer or shorter time, into an ensemble, consisting of "innovators" of very different sorts,
as far as individual mentality and professional skills were

concerned. The general ensemble-mentality can well be characterized by the early workshop activities of the Open Theater, which later came to be one of New York City's best known theater groups. Although fighting against the so-called literary theater, the workshops of the group use and reinterpret some literary and cultural heritage selected as pertinent for them:

1. We sit through endless scenes of Chekhov, Williams, Beckett and then discuss performances and concepts.
2. A catalyst appears on the scene that spring (1963), Geraldine Lust, one of the producers of Genet's *The Blacks*.
3. The theater as a function of man: man in the community, man in the *polis*, and man in his collective unconscious. Brecht and Artaud out of Jung.
4. All of us consider it of paramount importance to develop what Grotowski was later to call the psychophysical life of the performer. [Here it must be noted that Grotowski's wide influence was somewhat belated in the United States; it can be traced back to his 1967 tour. Already a somewhat too laconic theorist, his experimental work with his "Laboratory Theatre" goes well back to the early sixties. For his American reception see *TDR,* vol. 13 (1), 24, 27, p. 30; 35, 41.]
5. Joe Chaikin is obsessed by the theme of alienation in modern society. . . . Ultimately the Absurd is incorporated predominantly as an idea for a counteraction. Unlike Ionesco and his *non-sequiturs,* exploration in the Open Theatre is not principally verbal but is *sometimes* through the word and more often through the body.[24]

In 1963, among the members of Open Theater, one finds Megan Terry, later author of *Viet Rock,* Gerry Ragni, later coauthor and performer of *Hair,* and young playwrights like Michael Smith and Sainer, who later became influential drama critics of the organ specializing in the field, *Village Voice*. The real profile of this group developed itself later when Joe Chaikin became the undisputed artistic director and leader and when Van Itallie became the leading dramatist, or rather, scriptwriter. Chaikin introduced the idea of spontaneous acting exercises derived form Stanislavsky's, Antonin Artaud's, and Jerzy Grotowski's teachings, whereas Van Itallie could build on the actors' improvizing power to help him express acute social criticism as well as psychological visions of postmodern *Weltanschauung*. Their unique collaboration together with the ensemble activity resulted in one of the main types of new performances, signifying the enthropy-shock of young intellectuals and artists, perhaps best manifested in *America, Hurrah!* (1966).

Almost parallel, the representatives of definitely different show and performance types also made their way to the stage. The first significant production of Bread and Puppet Theatre,[25] lead by Peter Schumann, sculptor and choreographer, resembles August Strindberg's work only in its title (*Totentanz*); in fact, a series of ancient rituals had been adapted for the stage. The same group soon easily shifted its interest to the medium of street theater: protest against the Vietnam War found its serial and improvised existence as well as the pacifistic and peace-demanding processions that were somewhat in the spirit of ancient pageants but corresponding to the looser events organized by youth, guerilla, and leftist organizations.

To portray the anguished and dwarfing effects of the various structures of society, they used in their performances almost every kind of puppetry imaginable: giant puppets (double or triple human size) as well as marionettes of all sizes. Actors often wore stylized masks and costumes of the Greek or commedia dell'arte type. Just as in the case of most ensembles, the barriers between the director, the playwright, the designer, the performer, and the various stage hands practically disappeared; everyone was ready to lend a hand anywhere, and almost everyone could play at least three or four musical instruments ranging from the kazoo to the harp.

It must be noted that Bread and Puppet Theatre is one of the few groups starting in the sixties that have managed to survive. In accordance with the more apathetic spirit of the seventies, they have migrated from New York City to a communally owned farm in Vermont. They are still able to accommodate old and new demands by organizing local festivals in a ritualistic spirit, conducting American and European tours, and making their living by farming. Being world-famous, they receive grants and awards that they often distribute among smaller groups and organizations. "Our God does not dwell in incense-smelling churches," says Schumann. "He is manifested in the garlicky smell of the toast make of our home-made bread asnd distributed freely among the spectators of our performances."[26] The theater historian cannot help reminiscing about the turn of the century's art theaters" and free theaters that had the same attitudes and hopes.

Parallel not only in time but also in their original stance, sixties' activity, and "survival", are the members of the San Francisco Mime Troupe. This group of young actors had broken with the famous and professional SF, ACT and experimented on their own. SF, ACT was at the time, going through a difficult period when both Herbert Blau and Jules Irving had left for New York City to help the newly formed Lincoln Center out of chaos. The first productions of the San Francisco Mime Troupe were typical "little theater" ventures (Jarry's *Pére Ubu;* Brecht's *The Exception and the Rule*). But under the leadership of Ronnie G. Davis, the group soon switched to open-air performances somewhat in the vein of commedia dell'arte. By then San Francisco had a long-standing tradition of open-air (park or street-corner) events with little or no admission fee (please, put a nickel in the artist's hat . . ."). The city had abounded in jazz concerts, beat literature recitals, and the like ever since the mid-fifties, well preceding the street theater practice of the sixties.

Mime has never been the sole activity of the troupe, although it does hint at the multidimensional nature of the productions. In their performances, they usually react to current political and social events. Their commitment makes the shows seem spontaneous, improvized. Nevertheless, the scripts are either deliberately structured collages or similar adaptations of classical material; the musical scores are as carefully composed or selected as the stage motions are well-rehearsed and choreographed. The result is a sort of popular theater, rich in tragicomic effects, offering leftist "politcomedies" in the Brechtian and, especially, Piscatorian tradition.

One must bear in mind that California is one of the places where the traditional (black and white), polarization is further complicated by the presence of Mexican-Americans. This certainly contributed to the rapid radicalization of the troupe. An inner break even occurred when some members formed the El Teatro Campesino elsewhere. But those who remained and the newcomers still stick to the definition of a multiracial group. The Campesino and the Troupe, just like Bread and Puppet Theatre, were frequent guests at the sixties' protest, guerilla, and peace demonstrations, processions, and events in New York City and elsewhere. "We are an artist *and* propaganda-group," say the group members. "Marginal propagandists but, as artists, also beyond propaganda, too."[27]

To complete these geographically extreme models, I will mention a famous midwestern group. Minneapolis must be considered an important regional theatrical center because of its significant repertory theater, the Guthrie. It was also the birthplace of an innovative group similar to those already mentioned called the Firehouse Theatre. Provocative as the name is, its origin is simple enough: the group had lived in a deserted firehouse near the University of Minnesota campus. They, also, started by "importing" the most pertinent Off-Broadway successes by (Gelber's *The Connection,* Pinter's *The Caretaker*), and their golden period was rich in technical experiments (multimedial Ionesco, Beckett in strobelights, an acrobatic Peer Gynt, street-theater Brecht). They also collaborated with the young American playwrights already mentioned: for example, one of the decisive events was the production of Terry's *Jack-Jack* with rock music, film inserts, strip-scenes, and the like. Their last production, before moving to San Francisco in 1969, was a passion play based on the motives of the Faustian legends.

Huge as the United States is, there still seems to be an almost symmetrical-geographical logic in the main "migrations" of the decade. The forum for innovative dramaturgical theories, *Tulane Drama Review* and its "motor," Richard Schechner, moved to New York City where the Kirby brothers joined them, forming its successor *The Drama Review.* Schechner, remaining coeditor and one of the major contributors, founded the most consistent representative of "environmental-ritual theatre," the Performance Group whose activity culminated in *Dionysus '69*. Although the decade saw a flourishing of regional theatrical cultures, especially that of repertory theaters (Washington, D.C., Arena Stage; Los Angeles, Mark Taper Forum; Minneapolis, Guthrie) alongside the dozens of new, innovative groups, contributing to a healthy decentralization, New York City still continued to be the *ultima ratio*—a testing area of scandal and concern. Simple yet appropriate labels, Off Broadway, Off-Off-Broadway, Beyond Broadway,[28] testify to this. But since the vast majority of American theaters are self-supporting, any alternative theatrical culture, from the beginning up to the present, has had to face the paradoxical dilemma of how to fight against the commercialism of Broadway without enjoying its profits and its often primary place in theater. This is all the more so because Broadway has never exclusively been the place for cheap hits (for example, *Under the Yum-Yum Tree*). It has also crowned authors like O'Neill, Thornton Wilder, Hellman, Miller, Williams, and Albee, not to mention the well-librettoed George Gershwin, Leonard Bernstein, and even John Lennon. Radical theater, in the form of amateur, regional, ethnic-political, communally oriented innovative, neo-avant-garde, or postmodern groups, found the "answer" in an artistic and social commitment verging on sacred insanity. "Sacred," cruel," and especially "poor" theater meant not only aesthetic key words but social protest and ontological determination.

The best example of this self-supporting and self-immolating Buddhist attitude is probably provided by the New York City oriented Living Theatre—at first Off Broadway, then picaresqueing around America and Europe, sometimes as the primary example of all theatrical innovators, at one time excommunicated by the not exactly prudish Avignon Festival of Free Expression, and so forth and so on. The actual beginnings of the artistic revolution, headed by the Becks can be traced back to the fifties. Just as in the case of Open Theater, workshop experiments meant a wide range of selected values. Productions of Christopher Marlowe, Brecht, and Beckett plays were mixed with mystery plays and adaptations of the Frankenstein and Antigoné-Kreon legends, respectively; premiering not only Gelber's frequently mentioned clarion but also Brown's *The Brig*—a jail play that in its choreography and artistic depth could probably rival in popularity the spontaneous concerts given by Johnny Cash to inmates, just as (quite the reverse) *Waiting for Godot* proved to be a prison and lunatic asylum hit. Brown's play, as performed by the Living Theater, seems to have been a strangling experience even for the American audience quite accustomed to everyday manifestations of violence. A ready European parallel offers itself in the Irish dissenter, Brendan Behan's *The Quare Fellow*. The American play and performance (where the stage was surrounded with wires) laid comparatively less trust in verbal confessions than in the mimetic (kinetic) possibility of subhuman *danse macabre,* portrayed by the "concrete music" and the "choreography" of the whistles, commands, and subsequent motions of the suggestive vision on stage.

The nomadic lifestyle, the loud successes, the persecution, the manifestations of counterculture, the experiments with Buddhist meditation as well as with drugs, all culminated in the 1968 performance series of *Paradise Now*. In fact, 1968 might in many respects be called the final year of the decade since it abounded in decisive events like the assassinations of Robert Kennedy and Martin Luther King, student protests in Berkeley and elsewhere, and the Yippie "Congress" in Chicago. *Paradise Now!*—apart form the demand for spontaneity and improvization—was theoretically based on the *I Ching* (*Book of Changes*) and embraced, of course, as many current elements as the performance could.

It was impossible then, and it would be absurd now, to document any performance in a form other than a highly impressionistic report with absolute statements of like or dislike. One thing is certain: any spectator, whether a man off the street or a sophisticated theorist pro or con (there are rumors of Schechner actually stripping himself when one of the cast complained of its not being allowed and of Eric Bentley enjoying a heavy verbal debate with the cast), became an active physical entity in the play either by giving in to mad enchantment and activity or by squarely withdrawing as if in a zoo or by actually leaving the premises. The spectators' provoked dialogue and participation were always mixed in nature, including extremists and middle-of-the-roaders. The former indulged in joining the stylized scenes of group sex, mass meditation, and protest marches, or in heavily rebuking the same in the name of Holy Spirit or Holy Reason. The latter tried spontaneously to point out the contradictions of the complaints. (A cast member: "I am not allowed to smoke marijuana." A spectator: "Don't be silly. We are all smoking it. Here's the joint for you.") At Yale Theatre there was a discussion between the cast

and the audience already admitted about the crowd outside waiting to gain admittance:

—Open the doors.
—Free the people.
—Don't go out into the street and put your head in front of
a police club. . . .
—Last night the Living Theatre went on. And tonight the
revolution is dead, right?
—The Living Theatre is a bunch of cowards.
—Wait a minute. . . . There are two people here, who, if the
doors open and there's a violation will go to jail for five years.
Let's think about human life.
—If you want someone to go to jail, if you want someone to
get clubbed, let that someone be you. But don't force that
penalty on others.
—Get those fucking liberals out of the house. I only want
revolutionaries here. . . .
—A Member of the Cast: Let me ask you a serious ques-
tion. . . . Who here is not going to pay his taxes this year?
—A Man in the Audience: I'm not.
—A Member of the Cast: Who here is not going to vote?
—Cries from the Audience: Me. Here. Here. Yeah.
—A Member of Cast: The rest of you please go outside and
let the other two hundred people in. (Cheers)[29]

The richness of the neo-avant-garde theater in the
sixties seems generally to parallel that of the classical
avant-garde of the turn of the century; as far as the
United States is concerned, I might even speculate about
a braver sweep. Apart from the few models already mentioned, other summaries ought to be dedicated to the
renaissance of the musicals, to ethnic theaters, to Off
Broadway (for example, Albee's organizing the Playwrights' Unit after the worldwide aesthetic and financial

success of *Who's Afraid of Virginia Woolf?*) and to Off-
Off-Broadway (Greenwich Village) groups like Caffé
Cino, La Mama, and Judson Corner. Not only the main
repertory theaters already mentioned but dozens of regional groups would demand attention. By the end of
the decade, the healthy decentralization of Beyond
Broadway found its New York City equivalent as well,
owing to the producing activity of Joseph Papp who, at
least for a time, seems to have solved the antagonism of
art threaters and commercial theaters by running both
and subsidizing the former with help of the latter. In
this way, a non-profitmaking undertaking (such as producing Shakespeare in Central Park) could develop.

All this raises the question as to what extent the theatrical revolution of the 1960s was an indigenous one
in America and in Europe. One may rightly suppose
some sort of continuous artistic revolution in the twentieth century wherein Europe may have had a traditionally innovative and America an adaptive and
reinterpretive function, the latter giving rise to new
qualities for new phases. As for the loosening of well-
established dramaturgical functions after World War II,
the first wave was British (the Angry Young Men) and
also international (French, British, American, and even
Slavic). The well-known periodization "Anger and After"
is somewhat misleading if one takes into consideration
the pre-sixties manifestations of the Theater of the Absurd and the events, intermedia, and happenings. Moreover, in digesting the main twentieth-century dilemmas,
the French ("active") existentialist theater and the American psychologizing theater of the fifties were not rivals
but rather coordinators and collaborators influencing
one another to a certain extent.

The Theater of Cruelty reached America by way of performances by the Royal Shakespeare Company, such as Weiss's *Marat/Sade,* with Brook, Marowitz, Kott, and the like, also changing the traditional image of Shakespeare. Brook, however, found the American audiences immensely responsive, and it took only a short time for American playwrights to produce their own visions and rituals of curelty at home. Grotowski's Poor Theater also contributed to the radicalist spirit always present Off or Beyond Broadway. It would be futile to forget that the American intellectuals, if not the politicians, have always been famous for an almost self-torturing clarity of self-criticism when pointing out the shortcomings (or sometimes the nonexistence) of the American Dream.

When a theorist tries to summarize the main factors in this development, he is usually confined to brave generalizations. Thus, James Roose-Evans, in his book *Experimental Theatre: From Stanislavsky to Today,*[30] considers Artaud the most influential European and Cage the most influential American factor in the area dealt with here. The effects of Artaud and Grotowski have filtered into American theater. Not so with Cage. His pioneering seems to be unquestionable in some spheres (for example, indeterministic compositional constituents, early I-Ching inspirations); nevertheless, he is not as lonely and overpowering a figure in the history of American avant-garde art, including abstract espressionism, action painting,[31] and the happenings, as O'Neill seems to be in American dramatic history. Introducing other arts is not irrelevant. Atonal music and nonobjective beaux-arts did not contribute primarily to the theatrical revolution as parts of innovative theater design but rather as sister arts showing some parallel features that could not be ignored. Cage would probably agree with the nonmusicians of the European Fluxus in maintaining that there should not be any boundaries between Life and Art, at least theoretically speaking, and that psychophysical intensity should be sought. The representatives of new performance theories in the theater are directed toward the same thing. There is not even a need technically for routine plotting, naturalist imitation, mechanical delay of tension, construction of a climax, and a didatic message. These things can be erased only in new manifestos—when new categories (fragmentation, discontinuity, multimedial sensation, shock-technique, significance instead of beauty, and so on) dominate the theoretical text.[32]

It takes a theorist, emigrating occasionally and briefly from the sphere of creation, to construct labels that impress the interested lay majority. Almost all manifestations of the alternative theater could be classified by one or another of Brook's basic categories. Theater is either Sacred, Direct, Profane, Cruel, Poor, or all of these. Some labels are likely to date. Such is the case with the Artaudian conception of the Theater of Cruelty. John Vaccaro (leader of one of the extremist groups in New York City, the Theater of the Ridiculous, and director of scandalous plays like Rochelle Owens' *Futz* or Tavel's *The Gorilla Queen*) summarizes it like this: "I have gone beyond Artaud. Artaud doesn't work, the cruelty is not an assault on the audience. In order to be cruel to the audience, you have to be cruel to yourself. I find it a very horrifying experience."[33] This may mean moving nearer to Grotowski, though I feel something else may also be deduced. A Marlowe, a Brecht, a Beckett, *mutatis mutandis* an O'Neill are always likely to be "rediscovered."

The kaleidoscope of the sixties becomes even more confusing if one tries to contrast it with the following decade. One may consider the survivors, like Bread and Puppet Theatre, San Francisco Mime Troupe, Mabou Mines, La Mama, Los Angeles Provisional Theatre, and the like; or the newcomers and/or chameleons like Manhattan Project, Ontological-Hysterical Theatre, and so on. One may be relatively safe in feeling that the ensemble mentality of the seventies is lingering in spite of the fact that it was not a golden age for drama, even if Sam Shepard, David Mamet, David Rabe, Ken Jenkins, and so on, are worth our attention (together with the survivors like Albee, Kopit and Guare). Some change in attitude might be deduced from the titles of two respective hits—*Paradise Now!* and *Apocalypse Now!*—and from the recent nostalgia for the fifties and sixties. Interim now? They said so in the fifties and sixties.

5

The Regional Alternative Theater

IT IS NOT THE VAST regional centers (like Guthrie, Arena Stage, and SF, ACT) that I want to deal with here. An almost complete map of regional theatrical culture of the American 1960s is offered by Julius Novick in his *Beyond Broadway*.[1] As the "flying reporter" of *Village Voice*, he has surveyed the major developments in theater. He seems to have been everywhere where a drum was being banged. Washington and Philadelphia, the South and Southwest, the Pacific Coast, Minneapolis and the Midwest, New England and New York all get a chapter in his book, not to mention his attention to nonresident professional theaters, university theaters, summer festivals, and poor people's theaters (most markedly The Free Southern Theater).

I was fortunate to be in close contact with three theater companies—Minneapolis Playwrights' Laboratory, Provisional Theatre, L.A., and San Francisco Mime Troupe—observing performances and their rehearsals, practices, exercises, and everyday life. The Playwrights' Laboratory—during my stay there—was chiefly occupied with presenting a play by a talented young play-wright, Henry Manganiello, that was a peculiar American version of Ionesco's *Exit the King*. In spite of this and because of it, I shall once again come back to the Bread and Puppet Theatre, because I think they are the best model for the sixties' upheaval and the seventies' revival. I had a shorter encounter with them than with the companies previously mentioned. They toured in Minneapolis with Josquin des Prés' *Ave Maris Stella*, but they accompanied it with happy jam sessions and workshop illustrations.

Like Albee, who thinks *Tiny Alice* is "derriére-garde," I am always amazed by prophets who slowly return to prototypes (Ginsberg to Blake), as in the case of Schumann who arrives at simplicity from complexity: "You cannot simply shock an audience. That will only disgust them. We don't necessarily have to revolutionize the theatre. It may be that the best theatre—if it comes—will develop from the most traditional forms. A theatre is good when it makes sense to the people."[2]

A fantastic modern showboat, that is what Bread and Puppet Theatre is. For want of a better summary, I again quote in anticipation of my experiences with the Provisional Theatre, L.A.:

The atmosphere of a "Bread and Puppet-" performance is set even before the play begins. In grubby white pants and shirts, colored bandanas round their foreheads or wearing an assortment of headgear, as though they all had been to a jumble sale, the actors process through the streets beating drums, rattling tambourines, blowing trumpets, some wearing giant masks. An actor in a pig's head rolls over and over the pavement, dances among the traffic, swings from a lamp-post, and bows to a dog who is at once terrified. The audience joins in the procession if so inclined, goes for a walk around the block, chatting with the actors. People pause, stare, then their faces light up, smile—the gaiety of the Company is infectuous![3]

In chapter 4 I referred to the San Francisco Mime Troupe's different phases with Davis and after: In the meantime, they collaborated with the happener, Jim Dine (stage-design and effects), they used musical background provided by Mendelssohn and Mahler, and their choice of scripts ranged from early Brecht, Williams, Molière, Boris Vian, and *A Midsummer Night's Dream* to Jarry and Michel Ghelderode. They maintain their "multiracial" composition, which accounts for my calling them "multimedial" rather than "intermedial." Theater has always been multimedial, as I stated, and these groups probably share the fluxus mentality of Europe and America. Person by person, group by group, they may, however, differ by putting to use different emphases. Multimedial in alternative, regional theaters' case may be equivalent to their being multiracial, whereas Megalopolis–New York City theater developments may call themselves intermedial, because of the world capital's close touch with the former capitals—Paris, London, and the like—as experimental centers.

Finally, coming to Provisional Theater, L.A., I must clearly state what I mean when talking about the survivors of the sixties and the relative continuity between the sixties and the seventies. Barry, the speaker for the Group, detests both the transcendental-artist attitude and the communal-like attitude of "transling together." He says they are cultural workers rather than exceptionalists. They confess that they used to belong to the Bad Kids of the sixties (cf. *What You Are Like, America?*).

They do not deny the sixties heritage, either; they still believe in Chaikin's exercises; they want as diverse an audience as possible. They, too, complete thousand-mile-tours and include into their improvised program folk songs, pantomime, masquerade, jam sessions, choreographed and improvised dance, and politically oriented collages.

They smilingly say they have seven actors and eight technical personnel, but the roles are interchangeable. Five couples rent two near-ruined houses and two small vans. Their theater, studio, rehearsal place, and office is below a bookshop. They make their own scenery and masks and create their own musical instruments. Systematically, they inform their "friends" about the tours to be undertaken and about the details of their daily life: art is always involved. In their circulars, the blissful clown's good humor and the administrator's sincerity are a "godfornotsaken" happy mixture. They say: we are acquainted with Brook, Grotowski, Brecht, Stanislavsky, Marx/Engels, and McLuhan/Lévi-Strauss, but none of them are considered while all are taken into consideration. Production atmosphere is in accordance with the day-to-day reaction of the audience. Accordingly, they keep a production on schedule as long as it earns relatively differing audience responses.

I happened to see several experiments and, specifically, several productions of *Inching through the Everglades* (or *Pie in the Sky and Something in Your Shoe*). It was a loosely organized, almost collage-like play about working-type models, both male and female, occasionally colliding with one another while looking for new jobs, occasionally mating with one another, occasionally quarreling, and so on. The scenic background was provided by a steelwork structure from which colored canvases could be pulled out in order to indicate changes of time and place. "Did you get this idea from Craig?" I asked Candy, the leading actress of the group. "Don't matter where it had come from," was the smiling answer again. "One of us simply happened to think if it and there you are. . . . "

The San Francisco Mime Troupe during my stay there was also preparing a play of a very similar nature. It took place, however, in a sort of computerized factory where the multicolored workers were preparing to strike against inhuman working conditions. In spite of this play having been more politically charged than the other— the Provisionals always reminded me more of wandering minstrels, whereas the SFMT (with no less fun involved), of commedia dell'arte—I was almost struck dumb by the sincerity of oriental meditation and by the high acrobatic quality of the flips, jumps, mime, aerobics, and so on that preceded their rehearsals.

Their rehearsal place was a huge barn with an improvised stage on one far side, in the middle a vast empty space for exercising, and the other far end for storage of furniture and carpets. "Off-duty" actors carved musical instruments there, mothers were breast-feeding their infants, small children were climbing on all fours, cats were meowing, and dogs were barking. In spite of all this, discipline of the rehearsal was no less severe than that I had witnessed in Grotowski's Laboratory Theater.

Post-Chaplinian figures as they are, they remind us of little everyday problems. The exact parameters of this dramaturgy may not be defined for quite a while. I am, sure, however, about the two "models" getting closer and closer; the more so because "rebellious drama" is trying to "imitate" the spontaneity of the "intermedia" as far as traditional dramaturgy allows it to do so.

The finest example of a conglomerate of classical literary text, atonal music effects, stroboscopic lights, self-torturing actor's attitude, and an almost happening-like atmosphere was the performance of Beckett's *The Lost Ones* by the Mabou Mines, with David Warrilow in the main role. Such little-theater ventures are proof that a healthy mixture of ever so many theatrical tendencies can point toward the desirable future of theater development.

6

Conclusion, Outlook, and Reminiscences

IN ITS FALL 1977 ISSUE,[1] the *Performing Arts Journal* asked those who started in Off-Off-Broadway in the 1960s and who are now leading theater personnel (playwrights, directors, and critics) in Greenwich Village— still a center of alternative innovations—if they perceived a definite decline between the sixties and the seventies.

Director Lawrence Kornfeld thinks the decade of the seventies was a period of artistic retrospection preceded by a most unusual audience reaction during the sixties. The playwrights Terry and Shepard say that present audiences are a genetic product of the sixties. Shepard—together with critic Stanley Kaufmann—also talks about a post-Vietnam period. Kaufmann states that it is still the monistic theatrical doctrines that are the most dangerous; he thinks everything that is rebelliously good must have its due place, from naturalism to Grotowski. Kostelanetz, eclectic artist and occasional critic, also believes in the organic continuity of arts.

Director Carl Weber, somewhat in contrast to the others, complains about the influence of the less socially oriented European theater in the American 1960s. The influence was refreshing because it conferred new, avant-garde techniques, but it was retrograde inasmuch as it brought the American theater toward non-American (esoteric, mystical, elitist) tendencies. The seventies seem to be more "committed" (more to ratio than to ritual), thus a comeback presents itself to attitudes like those of Brecht, Erwin Piscator, and Giorgio Strehler. Director Wynn Handman may be the most laconic in that he sees a continuity of the two decades in the blurring of the boundaries between the so-called professional and the so-called nonprofessional theater; the great foundations, state-support, and regional donors are also given attention. I should add that this served a better cause for the professionals because they had to attach themselves to the demands of a poorer, braver, more experimental theater attitude; it was good for the nonprofessionals or semi-professionals who, at last, received deserved attention. In the long run, however, the latter may have come out of it the worst, since one of the utmost dangers of a revolting company may be its being "overpatronized."

Those excluded from the interview might also have a say about all this. It is relatively understandable that the grand old dads of any sort (such as Miller, Williams, Kazan, Clurman, and Lee Strasberg) were not questioned and that the *TDR*'s leading experts (Kirby, Schechner, Esslin, Kott and Marowitz) were deliberately excluded. Less understandable is why *Village Voice* young prophets, the only exception being Michael Feingold, Michael Smith, Erika Munk, and Arthur Sainer, among others, were not given an opportunity to speak. The stinging comments by older theater-foxes like Bentley, Kerr, and Brustein may also have deliberately been excluded. The question remains, who now?

The Best of Off-Off-Broadway (1969), edited by Michael Smith, has one really superb play in it, Tavel's *The Gorilla Queen* (1967). Tavel made himself known in at least two ways: as a scenarist for some of Andy Warhol's films and as one of the leading playwrights of the Theater of the Ridiculous. The prolific Shepard and the talented Fornés do get a place, but better plays could have been chosen than Shepard's *Forensic and the Navigators* (1969) and Fornés's *Dr. Kheal* (1969).

I may disagree with Clurman's choice in *Famous Plays of the 1960s* but, at the same time, I have to give him a hand for his editorial introduction to the Dell book (1972). His overview of the entire horizon is far more satisfying than that of his younger colleagues. He at least mentions the basic musicals—which do not fit into the paperback but define the theatrical atmosphere of the period, such as, *Hair, Oh, Calcutta!*, and *Viet Rock;* plays of earlier genesis but belonging to the period like Hellman's *Toys in the Attic,* Williams's *The Night of the Iguana,* Miller's *After the Fall;* "black drama" like LeRoi Jones's *The Dutchman,* Charles Gordone's *No Place to Be Somebody;* actual appearances Off-Off-Broadway such as Living Theater, Van Itallie and Schechner's *Dionysus '69,* and even "pacifist" muscials like *Fiddler on the Roof* and *The Man of La Mancha.*

When talking about particular artistic events of this decade, we are in strong want of new terminology. Definitions fluctuate all the time. Graham does call some of her "dance-poems" dramatic achievements. A fake John

Cage concert, like 3'33, is just as much an event as a Jim Dine moving exhibition. "People get stoned and sculptures get mobile" is a relatively widely quoted statement of mine in Hungary. Even Broadway is trying to keep up with expectations when offering the umpteenth revival of *West Side Story* as well as *Godspell.* Almost all the theater sets, amateur or professional, have discovered the newly adaptable possibilities of the grotesque and black humor (the latter in its European meaning). It is only a question of terminology whether they call themselves (neo-)avant-garde one time and derriére garde the next or modern and postmodern.

It is not only the famous novelists of the decade, as referred to previously, who discovered the liberating surprises of the stage. Some poets also had a go at it, for better or worse (for example, Frank O'Hara's *Try! Try!* [1960] or Lawrence Ferlinghetti's *Unfair Arguments with Existence* [1963]. These, together with Lowell's *The Old Glory,* obviously enjoyed a lesser popularity than long-runners like *Hello, Dolly* or *The Fantasticks.*

The generational ensemble experimenters' activity (like the Becks, Chaikin, Tom O'Horgan, Schechner, Kaprow, Vaccaro, and Ellen Stewart) may have been the signs of a new (video?) culture as opposed to the dying Gutenberg Galaxy. One wonders which of those belonging to the latter culture will live on in posterity with Albee and company.

Quite a few critics say Albee creates an atmosphere of mystery and obscurity while dealing with essentially realistic problems and does not risk self-exposure, as, for example, does Williams. I do, however, see a genetic continuity in his sixties products; because of this, I cannot accept *All Over* and *Seascape* as outdoor experiments only because of the pater familias dying behind the coulisses in the first play and because of lizardlike creatures appearing from under the sea, in the second to signify that marital life is not without its problems even somewhere around "fair Atlantis." We all have seen braver experiments than that—just consider the Slavic Theatre of the Absurd and particularly the Polish Witkiewicz, Slavomir Mrožek, and Tadeusz Rozewicz, the Czech Vaclav Havel, the (non-Slavic) Hungarian István Örkény, and so forth.

For me, *Box and Quotations from Chairman Mao Tse Tung* (1968–1970) *Counting the Ways* (1976–1977), and *Listening* (1975–1977) are fugues just like the early one-acters. I do not think that the major dramas are "family" toccatas or symphonies and that the experimental short pieces are a different kind of jazz. The same theme is being varied upon, and it is not only the sterility of the American Family and the American Dream that is being criticized in a naturalist fashion but it is lonely voices speaking from all sorts of personal boxes, cages, and living rooms that dominate this kind of music.

That is why I have chosen "toccata" and "fugue"— the main idea here is variation upon the same major or minor theme. And I honestly believe that when we come to 1980, we again get a masterpiece from Albee (with possible, but not probable, echoes from Pinter's *The Birthday Party*, where a mysterious Kafkaesque "couple" come for the Man to punish or at least to take him to his "proper place"—a prison, a lunatic asylum, or something of that kind). It is *The Lady from Dubuque*, in which we once again realize who the families are and who the mysterious guest is (just as in Eliot's *The Family Reunion* or *The Cocktail Party*, and when we come to understand the connections, if any, we come to realize what is going to happen. The rest, I hope, is not silence.

The last inspiring thing we Hungarians were confronted with in this field was the exhibition "American Theatre Today" in 1983 at the American Embassy in Budapest, accompanied by videotapes and live performances by the Actors Theatre of Louisville. These performances were mainly monodramas written by an eighties' star, Ken Jenkins (*Rupert's Birthday, The Century Man*); *Double Gothic* as envisaged by Michael Kirby; *I was Sitting on my Patio; The Kipper Kids* as done by the Louisvilles; *The Red Horse Animation* by Mabou Mines; and *Andy Warhol's Last Love*. All were informative as far as my mania for continuity is concerned.

As long as I survive, I shall feel it is my duty to try to probe into the seventies output in America. Shepard's works in *Seven Plays* (New York: Bantam Books, 1981) have convinced me of his talent more than his sixties experiments did (but I should like to see them on stage). And I would like to check whether I could afffix myself to the second (rather than to the first) part of Kaprow's sardonic outcry "The Happenings Are Dead! Long Live the Happenings!" My last word to you, theater folks, is carry on with the good work and we shall see what happens.

Notes

Introduction

1. Jerome Klinkowitz, *The American 1960s: Imaginative Acts in a Decade of Change.* Ames: Iowa State University Press, 1980.
2. From the ample choice I select only two: Arthur Schlesinger, Jr., *Violence: America in the Sixties* (New York: New American Library, 1968); and Ronald Berman, *America in the Sixties: An Intellectual History* (New York: Harper and Row, 1968).
3. C. W. E. Bigsby, "Drama as Cultural Sign: American Dramatic Criticism 1945–1978." *American Quarterly,* 30, iii (Bibliography Issue), 331.
4. Walter J. Meserve, *An Outline History of American Drama.* Totowa, NJ: Barnes and Noble, 1970, xiii.
5. Bigsby, *Drama as Cultural Sign,* 332.
6. Martin Esslin, *The Theatre of the Absurd.* Harmondsworth: Penguin, 1968, chap. 5.
7. Cf. E. J. Czerwinski, (ed.), "Commentary." *Comparative Drama* 3, iii (Fall 1969), 219.
8. Cf. Auto-Performance Issue of *TDR* (March 1979).
9. Georg Lukács, *A modern dráma fejlödésének története* (The History of the Development of Modern Drama). Budapest: Magvetö, 1978, chap. 14 and passim from Maeterlinck on.
10. Gilbert Debusscher, "Jack Richardson, Dramaturge Amèricaine." *Revues des Langues Vivantes,* Bruxelles, 1969, 44–151.
11. Julius Novick, *Beyond Broadway: The Quest for Permanent Theatres.* New York: Hill and Wang, 1968.

1. Edward Albee: First among Equals

1. This statement is not to conceal my ignorance of the topic if it is treated in the now-fashionable "reception-aesthetics" manner. In my dissertation, which formed the basis of this book, I devoted a whole chapter to Albee's international reception. To avoid proto-German-like philologizing, I give only a list of monographers and essayists who have seriously dealt with Albee: C. W. E. Bigsby, Walter J. Meserve, Foster Hirsch, Richard Gilman, Harold Clurman, Martin Gottfried, John Lahr, Downer, James A. Robinson, Ruby Cohn, Allan Lewis, Tom F. Driver, Richard Kostelanetz, the Soviet Maria Koreneva, Lee Baxandall, Morris Freedman, Martin Esslin, Gilbert Debusscher, Clara Györgyey, Martin Duberman, Pierre Brodin, Gerald Weales, John Gould, Michael E. Rutenberg and Richard Amacher. From among the Hungarian popularizers I have to stress, among others, Almási: János, Elbert, Levente Osztovits, Tamás Ungvári, and Miklós translators, dramaturges and soothsayers of Albee and Case. See also Richard Amacher and Margaret Rule, *Edward Albee at Home and Abroad: A Bibliography.* New York: AMS Press, 1971.
2. Quoted with personal permission of the author.
3. Cf. Pierre Brodin, *Écrivains américains d'aujourd'hui des années 60.* Paris: Series "Presences Contemporaines," 1969, 13.
4. Hirsch and several Hungarian commentators agree on this.
5. The label is attributable to Martin Esslin, who compared Albee (not without reason) to the "parallels and proselytes" of the Absurdist Paris School, basing his analysis on Albee's starting one-acters. Strangely enough, he did not change his mind in the revised version of his basic book, republished in 1968, much after *Who's Afraid of Virginia Woolf?* and a *Delicate Balance.*
6. Cf. Albee's preface to *The Sandbox.* New York: Signet Books, New American Library, 1963, 21.
7. Charles Marowitz, *New American Drama.* Harmondsworth: Penguin, 1966, 21.
8. Ibid., Preface, 11.
9. Ibid., xi.
10. David Riesman et al., *The Lonely Crowd.* New York: Doubleday and Company, 1953.
11. Cf. John Gould, *Modern American Playwrights.* New York City: Dodd Mead & Co., 1970, 279–81.

12. It is difficult to get hold of this "FAM and YAM" trouvaille; it can, however, be found in a common volume with *The Sandbox* and *The Death of Bessie Smith*—see n. 6.
13. Cf. Martin Duberman, "Theater 69." *Partisan Review* 36, iii (1969), 483–500.
14. Cf. T. E. Kalem, "The Club Bore," *The Theater,* April 15, 1971.
15. Cf. Walter Kerr, "The Living are Dead, Too." *The New York Times,* April 4, 1971.
16. Alan S. Downer (ed.), *The American Theatre Today.* New York: Basic Books, 1967, epilogue, 19.
17. Albee interviewed in Alvin B. Kernan (ed.), *The Modern American Theater.* New Jersey: Prentice-Hall, 1967, 175.
18. Foster Hirsch, *Who's Afraid of Edward Albee?* Berkeley: Creative Arts Book Company, 1978, 108.

2. Varieties of the Albee Generation

1. Cf. Meserve, *An Outline History,* xiii.
2. Cf. W. Thorp, *American Writing in the 20th Century.* Cambridge, MA: Harvard University Press, 1960, passim and 63.
3. Meserve, *An Outline History,* 177.
4. Czerwinski, "Commentary" 219.
5. Marowitz, *New American Drama,* 10.
6. Martin Esslin, *Theatre of the Absurd.* Harmondsworth: Penguin Books, 1968, 30.
7. Ibid., 305.
8. *Variety,* December 7, 1961.
9. *Plays and Players,* February 8, 1961.
10. Cf. *Theatre World,* August 1961; *Dialog,* March 1964.
11. *Arts,* October 23, 1963.
12. *Variety,* February 15, 1965.
13. Prologue to O'Neill's *The Great God Brown.*
14. Esslin, *Theatre of the Absurd,* 306.
15. Playwrights of the Theatre of the Absurd rediscover the Chekhovian technique of "indirect dialogues." Cf. Esslin *Theatre of the Absurd,* 112.
16. Cf. James Vinson (ed.), *Contemporary Dramatists.* London: St. James Press, 1973, 648.

17. The play was a success in Dublin (*Plays and Players*, 1965/12); in Milan (*Il Drama*, 314); in Holland performed by Ensemble 14 and in West Germany's Kasemattentheater (*Theatre World*, 1964/10). *Die Welt* (June 1961) committed the characteristic mistake of attributing the play to Albee!

18. Jack Richardson in the Preface to *Gallows Humour*. Harmondsworth: Penguin, New American Drama Series, 1966, 65.

19. Ibid., 77.

20. Ibid., 85, 86, 88.

21. Ibid., 89.

22. Ibid., 107.

23. Ibid., 109.

24. Ibid., 117.

25. Marowitz, *New American Drama*, 13.

26. See his "Modern Masks of Orestes: The Flies and The Prodigal." *Modern Drama*, December 1969, 308–18.

27. Described to me by Mme. Brustein and Mme. Györgyey at Yale Drama School in 1978.

28. Kopit *The Day the Whores Came Out to Play Tennis*. New York: Grove Press, 1978.

3. Dramaturgical Kaleidoscope of the Sixties

1. Cf. Edward Albee, "Which Theater Is the Absurd One?" in Kernan, *Modern American Theater*, 170.

2. An account of the activity of the Group Theatre is given by Harold Clurman, *The Fervent Years* (New York: Knopf 1945) and a thorough analysis of the relevant heritage can be found in Christine Edwards's *The Stanislavsky Heritage* (New York: New York University Press, 1965).

3. Obviously, there were numerous other influences as well (Brecht, Artaud, Copeau, Scandinavian drama, German Expressionist drama, etc.).

4. Phyllis Hartnoll (ed.), *The Oxford Companion to the Theatre*. London: Oxford University Press, 1967), 916.

5. Edwards, *Stanislavsky Heritage*, 275.

6. Peter Brook, *The Empty Space*. London: McGibbon and Kee, 1968, passim.

7. Richard Gilman, "Art and History." *Partisan Review* 35, i (1968), 270.

8. Quoted in John Cruichshank, *Albert Camus and the Literature of Revolt*. London: Oxford University Press; 1959, passim.

9. Alan E. Knight, "The Medieval Theatre of the Absurd." *PMLA*, 1971/3, 189.

10. Gordon Craig, *On the Art of the Theatre*. London: Gollancz, 1968, 136.

11. For his American reception see Herb Shore, "Barrie Stavis, the Humanist Alternative. *Educational Theatre Journal*, December 1973, 520–44, and an interview in *Dramatics*, March/April 1978, 20–23.

12. *Dramatics*, March/April 1978, 23.

13. Cf. *Religion and Theatre* (August 1981), 9.

14. John Lewin, introduction to *Coat of Many Colors*. New York: Barnes & Co., 1968, 14.

15. The Hungarian translations of three plays by Stavis, under the collective title *Kard és Kiáltás* (The Sword and the Word) have been published in Budapest: Europa MK, 1982. *The Man Who Never Died* was translated by Erzsébet Bereczky; *Harpers Ferry* and *Coat of Many Colors* were translated by the present author.

16. Quoted, by permission of the author, from personal correspondence.

17. Cf. *Dramatics* interview, March/April 1978, 20.

18. Cf., e.g., James A. Robinson, "O'Neill and Albee." *Philological Papers*, West Virginia University Bulletin, vol. 25, series 79, no. 8/3 (February 1979), 38–45. See also Albee's comment in Downer, *American Theatre Today*, 121.

19. Tennessee Williams, *Dragon Country*. New York: New Directions, 1970.

20. See Julius Novick, *Beyond Broadway*. New York: Hill & Wang, 1968, chap. 9, 178–97. A real insider's comments can be found in Herbert Blau, *Take up the Bodies*. Urbana: University of Illinois Press, 1982.

21. See Marowitz, *New American Drama*, 12–13.

4. Happenings and New Performance Theories

1. See Ch. Caramello, and M. Benamou (eds.), *Performance In Postmodern Culture*. Madison: Coda Press, 1977.

2. Paul Walsh, in an unpublished essay entitled "Happenings and New Performance Theories" (University of Minnesota, 1978, MS), suggested that the following books should be studied with

care: Allan Kaprow, *Assemblages, Environments, and Happenings* (New York: Abrams, 1966); Michael Kirby, *Happenings* (New York: Dutton, 1965); Richard Kostelanetz, *The Theater of Mixed Means* (New York: Dial, 1968).

3. Kostelanetz, *Recyclings* (Brooklyn: Assembling Press, 1974).
4. See Kostelanetz, *Theater of Mixed Means.*
5. Richard Schechner, *Public Domain* (New York: Discus/Avon, 1970); and *Environmental Theatre* (New York: Hawthorn, 1973).
6. The other-oriented Sontag did have a say in this sphere, too.
7. Cf. Klinkowitz, *American 1960s,* 102.
8. *Liminalities* is a key word in Caramello and Benamou, *Performance in Postmodern Culture,* especially in part 1, 11–55.
9. Michael Kirby, *The Art of Time.* New York: Dutton, 1969.
10. Schechner, *Public Domain,* passim.
11. Allan Kaprow, "Happenings in the New York Scene" (*Art News,* May 1961), "Happenings are Dead; Long Live the Happenings" (*Artforum,* 4, March 1966).
12. Walsh, "Happenings and New Performance Theories."
13. See also Andy Warhol's and Woody Allen's experiments.
14. Ken Dewey, "Act of San Francisco at Edinburgh. "*Encore,* November/December 1963.
15. See Kaprow *TDR,* March 1979, (Auto-Performance Issue).
16. Michael Kirby, *Happenings.* New York: Dutton, 1966.
17. Franck Jotterand, Le nouveau thèâtre américain. Paris: Editions du Sevil, 1970.
18. See Bigsby, *Drama as Cultural Sign.*
19. Kostelanetz, *Theater of Mixed Means,* 41.
20. E. T. Kirby disregards the different kinds of cocktails different periods are likely to produce.
21. Schechner, *Public Domain* passim.
22. Walsh, "Happenings and New Performance Theories," passim.
23. Many American authors share this point of view.
24. Arthur Sainer, *The Radical Theatre Notebook.* New York: Avon Books, 1975, 18–20.
25. See chap. 5.
26. Schumann's personal interview with the author.
27. Personal interview with group members.
28. See Novick, *Beyond Broadway.*
29. Sainer, *Radical Theatre Notebook,* 74–75.
30. James Roose-Evans, *The Experimental Theatre: From Stanislavsky to Today.* New York: Avon, 1971.
31. See Klinkowitz, *American 1960s,* final chap.

32. Borrowed from the categories of all the aesthetes mentioned here: Michael Kirby, Richard Schechner, etc.
33. John Vaccaro, "I come from Ohio." *TDR*, fall 1968, 142.

5. Regional Alternative Theater

1. Novick, *Beyond Broadway*. Aside from his personal help in New York City, my book owes a lot to Mr. Novick's professional care.
2. Cf. Roose-Evans, *Experimental Theatre from Stanislavsky to Today*, 121–22.
3. Ibid., 124–25.

6. Conclusion, Outlook, and Reminiscences

1. This chapter was originally designed as a study for *NAGYVILÁG*, a Hungarian monthly publication of world literature, translations for foreign languages, book reviews, etc., the title of which could vaguely be translated into English as "All That Wide World".

Index